Anglo-Saxon Manuscripts and their Heritage

Edited by

PHILLIP PULSIANO

and

ELAINE M. TREHARNE

Routledge
Taylor & Francis Group
LONDON AND NEW YORK

First published 1998 by Ashgate Publishing

Reissued 2018 by Routledge
2 Park Square, Milton Park, Abingdon, Oxon OX14 4RN
711 Third Avenue, New York, NY 10017, USA

Routledge is an imprint of the Taylor & Francis Group, an informa business

A Library of Congress record exists under LC control number: 97051288

ISBN 13: 978-1-138-60779-8 (hbk)
ISBN 13: 978-1-138-60780-4 (pbk)
ISBN 13: 978-0-429-46056-2 (ebk)

Contents

List of Plates

Between pages 136 and 137

Preface

Current work on cataloguing, describing, photographing and interpreting Anglo-Saxon manuscripts attests to the advances within the area of codicology and serves to reaffirm how fundamental is the study of manuscripts within the field of Anglo-Saxon studies. Helmut Gneuss' 'A Preliminary List of Manuscripts Written or Owned in England up to 1100'[1] stands as the most important contribution to the discipline since N.R. Ker's magisterial *Catalogue of Manuscripts Containing Anglo-Saxon*, first published in 1957, and recently reissued with a supplement in 1990.[2] The task of cataloguing manuscripts is continued by Richard Gameson, who is currently preparing a handlist of post-Conquest manuscripts written and owned in England, *c.* 1066–*c.* 1125.[3] Other initiatives include an important project being undertaken by the British Library aimed at preparing a new catalogue of the entire Cotton collection. Complementing this initiative is the Anglo-Saxon Manuscripts in Microfiche Facsimile project under the direction of A.N. Doane and Phillip Pulsiano, the objective of which is to provide new descriptions of all extant manuscripts containing Old English, accompanied by microfiche facsimiles of the manuscripts.[4] New methods in the recovery of manuscripts have been spearheaded by Kevin Kiernan, whose electronic *Beowulf* project will soon be published. The project reflects a significant advance in the application of technology to codicology and has important implications for future research. And as the cataloguing, describing and recovery of manuscripts presses ahead, we see as well a continued substantial outpouring of studies on manuscripts: the 1995 bibliography compiled by Carl Berkhout for *Old English Newsletter* records *c.* 80 publications under the rubric 'Manuscripts, Illumination, Charters', roughly 30 more than listed in the 1994 or 1993 bibliographies.

It is within the arena of this active interest in manuscript studies that the present collection of new essays is offered. The title for the volume, *Anglo-Saxon Manuscripts and their Heritage*, bespeaks an intentional ambiguity, for the idea of *heritage* points in different directions as at once something that is transmitted or acquired, a legacy passed down or received.[5] When we thus speak about manuscripts and their contexts, it is not only the immediate manuscript context that commands attention but often broader cultural contexts that bear consideration, those within which a manuscript was written as well as those shaped by contemporary and subsequent readers.[6] At base, however, the physical artifact remains a fundamental building stone of research. Recent publications such as Patrick W. Conner's *Anglo-Saxon Exeter: A Tenth-Century Cultural History*, Teresa Webber's *Scribes and Scholars at Salisbury Cathedral c.1075–c.1125*, Richard Marsden's *The Text of the Old Testament in Anglo-Saxon England*, along with studies that focus upon specific codices or groups of codices, such as Margaret Gibson, T.A. Heslop, and Richard W. Pfaff's *The Eadwine Psalter: Text, Image, and Monastic Culture in Twelfth-Century Canterbury*, Richard Gameson's *The Early Medieval Bible: Its Production, Decoration and Use*, Robert Deshman's *The Benedictional of Æthelwold*, William Noel's *The Harley Psalter* and Michelle P. Brown's *The Book of Cerne: Prayer, Patronage and Power in Ninth-Century England* underscore both the necessity of fresh examination of the original manuscripts and the importance of such work for our understanding of the manuscript culture.[7]

The present collection of essays seeks to extend our understanding of specific codices, their contents, use, audience and context within the broader culture that produced these works. The individual studies affirm the importance of close and sustained examination of the manuscripts themselves and in many cases stand as reminders that the filters through which these codices have passed — in effect undergoing over time a process of scholarly dismemberment — have on occasion obscured our understanding of the manuscripts and the larger issues pertaining to culture, audience and transmission.

Gernot Wieland returns to an examination of the use of glossed and illustrated manuscripts as classbooks, first advanced in an article he published in 1985.[8] In his discussion of illustrated *Psychomachia* manuscripts, Wieland argues that the boundary between 'art book' and 'classbook' cannot be rigidly enforced, for the *Psychomachia* manuscripts raise the possibility that glossed and illustrated manuscripts could well have been used as classbooks (particularly since the provenance of the illustrated manuscripts can be traced to centres with schools), and that the illustrations as well as the glosses were used in teaching in the classroom.

How manuscripts were used and what they reveal about the practices of a late Anglo-Saxon monastery forms the central concern of Timothy Graham's detailed discussion of the collection of Latin Benedictine texts in Cambridge, Corpus Christi College 57. Through a discussion of the manuscript's contents and codicological aspects, origins, intended use, glossing and additions to martyrology (such as entries, obits, prompts and construe marks) Graham is able to chart the use of the manuscript by numerous readers through the twelfth century.

D.G. Scragg offers insight into the creation of a vernacular homiliary in his examination of Cambridge, Corpus Christi College 162. Through a detailed discussion of the contents and compilation of the manuscript, he demonstrates that the manuscript is a clearly organised temporale in which we are given a glimpse of the compiler at work arranging and adjusting his material as he wrote. Such study opens the way to future investigation of the manuscript's audience. Manuscripts containing Anglo-Saxon homilies also stand at the center of Mary Swan's discussion of London, British Library, Cotton Cleopatra B. xiii, Oxford, Bodleian Library, Auct. F. 4. 32 and Cambridge, Corpus Christi College 303. Here she studies textual variations as evidence of a scribe's working from juxtaposed written copies and/or from memory, positioning the analysis within the context of scholarship on reception theory and medieval training in memorisation techniques. The essay calls for a reexamination of suppositions concerning theories of transmission and suggests that the homilies may well stand as vital witnesses to a more dynamic process of reception than has been fully recognised.

Questions concerning a manuscript's use also inform the essays by Phillip Pulsiano, Katherine O'Brien O'Keeffe and Kathryn Lowe. For Pulsiano, the prefatory matter of London, British Library, Cotton Vitellius E. xviii offers suggestive clues as to the manuscript's use within the monastic and larger lay communities. Among psalters written or owned in Anglo-Saxon England, it is unique in its compilation of preliminary texts, which display a certain focus and overarching sense of organisation. Further, in view of the correspondences between the *Vitellius Psalter* and 'Ælfwine's Prayerbook' and a key name embedded in a passage on secret writing, Pulsiano suggests that the prefatory matter may well reflect two periods of composition and compilation, that of the period of Ælfwine's abbacy *c.* 1030 and that of the period in which the psalter was written *c.* 1060.

With Katherine's O'Brien O'Keeffe's essay, codicology, the history of manuscript use and theory are unified in a discussion of London, British Library, Cotton Tiberius B. i, the Anglo-Saxon Chronicle. For the antiquarian Robert Talbot, the manuscript served as a mine for the identification of English place-names, whereas for John Leland the historical details in the Chronicle served 'to render the English countryside clear, identifiable and controllable for Henry VII', in the process reversing Talbot's translation glosses in favour of identification of the original lemmata. The larger implications concern the various uses which the manuscript served, whether for the twelfth-century writer who extended the record of 1066, for later writers such as Talbot and Leland, as an artifact on exhibition in the nineteenth and twentieth centuries, or as an electronic image: each use, each new context, transforms the nature of the artifact in both dramatic and subtle ways.

Later users of Anglo-Saxon manuscripts form the subject of Kevin Kiernan's discussion of the collations of the *Beowulf* manuscript made by John Josias Conybeare and Frederic Madden as he compares the two collations with the Thorkelin transcripts and with manuscript readings aided by digital photography. While the immediate results show Madden's collation to be more accurate than Conybeare's (although not without its own faults), the essay also reveals much about Madden through his diary and offers detailed study of over 40 readings in the *Beowulf* manuscript.

Kathryn Lowe offers new insight into the question of lay literary through the use of chirographs as highly visual documents that stand as central to the 'literacy event' and that, by their very design and use, bring the layman to participate in direct ways, both with regard to the physical artifact itself (which would be cut and whose halves can later be matched for authentication) and in terms of content (e.g., a will), which would be written in the vernacular and thus understood when read to the testator. Such documents become important in tracing the evolution of literacy as they attest to the growth of a literate mentality that was not confined to the arena of Church and State or to the post-Conquest period. Lowe sets this issue within the broader context of contemporary scholarship on literacy, particularly the work of Michael Clanchy, Jack Goody, Ian Watt, Brian Street, Susan Kelly and Simon Keynes. The essay concludes with an appendix detailing 64 extant chirographs.

Two essays treat from differing viewpoints the post-Conquest heritage of Anglo-Saxon manuscripts. E.C. Teviotdale focuses on London, British Library, Cotton Caligula A. xiv, fols 1–36 (the Caligula Troper), examining the work of a thirteenth-century Worcester annotator who provided directions for a number of the introit tropes for a scribe to copy. The scribe also added liturgical instructions, summarised in the appendix to the essay, which yield a contemporary dimension to the manuscript's use. Teviotdale's analysis provides further evidence of the interest in and continuing use of Anglo-Saxon manuscripts at this important monastic centre.

Elaine Treharne reassesses the evidence for dating and localising manuscripts that contain copies of Old English texts. She focuses, in particular, on London, British Library, Cotton Vespasian D. xiv, Oxford, Bodleian Library, Hatton 115, fols 148–155, Cambridge, Corpus Christi College 367 and Cambridge, University Library Ii. 1. 33 to propose that these manuscripts can be assigned to south-eastern centres of production in the mid- and later twelfth century. In providing detailed palaeographical, contextual and linguistic information, Treharne shows how research into these manuscripts might be advanced, but also indicates how much remains to be done before firm conclusions can be reached.

The final essay offers a fitting conclusion to a collection that treats manuscripts and their heritage. In 'The Ghost of Asser', Andrew Prescott examines the long and complex history of scholarship on the lost text of Asser's *Life of Alfred* that originally formed part of London, British Library, Cotton Otho A. xii. The essay is as much a scholarly detective story as it is an examination of the methods used and assumptions made by manuscript researchers; it is as well a study with a lesson concerning 'the potential dangers of relying uncritically on the testimony of experts when dealing with manuscripts' and a sobering reminder of how much new material can be brought to light on a topic that has supposedly been exhaustively researched.

NOTES

1. *Anglo-Saxon England* 9 (1981), 1–60. Prof. Gneuss is currently preparing a revised handlist.
2. Oxford: Clarendon Press. An important supplement to Ker's work is Mary Blocklye's 'Further Addenda and Corrigenda to N.R. Ker's *Catalogue*', *Notes and Queries* n.s. 29 (1982), 1–3; repr. in *Anglo-Saxon Manuscripts: Basic Readings*, Basic Readings in Anglo-Saxon England, 2; Garland Reference Library of the Humanities, 1434, ed Mary P. Richards (New York and London: Garland Publishing, Inc., 1994), pp. 79–85.
3. The work, which began as a lengthy article listing some 815 items, is being prepared as a book. We are grateful to Dr Gameson for allowing us access to a draft of the handlist in its earlier form.
4. The project, which is supported by grants from the National Endowment for the Humanities, has issued six volumes and will publish five or six volumes annually through Medieval and Renaissance Texts and Studies. Ideally, the project will be extended to include all manuscripts contained in Gneuss' handlist.
5. We are grateful to Richard Gameson for suggesting the volume's title to us.
6. Fred C. Robinson gave eloquent voice to the necessity of examining works in their immediate manuscript contexts in 'Old English Literature in Its Most Immediate Context', *Old English Literature in Context: Ten Essays*, ed John D. Niles (Woodbridge: D.S. Brewer; New Jersey: Rowman & Littlefield, 1980), pp. 11-29 (repr. in his *The Editing of Old English* [Oxford: Blackwell, 1994], pp. 3–24), and his '"The Rewards of Piety": Two Old English Poems in Their Manuscript Context', *Hermeneutics and Medieval Culture*, ed Patrick J. Gallacher and Helen Damico (New York: Garland Publishing, Inc., 1989), pp. 193–200. Recent publications that advance the study of manuscript contexts are numerous; one can mention here Katherine O'Brien O'Keeffe, *Visible Song: Transitional Literacy in Old English Verse* (Cambridge: Cambridge University Press, 1990); Sarah Larratt Keefer, 'Respecting the Book: Editing Old English Liturgical Poems in Their Manuscripts', *Florilegium* 11 (1992), 35–52; Graham D. Caie, 'Text and Context in Editing Old English: The Case of the Poetry in Cambridge, Corpus Christi College 201', *The Editing of Old English: Papers from the 1990 Manchester Conference*, ed D.G. Scragg and Paul E.

Szarmach (Woodbridge: D.S. Brewer, 1994), pp. 155–62; A.N. Doane, 'Editing Old English Oral/Written Texts: Problems of Method', *The Editing of Old English*, pp. 125–45.

7. Patrick W. Conner, *Anglo-Saxon Exeter: A Tenth-Century Cultural History*, Studies in Anglo-Saxon History IV (Woodbridge: The Boydell Press, 1993); Teresa Webber, *Scribes and Scholars at Salisbury Cathedral c.1075–c.1125*, Oxford Historical Monographs (Oxford: Clarendon Press, 1992); Richard Marsden, *The Text of the Old Testament in Anglo-Saxon England*, Cambridge Studies in Anglo-Saxon England, 15 (Cambridge: Cambridge University Press, 1995); Margaret Gibson, T.A. Heslop, and Richard W. Pfaff, eds, *The Eadwine Psalter: Text, Image, and Monastic Culture in Twelfth-Century Canterbury* (London and University Park: The Modern Humanities Research Association in conjunction with Pennsylvania University State Press, 1992); Richard Gameson, *The Early Medieval Bible: Its Production, Decoration and Use*, Cambridge Studies in Palaeography and Codicology, 2 (Cambridge: Cambridge University Press, 1994); Robert Deshman, *The Benedictional of Æthelwold*, Studies in Manuscript Illumination, 9 (Princeton: Princeton University Press, 1995); William Noel, *The Harley Psalter*, Cambridge Studies in Palaeography and Codicology, 4 (Cambridge: Cambridge University Press, 1995); Michelle P. Brown, *The Book of Cerne: Prayer, Patronage, and Power in Ninth-Century England*, The British Library Studies in Medieval Culture (London: The British Library and University of Toronto Press, 1996).

8. 'The Glossed Manuscript: Classbook or Library Book?', *Anglo-Saxon England* 14 (1985), 153–73.

1 Gloss and Illustration: Two Means to the Same End?

Gernot R. Wieland

Two recent articles, one by R.I. Page, the other by J.A. Kiff-Hooper, raise the question of whether illustrated manuscripts were also used as classbooks.[1] Kiff-Hooper establishes the following criteria for illustrated manuscripts *not* used in the classroom: 'Elaborate initial forms; drawings of the author and the absence of extensive contemporary glossing'.[2] And Page, speaking about Cambridge, Corpus Christi College 23, an illustrated *Psychomachia* manuscript, gives the following point as one major reason why he does not consider the manuscript a classbook:[3]

> Possibly the most suggestive evidence that CCCC 23 was not a classbook (or at least not designed as such) is the nature of the manuscript itself ... . CCCC 23 is sumptuous. First its size: it is 360 x 285 mm, a largish volume, not very convenient for taking to and from class ... . There are 89 large pictures, and spaces for a few more that were never filled in. The illustrations are elegant line drawings in tinted inks, with captions in red or green. This does not look like a book intended for teaching ... .[4]

Both Kiff-Hooper and Page seem to agree that manuscripts with elaborate illustrations or initials would not have been intended for use in the classroom.

There is one major difference between the two arguments: while Kiff-Hooper establishes as one of her criteria 'absence of extensive contemporary glossing', Page contends that CCCC 23 is not a classbook despite extensive contemporary glossing. *A priori*, Kiff-Hooper's criterion seems to be the more valid one. If glosses are absent, we are, aside from the use to which the content can be put, left without any indication as to the intended uses of the manuscript. The only way to determine whether a manuscript was *designed* for use in the classroom is through the glosses, since they provide the information concerning the manner in which the text was to be read. If the glosses reflect the concerns of the schoolroom, that is, if they are prosodic, lexical, morphological, and syntactical, and if they provide sources or explanations for culturally foreign objects,[5] then the assumption is justified that the manuscript was destined to be a teaching text. The presence of glosses does not allow the assumption that the manuscript was subsequently actually used as such since books are portable property and can be alienated from their intended purpose; conversely, many manuscripts not containing glosses may have been used as teaching texts, but such use cannot be proven.

Kiff-Hooper specifies 'contemporary' glosses, and thereby begs the question of what happens when a manuscript is glossed later on. It would seem that a manuscript that did receive glosses after its original compilation could still be considered a classbook, one that perhaps originally was not intended for classroom use, but one that was appropriated for the school at a later date. This in turn raises the possibility that the book received the glosses at a later date because it had already been used as a classbook. If that possibility is accepted, then the boundary between 'classbook' and 'art book' cannot be drawn as strictly as Kiff-Hooper does explicitly and Page implicitly. It would seem that the question of whether the two are mutually exclusive needs to be explored further.

The present essay intends to do just that, and it will do so with special reference to illustrated *Psychomachia* manuscripts. Kiff-Hooper has examined manuscripts containing Aldhelm's *De laudibus virginitatis*, both the prose and the verse, and even the most elaborately illustrated of these manuscripts contains at the most two illustrations and some elaborate initials. The case is entirely different with the illuminated *Psychomachia* manuscripts which contain as many as 89 illustrations,[6] the sheer number of which would, in comparison to the Aldhelm manuscripts, turn them into *de luxe* codices and therefore, if we follow Page's and Kiff-Hooper's criteria, disqualify them from use in the classroom. As it happens, however, all extant illustrated *Psychomachia* manuscripts from Anglo-Saxon England are also extensively glossed with exactly the types of glosses one would expect a teacher to use, and on the strength of these glosses they could all be classified as classbooks.[7] Does the evidence of the illustrations contradict the evidence of the glosses? Or are they two different means to the same end?

An answer to these questions has to examine what we know about Anglo-Saxon illustrated manuscripts generally; it needs to discuss the relationship of illustrated to non-illustrated *Psychomachia* manuscripts. It needs to focus on the relationship between text and illustration in order to determine whether the illustrations function as a type of gloss; and finally, it needs to discuss the relationship between glosses and illustrations in order to see whether the one influenced the other.

Temple's catalogue of illustrated Anglo-Saxon manuscripts between 900 and 1066 is the best place to start.[8] Of the more than 100 manuscripts listed by her, several can be considered teaching texts.[9] Among them are Aldhelm's *De virginitate*,[10] Arator's *Historia apostolica*,[11] Sedulius' *Carmen Paschale*,[12] Juvencus' *De evangelio*,[13] and Boethius' *De consolatione*

Philosophiae.[14] All these manuscripts have only very few illustrations: in the Aldhelm manuscripts, the illustrations are limited to a dedicatory page and some elaborate initials; the Boethius manuscripts usually contain no more than a portrait of Philosophy and again some elaborate initials; and the manuscripts with the other authors have only elaborate initials. Nonetheless, as the list shows, teaching texts were sometimes considered worthy of special attention in the form of elaborate initials and drawings.[15] I might add here that Ælfric's Grammar, fols 56–127 in Durham Cathedral Library B. III. 32 (Temple no. 101), is prefaced by a full-page drawing of two men disputing with each other while a third man looks on. Why should this manuscript have deserved special treatment? If a grammar is not a text to be used in school, which text is?

Although like the other texts mentioned above the *Psychomachia* is a teaching text, yet with potentially 90 illustrations it differs significantly from them. Because of the large number of illustrations, it really ought to be considered in connection with manuscripts having cycles of illustrations. According to the manuscripts presented by Temple, the Anglo-Saxons possessed such cycles in psalters,[16] in Old English biblical texts,[17] in *The Wonders of the East*,[18] in the *Herbarium*,[19] in the *Aratea*,[20] and in Hrabanus Maurus' *De laude s. crucis*.[21] None of these texts except for the psalters is usually considered part of the curriculum. The *Psychomachia* thus occupies a singular place among illustrated Anglo-Saxon manuscripts: despite possessing a cycle of illustrations, it differs from other such manuscripts in that its text forms part of the curriculum; and despite forming part of the curriculum, it differs from other teaching texts because of the presence of a cycle of illustrations. Its hybrid form contributes largely to the confusion of whether a particular glossed and illustrated manuscript should be considered a classroom text or not.

In order to gauge fully the classbook potential of the illustrated *Psychomachia* manuscripts, one must examine them together with the non-illustrated manuscripts. Ten *Psychomachia* manuscripts written or owned in Anglo-Saxon England are still extant. They are (in roughly chronological order):

1. *Non-illustrated manuscripts*:

   Oxford, Bodleian Library, Rawlinson C. 697 (s. ix ex.), written in north-eastern France and later owned at Bury St Edmunds (HG 661).[22]

   Cambridge, Corpus Christi College 223 (s. ix/x), written at St Bertin and in England by the tenth century (HG 70).

   Cambridge, Trinity College O. 2. 51 (s. x) of unknown origin and provenance (HG 191).

Durham, Cathedral Library B. IV. 9 (s. x med.) of unknown origin and provenance (HG 246).

Oxford, Bodleian Library, Auctarium F. 3. 6 (s. xi in.), written at Exeter (HG 537).

Cambridge, University Library, Gg. 5. 35 (s. xi med.) written and owned at St Augustine's, Canterbury (HG 12).

2. *Illustrated manuscripts*:

Cambridge, Corpus Christi College 23 (s. x ex.), written in England (possibly at Christ Church, Canterbury?) and later owned at Malmesbury (HG 38).

London, British Library, Additional 24199 (s. x ex.) of unknown origin and later possibly owned at Bury St Edmunds (HG 285).

London, British Library, Cotton Cleopatra C. viii (s. x/xi), written at Christ Church, Canterbury (HG 324).

Munich, Bayerische Staatsbibliothek, clm 29336/1 (formerly 29031b, s. xi in.) of unknown origin and provenance (HG 852).

Ten surviving manuscripts of a teaching text is a large number as a comparison with other teaching texts will show: Arator's *Historia apostolica* survives in six manuscripts, Juvencus' *Libri Evangeliorum* in six as well, Sedulius' *Carmen Paschale* in seven manuscripts, and only Boethius' *De consolatione Philosophiae*, which survives in sixteen manuscripts, surpasses the number of *Psychomachia* manuscripts.[23] As can readily be seen, four of the *Psychomachia* manuscripts are illustrated, while six are not. This would appear to be a high percentage of illustrated manuscripts. Partly their large number can no doubt be accounted for by the fact that later ages considered illustrated manuscripts more valuable and would therefore more readily have preserved them. For the other part, the large number of illustrated manuscripts suggests that the Anglo-Saxons did not, except for the illustrations, consider them essentially different from their non-illustrated counterparts.

Since it seems to be easier to accept that non-illustrated manuscripts were used as classbooks, let us first examine their classbook potential. The two manuscripts originally written in France and then brought to England do not contain enough glosses to classify them as classbooks. The *Psychomachia* of Rawlinson C 697 is not glossed at all. The *Psychomachia* in CCCC 223 is extensively glossed in only the first four lines; thereafter occasional Latin and Old English glosses in both ink and drypoint appear;[24] it should be emphasised that all the glosses are added by later hands, presumably in England. The glossing is, however, not consistent or extensive enough to define unambiguously the manuscript as a classbook. Possibly once we find out more about the role of the mainly drypoint Old English glosses, we can revise that judgment, but as it stands now, the *Psychomachia* of CCCC 223 cannot be shown to be destined for use in the classroom. Of the four non-illustrated *Psychomachia* manuscripts written in England, three are extensively glossed; the one exception is the *Psychomachia* in Trinity College O. 2. 51, which is heavily glossed on only the first three folios, and then the glosses abruptly cease and are not resumed again. In CUL Gg. 5. 35, Durham B. IV. 9, and Auct. F. 3. 6, the glosses are of the type one would expect a teacher to use: lexical, prosodic, morphological, syntactical, and commentary glosses. There is more: the placement of the glosses also suggests that the manuscripts containing them were intended for the classroom. Speaking about glossed psalters, Gibson contends that if a gloss is 'set adjacent to the text in a smaller script, the annotation is a planned element in the *mise-en-page* [and hence the manuscript is a *de luxe* manuscript]. A gloss of this kind is sharply distinct from the marginal and interlinear notes in a school text',[25] which, it would appear, are not added with a definite plan, but are squeezed in wherever they are needed. Gibson's distinction between *de luxe* glossed psalters and glossed psalters for the schoolroom is useful for the *Psychomachia* manuscripts as well. If we accept her criteria, then we find that the non-illustrated English *Psychomachia* manuscripts, with the exception of Trinity College O. 2. 51, are designed as classbooks. The glosses in CUL Gg. 5. 35 and Durham B. IV. 9 are added rather haphazardly either in the margin or between the lines, sometimes with one gloss above another. Little thought was given to a careful *mise-en-page*; the primary purpose clearly was to present information as close to the lemma as possible without being overly concerned about the aesthetic appeal of the placement of the gloss. Auct. F. 3. 6 differs from this pattern on the first few pages, which are carefully laid out with the glosses neatly arranged in the margins. After a few pages, however, this neatness partly breaks down, since interlinear glosses, sometimes one above another, begin to appear next to the marginal ones, and while the marginal scholia maintain their neatness, the interlinear glosses do not, and the manuscript approaches the rather haphazard look of the other glossed non-illustrated *Psychomachia* manuscripts. The following pattern thus establishes itself: the French imports, Rawlinson C 697 and CCCC 223, are not, or were not originally, glossed, and can therefore not be proven to be classbooks, although the addition of glosses to CCCC 223 at a later date makes it entirely possible that this manuscript was used as a classbook all along. All but one of the four non-illustrated manuscripts written in England, i.e., CUL Gg. 5. 35, Durham B. IV. 9, and Auct. F. 3. 6, are consistently and extensively glossed, and these contain the types of glosses necessary to identify them as classbooks, and the placement of these glosses is such that they are more typical of a classbook than a *de luxe* manuscript. Only three of the six non-illustrated *Psychomachia* manuscripts in Anglo-Saxon England can be shown to be classbooks; of the other three, one has no glosses at all, and the other two do not have enough glosses to prove their use in the classroom.

Except for the illustrations, the extant illustrated manuscripts do not essentially differ from their non-illustrated counterparts. Illustrated and non-illustrated manuscripts share textual variants, captions and glosses. The illustrated Cleopatra C. viii, for instance, shares its textual class III with the non-illustrated manuscripts CUL Gg. 5. 35 and Auct. F. 3. 6; the illustrated CCCC 23 shares its text with the non-illustrated Rawlinson C 697, both belonging to the textual class II.[26] Illustrated and non-illustrated *Psychomachia* manuscripts also overlap in the use of captions. These identify and partly explain the illustrations in the illustrated manuscripts, and they appear in the non-illustrated manuscripts to serve as chapter headings.[27] Glosses are also shared by illustrated and non-illustrated manuscripts. The two categories of glosses[28] available to the Anglo-Saxons can be found in both illustrated and non-illustrated manuscripts: the illustrated Additional 24199 and CCCC 23 share their gloss group B with the non-illustrated Auct. F. 3. 6., and the illustrated Cleopatra C. viii[29] and clm 29336/1 share their gloss group A with the non-illustrated CUL Gg. 5. 35 and — as far as it contains glosses — with Trinity College O. 2. 51. This strong connection between the glosses of illustrated and non-illustrated manuscripts would suggest that to whatever uses the glosses were put in non-illustrated manuscripts are also the uses to which they were put in the illustrated manuscripts. Moreover, the placement of the glosses in the illustrated manuscripts does not suggest that they are *de luxe* codices. In Cleopatra C. viii and clm 29336/1 there is no careful *mise-en-page*; the glosses are squeezed in wherever necessary, and hence suggest a classbook rather than a *de luxe* manuscript. The case for CCCC 23 and Additional 24199 is slightly different: both manuscripts contain neatly presented marginal glosses, but the *de luxe* effect is spoiled by interlinear glosses which, as in the non-illustrated manuscripts, sometimes are crammed in one above another. Hence, both the content of the glosses as well as their placement suggest that, like their glossed non-illustrated counterparts, the illustrated manuscripts were intended for the schoolroom. At this point it should be emphasised that while only half of the non-illustrated manuscripts are glossed in a way suggestive of classroom use, all of the illustrated manuscripts are so annotated. That fact alone would seem to argue that the Anglo-Saxons fully recognised the educational possibilities of the illustrations.

Let us now turn from a comparison of illustrated with non-illustrated manuscripts to the illustrated manuscripts themselves. The illustrations of the four manuscripts fall into two groups, group (a), consisting of Cleopatra C. viii and clm 29336/1, group (b) of Additional 24199 and CCCC 23.

Stettiner and Woodruff[30] have established these two categories, and as far as the general classification is concerned, they are no doubt correct. These two manuscript groups, based entirely on the illustrations, can be confirmed by further similarities between the manuscripts. Cleopatra C. viii and clm 29336/1, as we have seen above, also share the same textual variants as well as the same glosses. Moreover, their sizes, with approximately 260 x 180 mm. for the Munich fragment and with 215 x 180 mm. for Cleopatra C. viii, differentiate these two manuscripts from CCCC 23 and Additional 24199, with 365 x 287 mm. and 320 x 240 mm. respectively.[31] Cleopatra C. viii and clm 29336/1 have the same type of text, approximately the same size, the same type of glosses, and the same type of illustrations. And while Additional 24199 and CCCC 23 do not share the same text, they do have approximately the same size, the same type of glosses, and the same type of illustrations.[32] The fact that, whatever the groups, gloss types and illustration types travel together (gloss group A with illustration group a, and gloss group B with illustration group b) suggests a strong relationship between glosses and illustrations, a suggestion which will be treated in greater detail below.

Let us briefly return to the sizes of the manuscripts. Page thinks that because of its size CCCC 23 is 'not very convenient for taking to and from class'. The size of the manuscript need not be any problem if we assume that the teacher did not take the volume 'to and from class', but that the class came to the manuscript, i.e., that classes were held in or near the library. The relative sizes also suggest that if CCCC 23 is to be disqualified as a classbook, then Additional 24199 needs to be disqualified as well, or conversely, if Additional 24199 is accepted as a classbook, then CCCC 23 needs to be accepted as well.

The dates at which the illustrated manuscripts were produced, i.e., at the end of the tenth or the beginning of the eleventh century, also help to strengthen the case for classroom use of the illustrated *Psychomachia* manuscripts. In an article which appeared in 1990, T.A. Heslop argued that many of the late Anglo-Saxon *de luxe* manuscripts, usually dated *c.* 990–1030 actually were produced between 1017 and 1027, i.e., during the reign of Cnut and Emma, and that they were commissioned by them to be used as gifts for monasteries and bishoprics.[33] Heslop concentrates on liturgical books, but there is some reason to suppose that Cnut and Emma would also have commissioned illustrated manuscripts of educational works such as the *Psychomachia*. The strongest indication is this: the artist responsible for the first ten illustrations (fols 4v–7v, upper illustration) in Cleopatra C. viii is also the artist of one of the *de luxe* manuscripts commissioned by Cnut and/or Emma, namely of the York Gospels.[34] If he illustrated the York Gospels on orders, or certainly with the financial backing, of the king or queen, it certainly would seem reasonable to assume that he did likewise when he illustrated the *Psychomachia* in Cleopatra C. viii. The case for the other illustrated *Psychomachia* manuscripts also being produced under Cnut's or Emma's royal patronage is not quite as strong, since there is no artist common to them and the *de luxe* manuscripts examined by Heslop, but the dates at which clm 29336/1, Additional 24199, and CCCC 23 are produced all come close to the period of Cnut's and Emma's patronage. Moreover, the illustrations of Cleopatra C. viii and clm 29336/1 resemble each other closely, as do the glosses and relative sizes of the two manuscripts, so that there must be a strong link between the two. If, therefore, one was produced under royal patronage, the other in all likelihood was produced under the same circumstances. For the more sumptuous Additional 24199 and CCCC 23, we have only their dates of origin to make them candidates for the royal patronage of Cnut and Emma. But one also has to ask who else would or could have provided the money for their production at that time?

The known origins of the illustrated *Psychomachia* manuscripts, namely Christ Church, Canterbury (although Christ Church may not be correct for CCCC 23, as outlined above), also place them at a centre which produced *de luxe* manuscripts. More important for our argument here is the fact that the known places of origin and provenance of these manuscripts, namely Canterbury(?)/Malmesbury for CCCC 23, Bury St Edmunds for Additional 24199, and Canterbury for Cleopatra C. viii (and because of the closeness of size, text, gloss, and illustrations quite possibly Canterbury for clm 29336/1 as well), are all monasteries or bishops' seats, in other words places at which we can expect to find a school. If there were any clear evidence, for instance, that any or all of these manuscripts were in the hands of lay owners, the case for their being teaching texts would obviously be weakened. Since, however, they can be shown to come from centers that had schools, there is, especially in view of the points mentioned above, a strong possibility that they were actually used in the classroom.

This possibility can be strengthened if the illustrations themselves can be shown to be didactic. The modern cliché that 'a picture is worth a thousand words' was not known in those words to the early Middle Ages, but they knew sentiments very close to it.[35] We do not know what originally motivated the Carolingians to illustrate the *Psychomachia*, whether they copied late classical models or whether they originated the illustrations, but their didactic potential must have been obvious to them. And when the Anglo-Saxons in turn began to copy the Carolingian illustrations, they must also have been aware of their pedagogic possibilities. The illustrations form a commentary on the text in several ways: aside from translating the text into pictorial form, they provide detail for elements which Prudentius had not described fully, they provide a pictorial representation for unfamiliar objects or characters, and they anticipate sections that are to follow later.

Let us look at these points in detail. The illustrations generally focus quite narrowly on the sections of the text to which they provide the image. We see, for instance, Patientia in the typical dress of a Virtue in all twelve illustrations of her encounter with Ira, the dress consisting of a long flowing robe and a veil. The pattern is broken only once, in order to illustrate lines 140–3 (*Aerea sed cocto cassis formata metallo / tinnitum percussa refert aciemque retundit / dura resultantem, frangit quoque uena rebellis / inlisum chalybem*)[36] where Patientia's veil clearly would not suffice to break the brandished sword, and where the text demands a *cassis* (Woodruff's no. 23). The change from veil to helmet and back to the veil again[37] draws our attention to the narrow focus the illustrator has for the most part. The illustration thus can serve as an immediate commentary on a rather limited section.

A similarly narrow focus appears in the next few illustrations mentioned, even though I shall concentrate on other types of commentary these illustrations provide. *Metus et Labor et Vis*[38] are not described any further by Prudentius; nonetheless, the illustrator gives them attributes by which they can be recognised: Labour is shown carrying a heavy sack or rock on his shoulder, Vis is represented in full armour with helmet, shield, and sword, and Metus as a frightened young man.[39] Here the artist, much like a glossator, provides illustrative details and so supplements the sparse information given by Prudentius.

Yet a different purpose can be gleaned from the pictorial representations of Iocus, Amor, and Pompa, none of whom features largely in the narrative.[40] They probably owe their existence to the illustrator's desire to make the unfamiliar familiar. Iocus is shown as throwing away his cymbals, a musical instrument with which the Germanic people were not familiar.[41] Amor is represented as a winged and naked young man discarding his quiver and bow (plus arrows in Cleopatra C. viii): again, the classical divinity would not be a figure familiar to the Germanic audience. Nor is the Greek *peplum* (l. 440), which Pompa sheds, and which is a garment not worn by the Germanic people. The artists of Cleopatra C. viii and Additional 24199 here strive to make the unfamiliar familiar; the artist of CCCC 23, however, goes one step further: by assimilating Pompa's *peplum* to the ceremonious robes of a priest or a bishop,[42] he attacks the clerics who love elaborate robes;[43] in other words, he practices a bit of contemporary social criticism.

The anticipatory technique can be seen in, for example, the illustration in which Loth is led away captive.[44] The text laconically reports:

> Victum feroces forte reges ceperant
> Loth inmorantem criminosis urbibus
> Sodomae et Gomorrae, quas fouebat aduena
> pollens honore patruelis gloriae. (Praef. ll. 15–9)

In two manuscripts, the kings lead not only Loth but also members of his household and some cattle.[45] Here the illustrations anticipate the list of ll. 30–1 in which Prudentius states that Abraham freed not only Loth but also

> aurum puellas paruulos monilia
> greges equarum uasa uestem buculas.

Obviously the illustrators worked on the principle that if Abraham freed all these people and things, then they must originally have been captured by the kings.

In this last example, the illustrator steps outside of the narrow confines of the passage he is illustrating by letting the larger context influence him. Nonetheless, one can argue that in such an illustration it is still the *Psychomachia* that comments on the *Psychomachia*. Occasionally, however, the illustrator transcends the boundaries of the *Psychomachia* altogether and introduces details not found anywhere in its text. One such example would be the illustration showing the victorious Abraham with Melchisedech (Woodruff no. 5). The text reads as follows:

> Adhuc recentem caede de tanta uirum
> donat sacerdos ferculis caelestibus,
> dei sacerdos rex et idem praepotens
> ...
> Melchisedec. (Praef. ll. 38–43)

Prudentius says nothing here of Abraham offering anything to God or to Melchisedech, and yet the illustrations show him holding up a lamb toward Melchisedech, and the captions reinforce the message of the illustrations, namely that Abraham offers either tithes or a lamb as a sacrifice.[46] Clearly the illustrator sought his inspiration for the image not only in the *Psychomachia*, but in another source, here the Bible as well.[47] One other point should be noted here: the illustrations form the basis of the captions. The illustrations show Abraham offering a lamb to either God or Melchisedech, a feature mentioned in neither the Bible nor the *Psychomachia*. When the caption of CUL Gg. 5. 35 therefore specifies a lamb, it can take its information only from an illustration, and since CUL Gg. 5. 35 is not illustrated, it must be from the illustration of an earlier manuscript.

The preceding points show the illustrator as a type of glossator: he clarifies the text; he supplements it; he anticipates later portions; he makes unfamiliar things familiar. All of this is teaching activity; all of this is the same activity as that of the glossator, only in a different medium. One may object that there is a difference between the original illustrator of either the late classical or the Carolingian era and the Anglo-Saxon copyists: there is no denying this difference, but it also holds true that if there is a didactic potential in the original illustrations, then that potential is still there in the copies. The effect of the illustrations may not be the same: a late antique audience would presumably learn different things from, e.g., an illustration of Amor or a figure with a Greek *peplum* than a Germanic audience, but both audiences are taught something about Prudentius' and the artist's conception of those two figures. I am fully aware that the fact that illustrations teach something does not turn a manuscript containing illustrations into a classbook. But these illustrations do not appear in isolation: each one of the illustrated manuscripts also has extensive glosses. Hence two different forms of teaching are coinciding in these manuscripts.

Are these two different forms of teaching independent of each other, or do they reinforce each other? In other words, are they different means to the same end? It would seem that they do reinforce each other, since Cleopatra C. viii and clm 29336/1 share both gloss type A and illustration type (a), and CCCC 23 and Additional 24199 share gloss type B and illustration type (b). This overlap may be fortuitous. If, however, gloss and illustration can be shown to differ from the text and to agree with each other, then we would have the strongest indication that the two can be seen as different means to the same end. By necessity, there will be only a few illustrations and glosses of this kind, since both gloss and illustration usually derive from the text and hence the possibilities are limited. One such detail appears in the scene usually entitled *Avaritia spolia in sinistro latere protegit*,[48] in which Avaritia is shown carrying a solid (metal or wood) container with a handle, similar to a bucket. The scene illustrates Prudentius' lines 459–62:

iuuat infercire cruminis
turpe lucrum et grauidos furtis distendere fiscos,
quos laeua celante tegit laterisque sinistri
uelat opermento.

Fiscos is usually glossed with the words *saccos publicos*,[49] a gloss that fits the implicit description of the item as being capable of expanding (*distendere*). The illustration, however, is at odds with the text since buckets (or baskets) do not expand when they are stuffed. In Auct. F. 3. 6 *fiscos* is not glossed with the expandable *saccos publicos* but with *uasa*, a gloss that allows the interpretation of a solid, rather than an expandable, container, and that seems to be a reaction to the illustration. Since Auct. F. 3. 6 does not have illustrations, and since its gloss nonetheless seems to be derived from the illustration, we can only conclude that the gloss in Auct. F. 3. 6 is a copy of a gloss that was originally found in an illustrated manuscript. This in turn means that the original glossators studied not only the text, but also the illustrations when they composed their teaching aids and that sometimes the illustrations rather than the text actually were the sources for glosses.

Another instance in which gloss and illustration agree against the text appears in the scene usually entitled *Ubi quinque reges predati sunt loth*,[50] where five men are shown leading Loth into captivity. The text of the *Psychomachia* does not specify the number of the victorious kings; Prudentius simply writes that *feroces...reges* (l. 15) had captured Loth. The Bible, however, from which Prudentius had taken the story (Gen. 14:9), gives both the names and the number of the attackers: Chodorlahomor, Thadal, Amraphel, and Arioch, i.e., four kings. Why then do the illustrations show five men, and in their wake why do the captions mention *quinque reges*? Five kings are mentioned in the Bible, but they are the overlords rather than the conquerors of Loth: it is the defeat of the five kings that allows the four kings to capture Loth. Stettiner and Woodruff[51] trace the history of this mistake and come to the conclusion that the error was already present in the archetype of the illustration and goes back to Isidore of Seville.[52] Most glosses speak of four kings, and hence seem to ignore the illustration. In Auct. F. 3. 6 and Durham B. IV. 9, for example, the gloss reads:

> Antequam immolaret filium bellum gessit cum iiii.or regibus. sic nos antea non possumus immolare filium deo. i. animam quousque bellum cum uitiis geramus sicut idem fecit.

In Trinity College O. 2. 51, however, the gloss reads: *cum profanis gentibus*: *.i. regibus quia contra .v. reges pugnauit.* And the following gloss: *Quinque reges .v. sensus corporis signant. Visus. Auditus. gustus. odoratus. tactus.* The text is reminiscent of that in Ambrosius, *De Abraham*, which reads: *Quinque reges, quinque sensus corporis nostri sunt, visus, odoratus, gustus, tactus, auditus*,[53] but because of the different order of the five senses not close enough to argue for an immediate copy. There is no reason for the gloss with its mention of a specific number of kings to become attached to the non-illustrated Trinity College O. 2. 51, since the *Psychomachia* is silent on the number of the kings. The gloss thus must derive from a manuscript that specifies their number. This earlier manuscript could be one with the caption *Ubi quinque reges predati sunt loth* or with the illustration showing five kings. Captions, however, as we have seen above, ultimately derive from illustrations and can therefore only be regarded as intermediate steps. Trinity College O. 2. 51 cannot be shown to be a teaching text, but even though the gloss concerning the five kings appears uniquely in that manuscript, it cannot be original with it. It must be a copy of a gloss that first appeared in a manuscript with an illustration or a caption. Since illustrations give rise to captions, and illustrations or captions (which themselves are based on illustrations) give rise to glosses, we can only conclude that illustrations were seen as commenting on the text, much in the manner of glosses. In a few instances the illustrations give rise to glosses either in contradiction to the text or in specifying something that is not specified in the text but in the illustration. This shows that illustrations and glosses were used for the same purposes. If we accept glosses as teaching techniques, then we must also accept illustrations that give rise to glosses as teaching techniques. This in turn means that illustrations, especially when they appear together with glosses, can help characterise a manuscript as a classbook. Illustrations thus do not necessarily and automatically turn a manuscript into a *de luxe* codex, but can occur in books designed for use in the classroom.

As far as the illustrated *Psychomachia* manuscripts are concerned, we reach the following conclusions. The provenance of these manuscripts suggests schools, and the dates at which they were written suggests royal patronage, which could serve equally well for schools as for churches. The illustrated manuscripts share texts, captions, and glosses with their non-illustrated counterparts, i.e., except for the illustrations there is no significant difference between them. If glossed non-illustrated manuscripts are classbooks, then glossed illustrated ones are as well. All of the Anglo-Saxon illustrated *Psychomachia* manuscripts are glossed, and both placement and content of the glosses imply classroom use. Moreover, the illustrations can be shown to act like commentaries, and a few illustrations can be shown to make common cause with glosses rather than the text, and even give rise to the glosses. This last connection between illustration and gloss is the strongest indication that the illustrations were used for the same purposes as the glosses, namely for teaching in the classroom.

The present argument seeks to reclaim CCCC 23 to the ranks of classbooks, from which Page wanted to see it excluded. It does not extend its claim to the Aldhelm manuscripts which Kiff-Hooper had examined. The 'absence of extensive contemporary glossing' prevents us from considering them any further since, as I hope I have shown, the glosses, and the interplay of the glosses with the illustrations, can show us what the Anglo-Saxons taught in their classrooms.

NOTES

1. R. I. Page, 'On the Feasibility of a Corpus of Anglo-Saxon Glosses: The View from the Library', *Anglo-Saxon Glossography: Papers Read at the International Conference held in the Koninklijke Academie voor Wetenschappen Letteren en Schone Kunsten van België*, ed. R. Derolez (Brussels: Paleis der Academien, 1992), pp. 77–95; J. A. Kiff-Hooper, 'Class Books or Works of Art?: Some Observations on the Tenth-Century

Manuscripts of Aldhelm's *De Laude Virginitatis*', *Church and Chronicle in the Middle Ages: Essays presented to John Taylor*, ed. Ian Wood and G. A. Loud (London: Hambledon Press, 1991), pp. 15–26.

2. Ibid., p. 25.

3. Page's other reasons are these: (a) the base text is often inaccurate, and the word division is idiosyncratic; (b) since the glosses are sometimes displaced, they often do not help the teacher; (c) scholia are often confused and hard to align with their lemmata; (d) glosses are often absent where one would expect them (pp. 90–1). I shall briefly respond to these. To points (b) and (d): displaced glosses are no difficulty for a teacher who prepares himself; often the displacement is minimal and a teacher reading through the text the night before the class could quickly correlate lemma and gloss or scholion. The absence of glosses means nothing; as I have argued in *The Latin Glosses on Arator and Prudentius in Cambridge University Library Ms. Gg. 5. 35*, Studies and Texts, 61 (Toronto: Pontifical Institute of Mediaeval Studies, 1983), p. 192, in theory the teacher should not need any glosses at all, but in practice he will be pleased to have them as reminders to explain or to ask questions. Point (a), the base text often being inaccurate and word division idiosyncratic, would require clarification. What does 'often' mean — a mistake per line, per page, per folio? As Page himself points out (p. 81, *parenti* corrected to *parente*), several of the mistakes have been corrected so that at least one educated reader (at a school?) noticed some errors. If only error-free manuscripts could be considered as classbooks, then the medieval school system would have had very few books to work with. The other question to be asked is whether the word division is really as idiosyncratic as Page would have it. Spot checks in other Anglo-Saxon *Psychomachia* manuscripts reveal similar word divisions as those in CCCC 23, so that the 'idiosyncracy'seems to be Anglo-Saxon rather than that of the scribe of CCCC 23 (examples are *Sedcadit infoueam praeceps quacallida forte*, *Psych*. l. 257 in Durham B. IV. 9, or *Nontrepidantemanu. uindex mea celitus audax*, *Psych*. l. 65 in Additional 24199). Though Page's points a-d certainly do not always make the Anglo-Saxon teacher's task of explicating the text to his students an easy one, nonetheless, on balance, the glosses provide more help than hindrance for the teacher.

4. Ibid., p. 91.

5. On the types of glosses that characterise a manuscript as a classbook, see Gernot R. Wieland, 'The Glossed Manuscript: Classbook or Library Book?' *Anglo-Saxon England* 14 (1985), 153–73.

6. On the number and short titles of the illustrations in *Psychomachia* manuscripts, see H. Woodruff, 'The Illustrated Manuscripts of Prudentius', *Art Studies: Medieval, Renaissance and Modern* 7 (1929), 33–79, at pp. 34–5, n. 3. None of the Anglo-Saxon illustrated manuscripts has all 90

illustrations. CCCC 23, which contains the most compete cycle, lacks only one picture, namely *Fides idolatriam conculcat* (Woodruff's scene 9). Clm 29336/1, being a fragment, has only three (Woodruff's 8–10). Because of the lacuna of lines 705–45, Cleopatra C. viii lacks six illustrations (Woodruff's 80–5). In Additional 24199, all the scenes are complete up to *Auaritia se ornat ut facilius uirtutes fallat* (Woodruff 61); the remaining illustrations have been begun but not completed, and four pictures (Woodruff's 83, 84, 86 and 87) had space left for them, but the artist did not fill them in.

7. See Wieland, 'The Glossed Manuscript', p. 171.
8. Elzbieta Temple, *Anglo-Saxon Manuscripts 900-1066*, A Survey of Manuscripts Illuminated in the British Isles, 2 (London: Harvey Miller, 1976).
9. I make a distincton between 'teaching text' or 'texts for the curriculum' and 'classbooks'. The first two terms refer to texts that we know were read in schools, but without any indication that a particular manuscript was actually used in the classroom. The term 'classbook' denotes a manuscript designed for use by a teacher, regardless of whether it was later actually used as such or not.
10. Illustrations can be found in the following Aldhelm manuscripts: London, British Library, Royal 5 F. iii (Temple no. 2: initials), London, British Library, Royal 7 D. xxiv (Temple no. 4: initials + full-page miniature showing Aldhelm [?]); Oxford, Bodleian Library, Bodley 49 (Temple no. 19 [i]): initials); Cambridge, Corpus Christi College 326 (Temple no. 19 [iv]: initials); Salisbury, Cathedral Library 38 (Temple no. 19 [v]: initials); Oxford, Bodleian Library, Digby 146 (Temple no. 19 [vi]; initials); London, British Library, Royal 15 E. xi (Temple no. 19 [ix]: initials); London, British Library, Royal 12 C. xxiii (Temple no. 30 [iii]; initials: Aldhelm, Riddles); London, British Library, Royal 6 A. vi (Temple no. 30 [xi]; initials); London, Lambeth Palace 200 (Temple no. 39; initials and drawing); Oxford, Bodleian Library, Bodley 577 (Temple no. 57; two drawings).
11. Illustrations can be found in the following Arator manuscripts: Oxford, Bodleian Library, Rawlinson C 570 (Temple no. 30 [iv]; initials) and Cambridge, Trinity College B. 14. 3 (Temple no. 34; initials).
12. Illustrations can be found in the following Sedulius manuscripts: London, British Library, Royal 15 B. xix (Temple no. 19 [iii]; initials) and Paris, Bibliothèque Ste Geneviève 2410 (Temple no. 30 [xvi]; initials).
13. Illustrations can be found in the following Juvencus manuscript: Paris, Bibliothèque Ste Geneviève 2410 (Temple no. 30 [xvi]; initials).
14. Illustrations can be found in the following Boethius manuscripts: Cambridge, Trinity College O. 3. 7 (Temple no. 20; full-page drawing of Philosophy + initials); Paris, Bibliothèque Nationale lat. 6401A (Temple

no. 30 [viii]; initials); Paris, Bibliothèque Nationale lat. 17814 (Temple no. 30 [xii]; initials); Oxford, Bodleian Library, Auctarium F. 1. 15 (Temple no. 37; initials).

15. Martin Irvine (*The Making of Textual Culture: 'Grammatica' and Literary Theory, 350–1100*, Cambridge Studies in Medieval Literature, 19 [Cambridge: Cambridge University Press, 1994]), in his chapter 'The Semiology of the Page and the Layout of Glosses', speaks about the 'hierarchy of scripts' (p. 383), including elaborate initials, but is unfortunately silent about other illustrations.

16. E.g., in London, British Library, Harley 603 (Temple no. 64); in Vatican City, Biblioteca Apostolica Reg. lat. 12 (Temple no. 84); and in London, British Library, Cotton Tiberius C. vi (Temple no. 98).

17. E.g., in the Old English Genesis account in the Junius 11 manuscript (Temple no. 58), and in Ælfric's paraphrase of the Pentateuch and Joshua in London, British Library, Cotton Claudius B. iv (Temple no. 86).

18. London, British Library, Cotton Vitellius A. xv (Temple no. 52).

19. E.g., in London, British Library, Cotton Vitellius C. iii (Temple no. 63), with hundreds of coloured drawings.

20. London, British Library, Cotton Tiberius B. v (Temple no. 87) and London, British Library, Harley 647 (no Temple number, since the manuscript was not illustrated in the British Isles).

21. Cambridge, Trinity College B. 16. 3 (Temple no. 14); Cambridge, University Library Gg. 5. 35 (no Temple number, although it should have one).

22. 'HG' numbers refer to Helmut Gneuss, 'A Preliminary List of Manuscripts Written or Owned in England up to 1100', *Anglo-Saxon England* 9 (1981), 1–60.

23. The Anglo-Saxon manuscripts of Arator's *Historia apostolica* are Cambridge, University Library Gg. 5. 35 (HG 12), Cambridge, Trinity College B. 14. 3 (HG 175), London, British Library, Additional 11034 (HG 280), London, British Library, Royal 15 A. v (HG 488), Oxford, Bodleian Library, Rawlinson C 570 (HG 660), and Paris, Bibliothèque Nationale, lat. 8092 (HG 890); of Juvencus' *Libri Evangeliorum* Cambridge, University Library Ff. 4. 42 (HG 7), Cambridge, University Library Gg. 5. 35 (HG 12), Cambridge, Corpus Christi College 304 (HG 87), London, British Library, Royal 15 A. xvi (HG 489), Oxford, Bodleian Library, Barlow 25 (HG 540), and Paris, Bibliothèque Ste Geneviève 2410 (HG 903); of Sedulius' *Carmen Paschale* Cambridge, University Library, Gg. 5. 35 (HG 12), Cambridge, Corpus Christi College 173 (HG 53), Edinburgh National Library, Advocates' 18. 7. 7 (HG 253), Oxford, Bodleian Library, Lat. th. c. 4 (HG 652), Paris, Bibliothèque Nationale, lat. 8092 (HG 890), Paris, Bibliothèque Ste Geneviève 2410 (HG 903); of Boethius' *De consolatione philosophiae* Cambridge, University Library,

Gg. 5. 35 (HG 12), Cambridge, University Library Kk. 3. 21 (HG 23), Cambridge, Corpus Christi College 214 (HG 68), Cambridge, Trinity College O. 3. 7 (HG 193), London, British Library, Egerton 267 (HG 408), Oxford, Bodleian Library, Auctarium F. 1. 15 (HG 533), Oxford, Corpus Christi College 74 (HG 671), Oxford, Merton College E. 3. 12 (HG 678), Antwerp, Plantin-Moretus Museum 16.8 (formerly 190) (HG 776), El Escorial, Real Biblioteca E. II. 1 (HG 823), Geneva, Bibliotheca Bodmeriana, 175 (HG 829), Paris, Bibliothèque Nationale, lat. 6401 (HG 886), Paris, Bibliothèque Nationale, lat. 6401A (HG 887), Paris, Bibliothèque Nationale, lat. 14380 (HG 899), Paris, Bibliothèque Nationale, lat. 17814 (HG 901), and Vatican City, Biblioteca Apostolica Vaticana, lat. 3363 (HG 908).

24. The Latin glosses of the *Psychomachia* in CCCC 223 have not been published. For the Old English glosses of that manuscript, see Herbert Dean Meritt, ed., *Old English Glosses (A Collection)* (New York: Modern Language Association of America; London: Oxford University Press, 1945), pp. 28–9, and R. I. Page, 'More Old English Scratched Glosses', *Anglia* 97 (1979), 27–45, at pp. 32–43.

25. Margaret Gibson, 'Carolingian Glossed Psalters', *The Early Medieval Bible: Its production, decoration and use*, ed. Richard Gameson, Cambridge Studies in Palaeography and Codicology, 2 (Cambridge: Cambridge University Press, 1994), pp. 78–100, at p. 79.

26. On the textual classes, see Gernot R. Wieland, 'The Anglo-Saxon Manuscripts of Prudentius's *Psychomachia*', *Anglo-Saxon England* 16 (1987), 213–31, at pp. 218–21. Only Additional 24199 is in a textual group by itself, but it shares its illustrations with CCCC 23, and its glosses with CCCC 23 and Auct. F. 3. 6, so that it can be demonstrated to be linked with the other manuscripts.

27. E.g., in non-illustrated manuscripts: CUL Gg. 5. 35: *Pudicitia libidinem extinctam increpat*; Rawlinson C 697: *Pudicitia extinctam libidinem uituperat*; Auct. F. 3. 6: *Extinctam libidinem laetanti ore increpat pudicitia*; CCCC 223: *Pudicitia libidinem extinctam increpat*; Trinity College, O. 2. 51: *Pudicitia libidinem extinctam increpat*; Durham B. IV. 9 does not have this caption. In illustrated manuscripts: Cotton Cleopatra C. viii: *Pudicitia libidinem extinctam increpat*; CCCC 23: *Pudicitia libidinem extinctam increpat*; Additional 24199 does not have captions, clm 29336/1 does not have this picture.

28. On these two categories, see Wieland, 'The Anglo-Saxon manuscripts of Prudentius's *Psychomachia*', pp. 225–8.

29. Cleopatra C. viii actually contains glosses of both groups A and B: those of group A are written in the hand that wrote the text while those of group B were added later; the glosses of group A outnumber those of group B, and hence the manuscript can be seen as originally, and basically, a gloss

group A manuscript. Durham B. IV. 9 also has glosses from both groups.

30. R. Stettiner, *Die illustrierten Prudentiushandschriften* (Berlin: J. S. Preuss, 1895), p. 170, and H. Woodruff, 'The Illustrated Manuscripts of Prudentius', pp. 50–1.

31. These measurements are Temple's. Page's measurements for CCCC 23, 360 x 285 mm., differ slightly.

32. Cleopatra C. viii has definitely, and CCCC 23 has tentatively been assigned to the Christ Church scriptorium in Canterbury. On the basis of the differences just outlined, I would suggest that CCCC 23 has not been written at the same scriptorium as Cleopatra C. viii.

33. T. A. Heslop, 'The Production of *de luxe* Manuscripts and the Patronage of King Cnut and Queen Emma', *Anglo-Saxon England* 19 (1990), 151–95, at pp. 153 and 172 respectively.

34. Heslop, '*De luxe* Manuscripts', p. 167, n. 45; Temple no. 61, although Temple does not mention that the artist of the York Gospels is identical with that of the first ten illustrations of Cleopatra C. viii.

35. The *Anticlaudianus*, admittedly a text written after the Anglo-Saxon period, contains the line: 'Quod lingua nequit, pictura fatetur', which comes closest to our modern sentiment (*Alain de Lille: Anticlaudianus. Texte critique avec une introduction et des tables*, ed. R. Bossuat [Paris: Vrin, 1955], 5. 118). The earlier Middle Ages could draw on the *Ad Herennium*, which contains the following statement: 'Poema loquens pictura, pictura tacitum poema debet esse' (*Rhetorique à Herennius*, ed. and trans. Guy Achard [Paris: Belles Lettres, 1989], p. 177).

36. *Aurelii Prudentii Clementis Carmina*, ed. Maurice P. Cunningham, Corpus Christianorum, Series Latina, 126 (Turnhout: Brepols, 1966), p. 156. All other quotations are taken from this edition as well.

37. This change is not present in all the manuscripts; it occurs in Additional 24199 and CCCC 23 in the illustration preceding l. 145, but the Patientia of the same scene in Cleopatra C. viii does not wear a helmet.

38. Woodruff no. 71, preceding l. 629.

39. In CCCC 23 and Cleopatra C. viii the illustration is complete, although the ink has faded somewhat in Cleopatra C. viii. In Additional 24199 the illustration is incomplete; only Vis and Labour are shown, and the inscription incorrectly reads *LABOR METUS FRAUS dispersi fugiunt*.

40. The illustration of Iocus (Woodruff no. 50) precedes l. 432; of Amor (Woodruff no. 51) l. 436; and of Pompa (Woodruff no. 52) l. 439.

41. The Anglo-Saxon's lack of familiarity with the musical instrument can be demonstrated by the Old English translation of the Latin caption in Cleopatra C. viii. The Latin *Iocus cymbala proiciens fugit* is translated as *Her þara cymbala stow aworpen was*. Aside from the fact that *Iocus* is misread as *locus* and *fugit* as *fuit* (which it originally was before it was corrected), the Old English translation keeps the word *cymbala* and

considers it genitive plural. See. J. Zupitza, 'Englisches aus Prudentius-handschriften', *Zeitschrift für deutsches Alterthum und deutsche Litteratur* 20 (1876), 41. Despite their efforts, the illustrators were not successful in making the instrument familiar; in all three manuscripts the cymbals look like two wheels mounted on a stick.

42. The illustrator of CCCC 23 has added a cross on the end of the stole. There is no such cross in the illustration of Additional 24199, although there Pompa does remove a stole. In Cleopatra C. viii Pompa seems to wear an elaborate necklace rather than a stole.

43. In so doing he follows writers like Alcuin who in letter 19, addressed to the monks of Jarrow and Monkwearmouth, writes: 'Nolite conformare vos saeculi hominibus in vestimentorum vanitate' (p. 54) and later in the same letter: 'Vos decet, ut filios Dei...vestimentorum modestia' (p. 54). And in letter 21 to Higbald, bishop of Lindisfarne, he expresses a similar sentiment: 'Dum a pompis feminas prohibere curavit, de pretiosis vestimentis, quanto magis viros non decet vanitas vestimentorum, et maxime Deo servientibus sub nomine monachciae vitae nocet' (p. 59). See MGH *Epistolae Karolini Aevi* 2, ed. E. Duemmler (Berlin: Weidmann, 1895, repr. 1974).

44. Woodruff no. 2, *Praef.* l. 15.

45. Eight people accompany Loth in Additional 24199 and two in CCCC 23. In both these manuscripts some cattle are shown as well. In Cleopatra C. viii Loth is accompanied by only one woman, and there is no cattle.

46. The captions read: CUL Gg. 5. 35: *Abraham offert agnum. Melchisedech panem et uinum*; Cleopatra C. viii: *Ubi abraham decimas offert et Melchisedech offert habrahe panem et uinum. Melchisedech rex et sacerdos dei summi*; Rawlinson C. 697: *Ubi Abraham decimas offert et Melchisedech panem et uinum. Melchisedech rex et sacerdos summi dei*; CCCC 23: *Abram decimas offert et Melchisedech Abrahe panem et uinum. Melchisedech rex et sacerdos dei*; CCCC 223: *De Melchisedech*; Trinity College O. 2. 51: *Ubi Abraham decimas offert et Melchisedech.* Durham B. IV. 9, Additional 24199, and Auct. F. 3. 6 do not have a caption for this scene or paragraph; clm 29336/1 does not contain this text.

47. Gen. 14:20: *et dedit ei decimas ex omnibus*, although the context does not make it entirely clear whether Abraham or Melchisedech is the subject of *dedit*.

48. Woodruff no. 56. The captions read: CUL Gg. 5. 35: *Auaritia spolia in sinistro latere protegit*; Cleopatra C. viii: *Auaritia spolia in sinistro latere protegit*; CCCC 23: *Auaritia spolia in sinistro latere protegit*; CCCC 223: *Auaritia spolia in sinistro latere tegit*. The other manuscripts do not have captions for this scene or paragraph.

49. This gloss appears in Cleopatra C. viii, CCCC 23, and Additional 24199. In Gg. 5. 35 the gloss reads *publicos saccos.* CCCC 223, Trinity College

O. 2. 51, and Rawlinson C 697 are not glossed. Clm 29336/1 does not have this text, and hence no gloss, and Durham B. IV. 9 has only *saccos*.

50. Woodruff no. 2. The captions read: Gg. 5. 35: *Loth captus de sodomis*; Cleopatra C. viii: *Ubi quinque reges predati sunt loth*; Rawlinson C 697: *Ubi quinque reges predati sunt loth*; CCCC 23: *Ubi quinque reges predati sunt loth*; CCCC 223: *De Lot capto*. The other manuscripts do not have captions for this scene or paragraph.

51. Stettiner, *Die illustrierten*, pp. 161, 204, 214–5, and 222–4; Woodruff, 'The Illustrated Manuscripts of Prudentius', pp. 48 and 77–8.

52. Isidore of Seville, *Quaestiones in vetus testamentum: In Genesin*, PL 83, col. 239: Deinde a quinque regibus, qui Sodomis irruerant, captum Lot liberat, habens secum in praelio trecentos decem et octo vernulas. Sed quid haec victoria Abraham de quinque reges indicabat, quos ille fidei pater mysterio superavit, nisi quod fides nostra, si confirmata sit in spiritu principali, totidem corporis nostri sensus verbo Dei subigat? Nam sicut ille de proximo in regibus victor, ita et fides nostra per animam victrix de exteriore homine triumphat.

53. PL 14, col. 497.

2 Cambridge Corpus Christi College 57 and its Anglo-Saxon Users

Timothy Graham

Cambridge, Corpus Christi College 57 contains a collection of Latin Benedictine texts suitable for public reading, and dates from the late tenth or early eleventh century.[1] While its place of origin is uncertain, added texts show that it was at the abbey of St Mary, Abingdon, by the 1040s. It attracted considerable attention from readers, as is demonstrated by the many added glosses, notes, marks of various forms and sketches. Close study of the manuscript and its additions reveals much about its intended purpose and actual usage, and provides illuminating insights into the practices of a late Anglo-Saxon monastery.

CONTENTS

The manuscript now contains 163 leaves, the original contents of which are as follows:

fols 2r–32v|11: the *Regula sancti Benedicti.*

fol. 32v|12–17: a brief excerpt from the end of the *Liber de conflictu uitiorum et uirtutum* by the Frankish theologian Ambrosius Autpertus (d. 784), monk of the Benedictine abbey of San Vincenzo al Volturno in south central Italy. The manuscript misattributes the text to St Fulgentius.

fols 33r–37v|12: the text known as the *Memoriale qualiter*. The manuscript divides this into two separate texts, with the first (fols 33r–34v|16) entitled *Memoriale qualiter in monasterio conuersari debemus* and the second (fols 34v|17–37v|12) *Epitoma Lothuuici imperatoris super regulam beati Benedicti.*

fol. 37v|12–22: Canon XXXVI of the Council of Mainz of 813, here entitled *De festiuitatibus anni* without indication of its source.

fols 37v|23–40v: a collection of monastic decrees passed at Aachen under the emperor Louis the Pious, here entitled *Adbreuiatio eius qui supra.*

fols 41r–94r: *Martyrologium* of Usuard of Saint-Germain-des-Prés.

fols 95r–163v: *Diadema monachorum* of Smaragdus of Saint-Mihiel. The text ends abruptly within chapter LXXXIV. In the lower margin of fol. 163va sixteenth-century hand has commented that a complete quire is missing from the manuscript.

The contents thus comprise the Rule of St Benedict, the central prescriptive text for all Benedictine monks, combined with a group of texts produced during the period of the Carolingian Benedictine renewal. Together the texts direct the monk how to behave in the monastery and to conduct his daily life, and provide a core of edifying reading.

St Benedict's Rule, composed in the second quarter of the sixth century, recommended itself to communities by the concision with which it dealt with a comprehensive range of aspects of monastic life, including the qualities required of every monk, the duties of office-holders, the programme for the daily celebration of the divine office and for the monks' daily labour, and procedures for conducting the communal aspects of life and for correcting wrongdoers.[2] The excerpt from Ambrosius Autpertus that follows the Rule in MS 57 clearly functions as a tailpiece to it, for it immediately follows the *explicit* of the Rule and the rest of the page is left blank following the excerpt. The brief text recommends adherence to the Rule of St Benedict above all other Rules, directs followers of the Rule not to deviate from it in any matter as it contains all that is requisite, and proclaims that its words lead its followers to the palaces of heaven.[3]

The texts grouped on fols 33–40 are for the most part linked with the movement of Benedictine reform promoted under the emperor Louis the Pious (814–840) by his adviser Benedict of Aniane (750–821). The *Memoriale qualiter* was probably composed in the late eighth century, perhaps in middle Germany.[4] It is thought that Benedict of Aniane may have come upon it in a Frankish monastery, and that he perhaps circulated it by appending it to the Acts of the Council of Aachen of 817.[5] Like the *Regula sancti Benedicti*, the text is prescriptive. It falls into three sections, of which the first directs how the monk should conduct his day from the moment of rising for the night office until the time of manual labour, while the third covers the period from the evening meal until the time to retire to bed after compline. Sandwiched between these sections is an interpolated set of general directions about monastic behaviour, covering such issues as how juniors are to act towards seniors and vice versa, what the monk should do if he breaks or damages anything while working in the refectory or kitchen, and the importance of obedience. Morgand and Wandrille concluded that this middle section of the text was a compilation from other sources made by the author of the *Memoriale qualiter*, and intentionally interpolated.[6] The presentation of the *Memoriale* in MS 57 as two separate texts, each with its own title, is unusual,[7] although it is clearly somehow connected with the interpolation. The division in MS 57 comes one sentence before the general directions begin. The division interrupts the flow of the text: the first sentence following the division, which stipulates the hours at which, during the two principal seasons of the year, the monks should break off from their manual labour for the divine office, relates back to the last sentence before the division, which directs what the monks should do when during their manual labour, at the canonical hours, they hear the bell summoning them to office. Despite this link between the two sentences, Morgand and Wandrille concluded that the sentence that in MS 57 follows the division was probably interpolated into the *Memoriale* along with the general directions.[8] If correct, this would help to explain why it is at this point that MS 57 divides the *Memoriale*. It is notable that other Anglo-Saxon copies of the *Memoriale* mark the same point in the text with a major initial and the use of capitals, despite the disruption to the continuity of the text that this entails.[9]

The brief text that MS 57 entitles *De festiuitatibus anni* comprises Canon XXXVI of the Council of Mainz of 813.[10] This was one of five regional councils that Charlemagne caused to be convened in the late spring and early summer of 813, to reform the Frankish Church and eliminate abuses. Canon XXXVI, which may have acquired general acceptance, stipulates which feast days, beginning with Easter and ending with the Purification, are to be celebrated each year in all churches.

The preamble to the text that MS 57 entitles *Memoriale eius qui supra* states that the text comprises the proceedings of a monastic council held at Aachen in 817. Semmler, the modern editor of the text (which occurs in numerous manuscripts), has shown that it is more likely that it combines, and partly modifies, the monastic decrees of the two Aachen councils of 816 and 817.[11] This combined text may have been compiled at the council held at Aachen in the winter of 818–819. The purpose of the Aachen councils, summoned by Louis the Pious and presided over by Benedict of Aniane, was to establish norms of religious observance throughout the Carolingian empire for both secular clergy and monks. If Semmler's analysis of the Aachen legislation and its manuscript witnesses is correct, the monastic decrees of the 817 council both modified some of the 816 decrees, and regulated many matters not covered in the latter; the combined text of 818–819 places the 816 decrees first, but omits those that were modified in the council of 817. Semmler gave the combined text the title *Regula sancti Benedicti Anianensis siue Collectio capitularis*. Its decrees regulate such aspects of monastic life as clothing, food, hygiene, the admission of novices, the hierarchy of officers within the monastery, and the daily celebration of the office.[12] In some respects the decrees modify the provisions of the Rule of St Benedict.

The *Martyrologium* that occupies fols 41r–94r of MS 57 commemorates martyrs and confessors day by day throughout the year, from 1 January to 31 December. The individual entries name the saints for each day and state where they died, and frequently provide brief information about the manner of their death. By supplying such information, the text falls within the genre of the historical Martyrology.[13] It is the work of Usuard, monk of Saint-Germain-des-Prés (d. *c.* 877), and was compiled between *c.* 850 and *c.* 865.[14] Usuard's Martyrology, which drew on those of pseudo-Jerome, Bede, Florus of Lyons (d. 860) and Ado of Vienne (*c.* 800–875), was the first to have an entry for every single day of the year. The copy in MS 57 lacks the preface that Usuard addressed to Charles the Bald, King of the West Franks (840–877). Otherwise, it presents (in its original form, before marginal and interlinear additions were made) an almost unmodified version of Usuard's text, unlike other copies which extensively modify Usuard's text to local requirements.[15]

The last text in MS 57, the *Diadema monachorum*, is by Smaragdus, who became abbot of Saint-Mihiel in the diocese of Verdun by 809, and remained in office until his death some time between 826 and 841.[16] He had close links with Benedict of Aniane. He wrote the *Diadema* probably shortly before or around 816. It is a compilation from earlier works, notably the *Sententiae* of Isidore of Seville (*c.* 560–636), the *Expositio super epistolas catholicas* of Bede, the *Sententiae* of Taio, bishop of Saragossa (651–after 653), and various works by Pope Gregory the Great (*c.* 540–604). Smaragdus intended the book to provide edifying reading for monastic communities. It discusses practices and virtues that should be cultivated by monks, and describes the ensuing benefits. For example, the first chapter, on prayer, notes that prayer is the soul's remedy for one who is beset by temptations, and observes that true prayer proceeds from the heart, not the lips. Smaragdus also describes the pitfalls that may present themselves to the aspiring monk, and how to avoid them. The individual chapters frequently begin with a quotation from the Scriptures, often from the epistles of St Paul or the Catholic epistles. Altogether the work comprises one hundred chapters, but the copy in MS 57 breaks off abruptly within chapter LXXXIV, at the end of a quire. The sixteenth-century comment in the lower margin of the last page (fol. 163v), observing that a whole quire is missing, may well be accurate. Continuing at the same rate of script, it would probably have taken the scribe between 17 and 18 pages to complete the text.

The contents of MS 57 thus form a coherent body of texts — variously prescriptive and edifying — suitable for a community of Benedictine monks.

The link with the Carolingian Benedictine reform is striking. The manuscript's version of the Rule of St Benedict itself belongs to that branch of the text (known as the *textus receptus*) that originated in the Carolingian empire toward the mid-ninth century as a result of contamination between the version that had prevailed in the seventh and eighth centuries (the *textus interpolatus*) and the version that supposedly represented St Benedict's original (the *textus purus*), whose diffusion Benedict of Aniane encouraged.[17] All other texts in the manuscript belong to the late eighth or ninth century; several of them were actively promoted by Benedict of Aniane or, as with the *Diadema monachorum*, are the work of someone within his milieu. The original contents of MS 57 include no text that is not Continental or that is later than the second half of the ninth century.

The group of texts that follows the Rule on fols 32v–40v links MS 57 with four other Anglo-Saxon manuscripts of the Rule of St Benedict in which all or some of the same texts follow the Rule.[18] The manuscripts are: London, British Library, Harley 5431, fols 4–126, made at St Augustine's Abbey, Canterbury, in the second half of the tenth century; Cotton Tiberius A. iii, made at Canterbury in the mid-eleventh century; Cotton Titus A. iv, made perhaps at Winchester in the mid-eleventh century; and Cambridge University Library Ll. 1. 14, fols 70–108, of unknown provenance but datable to the second half of the eleventh century. The closest link is with Tiberius A. iii in which, on fols 163v–173r, the texts occur in exactly the same order as in MS 57, although Tiberius A. iii lacks the first portion of the *Memoriale qualiter*, having only the portion that in MS 57 appears as a separate text with the title *Adbreuiatio eius qui supra*. Harley 5431 includes all the texts, but in a different order, and with the text attributed to Fulgentius as a thirteenth-century addition.[19] Titus A. iv, which lacks the pseudo-Fulgentius text, has the others in the same order as Harley 5431. CUL Ll. 1. 14 has only the *Memoriale qualiter* and the Aachen Capitulary, and separates them by inserting another item between them.[20] These texts, in varying orders and combinations, were evidently seen as a fitting complement to the Rule of St Benedict in the late Anglo-Saxon monastic context.

However, the complete range of the contents of MS 57 is paralleled in no other surviving Anglo-Saxon manuscript. There is no other Anglo-Saxon copy of Usuard's *Martyrologium*; the next earliest surviving English copies date from the post-Conquest period.[21] Smaragdus' *Diadema monachorum* occurs in one other Anglo-Saxon manuscript: Cambridge University Library Ff. 4. 43, made at Christ Church, Canterbury, in the late tenth century. It is there presented on its own, with no accompanying texts, as it is in a post-Conquest copy of unascertained origin; in another post-Conquest copy, from Nunnaminster, Winchester, it is combined with a moral treatise *De superbia et fornicatione* and a set of sermons.[22] In addition to these surviving copies, the *Diadema* is mentioned in three booklists dating between the third quarter of the eleventh century and *c.* 1100.[23] The wording of two of these — the list of books that Bishop Leofric (1050–1072) procured for Exeter Cathedral, and a list of *c.* 1100 perhaps from Peterborough — suggests that in the listed copies, the *Diadema* occurred on its own. The third — the list of books given *c.* 1070 by Sæwold, sometime abbot of Bath, to the abbey of Saint-Vaast, Arras — indicates that the *Diadema* was coupled with the Rule of St Benedict: *Librum regule sancti Benedicti et Diadema monachorum.* MS 57, by combining the *Diadema* with both the Rule and the other accompanying texts, presents a highly functional volume whose purpose will be discussed below.

PALAEOGRAPHICAL AND CODICOLOGICAL ASPECTS OF THE MANUSCRIPT

MS 57 has a large, squarish format. Its leaves now measure *c.* 328 x 254 mm but were formerly somewhat larger, as is shown by the trimming of an entry in the upper margin of fol. 2r and of entries in several outer margins, for example fols 3r, 10r and 15v. Apart from three replacement leaves and a replacement patch, all described below, the leaves are brownish cream-coloured, with flesh-sides appearing somewhat lighter. The grain pattern of the skin is clearly visible in areas of the hair-sides of numerous leaves, for example the lower right area of fols 11r and 57r, the lower left area of fols 14v and 61v, and the upper area of fol. 88v. Patterns of veins can be seen on the flesh-sides of several leaves, for example fols 36v (outer margin) and 124v (upper and lower areas; see Plate 1). The membrane is calf-skin for all leaves.[24] In several places it is possible to see the parallel grooves made by the comb-like instrument used to scrape the skins: for example, in the lower left area of fols 21v and 48v, the upper right area of fol. 41r, and the outer right area of fols 83r and 97r. The leaves are arranged with the hair-side on the outside, so that, except between quires and mid-quire, hair-side faces flesh-side across the openings. The only exception occurs in Quire 6 (fols 41–48), where the central bifolium (fols 44–45) has its flesh-side turned outwards. The arrangement with hair-side on the outside corresponds with the Insular practice that in late tenth- and early eleventh-century England was giving way to the Continental practice in which the leaves were arranged so that hair-side faced hair-side and flesh-side faced flesh-side across the openings.[25] By the arrangement of its leaves, MS 57 looks backwards rather than forwards.

Pricks to guide the horizontal rulings on the leaves were made in the outer margin only, not in both margins as had been the earlier Insular practice.[26] The later trimming of the leaves has removed the pricks in the outer margins of all except the three replacement leaves, fols 8, 19 and 22. The leaves are ruled in drypoint for 27 lines of text. Unusually, there are two horizontal rulings — both a base-line and a head-line — for each line of text. The two rulings are generally *c.* 3 mm apart, and those letters that are minim-high are entered between them, while those with ascenders or descenders project above the head-line or below the base-line. Ker noted a handful of Anglo-Saxon manuscripts that are similarly ruled with pairs of horizontal lines. Most of these date to the early eleventh century and all are carefully written; where their place of origin is known or can be surmised, it tends to be within south-east England.[27] In MS 57, the distance between consecutive base-lines is *c.* 10.5–12 mm. This leaves a generous amount of space between lines of script, so that the text appears uncramped. There are pairs of vertical bounding-lines at each side of the column. These guided the entering of coloured initials at the left of the text-columns, although the initials usually extend beyond the inner line of the pair. On fols 3v–4v and 95v–97r there is an extra vertical line to guide the entering of the small ink initials of the chapter-lists on those pages; and on fols 3v–4r, but not fols 95v–97r, there are further vertical lines to guide the entering of the chapter-numbers of the list. Throughout the manuscript, the pairs of horizontal rulings for the top line and the bottom line of text extend the full width of the leaf; on fol. 17 (but not its conjoint, fol. 24), the pairs of rulings for the bottom two lines of text extend the full width. The other horizontal rulings extend between the inner lines of the pairs of vertical bounding-lines (and frequently project somewhat beyond).

The text on the leaves occupies an area of *c.* 280 x *c.* 203 mm, including the area at the left of the page that is reserved for the coloured initials. All the original contents were copied by a single scribe writing a late version of Anglo-Saxon Square minuscule datable to the late tenth or early eleventh century.[28] The square aspect of the script is emphasised by the horizontal stroke that provides a flat top to the letters *a*, *n*, *q* and *r*, to the two halves of *m*, and to the arm of *h* (see Plates 1–3, 5–7 and 9–10). As is normal for Square minuscule, the scribe employed the Insular forms of the letters *f*, *g* and *r*. The letter *d* occurs in both round-backed and straight-backed forms, with round-backed predominating. High *e* is used regularly in ligature with *t* for the word *et*; otherwise high *e* occurs only occasionally, linking with the next letter, usually to save space at line-ends (for example, on fols 2v|1, 6r|5 and 10, 98r|24 and 163v|16). High *i* occurs frequently in initial position before *n*, but not otherwise. Whether initial, medial or final, the letter *s* is usually low-set, with the stem descending below the base-line and the head of the letter not rising above the head-line. Tall *s* occurs very infrequently, for example in *spreuerunt*, fol. 5v|17–18, and *posterioribus*, fol. 13r|23–24. The round, half-uncial form of *s* occurs quite commonly within the *Diadema monachorum* (for example, fol. 97v|4, 7–9 and 13–14; see Plate 3), but not otherwise. Ligatures are used for the digraphs *æ* and *œ* and, as mentioned above, for the word *et*, where a single stroke serves for the tongue of *e* and the headstroke of *t*; otherwise ligatures are not a characteristic of the script. The tops of the minims of *i* and *u*, of the first minims of *m* and *n*, of the left stem of *f*, *p*, *r* and *s*, and of ascenders, end in emphatic wedge-shaped serifs. Descenders extend only a short distance below the base-line, which enhances the compactness of the appearance of the script. Abbreviations include the Insular abbreviation for *autem*, consisting of a letter *h* with a curving stroke rising diagonally to the right from the top of its short right limb (see, for example, fols 33v|19, 98r|12 and 26, 121v|2 [Plate 7] and 135r|8). Word separation is generally quite clear, although, as is normal at this period (and later), monosyllabic prepositions are run into the following word without separation. Punctuation (which in places has undergone later adjustment) includes the *punctus* for minor pauses, the *punctus elevatus* for pauses of medium strength, the *punctus versus* for major pauses (at the end of a sentence or of a section), and the *punctus interrogativus* for questions.[29]

The decoration of the manuscript is mostly rather simple. Titles, chapter-numbers, initials that begin texts or chapters within the texts, and the first line of several texts (including the first line of each month in the Martyrology) are written in metallic red lead pigment which in many cases has corroded and darkened. The initial on fol. 2r beginning the preface to the Rule of St Benedict is in green pigment (with ink additions). The height of the initials varies between two and four lines. The letters of the coloured first lines generally extend between two consecutive ruled base-lines or (as in several cases within the Martyrology) between two consecutive head-lines. Chapter I of the *Diadema monachorum* begins on fol. 97v with two lines of somewhat shorter coloured capitals, the letters being 'suspended' from one ruled head-line and extending down about half the distance to the next. The letters of all these coloured titles, initials and first lines are usually undecorated capitals. However, within the Martyrology, the initial *K* of the word *Kalendae* that begins the entries for each month usually has simple foliate decoration and/or has one or more areas left uncoloured (Plate 2). The initial beginning the preface of the *Diadema* on fol. 95r similarly has bare areas and a simple decorative curl.

The initial that begins chapter I of the *Diadema* on fol. 97v is the only element in the manuscript to include major decoration (Plate 3). With its outlines drawn in ink, the initial includes one animal-head, two bird-heads, band-like interlace, and foliate elements, and thus falls within Francis Wormald's Type IIb of late Anglo-Saxon initials.[30] Within the ink outlines, some features of the bird-heads and of the foliate elements are drawn in red pigment.

Throughout the manuscript, within the body of the text, sentences begin with thickened ink initials built up by several strokes of the pen. Frequently these initials have a filling of yellow pigment. In certain initials on fols 11v, 12r, 12v, 108v, 124v, 144v, 146v, 147r and 160r, the features of a human face have been entered in ink within the rounded bow of the letter (Plate 1). Several of these faces include a convex line near the top of the head. The line appears to indicate a tonsure and the faces seem therefore intended to be monastic. Examination under a microscope of the face within the initial *O* on fol. 146v|17 shows that the yellow infilling overlies the ink lines of the face, and was therefore added after the face had been drawn.

In significant respects, the appearance of the manuscript presents a paradoxical contrast to its contents. The latter associate the manuscript firmly with the movement of Benedictine reform initiated in England in the third quarter of the tenth century under the impetus of Sts Dunstan, Æthelwold and Oswald. That movement looked to the Continent, and to Carolingian precedent, for much of its inspiration. It was in association with the reform movement that the use of Caroline minuscule for Latin texts spread in England, and it was also from the late tenth century that English scribes began to adopt the practice of arranging the leaves of their quires in the Continental manner, with hair-side facing hair-side and flesh-side facing flesh-side. MS 57, however, uses a version of a more traditional English script despite its contents being in Latin, just as it also looks back to the English past by the arrangement of its leaves.

By the mid-eleventh century some leaves of the manuscript must have been lost or have become significantly damaged, for at that time three leaves were replaced (the replacements being the present fols 8 [Plate 4], 19 and 22), while a replacement patch, carefully shaped to fit the space that it fills, was sewn in the lower inner area of fol. 85 (Plate 5). The lost leaves were the last leaf of Quire 1, presumably originally conjoint with fol. 1, and the third and sixth leaves of Quire 3; these latter could have been a bifolium or two single leaves. The replacements are lighter in colour than the original leaves. They were arranged so that the disposition of their hair- and flesh-sides accorded with the pattern of the original manuscript. The hair-sides are thus fols 8v, 19r and 22v. The patch on fol. 85 has its hair-side turned to the recto, to match the leaf into which it fits. Like the original leaves, the replacements have 27 lines to the page. However, their ruling differs from that of the original leaves by having only a single ruled horizontal line for each line of text. The three replacement leaves are all written by a single scribe. The script on the replacement patch appears somewhat unsteady, and is perhaps the work of another scribe. On all four replacements, the script self-consciously imitates the script of the original manuscript by using Insular letter-forms and (on fol. 19v|21 and 22) the Insular abbreviation for *autem*. However, the script is more rounded than the original. It uses *ct* and *st* ligatures (for example, on fol. 8r|6, 11 and 23 [Plate 4]), which do not occur in the original scribe's work. Again, when the letter *r* follows *o*, it is often given the 2-shaped form (for example, fol. 8r|3, *amore*, and 15, *gloria* [Plate 4]). Further, in several places the scribe lapsed into Caroline minuscule letter-forms that do not occur on the original leaves. Thus on fol. 8r, Caroline minuscule *a* occurs in lines 1 (*inuidia*m) and 5 (*haec*); Caroline minuscule *g* in line 19 (*Ergo*); and Caroline minuscule *r* in lines 17 (*imperetur*) and 19 (*Ergo*) (Plate 4).[31] The decoration of the replacement leaves also imitates that of the original. Chapter titles are in plain red capitals, and chapters begin with unadorned red initials. Within the chapters, sentences begin with thickened ink initials. However, there is no infilling of yellow pigment such as occurs on the original leaves. Within the upper curve of the red initial *S* beginning chapter XLV of the Rule of St Benedict on fol. 22v|10 is the ink outline of a human head. This presumably imitates the human faces within some initials of the original leaves, although those faces occur only within ink initials of the main body of the text, never within the coloured initials that begin chapters or sections.

The replacement leaves and patch present a fascinating exercise in deliberate archaism aimed at preserving the original character of the manuscript. In the same vein are several corrections over erasure where the script of the correction imitates the original. Among the fairly frequent examples are those on fols 39r|19, 75r|15 and 24, 91r|26–27, 100v|10, 101v|16–17,[32] 102r|8–10 (Plate 6) and 106r|20. Similarly, several additions in interlines, in margins, and within the lines in areas originally left blank, are also in imitative Square minuscule (although many other additions are not). Examples of such Square minuscule additions, which are the work of more than one hand, occur on fols 38v (above line 27), 49v (above line 7), 55r (above line 6) and 76r (in lines 26–27).

In marked contrast to this respect for the character of the original script are adjustments to the script on fols 119v–122r, in chapters XXVI–XXIX of the *Diadema monachorum*. Within these chapters, most of the Square minuscule *a*'s have been altered to Caroline minuscule *a*'s. In most cases the adjustment was effected by adding a short, sharply curved stroke to the top right of the original letter. In some cases, particularly on fol. 121v (Plate 7), the complete letter has been overwritten (without the original letter being erased); several other letters on fol. 121v have also been reinked. On fol. 120r, the Insular *g* that begins line 11 (the second *g* within the word *congregant*) has been altered to Caroline *g*. On fol. 120v|13, the Insular *r* at the end of *efficitur* has been altered to Caroline *r* by partial erasure and rewriting. In line 22 on the same page, the flat-topped *c* that begins *cursus* has been altered to rounded *c*. A further group of adjustments to the script occurs in the lower area of fol. 124r, within chapter XXXII. In lines 16–21, the flat top stroke of the low-set *s* of the original script has in several cases been erased, and a curved stroke added to convert the letter into tall *s* that rises above the head-line. For the two consecutive words *iniustis iusti* in line 21, after the flat top of the first *s* in each word had been erased, the letters *st* were joined in a ligature rising high above the head-line. These various adjustments to the script may have been made by someone studying the manuscript privately. On the other hand, they may have been intended to assist someone reciting these chapters aloud. In the latter case they would be in line with other adjustments that were made to prepare the manuscript for public recitation.[33]

THE ORIGIN OF THE MANUSCRIPT

Two texts added on the originally blank fol. 94v, between the end of the Martyrology and the beginning of the *Diadema*, indicate that at the time they were entered, the manuscript was at the abbey of St Mary, Abingdon (Plate 8). The first text is a formula for announcing the death of a member of the Abingdon community to the church at large. It begins with the words *Domnus abba .N. totaque Abbandoniensis coenobii caterua regulari annuente domino disciplinę subiecta*. The second text, in a different hand of similar character, provides a formula for announcing the death of a member of another community to Abingdon,[34] and is more specific than the first formula in that its opening words of address name the abbot of Abingdon: *karissimo domno Æþelstano. & cunctis fratribus Abbanduniensis monasterii*. Æthelstan was abbot probably from 1044 until his death in 1047. The presence of the manuscript at Abingdon in the mid-1040s is therefore certain.

The abbey at Abingdon had been restored *c.* 954 by St Æthelwold, who remained there as abbot until his appointment to the see of Winchester in 963. Given the associations of the contents of MS 57 with the Carolingian Benedictine reform movement, and Æthelwold's strong sympathies with Continental Benedictine practice, it is tempting to see MS 57 as having been produced at Abingdon a generation or so after Æthelwold's departure, under the influences that he had introduced there. As was noted by Æthelwold's biographer Wulfstan the Cantor, writing at Winchester in the late tenth or early eleventh century, Æthelwold had himself wished to travel to the Continent to experience its reformed Benedictine practice, but had been prevented from doing so by King Eadred (946–955), who appointed him to Abingdon instead.[35] While at Abingdon, Æthelwold sent the monk Osgar to the abbey of Fleury — a principal centre of reform — to observe the customs there and report back.[36] Osgar was to succeed Æthelwold as abbot of Abingdon in 963, continuing in office until his death in 984. He may have brought back from Fleury a copy of the Rule of St Benedict, for the late twelfth- or early thirteenth-century *De abbatibus Abbendoniae* implies that Æthelwold had a copy brought from there: *Fecit...enire regulam Sancti Benedicti a Floriaco monasterio*.[37] Nor was Fleury the only Continental house with which Æthelwold established links while at Abingdon. According to the *Historia monasterii de Abingdon*, compiled in the late twelfth century, Æthelwold summoned to St Mary's a group of monks from

Corbie in north-eastern France to instruct his monks in reading and chanting.[38] It would not be surprising if Abingdon had produced in the late tenth or early eleventh century its own compilation of Continental Benedictine texts based on models acquired during Æthelwold's abbacy.

However, aspects of the appearance of MS 57 complicate the possibility of an Abingdon origin. The most notable palaeographical feature of the manuscript is that its scribe copied Latin texts in an uncompromisingly traditional Anglo-Saxon script at a time when English Caroline minuscule was commonly used in various centres for the copying of Latin texts.[39] T.A.M. Bishop, indeed, saw Abingdon as the principal centre for the early adoption and diffusion of the Caroline script in England.[40] His view has been questioned by David Dumville on the grounds that the place of origin of certain charters and manuscripts that Bishop attributed to Abingdon is more uncertain than Bishop admitted.[41] Nonetheless, while the status of Abingdon in the history of the origin and diffusion of English Caroline minuscule may be questionable, it remains true, as Dumville has also pointed out, that the houses associated with Æthelwold appear generally to have adopted Caroline script for copying Latin texts.[42] Further, Latin manuscripts of approximately the same date as MS 57 that have Abingdon associations are written in developed English Caroline minuscule that sets them quite apart from MS 57. The manuscripts include Antwerp, Plantin-Moretus Museum 16.2 (formerly 47) + London, British Library, Additional 32246, a copy of the *Excerptiones de Prisciano*; Antwerp, Plantin-Moretus Museum 16.8 (formerly 190), a copy of Boethius' *De consolatione Philosophiae*; Brussels, Bibliothèque Royale 1650, a copy of the prose version of Aldhelm's *De laudibus uirginitatis*; Cambridge University Library Kk. 3. 21, another copy of the *De consolatione*; and Oxford, Bodleian Library, Digby 146, another copy of the prose *De uirginitate*.[43] The three manuscripts now in Antwerp and Brussels (together with the fragment in London) are believed originally to have formed a single codex. All five manuscripts belong to the late tenth or early eleventh century. It must be acknowledged, however, that the place of origin of none of them is assured; their link with Abingdon is established by eleventh-century additions mentioning estates, individuals or saints associated with Abingdon, or by intertextual relationships. Nonetheless, it remains striking that those Latin manuscripts roughly contemporary with MS 57 that have links with Abingdon within the Anglo-Saxon period differ so noticeably from MS 57 in the character of their script. This, coupled with what is known of scribal practice in Æthelwoldian houses, suggests that the possibility of an Abingdon origin for MS 57 should be treated with some caution.

Dumville, noting Mechthild Gretsch's evidence that the text of the Rule of St Benedict in MS 57 showed some influence from the *textus interpolatus* tradition as represented by the eighth-century manuscript, Oxford, Bodleian

Library, Hatton 48, which has a Worcester provenance, alluded to the possibility that MS 57 might have originated at Worcester.[44] There is, however, nothing in the appearance of the manuscript to link it with Worcester, nor any known evidence of significant connections between Abingdon and Worcester, and what influence there may be from the *interpolatus* tradition does not have to be attributed directly to the Hatton manuscript.[45] Of greater weight are textual and artistic aspects of MS 57 that point towards Canterbury. As noted above, two of the manuscripts that accompany the Rule of St Benedict with some or all of the texts that occur on fols 32v–40v of MS 57 have a Canterbury origin. It is with one of these Canterbury manuscripts, the mid-eleventh-century Tiberius A. iii, that this group of texts in MS 57 has the strongest links. Further, the Rule of St Benedict in MS 57 includes an added set of glosses that is substantially the same as that in a mid-tenth-century manuscript (Cambridge, Trinity College O. 2. 30, fols 129–172) written by a scribe known to have been active at St Augustine's Abbey, Canterbury.[46] Another Canterbury association may be provided by the text of the Martyrology of MS 57. T.A. Heslop has discovered that in its original state — before the many marginal and interlinear additions were made — the Martyrology differed from the text as compiled by Usuard by including certain saints associated with Glastonbury and Flanders.[47] This suggests the possible influence of St Dunstan (d. 988), who had been abbot of Glastonbury in the 940s and 950s before being exiled to Flanders in 956–957. After brief spells as bishop of Worcester and of London following his recall in 957, Dunstan became archbishop of Canterbury in 959, and it is possible that the Martyrology in MS 57 derives from an exemplar dating from, or modified during, Dunstan's archiepiscopate. In any event, it is towards Canterbury that MS 57's one significant decorated initial points. Type IIb initials are found commonly in Canterbury manuscripts of the late tenth and early eleventh centuries, but only rarely in manuscripts produced elsewhere.[48] The skilled example that begins the *Diadema monachorum* in MS 57 includes several specific features that can be well paralleled in Canterbury examples; such features include the thin, flat bottom jaw of the creatures' heads, the delicate delineation of the eyebrows and other details of their faces, and the manner in which the interlace weaves around the trellis-like structure of the stem of the initial. In view of these possible Canterbury associations of MS 57, it should be borne in mind that both St Augustine's and Christ Church continued to practise Square minuscule script for Latin texts into the late tenth century.[49]

It is noteworthy that there was interchange between Abingdon and Canterbury both around the time that MS 57 was produced and around the time when its presence at Abingdon is assured. In 995, Ælfric, bishop of Ramsbury and apparently a former monk of Abingdon, became archbishop of Canterbury.[50] He died in 1005, and made a bequest to Abingdon by his will.

In 1044, Abbot Sigeweard of Abingdon — immediate predecessor of the Abbot Æthelstan named in the added text on fol. 94v of MS 57 — was appointed assistant bishop to Eadsige, the infirm archbishop of Canterbury.[51] Sigeweard remained in Canterbury for a few years, finally returning to Abingdon to die in 1048. Not only was there movement of individuals between Abingdon and Canterbury; manuscripts and texts also seem to have passed between the two centres. Despite some views to the contrary, MS B of the Anglo-Saxon Chronicle (London, British Library, Cotton Tiberius A. vi, fols 1–34 + Tiberius A. iii, fol. 178) was most probably written at Abingdon in 977/78.[52] It seems to have served as exemplar for parts of MS C (Cotton Tiberius B. i, fols 115v–164r), most of which is believed to have been copied at Abingdon in 1045/46. If so, this would indicate B's continued presence at Abingdon until that time. At some time before *c.* 1100, however, MS B reached Canterbury, and apparently Christ Church (although it later belonged to St Augustine's), for it includes additions of the late eleventh or early twelfth century by a known Christ Church scribe.[53] MS B may not have been the only annalistic text to travel from Abingdon to Canterbury, for Dumville has suggested that a set of annals covering the period from 983 may have been transferred from Abingdon to Canterbury in 1045, to be continued at St Augustine's Abbey.[54] As for the passage of texts in the opposite direction, the Abingdon additions in Plantin-Moretus 16.2 include a copy of the epitaph of Archbishop Ælfric who was presumably buried at Christ Church.[55]

Textual and artistic aspects of MS 57 therefore combine with the demonstrable links between Abingdon and Canterbury to suggest that, should the manuscript not have originated at Abingdon itself, Canterbury offers a possible alternative. However, only after a full weighing of all the textual, palaeographical and artistic affiliations of MS 57 might it prove possible to determine its place of origin; and it may be that insufficient comparative evidence of known origin survives to allow the question to be settled.

THE INTENDED USE OF THE MANUSCRIPT

There can be no doubt that MS 57 was intended for public recitation in the monastic chapter-house. The large format and clear script of the manuscript suit it admirably for the purpose, and the texts that it contains confirm the intention for such usage.

The Rule of St Benedict itself does not refer specifically to a daily meeting of the monks *in chapter*. It does, however, stipulate that after the evening meal, or shortly after Vespers on days of fasting, the brethren are to gather together in one place, and one of them is to read aloud from Cassian's *Collationes*, from the Lives of the Fathers, or from some other edifying text:

> Mox ut surrexerint a caena, sedeant omnes in uno loco; et legat unus Collationes uel Uitas patrum aut certe aliquid quod aedificet audientes.... Si autem ieiunii dies fuerint, dicta uespera, paruo interuallo mox accedant ad lectionem Collationum ut diximus; et legantur iiii aut quinque folia uel quantum hora permittit.[56]

This passage provided the germ for the development of a more formalised chapter office in which reading from the Rule of St Benedict itself formed a major element. The *Memoriale qualiter* provides for the monks to meet together for public reading in chapter both in the morning and in the evening. The morning meeting was the longer and more structured, and included not only readings, but also the recitation of specified verses and a session in which those brothers who had committed faults were to ask mercy and receive judgment. It was to take place after Prime. The version of the *Memoriale* in MS 57 is more detailed than most other copies of the text in its description of the morning meeting. It notes that once the brothers have entered the chapter-house and humbled themselves before one another, the lector for the week is to read a chapter from the Rule of St Benedict, and is then to recite the names (and, if available, accounts of the passions) of the saints whose feasts are commemorated on the day in question; then he should name the saints whose feasts are to be celebrated on the following day:

> Post hæc *autem* legat lector ebdomadarius lectione*m* de regula; et hac lecta nomina *sanct*orum recitet, *ue*l passiones si habeantur, quorum festa illa die celebrantur. His *per*lectis crastinam festiuitate*m* insinuet dicens, 'Et cras erit festiuitas *sancti* *ill*ius'.[57]

Other copies of the *Memoriale*, including the other Anglo-Saxon copies,[58] do not specify that the initial reading is to be from the Rule, and stipulate the announcement only of the names of those saints whose feasts are to be celebrated on the following day.[59] The names of those commemorated would be read out from a Martyrology, Usuard's and other Martyrologies having been designed to fulfil precisely this purpose.[60] Following this reading, various verses and a prayer would be recited, the guilty brothers would request mercy, further verses and the Lord's prayer would be said, and the brothers would then proceed to their manual labour.

The *Memoriale* provides for an evening chapter meeting that would be simpler and more akin to the meeting described in the Rule. It was to take place after Vespers, and to consist of the reading of some unspecified edifying text. As the copy of the *Memoriale* in MS 57 puts it:

> Post ues*per*tinam horam competenti facto signo omnes in unum *con*ueniant in capitulo ues*per*tino, et legatur scriptura q*uae* ędificet

audientes, quantum hora permittit.[61]

After a concluding verse, the brethren were to proceed to Compline.

The Aachen monastic legislation also envisaged daily meetings in chapter, and used the terms *capitulum* and *collatio* to refer to the morning and evening gatherings respectively. The version of the legislation that appears in MS 57 — the version now known as the *Regula sancti Benedicti abbatis Anianensis siue Collectio capitularis* — includes two relevant canons. The first of these (Canon LXVI), which happens to be omitted in the copy of the text in MS 57, reverses the *Memoriale*'s order of events for the morning meeting by stipulating that the reading from the Martyrology is to come first, to be followed by a reading from the Rule or some homily: *Ut ad capitulum primitus martyrilogium legatur et dicatur uersus, deinde regula aut omelia quaelibet legatur.*[62] Canon LXX briefly stipulates that there is to be an explication of the texts read at both the *capitulum* and the *collatio*, although in the latter case this is to happen only if time permits: *Ut ad capitulum lectio tradatur, similiter ad collationem si tempus fuerit oportunum.*[63]

The norms for English Benedictine practice in the reform period were laid down in the *Regularis concordia*, the document that was drawn up, probably by St Æthelwold, in the wake of the council held at Winchester *c.* 970 x 973, and that was intended to hold force in monasteries throughout the kingdom. According to the *Regularis concordia*, the morning chapter office was to take place after the Morrow Mass, which itself followed Tierce. The detailed description of the chapter office specifies that there is to be a reading from the Martyrology and from the Rule, or, if it is a feast day, from the Gospel for the day, and that the prior should expound upon the reading from the Rule or Gospel:

> Hoc [sc. the Morrow Mass] expleto, facto signo a priore, conuenientes ad Capitulum ipso praecedente, uersa facie ad orientem salutent crucem et ceteris undique fratribus se uultu inclinato humilient; cuius humiliationis ratio et in omni conuentu custodienda est. Tunc residentibus cunctis legatur martyrologium, quo dicto surgentes omnes dicant uersum *Pretiosa in conspectu Domini* cum oratione ac uersu *Deus in adiutorium meum intende*, qui uersus tertio repetatur ab omnibus, priore incipiente, subiungentes *Gloria* et flectentes genua si tempus ita dictauerit. Dicente uero priore *Et ne nos inducas* surgant omnes erectoque uultu dicant uersum *Respice in seruos*, subiungentes *Gloria* humiliato capite. Sequitur oratio *Dirigere et sanctificare* et *Adiutorium nostrum in nomine Domini: qui fecit caelum et terram.* Iterum autem residentibus legatur regula uel, si dies festus fuerit, euangelium ipsius diei, de qua lectione a priore prout Dominus dederit dicatur.[64]

The *Regularis concordia* also refers to the evening *collatio* which is to take place before Compline. It does not specify what material should be read. On Saturdays, the *collatio* is to start within the church and is to be punctuated by the *caritas*, that is, the provision of a measure of drink for which the brethren will retire to the refectory. On other days, the reading at the *collatio* should continue for as long as time allows and as shall seem good to the prior:

> Si sabbatum fuerit...facto signo, in ecclesia initietur collatio rursumque dato tintinnabuli signo refectorium introeant caritatis gratia. Quotiescumque fratribus caritas interim dum collatio legitur praebetur, lectione finita omnibusque surgentibus, dicat prior uersum *Sit nomen Domini benedictum* et *Benedicamus Domino*, ceteris ut mos est respondentibus. Reliquis uero diebus...cum signo collationem adeant, quae prout tempus permiserit utque priori uisum fuerit legatur, et sic accedant ad Completorium.[65]

MS 57 contains the two principal texts required for the readings at the morning chapter office, namely the Rule and the Martyrology. Further, the longest text in the manuscript, Smaragdus' *Diadema monachorum*, furnished precisely the type of edifying material suitable for the evening meeting. Indeed, Smaragdus in his preface wrote that he intended his work for just this purpose:

> Et quia in regula beati Benedicti scriptum est, Mox ut surrexerint fratres a coena, sedeant omnes in unum, et legat unus collationes uel uitas Patrum, aut certe aliquid quod aedificet audientes: ideo nos et de collationibus Patrum, et de conuersationibus et institutionibus eorum modicum, et de diuersis Doctoribus in hoc libello congessimus plurimum, et sic eum in centum capitulis consummauimus totum. Et quia mos est monachorum, ut regulam beati Benedicti ad capitulum legant quotidie matutinum: uolumus ut iste libellus ad eorum capitulum quotidie legatur uespertinum.[66]

MS 57 thus provides requisite and suitable material for both the morning and the evening meetings. It is possible that the other prescriptive texts in the manuscript, the *Memoriale qualiter* and the Aachen legislation, were also read aloud in the chapter, although there is no evidence that such was customary in Anglo-Saxon times. Alternatively, these texts may have been intended for private study; in this connection it is noteworthy that the *Memoriale* ends with the recommendation that its tenets are to be committed to memory: *Hi affectus in unum collecti ad memoriam reducantur*.[67]

The Martyrology in MS 57 was provided, apparently at the time of writing, with marginal apparatus designed to increase its practical value (see Plates 2 and 5). In the left margin next to the beginning of each day's entry are two letters, one in ink, the other, immediately to its right, in red pigment. In the right margin alongside many entries is a Roman numeral in ink. Most of these Roman numerals were first written in red pigment within the line (i.e., not in the margin), immediately following the rubricated date for each day. Most of the red numerals were then erased and substituted by the ink numerals in the margin, which themselves may be the work of the original scribe. (The erasure is visible in Plate 5.) The erasure and rewriting in ink probably resulted from the red numerals being difficult to distinguish from the rubricated dates; that difficulty can still be assessed in several places in Quire 8 where the red numerals have been left to stand (fols 57r|26, 61v|6, 62v|14, 63r|6, 12 and 27, 63v|17 and 24, and 64r|12 and 18).

The red letters entered in the left margin run in sequence from *A* to *G*, then start again at *A*. They are so-called Dominical letters, and serve to indicate the day of the week on which each day of the year falls. Thus in a year for which the Dominical letter is *A*, any day with an *A* next to it will be a Sunday, days marked *B* will be Mondays, and so on; whereas in years for which the Dominical letter is *B*, Sunday will fall on all those days marked *B*. The Roman numerals, known as Golden Numbers, indicate on which days the first day of the moon will fall in each year of the 19-year cycle that was the basis for most medieval computistics.[68] The numbers range from *I* to *XIX*, but do not run in consecutive sequence. Rather, each number entered alongside a date is 11 less than the preceding number; if the preceding number is below *XII*, then the next number is calculated by beginning the sequence again at 19, so that *XI* is followed by *XIX*, *X* by *XVIII*, and so on. Not every day has a number entered next to it, for, given that the basis of the system was the 19-year cycle, within the cycle there would be only 19 possible days on which the new moon of each lunar month could fall.[69]

The letters entered in ink are so-called lunar letters that further assist lunar calculations. They comprise three repeating consecutive sequences. The first runs from *A* to *V* (20 letters), the second from *A.* to *V.* (20 letters), and the third from *.A* to *.T* (19 letters). After *.T*, the first sequence recommences, and so on. The total of 59 letters from *A* to *.T* represents the number of days in two lunar months, for the length of the lunar month alternates between 30 and 29 days.[70] The letters enable the day of the moon to be identified for any day of the year. The system is described by Bede in chapter XXIII of his *De temporum ratione*.[71] Bede, however, did not approve of its use, preferring that students should use the means for calculating the day of the moon described in his chapter XXII; in his opinion the lunar letters should be used only by those who were too idle or dim-witted to learn the method of calculation.[72]

The marginal apparatus could be used for calculating the date of Easter and the other movable feasts of the church year. Easter fell on the Sunday following the first full moon in spring, the earliest possible date for that full moon being 21 March (the vernal equinox), the latest possible date 18 April.[73] In MS 57, both the Golden Numbers and the lunar letters would assist in calculating when the relevant full moon occurred, while the Dominical letters would indicate which of the following days was a Sunday. Over and beyond this, it was normal practice that when the reading from the Martyrology took place each day, the reader would state both the calendar date and the day of the moon. This is not mentioned in any of the prescriptive texts in MS 57, but is stated, for example, in the Rule for canons by Chrodegang of Metz (712–766), which directs that each day, in the chapter-house, *post lectionem recitetur etas mensis et lune, et nomina sanctorum quorum festa crastinus excipiet dies.*[74] Additions to MS 57, described below, establish that the daily readings from its Martyrology were accompanied by the announcement of the day of the moon.

However, the marginal apparatus in MS 57 is not of itself sufficient for the necessary calculations to be made. In order for the Dominical letters and the Golden Numbers to be serviceable, there would need to be available a table of years identifying each year's number within the 19-year cycle, and the Dominical letter for each year. For the use of the lunar letters there would need to be a table correlating the letters for the 59 days of a cycle of two lunar months with each year of the 19-year cycle.[75] Such tables might perhaps have been contained in a calendrical manuscript that could have been used in conjunction with the apparatus of the Martyrology. However, the usefulness of the apparatus is compromised by the occurrence of several mistakes. Most of these occur in the Golden Numbers, some of which are omitted (for example, on fols 45v|20 and 50r|11),[76] while others are incorrect (for example, *IX* instead of *XI* on fol. 41r|26, and *XI* instead of *IX* on fol. 48v|4).[77] In the lunar letters, error occurs at the end of the year, where, following 20 December (XIII Kl. Ian.), which is correctly lettered *.T*, there begins a new sequence preceded by dots, instead of an undotted sequence.

EVIDENCE OF USE

MS 57 bears signs of use by many different readers, most of whom worked within the Anglo-Saxon period, although some additions date to the twelfth and thirteenth centuries.[78] The manuscript provoked various types of attention and inattention from its readers. Several added entries are casual, distracted, or even destructive. For example, on fol. 54r|21 occurs the casual alphabetical pen-trial *ghik* scratched into the page in drypoint next to the date *.XVII. KL. MAI* within the Martyrology, while in the outer margin of fol. 30v, alongside lines 6–7, is a drypoint runic entry similarly unrelated to the adjacent text and apparently recording a Scandinavian personal name; the entry may be connected in some way with Abbot Rodulf (1051–1052), who before taking up his post at Abingdon had served as bishop in Scandinavia for 19 years.[79] In the upper margin of the originally blank fol. 94v is an elegant alpha-omega monogram written in ink and outlined with dots of red pigment (Plate 8). On the same page, immediately following the formula for the Abingdon community to announce the death of one of its members, is the beginning of an antiphon for the feast of St Lucy (13 December): *In tua paciencia possedisti animam tuam LVCIA sponsa* Christi (Plate 8).[80] Also on this page is a large, uncompleted plummet sketch perhaps of an angel, while in the lower part of fol. 96r is a dynamic uncompleted drypoint sketch of a warrior brandishing sword and shield; the sketch bears no relation to the adjacent text, which is a portion of the chapter-list of the *Diadema monachorum*.[81] Destructive as opposed to distracted tendencies are visible on fols 16–18 and 78–81, where cut-outs of three different shapes have been made in the margins of consecutive leaves. The knife used to cut the shapes penetrated through two or more leaves at once, and on fols 16rv and 18r the cutting has removed parts of the marginal glosses added to the Rule of St Benedict. A different type of deliberate damage has taken place in lines 2–4 of fol. 2r, the first lines of the preface of the Rule of St Benedict that are written in the normal text-script, following the opening line of capitals. Here, portions of the specifically Anglo-Saxon letter-forms of the Square minuscule script have been erased, presumably by someone who was unsympathetic to that script or who had difficulty in reading it. The letters affected are flat-topped *a*, high *e*, Insular *f* and *r*, and low-set *s*. For example, for each occurrence of Insular *r* within these lines, the right arm of the letter and the portion of the left stem that descends below the base-line have been erased.[82] Once the erasures had been made, no substitute strokes were added to modify the letter-forms, so the result is to make these lines difficult to read. Possibly whoever made these erasures initially planned to make extensive adjustments to the script of the manuscript, but swiftly abandoned his intention.

Other Anglo-Saxon additions to the manuscript confirm and illustrate its service for public recitation within the chapter-house, while also suggesting that it may have been used for study. The relevant evidence includes glosses added to the Rule of St Benedict, various additions made to the Martyrology, and construe marks added to the Rule, to part of the *Memoriale qualiter*, and to the *Diadema monachorum*.

(1) *The Glossing of the Rule of St Benedict*

The Rule of St Benedict is by far the most heavily glossed text in the manuscript. It has attracted interlinear and marginal additions by several hands. However, the great majority of the glosses are by a single hand writing a neat English Caroline minuscule of the first half of the eleventh century (Plate 9). This glossator carried out his work before the manuscript acquired its replacement leaves, fols 8, 19 and 22, for on fols 19 and 22 there are no glosses, while on fol. 8 the glosses are in the hand of the scribe who wrote the main text of the leaf (Plate 4); he may have copied the glosses from the damaged leaf that he was replacing.[83] The glosses of the principal glossator are primarily lexical; that is, they provide one or more Latin alternatives to words in the text. These glosses are added immediately above their lemmata, but when more than one alternative is given, as is frequently the case, the glosses extend above the following words also. It is not uncommon for as many as four alternatives to be given, as over *proterue* on fol. 7r|12,[84] where the glosses are *superbe. aut peruerse.* uel *inpudenter. uerbose*. Occasionally, lexical glosses are placed in the outer margins rather than over their lemmata, as with *Laqueu*m. *dolu*m alongside fol. 10v|2 (actually referring to a word that occurs on fol. 10r|27), while the margins are also used for longer explanations, such as that providing the meaning and etymology of *gehenna* alongside fol. 7v|13–18. The principal glossator seems to have added his glosses in at least two campaigns, for frequently the same lemma has glosses entered in two different shades of ink, but apparently in the same hand. The gloss first entered is usually in a dark brown ink, the later gloss in a lighter ink. That the two campaigns are the work of the same hand appears from a comparison of their scripts. For example, the glosses *adiungentur* and *addantur* above [*ad*-]*icientur* on fol. 6v|16[85] are respectively in dark and light ink, but the letter forms match well, notably the initial *a* with bowl descending to the left and the final *r* with its arm ending with an extended diagonal rise to the right. This glossator also worked as occasional corrector, for on fol. 6v|23, for example, he has added in the interline the originally omitted *reddatur*.[86]

This glossator's work does not represent his personal response to the text of the Rule. Rather, he copied from an existing set of glosses to the Rule. Paul Meyvaert has noted that substantially the same set of glosses occurs in two earlier manuscripts: Cambridge, Trinity College O. 2. 30, fols 129–172, written in the mid-tenth century by a scribe active at St Augustine's Abbey; and London, British Library, Additional 30055, a tenth-century Spanish manuscript in Visigothic script.[87] As Meyvaert aptly commented, this broad geographical spread within the tenth century points to 'a much earlier date of origin' for the glosses.[88] The copying of the glosses resulted in some errors in MS 57. For example, the false gloss *addalamus*, in error for *addamus*, occurs over *augeamus* on fol. 23v|2.[89] On the same page, the second gloss above con*datur* in line 26[90] originally read, quite inappropriately, *reprobatur*, and has been corrected to *reparatur*.[91] The copying also caused the misplacement of several of the marginal glosses, which sometimes fail to stand adjacent to the text to which they relate. The misplacement of

Laqueum. dolum on fol. 10v has been noted above. A further example is the set of three glosses alongside fol. 24v|14–15: they relate to words occurring on fol. 24r|27 and 24v|1–2.[92]

The wealth of glosses entered by this glossator could have assisted private study of the manuscript. Alternatively, the glosses could have guided the exposition that the *Regularis concordia* stipulated that the prior should make after the daily reading from the Rule.[93] Similar purposes could have been served by the scattering of suppletive glosses added to the Rule and also to the *Diadema monachorum.*[94] These suppletive glosses are always preceded by the abbreviation *s.* for *scilicet.* Most of them, including those in the *Diadema*, appear to be the work of a single hand, seemingly not that of the main glossator. In some places it can clearly be seen that the suppletive glosses stood on the page before the main glossator entered his lexical glosses, for he has been obliged to enter certain glosses either above a suppletive gloss, or to its right with the result that his lexical gloss does not stand directly above its lemma.[95] The suppletive glosses clarify the sense by supplying words omitted from the original text through ellipsis. Such ellipsis includes the omission of the subject of a verb when that subject is the same as for the previous verb, the omission of the auxiliary verb to accompany the past participle, and so on. Thus on fol. 5v|21–22, the suppletive glossator has twice supplied the gloss *s. debet*, respectively above the infinitives *ostendere* and *preponere*; *debet* had not been included at these points in the original text because it occurred before the first infinitive in the string, *preesse* in line 20.[96] The suppletive glossator also favoured adding the gloss *s. o* above vocatives to distinguish them from nominatives, as on fol. 2r|21 (above *filii*) and fol. 9r|5 and 12 (above *fratres* in both cases).[97] The suppletive glosses would have aided study and explication of the text.

A different purpose is served by sets of glosses on fols 12v–13r, 14rv and 21r. On these pages, within chapters XII–XIII, XVIII and XLIII, several Roman numerals (identifying psalms) occur within the text. In each case where such a numeral occurs, it has been glossed with the Latin word for the numeral: thus *sexagesimus sextus* for *LXVI* (fol. 12v|17), and so on. For each chapter within which they occur, these 'numerical glosses' are the work of a different hand.[98] It seems very likely that these glosses were entered to prepare the text for recitation, to save the reader from having to work out the words for the numbers as he read aloud. The different hands responsible for these glosses are presumably those of readers who recited these chapters, and who entered the glosses as they read the text privately in advance of recitation. Similar glosses constitute one of the several types of additions that were made to the Martyrology.

(2) *Additions and Glosses to the Martyrology*

(a) Additions to the Contents of the Martyrology

Usuard compiled his Martyrology in the third quarter of the ninth century for a Continental audience. It includes few references to English saints; among the few mentioned are St Cuthbert (20 March; fol. 51v|6–9) and St Æthelthryth of Ely (23 June; fol. 65r|16–18). The original text of the Martyrology in MS 57 is an only slightly modified copy of Usuard's text. To make the Martyrology more relevant to an Anglo-Saxon audience, it was provided with some 21 additions within the Anglo-Saxon period (there are also several additions dating from the twelfth century). The additions were made in available blank spaces in the last lines of the entries for the relevant days, in interlines, and in outer margins. They are the work of several different hands. About half of the Anglo-Saxon additions are in versions of Square minuscule that imitate the original script, the quality of the imitation varying from the neatly executed additions of St Dunstan on fol. 60r|18 and St Cuthburga on fol. 76r|26–27 to the somewhat unsteady and unattractive script of the addition of St Ælfheah on fol. 55r|6. The saints commemorated by the Anglo-Saxon additions are Oswald, archbishop of York (28 February; fol. 49r|20–21); Ceadda (2 March; fol. 49v|7); King Edward the Martyr (18 March and 18 July, the latter commemorating his accession; fols 51r|25 and 69r|9); Ælfheah (19 April; fol. 55r|6); Bertin (2 May, 16 June, 16 July and 5 September; fols 57r|lower margin, 64r|26, 68v|lower margin and 77r|16);[99] Dunstan (19 May; fol. 60r|18); Grimbald (8 July; fol. 67v|11); Swithun (2 July and 15 July; fols 66v|11 and 68v|21); Kenelm (17 July; fol. 69r|4); Cuthburga (31 August; fol. 76r|26–27); Edith (16 September; fol. 79r|outer margin); Frideswide (19 October; fol. 83v|outer margin); Edmund (20 November; fol. 88v|outer margin); Birinus (3 December; fol. 90v|outer margin); the ordination of St Ambrose and the octave of St Andrew (7 December; fol. 91r|4); and Judoc (13 December; fol. 92r|upper margin). The bias of the additions is strongly southern English. St Oswald and his contribution to the Benedictine reform are commemorated by the additions of Oswald himself and of Kenelm, revered at the monastery that Oswald revived at Winchcombe. Canterbury is represented by Sts Dunstan and Ælfheah. But the strongest influence is from Winchester and its milieu: Birinus was apostle of Wessex; Swithun was bishop of Winchester; Grimbald, originally from Saint-Bertin, was buried at New Minster, Winchester; and the relics of the Breton Judoc had been translated to Winchester *c.* 902. Æthelwold, Abingdon's own abbot who had transferred to Winchester in 963, is mentioned in an obit for 1 August added in the outer margin of fol. 71r.[100]

The most notable feature of the additions is the high status accorded to St Bertin (d. *c.* 700), evangeliser of the Morini in north-eastern France and second abbot of Sithiu (later renamed Saint-Bertin). In three of the four additions that concern him, his name is written in capitals. The additions relating to him probably reflect the acquisition by Abingdon of some of his relics. The date of the acquisition is unrecorded, the earliest reference to the relics apparently occurring in the account of the inspection of all the house's relics carried out by Abbot Faritius in 1116; the relics seen by Faritius included *de costa et aliis ossibus Sancti Bertini abbatis*.[101] All four additions for St Bertin are in a single Anglo-Saxon hand writing a rounded English Caroline minuscule. The addition for 2 May refers to the second translation (*eleuatio & translatio secunda*) of the saint, and must therefore be later than 2 May 1052 when that translation took place.[102] The body of Bertin had been removed from its tomb and secretly reburied in 846 in order to safeguard it from discovery by the Vikings. It was then rediscovered by chance during building work at the abbey of Saint-Bertin in 1050, and was translated with magnificent ceremony by Abbot Bovo (1043–1065) two years later.[103] In his written account of the translation, Bovo recorded that at the end of the ceremony a relic was given to each of the bishops and abbots who attended.[104] The list of those present does not include anyone from or connected with Abingdon, nor indeed anyone from England.[105] However, it seems most likely that Abingdon acquired its relics of St Bertin as a result of and soon after the translation, and that this swiftly led to the addition to the Martyrology of the four entries naming him. The entries may be the unique surviving evidence for a significant event in the mid-eleventh-century history of Abingdon.

All the Anglo-Saxon additions to the contents of the Martyrology could have been made at Abingdon. The Canterbury and Winchester elements in the additions could have resulted from Abingdon's known connections with those two centres. The work of several individuals, the additions amount to a sustained effort to adapt the Martyrology in MS 57 to its specific English audience.

(b) Obits

Another sizable batch of additions to the Martyrology provides obits for monks and abbots of Abingdon and for other religious and lay figures linked with Abingdon. These obits, all of which stand in the outer margins and many of which have been partly lost as a result of the trimming of the margins, have been studied in detail by Gerchow.[106] Most of the obits were added in a single campaign by one individual. As Gerchow showed, his work appears to be datable between summer 1046 and spring 1047, for the obit for Abbot Ælfstan that he entered under 5 July on fol. 67r probably refers to Ælfstan, abbot of St Augustine's, Canterbury, who died on 5 July 1046, while the entry under 29 March (fol. 52v) for Abbot Æthelstan of Abingdon, who died in 1047, is by another hand.[107] The principal hand of the obits made entries for only part of the year, and this indicates that he was copying from another source — perhaps a necrology or a calendar in which obits had been entered — and that for some reason he abandoned his copying.[108] Apart from a handful of entries for early November that may be by him, his last obit is that for 17 July on fol. 69r, just over halfway through the year. Nonetheless, his entries provide invaluable evidence of the composition of the Abingdon community from the restoration of Abingdon in the mid-tenth century until the time the obits were added to the Martyrology in the mid-eleventh, for, as Gerchow has calculated from the numbers involved, it would seem that the list from which the obits were copied must have provided a more or less comprehensive record of those members of the community who had died since the restoration.[109] Presumably the obits would have been read out at the morning chapter office;[110] their entry in the margins of the Martyrology would fit well with such a purpose.

(c) Prompts

Like the Rule of St Benedict, the Martyrology includes additions that appear to be readers' prompts. More numerous than for the Rule, some are written in ink, while others are in drypoint, scratched into the surface of the page with a stylus. These drypoint entries frequently reveal themselves by the chance fall of light on to the page at a certain angle. Once discovered, the reading of them can be assisted by the use of fibre-optic light, for the light-tubes can be directed across the page at different angles to throw different parts of the entries into relief. Many drypoint entries have been found in MS 57, but no doubt there are others still awaiting discovery. Given the difficulty — at least for the modern eye — of reading drypoint, it can be hard to understand the rationale for the use of this medium. It is true, however, that the discreet presence of drypoint has the advantage of not cluttering the page and interfering with the main text as interlinear ink entries can. Further, many drypoint entries may have been intended specifically for the benefit of the one who actually wrote them. If so, reading them would have been assisted by the memory of having written them.

Several of the readers' prompts in the Martyrology follow the pattern of those in the Rule by supplying the fully worded forms of Roman numerals within the text. Such entries are by a variety of different hands and again appear to represent the work of different readers preparing the text for reading aloud. Most of these entries are in ink, but on fol. 44v|13 and 15, entries occur both in drypoint and in ink over the numerals *XII* and *XXXVI*. In these cases, the drypoint and the ink entries are the work of different hands: thus the drypoint *duodecim* over *XII* uses the round-backed *d*, but the ink version uses straight-stemmed *d*. Presumably the drypoint entries came first, and a subsequent reader felt the need for a prompt that was more easily legible. On fol. 55r|26 the prompt is abbreviated, with *unde* (for *undecim*) standing over *XI*. On fol. 48v|10 the prompt is incorrect, for *XXXVI* is glossed by *triginta septem* entered alongside it in the outer margin.[111]

Several drypoint cues supply the day of the moon, which the reader had to announce, along with the calendar date, at the beginning of his recital from the Martyrology.[112] These cues stand either next to the rubricated date, or alongside in the outer margin. Thus on fol. 58v|25, *luna XXIII* stands to the left of *.IIII. ID MAI.* (Plate 10); and in the outer margin of fol. 84v, alongside lines 7–9 and the entry for IX Kl. Nov., is *luna sexta uicessima*. Frequently only the number is written, without the preceding *luna*: thus *XVII* in the outer margin of fol. 45v, alongside line 1 (Kl. Feb.);[113] *XII* on fol. 48r|18 (VIII Kl. Mar.); *XXVII* (with more digits perhaps trimmed away) in the outer margin of fol. 51r, alongside lines 7–8 (XVII Kl. Apr.); *XVIIII* on fol. 51v|11 (XII Kl. Apr.); *XXIIII* (with the last digit partly trimmed away) in the outer margin of fol. 58r, alongside line 7 (Non. Mai.); *X*, *XI*, *XII*, and *XIII* in the outer margin of fol. 83v, alongside lines 5, 10, 17 and 26 (XVI–XIII Kl. Nov.); and *XXV* in the outer margin of fol. 92v, alongside line 10 (XII Kl. Ian.). The drypoint *duodema uigesima* on fol. 64v|18 (to the left of the date *.XII. KL. IUL.*) is probably also a lunar cue; the Latin is faulty, but is perhaps meant to signify 'eighteenth', and could result from a false formation of the ordinal from the cardinal *duodeuiginti*. There appears to be no case where more than one lunar cue is entered for any given date. This is perhaps surprising, for in each year of the 19-year cycle the age of the moon on a particular date is different. This could have led to an accumulation of several lunar cues for individual dates, but it has not. The cues that have been entered cannot all have been written in the same year. This is shown, for example, by the entry of *XXVII* (with other digits perhaps trimmed away) for XVII Kl. Apr. (16 March) and *XVIIII* (clearly in a different hand) for XII Kl. Apr. (21 March, that is, five days later) on fol. 51rv. 21 March would have been the nineteenth day of the moon in the eleventh year of the 19-year cycle.[114] 16 March is the twenty-seventh day of the moon in the fourth year of the cycle, and the twenty-eighth day in the fifteenth year; the twenty-ninth day of the moon cannot occur on 16 March, which means that, if the cue for XVII Kl. Apr. has been partly lost through trimming, and if the cue was accurate, no more than one digit can have been lost. These two cues, then, provided that they were correct, applied to years that were either four or seven years apart. A clue to one year in which drypoint entries were being added to the Martyrology is provided by the entry *hic erit pascha* on fol. 54v|2, next to the date XVI Kl. Mai. (16 April). Between 950 and 1100, Easter occurred on 16 April in the years 971, 982, 993, 1004, 1055, 1066, 1077 and 1088.[115] Given the character of the script of this entry, and the evidence that the manuscript was acquiring other entries in the mid-eleventh century — and assuming that the comment was accurate — 1055 is the most likely date for the entry.

(d) Additions Concerning the Status of Feast Days

A further set of additions to the Martyrology indicates the status accorded to different feast days at Abingdon. Most of these additions take the form *XII R* or *III R* (see Plate 2), although some that are datable to the twelfth century are in the form *XII Lc* or *III Lc*. *R* and *Lc* respectively abbreviate *Responsoria* and *Lectiones*. The additions thus differentiate between feast days in which the night office would include either twelve or three lections, each of which would be followed by a respond.[116] The additions do not always occur alongside the first line of the Martyrology entry to which they apply. Rather, they are entered next to that line in which occurs the name of the saint in whose honour the feast day would be. For example, on fol. 43v, *XII R* is entered alongside the fourth line of the entry for XII Kl. Feb. (21 January), the line in which there is a reference to St Agnes, whose feast is celebrated on that day; and on fol. 46r, *XII R* is entered next to the fifth line of the entry for VIII Id. Feb. (6 February), the line in which begins the reference to Sts Vedastus and Amandus. The additions thus indicate which saints were honoured at Abingdon, and thereby assist the reconstruction of the early form of the Abingdon calendar (there survives no Abingdon calendar earlier than the late thirteenth century).[117]

However, the additions are in more than one hand, and since each addition includes only a numeral followed by one or two letters, the date of the scripts is difficult to assess. Nonetheless, a significant number of these additions can be attributed to the late Anglo-Saxon period. One of them occurs in the upper margin of fol. 92r, at the end of the addition to the Martyrology of a reference to St Judoc. The added entry for Judoc, which uses Insular *r* in imitation of the original script, looks mid-eleventh-century, and the *XII R* that concludes it is in the same ink and hand as the entry itself. The *R* includes a diagonal abbreviation stroke through its right limb. A similar form of abbreviation, and similar forms for the Roman numerals, occur in many of the other additions of *XII R* and *III R*, which suggests that they also (although the work of a different hand) are to be dated within the Anglo-Saxon period. Other additions, however, can be assigned to the twelfth century. These include the additions of *III R* and *XII R* that are entered above, and relate to, the added twelfth-century references to St Giles (Plate 2) and the Ordination of Pope Gregory in the outer margin of fol. 76v; the *XII R* for Gregory is apparently in the same ink and hand as the actual reference to Gregory. These two additions occur at the end of a whole block datable to the twelfth century and spanning fols 69r–76v and the period 21 July–3 September.[118] Characteristic features of this block are the use for many entries of a horizontal abbreviation bar over the top of *R*, instead of a diagonal through its right limb; and the manner in which the final *I* of the Roman numeral descends below the base-line and curves back toward the left. The absence from these pages of Anglo-Saxon additions citing the number of responds shows that the first, Anglo-Saxon phase of this work did not cover the whole year. All the *Lc* additions — several of which occur within the block on fols 69r–76v — are assignable to the twelfth century.

For one day (24 August) the format varies from the normal assignment of three or twelve responds. In the outer margin of fol. 74v a twelfth-century hand has entered, above the added marginal reference to St Bartholomew the Apostle,[119] *VIII R 7 Al*, indicating that there would be eight responds and an Alleluia in honour of St Bartholomew. Three lines further down, still within the entry for 24 August, the same hand has written *IIII R* next to the mention of St Ouen within the text: the total of 12 responds would thus be completed by four for Ouen. Two other variations from the normal pattern occur in the outer margins of fols 72v and 73r, with reference to the feasts of St Laurence (10 August) and the Assumption of the Virgin (15 August). Here, rather than noting the number of responds, a twelfth-century hand has written *cap*, abbreviating *cappis* and signifying that the celebration of these two feasts would be marked by the wearing of copes.[120] Both the Virgin and St Laurence (the third-century Roman deacon) were held in high honour at Abingdon: the abbey was dedicated to the former, and by 1116 possessed two relics of the latter.[121]

The additions assigning the number of responds have not previously been listed in descriptions of MS 57. Given their importance in identifying which saints were honoured at Abingdon in the period prior to its earliest surviving calendar, it is worthwhile to list them here.[122] In the table that follows, I note within parentheses the saint to whose feast each addition applies; as mentioned above, it is possible to identify the saint in question from the positioning of the addition. The footnotes indicate which additions belong to the twelfth century.

XII R	*III R*
	14 January (Felix of Nola)
15 January (Maurus)	
	16 January (Marcellus)
	18 January (Prisca)
20 January (Fabianus and Sebastianus)	
21 January (Agnes)	
22 January (Vincent)	
25 January (Conversion of Paul)	

XII R	*III R*
	28 January (second feast of Agnes)
	29 January (Octave of Vincent)
30 January (Baltild)[123]	
1 February (Brigit)	
2 February (Purification of the Virgin/Cornelius)[124]	
5 February (Agatha)	
6 February (Vedastus and Amandus)	
	25 May (Urbanus)
26 May (Augustine of Canterbury)	
	1 June (Nicomedes)
	2 June (Marcellinus and Peter the exorcist)
	9 June (Primus and Felicianus)
11 June (Barnabas)	
	12 June (Basilides, Cirinus and Nabor)
	14 June (Basil)[125]
	16 June (Cyricus and Julitta)[126]
	18 June (Marcus and Marcellianus)
22 June (Alban)	
23 June (Æthelthryth)	
24 June (Nativity of John the Baptist)	
	26 June (John and Paul the brothers)
29 June (Peter and Paul)	
30 June (Paul)	
2 July (Swithun)	
4 July (Translation of Martin)	
6 July (Octave of Peter and Paul)	
8 July (Grimbald)[127]	
	10 July (the seven brothers, sons of St Felicity)
11 July (Translation of Benedict)	
	21 July (Praxedes)[128]
22 July (Mary Magdalene)[129]	

XII R	*III R*
23 July (Apollinaris)[130]	
	31 July (Germanus of Auxerre)[131]
3 August (Invention of Stephen)[132]	
5 August (Oswald king and martyr)[133]	
	6 August (Sixtus, Praetextatus, Felicissimus and Agapitus)[134]
	7 August (Donatus)[135]
	11 August (Taurinus)[136]
	13 August (Hippolytus)[137]
24 August (Bartholomew/Ouen)[138]	
	27 August (Rufus)[139]
29 August (Decollation of John the Baptist)[140]	
	1 September (Giles)[141]
3 September (Ordination [*sic*] of Gregory)[142]	
14 September (Exaltation of the Cross)	
	15 September (Nicomedes)
	17 September (Lambert)
21 September (Matthew)[143]	
	22 September (Maurice and companions)
	27 September (Cosmas and Damian)
29 September (Michael)[144]	
30 September (Victor and Ursus)[145]	
1 October (Translation of Germanus and Remigius)	
	2 October (Leodegar)
	7 October (Marcus)
9 October (Dionysus, Rusticus and Eleutherius)	
	14 October (Callixtus)
18 October (Luke)	
28 October (Simon and Jude)	
	31 October (Vigil of All Saints)
1 November (All Saints)	

XII R	*III R*
	2 November (Eustace)[146]
	8 November (Claudius and companions)
	9 November (Theodore the martyr)
11 November (Martin)	
21 November (Columbanus)	
22 November (Cecilia)	
23 November (Clement)	
	24 November (Chrysogonus)
	29 November (Saturninus)
30 November (Andrew)	
	1 December (Chrisantus and Daria)
6 December (Nicholas)[147]	
13 December (Judoc)	

XII Lc	*III Lc*
[All these entries are twelfth-century additions]	
	15 June (Vitus, Modestus and Crescentia)
19 June (Gervase and Protase)	
	24 July (Christina)
25 July (James)	
	9 August (Romanus)
	14 August (Vigil of the Assumption)
	30 August (Felix)
31 August (Aidan)	
31 December (Sylvester)	

(3) *Construe Marks*

Throughout much of MS 57, marks consisting of ink dots and strokes have been added below or above certain words of the text (Plates 1, 3, 6 and 9). These marks occur on most pages of the Rule of St Benedict, on the first three pages of the *Memoriale qualiter* (fols 33r–34r), and on most pages of the *Diadema monachorum*. Their function is to assist the reader to construe the Latin correctly.

Construe marks occur in several Anglo-Saxon (and other) copies of Latin texts, and take various forms.[148] One system consisted of entering letters of the alphabet above the Latin words: *a* might be entered above the main verb, *b* above the subject, *c* above the direct object, and so on, and the reader should then take the words in the order indicated by the alphabetical sequence.[149] A second system involved entering varying numbers of dots (usually not exceeding five or six, and supplemented by other indicators) below or above words of the text; in construing, the reader should first take the word marked with one dot, then that marked with two dots, and so on.[150] In yet a third system, marks were entered above or below just a few words in a sentence, the marks serving to pick out the principal elements in the sentence and to establish syntactical links.[151] As Robinson noted, this system is more sophisticated than the other two, as it 'helps the Anglo-Saxon reader to understand the Latin syntax rather than showing him how to rearrange the Latin words mechanically into common Old English word-order'.[152]

It is this third system — although in one of its simpler forms — that occurs in MS 57. Whereas this system frequently employs a variety of types of marks, MS 57 uses just two principal marks. One of these comprises two dots aligned vertically and followed by a stroke that rises toward the right; the other consists of two dots aligned horizontally. Sometimes one of these marks will be used for the main clause in a sentence and the other for a subordinate clause, but the practice is not consistent. A few other marks occur sporadically, and only within the *Diadema monachorum*. The most frequent of these marks comprises two dots aligned vertically, like a modern colon; this occurs, for example, on fols 95r, 97v, 98v, 106v–107r, 128r, 146rv, 147v and 161r. A similar mark with a third dot placed to the right of the upper dot occurs on fols 109v|10 and 110r|10. Finally, a fifth type of mark, comprising two dots aligned horizontally or diagonally with a stroke rising to the right above them, occurs on fols 106v|26, 111v|8 and 116r|21 and 23. In other manuscripts that use this system, it is often significant whether a mark is placed below or above the word: if two or three syntactically related words are linked by the same mark, the mark is usually placed below the first one or two words, but above the last word to indicate that the end of the sense-unit has been reached.[153] In MS 57 this distinction is not made. On the other hand, there is a distinction between the positioning of the two principal marks: the first mark described above always occurs below words, the second above.[154] This difference in positioning is not syntactically meaningful except that, when the two different marks are used respectively for main and subordinate clauses, the positioning provides a further means of distinguishing between the two types of clause.

Two examples will demonstrate the relative simplicity of the system in MS 57, and the variation in the method of use. In Plate 3, in the sentence extending from *Tam perseueranter* in line 5 to *uincamus* in line 9, the first principal mark serves only to signal the impersonal main verb *oportet*; the second principal mark indicates the relative adverb *quousque* that introduces the first subordinate clause, and the verb *superemus* within that clause. In Plate 9, in the sentence extending from *Tertium uero monachorum* to *per tonsuram noscuntur* (lines 2–6 in the Plate), only the first principal mark is used. It serves to pick out the subject (*Tertium...genus*) and the main verb (*est*), although not the adjective (*teterrimum*) qualifying the subject;[155] it also marks the relative pronoun (*qui*) that is the subject of the subordinate clause, and the verb within that clause (*noscuntur*). In this case, the marks isolate the principal elements within the sentence, but do not distinguish elements within the main clause from elements within the subordinate clause. A more refined version of the system would use different marks within the two clauses, and would place marks above rather than below the two verbs, to indicate in each case that the end of the sense-unit has been reached.

Most of the construe marks in MS 57 appear to be the work of a single hand. On fol. 6v|23, a construe mark is entered below the interlinear correction *reddatur* which, as noted above, is attributable to the principal glossator of the Rule of St Benedict.[156] The construe marks therefore postdate this scribe's work, or at least part of his work. On fols 101v–102r (see Plate 6), construe marks are entered below a portion of text written over erasure in imitation Square minuscule script. Again, the marks must postdate this phase of work. On the other hand, they must have been entered before the manuscript acquired its supply leaves, for there are no construe marks on those leaves. Like the lexical glosses to the Rule of St Benedict, the marks would presumably have assisted private study of the manuscript, and perhaps also the public explication of its texts.

CONCLUSION

The various types of addition to MS 57 demonstrate the use of the manuscript in different ways by numerous readers over a prolonged period. Twelfth-century additions to the Martyrology indicate the continuation of its public use, while a handful of annotations to the Rule of St Benedict shows that that text was still studied privately in the second half of the thirteenth century.[157] The majority of the additions, however, cluster within the late Anglo-Saxon period, some being datable from their content to the middle 1040s and to the early 1050s. These Anglo-Saxon additions, while also pointing to casual use and use for private study and/or public explication, primarily show that MS 57 served the purpose for which its contents indicate that it was intended, namely public recitation within the chapter-house. Through the character of its contents and the evidence for its use, the manuscript can justly claim to be the outstanding surviving example of an Anglo-Saxon chapter-house book.

NOTES

The research underlying this article was begun during the Leverhulme Trust-funded project on 'The Archaeology of Anglo-Saxon Manuscripts' based at Corpus Christi College, Cambridge, from 1989 to 1994, and was completed with the financial assistance of Prof. Shuji Sato of Chuo University, Tokyo.

1. Descriptions of the manuscript occur in Montague Rhodes James, *A Descriptive Catalogue of the Manuscripts in the Library of Corpus Christi College Cambridge*, 2 vols (Cambridge: Cambridge University Press, 1912), vol. 1, no. 57; Mildred Budny, *Insular, Anglo-Saxon, and Early Anglo-Norman Manuscript Art at Corpus Christi College, Cambridge*, 2 vols (Kalamazoo: Medieval Institute Publications, forthcoming), no. 25; and in the first Corpus Christi issue of *Anglo-Saxon Manuscripts in Microfiche Facsimile* (Binghamton: Medieval and Renaissance Texts and Studies, forthcoming).
2. For an authoritative edition of the Rule, see Rudolf Hanslik, ed., *Benedicti Regula*, Corpus Scriptorum Ecclesiasticorum Latinorum, 75 (Vienna: Hoelder, Pichler, Tempsky, 1960). The copy in MS 57 has been edited with an introduction in John Chamberlin, *The Rule of St. Benedict: The Abingdon Copy*, Toronto Medieval Latin Texts (Toronto: Pontifical Institute of Mediaeval Studies, 1982).
3. The text is printed in PL 40: 1106 and in Hans Sauer, 'Die Ermahnung des Pseudo-Fulgentius zur Benediktregel und ihre altenglische Glossierung', *Anglia* 102 (1984), 419–25, at p. 423.
4. The text is edited by Morgand and Wandrille in Peter Becker et al., ed., *Initia consuetudinis Benedictinae: consuetudines saeculi octavi et noni*, Corpus Consuetudinum Monasticarum, 1 (Siegburg: F. Schmitt, 1963), pp. 229–61. On the likely late eighth-century origin and on the possible role of Benedict of Aniane in the diffusion of the text, see ibid, pp. 224–5.
5. Ibid., p. 225.
6. Ibid., pp. 222–3.
7. Exactly the same division occurs in a closely related thirteenth-century manuscript from the Abbey of Saint-Victor in Paris (Paris, Bibliothèque Nationale, lat. 15025, fols 113v–116r), on which see ibid., pp. 180 and 188. London, British Library, Cotton Tiberius A. iii, a mid-eleventh-century Canterbury manuscript, contains on fols 164r–168v only that

portion of the text that follows the division in MS 57; it is treated as an independent (although untitled) text. See ibid., p. 183, and N.R. Ker, *Catalogue of Manuscripts Containing Anglo-Saxon* (Oxford: Oxford University Press, 1957), no. 186, art. 3.

8. Becker et al., *Initia consuetudinis Benedictinae*, p. 223.

9. Ibid., critical apparatus on p. 240. The manuscripts are Cambridge University Library Ll. 1. 14 and London, British Library, Cotton Titus A. iv and Harley 5431, all discussed further below.

10. Printed in Albert Werminghoff, ed., *Concilia aevi Karolini* I, Monumenta Germaniae Historica, Concilia 2:1 (Hanover and Leipzig: Hahn, 1906), pp. 269–70. On the councils of 813, see Carlo de Clercq, *La Législation religieuse franque de Clovis à Charlemagne: étude sur les actes de conciles et les capitulaires, les statuts diocésains et les règles monastiques (507–814)*, Université de Louvain, Recueil de Travaux publiés par les Membres des Conférences d'Histoire et de Philologie, 2nd ser., 38 (Louvain: Bibliothèque de l'Université; Paris: Sirey, 1936), pp. 231–47.

11. Semmler's edition is in Becker et al., *Initia consuetudinis Benedictinae*, pp. 515–35. On the date of the text, see ibid., pp. 430–1, and Josef Semmler, 'Zur Überlieferung der monastischen Gesetzgebung Ludwigs des Frommen', *Deutsches Archiv für Erforschung des Mittelalters* 16 (1960), 309–88, at pp. 362–5.

12. For an overview of the Aachen legislation as a whole, see Rosamond McKitterick, *The Frankish Kingdoms under the Carolingians, 751–987* (London: Longman, 1983), pp. 112–17.

13. On the genre, see Henri Quentin, *Les Martyrologes historiques du Moyen Âge: étude sur la formation du Martyrologe romain* (Paris: J. Gabalda, 1908), pp. 1–4.

14. Usuard's text is edited by Jacques Dubois, *Le Martyrologe d'Usuard: texte et commentaire*, Subsidia Hagiographica, 40 (Brussels: Société des Bollandistes, 1965).

15. Examples of such modified texts include the late eleventh-century copy from Durham (Dean and Chapter Library B. IV. 24, fols 12–39) and the late eleventh- or early twelfth-century copy fom St Augustine's Abbey, Canterbury (London, British Library, Cotton Vitellius C. xii, fols 114–56). Dr T.A. Heslop, who is working on the text of the Martyrology in MS 57, has kindly informed me that it includes one or two modifications to Usuard's basic text that suggest Glastonbury and Flemish influence (the possible significance of which is discussed below). The interpolation (under 24 August, on fols 74v|24–75r|2) of information relating to St Patrick and his burial at Glastonbury is noted and discussed by David N. Dumville, 'St Patrick in an Anglo-Saxon Martyrology', in his *Saint Patrick, A.D. 493–1993* (Woodbridge: The Boydell Press, 1993), pp. 243–4.

16. The text of the *Diadema* is printed in PL 102: 593–690. On Smaragdus' career and work see Fidel Rädle, *Studien zu Smaragd von Saint-Mihiel*, Medium Aevum, Philologische Studien, 29 (Munich: Wilhelm Fink, 1974); for the *Diadema*, ibid., pp. 68–77.
17. For a concise summary of these three branches of the text, see Mechthild Gretsch, 'Æthelwold's Translation of the *Regula Sancti Benedicti* and Its Latin Exemplar', *Anglo-Saxon England* 3 (1974), 125–51, at pp. 128–9. All surviving Anglo-Saxon copies dating from the third quarter of the tenth century onwards belong to the *textus receptus* tradition. Interestingly, however, the copy in MS 57 has numerous readings that suggest a link with the older *textus interpolatus* tradition; see ibid., p. 134, and Chamberlin, *Rule of St. Benedict*, pp. 9–10.
18. Cf. Sauer, 'Die Ermahnung des Pseudo-Fulgentius', pp. 419–21.
19. Most of the text of *De festiuitatibus anni* has been lost from Harley 5431. The beginning of its rubricated title survives on fol. 126v|14, but the rest of the page below has been erased, presumably at a time after the following leaf, which would have contained the conclusion of the text, had been lost (fol. 126 is now the last leaf of this part of the manuscript). The erasure has left visible the large green initial *F* that began the text. For a reproduction of the page, see Mildred Budny, 'Assembly Marks in the Vivian Bible and Scribal, Editorial, and Organizational Marks in Medieval Books', in *Making the Medieval Book: Techniques of Production*, ed. Linda L. Brownrigg (Los Altos Hills: Anderson-Lovelace; The Red Gull Press, 1995), pp. 199–239, at fig. 25.
20. A fifth, fragmentary Anglo-Saxon manuscript (Rouen, Bibliothèque Municipale, U. 107 [1385], fols 20–26) contains just the *Memoriale qualiter* and another set of Aachen decrees, the *Acta praeliminaria* of the council of 816. The fragment, which dates from the late tenth or early eleventh century, consists of a single quire that has lost its first leaf with the opening of the *Memoriale qualiter*. The fragment may come from a manuscript that once contained the Rule.
21. They are the two copies cited in n. 15 above.
22. The two post-Conquest copies of Smaragdus are Oxford, Bodleian Library, Bodley 451, and Cambridge, Clare College 17 (Kk. 4. 4). These and the two Anglo-Saxon copies are listed in Helmut Gneuss, 'A Preliminary List of Manuscripts Written or Owned in England up to 1100', *Anglo-Saxon England* 9 (1981), 1–60, nos 8, 31, 41 and 579; and Joyce Hill, 'Ælfric and Smaragdus', *Anglo-Saxon England* 21 (1992), 203–37, at p. 233.
23. Cf. Michael Lapidge, 'Surviving Booklists from Anglo-Saxon England', in *Learning and Literature in Anglo-Saxon England: Studies Presented to Peter Clemoes on the Occasion of his Sixty-Fifth Birthday*, ed. Michael Lapidge and Helmut Gneuss (Cambridge: Cambridge University Press, 1985), pp. 33–89, nos VIII.7, X.53 and XIII.43; repr. with corrections in

Anglo-Saxon Manuscripts: Basic Readings, ed. Mary P. Richards, Basic Readings in Anglo-Saxon England; Garland Reference Library of the Humanities, 1434 (New York and London: Garland Publishing, Inc., 1994), pp. 87–167.

24. For advice on this, I am grateful to Mr Nicholas Hadgraft, Conservation Officer of Corpus Christi College.

25. Cf. Ker, *Catalogue*, p. xxv.

26. Cf. ibid., p. xxiv.

27. Ibid., p. xxv, and nos 38, 162 (Quire 3), 227 (Quires 7–9), 243 and 309. One of the two fragments that make up no. 243 (London, British Library, Harley 5915, fol. 13) has a late fifteenth- or early sixteenth-century inscription on its recto showing that it then belonged to Thomas Dayly, vicar of Marcham near Abingdon. Stains on the verso indicate that at this time the fragment was in service as a pastedown. This fragment and its fellow (Cambridge, Magdalene College, Pepys 2981, no. 16) come from a collecton of Ælfric's homilies. David N. Dumville, in 'Beowulf Come Lately: Some Notes on the Palaeography of the Nowell Codex', *Archiv für das Studium der neueren Sprachen und Literaturen* 225 (1988), 49–63, at p. 59 n. 51, has written that the script of the two fragments 'seems related' to that of MS 57. In view of the shared connection with Abingdon and its region, this is of potential significance. The relationship is, however, more generic than particular. Both scripts are late versions of Square minuscule, but their individual idioms are unmistakably different.

28. This is the dating of Ker, *Catalogue*, p. 46 ('s. x/xi'). Cf. Dumville, 'St Patrick in an Anglo-Saxon Martyrology', p. 243, who describes MS 57 as 'written in Phase-VII Anglo-Saxon Square-minuscule script *ca* A.D. 1000: the dating is a rather precise one, for this flat-topped variety of Square minuscule seems to have been written for only a very few years, in the 990s and possibly in the succeeding decade'.

29. On these marks of punctuation and their use, see M.B. Parkes, *Pause and Effect: An Introduction to the History of Punctuation in the West* (Aldershot: Scolar Press, 1992), pp. 35–40.

30. For Wormald's categories, see his 'Decorated Initials in English MSS. from A.D. 900 to 1100', *Archaeologia* 91 (1945), 107–35; repr. in *Francis Wormald: Collected Writings*, ed. J.J.G. Alexander, T.J. Brown and Joan Gibbs, 2 vols (London: Harvey Miller; Oxford: Oxford University Press, 1984), vol. 1, pp. 47–75. The initial in MS 57 is there listed on p. 134 (p. 74 in the reprint). See also Elzbieta Temple, *Anglo-Saxon Manuscripts 900–1066*, A Survey of Manuscripts Illuminated in the British Isles, 2 (London: Harvey Miller, 1976), no. 30 (x).

31. The hybrid character of the script on the replacement leaves is noted by David N. Dumville, *English Caroline Script and Monastic History: Studies in Benedictinism, A.D. 950–1030*, Studies in Anglo-Saxon History, 6

(Woodbridge: The Boydell Press, 1993), p. 154.

32. Reproduced ibid., pl. XV.

33. See below, pp. 45–6.

34. There is later medieval evidence (from St Mary's, York) that formulae of this kind were read out at the morning chapter office. See J.B.L. Tolhurst, ed., *The Monastic Breviary of Hyde Abbey, Winchester*, Henry Bradshaw Society, 78, 6 vols (London: Harrison and Sons, 1932–1942), vol. 6, p. 54.

35. Wulfstan of Winchester, *The Life of St Æthelwold*, ed. Michael Lapidge and Michael Winterbottom, Oxford Medieval Texts (Oxford: Oxford University Press, 1991), p. 18.

36. Ibid., p. 27.

37. See Joseph Stevenson, ed., *Chronicon monasterii de Abingdon*, Rolls Series, 2, 2 vols (London: Longman, 1858), vol. 2, p. 278.

38. Ibid., vol. 1, p. 129.

39. On the origin and spread of English Caroline minuscule, see T.A.M. Bishop, *English Caroline Minuscule*, Oxford Palaeographical Handbooks (Oxford: Oxford University Press, 1971), pp. xi–xxiv; and Dumville, *English Caroline Script*, pp. 1–6.

40. Bishop, *English Caroline Minuscule*, pp. xix, xxi–xxii, and nos 11 and 15.

41. Dumville, *English Caroline Script*, pp. 18 n. 50, 58 n. 259, and 102 and n. 101. See also David Dumville, 'English Libraries before 1066: Use and Abuse of the Manuscript Evidence', in *Insular Latin Studies. Papers on Latin Texts and Manuscripts of the British Isles: 550–1066*, ed. Michael W. Herren, Papers in Mediaeval Studies, 1 (Toronto: Pontifical Institute of Mediaeval Studies, 1981), pp. 153–78, at pp. 163–4; repr. with revisions in Richards, *Anglo-Saxon Manuscripts: Basic Readings*, pp. 169–219 (see pp. 186–8).

42. Dumville, *English Caroline Script*, p. 153, where he remarks that from these houses 'we gain no evidence for the retention of Square minuscule as a vehicle for Latin texts'. In n. 78 he observes that MS 57, if it originated at Abingdon, would be the one exception to this pattern.

43. For descriptions of these manuscripts and their Abingdon connections, see Ker, *Catalogue*, nos 2, 3, 8, 24 and 320.

44. Dumville, *English Caroline Script*, p. 76 n. 349. According to Dumville, Gretsch 'hinted' that MS 57 'might have originated at Worcester'. Gretsch herself, however ('Æthelwold's Translation', p. 134), drew attention only to the link of MS 57 with the *textus interpolatus* tradition that is shown by the readings that MS 57 shares with the Hatton manuscript; she did not comment on the place of origin of MS 57.

45. Gretsch's view (ibid.) was that the readings shared with Hatton 48 by MS 57 and by the late eleventh-century Durham, Dean and Chapter Library B.

IV. 24, point to the general conclusion that 'this early English textual tradition must have survived for quite a long time after the *receptus* tradition had reached England as a consequence of the Benedictine reform'.

46. See below, p. 41.
47. Dr Heslop's work on the text of the Martyrology in MS 57 will be the subject of a future publication. I am most grateful to him for generously informing me of his discovery.
48. Cf. Temple, *Anglo-Saxon Manuscripts*, no. 30 and pls. 50, 103–14, 116–22, 130–1 and 138.
49. Bishop, *English Caroline Minuscule*, pp. xxii–xxiii and no. 5; Dumville, *English Caroline Script*, pp. 89, 100–1, 148 with n. 42, and 153. An additional, if minor, palaeographical link of MS 57 with Canterbury is the occasional use as an interlinear correction of a 'rough breathing' consisting of the left stem and crossbar of a capital *H*; it is entered above the initial *i* of *istoria* on fol. 56r|21 and of *ibernia* on fol. 75v|24. T.A.M. Bishop noted the use of such a breathing as a correction in three tenth-century manuscripts of probable St Augustine's origin; see his 'Notes on Cambridge Manuscripts Part IV: Manuscripts Connected with St Augustine's Canterbury', *Transactions of the Cambridge Bibliographical Society* 2.4 (1957), 323–36, at p. 325.
50. See Nicholas Brooks, *The Early History of the Church of Canterbury: Christ Church from 597 to 1066*, Studies in the Early History of Britain (Leicester: Leicester University Press, 1984), p. 279; and, on the bequest to Abingdon, Dumville, *English Caroline Script*, p. 82. Æthelgar, archbishop of Canterbury 988–990, was also a former monk of Abingdon, having departed thence to become abbot of New Minster, Winchester, in 964; see David Knowles, C.N.L. Brooke and Vera C.M. London, eds., *The Heads of Religious Houses: England and Wales 940–1216* (Cambridge: Cambridge University Press, 1972), pp. 80–1.
51. On this episode, see Brooks, *Early History*, pp. 299–300.
52. The Abingdon origin of MS B is accepted, and the case for it strengthened, in Simon Taylor, ed., *MS B*, The Anglo-Saxon Chronicle: A Collaborative Edition, 4 (Cambridge: D.S. Brewer, 1983), pp. xi and xxviii–l, where the relationship with MS C is discussed in detail. Taylor notes that, while textual evidence indicates that the manuscript was written in 977/78, 'in principle...MS B may be up to about twenty years later'. Cyril Hart's suggestion of a Ramsey origin for MS B ('The B Text of the *Anglo-Saxon Chronicle*', *Journal of Medieval History* 8 [1982], 241–99), has not won acceptance. However, Hart's persuasive argument for a link between the annals for A.D. 1–99 in MS B and Latin annals for those years in the lower margin of fol. 111rv of Oxford, St John's College 17 (ibid., pp. 274–78) has prompted the conclusion that MS B could have been loaned to Ramsey during the 990s; see the general editors' foreword to Taylor, *MS B*, p. viii,

and David N. Dumville, 'Some Aspects of Annalistic Writing at Canterbury in the Eleventh and Early Twelfth Centuries', *Peritia* 2 (1983), 23–57, at p. 40.

53. Ker, *Catalogue*, pp. 249–50; and Taylor, *MS B*, pp. xxi–xxii. Ker notes the sixteenth-century evidence for the presence of MS B at St Augustine's.

54. Dumville, 'Some Aspects', pp. 28–9.

55. The verses commemorating Ælfric (noted by Ker, *Catalogue*, pp. 2–3) were published by Max Förster, 'Die altenglische Glossenhandschrift Plantinus 32 (Antwerpen) und Additional 32,246 (London)', *Anglia* 41 (1917), 94–161, at p. 154. That the verses served as an epitaph is indicated by the first line referring to Ælfric's remains that 'emit a sweet odour here' (*Prȩsulis hic redolent Ælfrici lypsana summi*).

56. Ch. XLII; Chamberlin, *The Rule of St. Benedict*, p. 51: 'As soon as they have risen from the evening meal, all are to sit in one place; and one of them is to read the *Collationes* or the *Lives of the Fathers* or indeed anything that may edify the listeners.... On fast days, however, once Vespers have been said, they are after a short interval to proceed to the reading of the *Collationes* as we have said; and four or five pages are to be read, or as much as time permits.'

57. Fol. 33v|19–23: 'After this the reader for the week is to read a lesson from the Rule. Once this has been read, he is to recite the names, or, if available, the passions of those whose feasts are celebrated on that day. When these have been read out, he is to announce the feast of the following day, saying, "Tomorrow it will be the feast of such and such a saint."'

58. I.e., CUL Ll. 1. 14, Harley 5431, Titus A. iv, and Rouen U. 107. The text does not occur in Tiberius A. iii, as its partial copy of the *Memoriale* begins at a later point in the text.

59. See Becker et al., *Initia consuetudinis Benedictinae*, p. 235: 'Post lectionem uero recitata nomina sanctorum quorum festa crastinus excipiet dies, surgentes pariter dicant uersum *Pretiosa in conspectu domini.*'

60. On the early medieval use of the Martyrology, see Baudouin de Gaiffier, 'De l'usage et de la lecture du Martyrologe: témoignages antérieurs au XIe siècle', *Analecta Bollandiana* 79 (1961), 41–59.

61. Fol. 37r|17–20: 'After the hour of Vespers, when the appropriate signal has been given, all are to come together in one group in the evening chapter, and a text that will edify the listeners is to be read out, as much as time permits.' The opening of the passage differs slightly from the edited text in Becker et al., *Initia consuetudinis Benedictinae*, p. 259, where the wording is: *Post Uesperas hora competenti.*

62. Ibid., p. 532.

63. MS 57, fol. 40v|5–6; Becker et al., *Initia consuetudinis Benedictinae*, p. 533. I assume that *tradere* here refers to explication of the text, and this

was evidently Semmler's conclusion also; see ibid., p. 480, note on lines 6–7.

64. Thomas Symons, ed. and trans., *Regularis Concordia Anglicae Nationis Monachorum Sanctimonialiumque: The Monastic Agreement of the Monks and Nuns of the English Nation* (London: Thomas Nelson, 1953), p. 17: 'After the Morrow Mass, at a sign from the prior, all shall come together for the Chapter, the prior leading. Turning to the east they shall salute the Cross and with bared heads abase themselves before one another: this act of humility is to be observed whenever the brethren are assembled together. When the brethren are seated, the Martyrology shall be read; all shall then rise and say the verse *Pretiosa in conspectu Domini* with the collect and the verse *Deus in adiutorium meum intende*, this verse being given out by the prior and said thrice, with the *Gloria* at the end, the brethren making a genuflection if the season of the year demands it. When the prior says *Et ne nos inducas* all shall rise, and, with unbowed heads, say the verse *Respice in seruos*, adding the *Gloria* and bowing their heads. There follow the collect *Dirigere et sanctificare* and the *Adiutorium nostrum in nomine Domini: Qui fecit coelum et terram*. Then, all being seated again, the Rule or, on feast days, the Gospel of the day, shall be read and the prior shall explain what has been read according as the Lord shall inspire him' (Symons' translation).

65. Ibid., pp. 22–3: 'On Saturdays...the bell is rung and *collatio* is begun in the church. When the little bell rings again, the brethren shall enter the refectory for *caritas*. As often as *caritas* is provided for the brethren during the reading of the *collatio*, they shall all rise when the reading is finished, and the prior shall say the verse *Sit nomen Domini benedictum* and *Benedicamus Domino*, the brethren answering in the usual way. On the remaining days of the week...at the sound of the bell, they shall go to the *collatio*, at which the length of the reading shall be as time allows and as seems good to the prior; and so to Compline' (Symons' translation).

66. PL 102: 593: 'And because it is written in the Rule of blessed Benedict, "As soon as the brothers have risen from the evening meal, all are to sit together, and one of them is to read the *Collationes* or the *Lives of the Fathers*, or indeed anything that may edify the listeners"; therefore we have gathered together in this little book somewhat of the discourses of the Fathers and of their ways of life and institutes, and much from various teachers, and have brought the whole to completion in one hundred chapters. And since it is the custom of monks to read the Rule of St Benedict each day at the morning chapter, we wish that this little book may be read each day at their evening chapter.' In MS 57, this passage occurs on fol. 95r|14–23, and differs in small details from the text as published in PL: MS 57 has *uitam* for *uitas*, omits *et* before *de collationibus*, omits *centum*, and has *primitiuum* for *matutinum*.

67. MS 57, fol. 37v|11–12, differing slightly from Becker et al., *Initia consuetudinis Benedictinae*, p. 261: *Hi affectus in unum collecti citius ad memoriam reducuntur.*

68. Twelve lunar months of 29½ days make 354 days, eleven less than the solar year. Therefore, on the same date in two consecutive years, the moon will be eleven days older in the second year than in the first. After 19 years (235 lunar months), provided that one lunar day is omitted (the so-called *saltus lunae*), the sun and the moon are back in phase and the cycle repeats itself.

69. See also the explanation of Golden Numbers in Beate Günzel, ed., *Ælfwine's Prayerbook (London, British Library, Cotton Titus D. xxvi + xxvii)*, Henry Bradshaw Society, 108 (London: The Boydell Press, 1993), p. 18.

70. See also ibid., pp. 18–19.

71. See Charles W. Jones, ed., *Bedae opera de temporibus*, Mediaeval Academy of America Publication, 41 (Cambridge, Mass.: Mediaeval Academy, 1943), pp. 224–6.

72. Ibid., p. 224: *Quod si adeo quisque deses uel hebes est ut absque omni labore computandi lunae cursum scire uoluerit, innitatur alphabetis quae in annali uidet libello iuxta cursum distincta lunarem, ubi duos lunae circuitus, id est quinquagenos et nouenos dies, terna tenent alphabeta.*

73. Cf. Günzel, *Ælfwine's Prayerbook*, p. 23, and, for a very full and lucid explanation and history of the calculation of Easter, Jones, *Bedae opera de temporibus*, pp. 6–104.

74. Arthur S. Napier, ed., *The Old English Version of the Enlarged Rule of Chrodegang together with the Latin Original*, Early English Text Society, o.s. 150 (London: Kegan Paul, Trench, Trübner & Co., 1916), p. 27; also PL 89: 1067. See also Tolhurst, *The Monastic Breviary of Hyde Abbey*, vol. 6, p. 52, who notes that announcing the day of the moon is stipulated in the later recension of the *Memoriale qualiter*, for which see Becker et al., *Initia consuetudinis Benedictinae*, p. 270.

75. For such a table, see Jones, *Bedae opera de temporibus*, p. 225, discussed on pp. 358–59 and also in Charles W. Jones, *Bedae Pseudepigrapha: Scientific Writings Falsely Attributed to Bede* (Ithaca: Cornell University Press, 1939), pp. 65–8. Bede accompanied chapter XXIII of *De temporum ratione* with this table, but, as Jones notes (*Bedae Pseudepigrapha*, pp. 65–7), the table goes back beyond Bede and in medieval times was believed to be the work of St Jerome. Among Anglo-Saxon manuscripts, the table occurs in London, British Library, Cotton Titus D. xxvii, fol. 9rv, for which see Günzel, *Ælfwine's Prayerbook*, pp. 103–4, with explanation on pp. 19–20.

76. On fol. 45v|20, where the number *XIX* should appear next to the date III Non. Feb., the original rubricated number has been erased and no ink

number has been substituted. On fol. 50r|11, where *XVI* should be entered next to VII Id. Mar., there appears never to have been a number, rubricated or otherwise. For further omissions (or erasures resulting in omissions), see fols 58r|7, 61r|6, 62r|24, 62v|8, 65r|11, 68r|15, 71r|9 and 86r|14.

77. Other errors occur at fols 52v|13 (*XIII* instead of *XIIII*), 52v|17 (*II* instead of *III*), 64v|22 (*XI* instead of *IX*), 70r|14 (*XIII* instead of *XIIII*) and 87r|17 (*III* instead of *IIII*).

78. Some of the twelfth-century additions are discussed below. In the outer margin of fol. 6v occurs a note ([*D*]*e reddenda ratione*) in Anglicana script of the second half of the thirteenth century. The same hand has entered *Nota* marks both here and in the outer margins of fols 23v, 28v, 29r, 29v and 30r. Except for fol. 28v, each marked passage refers to the conduct required of an abbot; possibly the marks were made by an abbot of Abingdon.

79. See Timothy Graham, 'A Runic Inscription in an Anglo-Saxon Manuscript from Abingdon and the Scandinavian Career of Abbot Rodulf (1051–2)', *Nottingham Medieval Studies*, 40 (1996), 16–24. On other drypoint entries of script in MS 57, including a handful of Old English glosses to the *Diadema monachorum*, see R.I. Page, 'More Old English Scratched Glosses', *Anglia* 97 (1979), 27–45, at pp. 29–32.

80. For this antiphon, see Tolhurst, *The Monastic Breviary of Hyde Abbey*, vol. 4, fol. 406v.

81. The sketch extends from line 23 into the lower margin. The head of the figure is just to the right of the end of the word *corporis* in the title of chapter XLVIII; the left foot is below and to the left of the chapter number *LIII*. The figure has no right leg but is otherwise complete. For further drypoint sketches in the manuscript, see Budny, *Insular, Anglo-Saxon, and Early Anglo-Norman Manuscript Art* (cited n. 1 above), no. 25.

82. In the case of the *r* of *redeas* in line 4, the complete letter was erased (as were the initial *e* and the two *f*'s of *efficaciter* and the initial *o* of *oboedientię*, in line 3).

83. Like most of the glosses of the principal glossator, most of those on fol. 8 belong to the set of glosses on the Rule that also occurs in the tenth-century Cambridge, Trinity College 0. 2. 30 (on which see below). This suggests that the glosses on fol. 8 probably matched those on the leaf that it replaced.

84. Within ch. III, *De adhibendis ad consilium fratribus*; cf. Chamberlin, *The Rule of St. Benedict*, p. 24|21.

85. Within ch. II, *Qualis debeat esse abbas*; cf. ibid., p. 23|29.

86. Also within ch. II; cf. ibid., p. 24|3.

87. Paul Meyvaert, 'Towards a History of the Textual Transmission of the *Regula S. Benedicti*', *Scriptorium* 17 (1963), 83–110, at pp. 102 and 110. For the Trinity College manuscript, in which the glosses for each chapter

occur as a block at the end of the chapter, see Ker, *Catalogue*, no. 94, and T.A.M. Bishop, 'Notes on Cambridge Manuscripts Part IV', pp. 324–6. In the Visigothic manuscript, only the preface and chs. XVIIII–XLI and LXIIII–LXV have early glosses. The glossing in these chapters is not as dense as in MS 57, but the numerous shared glosses show that ultimately the glosses in both manuscripts depend upon a common original stock. The glossing of the Anglo-Saxon copies of the Rule of St Benedict is by Rohini Jayatilaka, 'The *Regula Sancti Benedicti* in Late Anglo-Saxon England: The Manuscripts and their Readers', unpubl. D. Phil. thesis, Oxford University, 1996.

88. Meyvaert, 'Towards a History', p. 102 n. 76.

89. Within ch. XLIX, *De Quadregisimae obseruatione*; cf. Chamberlin, *The Rule of St. Benedict*, p. 56|3.

90. Within ch. LII, *De oratorio monasterii*; cf. ibid., p. 56|30.

91. The correction is presumably intended to be *reparatur*, but looks more like *repanatur*.

92. The glosses, which have suffered loss through trimming, are [?*maxim*]*us*. *precipuus* | [*uiola*]*ri*. con*taminari*. uel *inquinari*. | [*prosequ*]*ant*ur. *deducant*ur. *perseuerent*; cf. Chamberlin, p. 58|3–4. The glosses also occur as interlinear glosses correctly placed over their lemmata.

93. See above, p. 36.

94. On the genre of suppletive glosses, see Gernot Rudolf Wieland, *The Latin Glosses on Arator and Prudentius in Cambridge University Library, MS Gg. 5. 35*, Studies and Texts, 61 (Toronto: Pontifical Institute of Mediaeval Studies, 1983), pp. 109–11.

95. See, for example, fol. 9v|8, where the main glossator's *rimaris* (in error for *rimans*), glossing *scrutans* (cf. Chamberlin, *The Rule of St. Benedict*, p. 29|4), has been displaced to the right by the suppletive gloss *s. est*; and fol. 11r|16, where the main glossator's *prompt*us, glossing *facilis* (cf. ibid., p. 32|5), has had to be squeezed in above the suppletive *s. monachus*.

96. This is within ch. II, *Qualis debeat esse abbas*; cf. ibid., p. 22|11–14.

97. These examples fall within the preface and ch. VII (*De humilitate*); cf. ibid., p. 18|23 and p. 28|4 and 13.

98. For chapter XIII the glosses are by three different hands, one of them identical with the hand that entered the numerical glosses for ch. XII.

99. The fourth addition for St Bertin, under 5 September, is an expansion of Usuard's original brief entry for him. The end of that entry has been erased and replaced by a new text that continues above the following date and into the outer margin.

100. I treat the entry for St Æthelwold as an obit rather than an addition to the Martyrology because of its wording, which is more appropriate to an obit. The trimmed addition reads: *Hic presentis uitę* [...] *& supernae lucis* [...]

beatus pater Æþ[elwoldus] episcopus sortitus est. Immediately below this is a twelfth-century addition supplying an entry for Æthelwold that would be suitable for inclusion in the Martyrology and that begins: *In anglia ciuitate [Wenta]na, natale adelwo[ldi]*.

101. Stevenson, *Chronicon monasterii de Abingdon*, vol. 2, p. 157.

102. As was pointed out by Jan Gerchow, *Die Gedenküberlieferung der Angelsachsen mit einem Katalog der 'libri vitae' und Necrologien*, Arbeiten zur Frühmittelalterforschung, 20 (Berlin: Walter de Gruyter, 1988), p. 246 n. 9. Gerchow wrongly relates this addition to the entry for 3 May. The pair of omission-insertion signs that key the addition into the text make it clear that it is to be inserted at the end of the entry for 2 May.

103. See O. Bled, 'Abbatiale et Collégiale: les reliques de saint Omer et les reliques de saint Bertin', *Mémoires de la Société des Antiquaires de la Morinie* 32 (1914–1920), 5–112, at pp. 18–28.

104. See *Inventio et elevatio corporis auctore Bovone abbate*, ed. Joannes Stilting, *Acta Sanctorum*, September II (Antwerp: Bernard van der Plassche, 1748), p. 623.

105. Bishops and abbots who attended the ceremony were listed in a document buried with the newly translated remains of Bertin and found within his shrine at the time of the next translation in 1237; see ibid., p. 583. All these bishops and abbots were from northern France or Flanders.

106. *Die Gedenküberlieferung der Angelsachsen*, no. 18 (pp. 245–52 and 335–8). Gerchow's study of the obits is fundamental. I must, however, take issue with his statement (p. 246) that MS 57 appears to have been taken to Normandy following the Conquest. He cites as evidence (p. 246 n. 9) the references to Sts Judoc and Bertin added to the Martyrology. Those additions, however, are (with the exception of the twelfth-century reference to the translation of Judoc on fol. 42r) in Anglo-Saxon script, and the importance to Anglo-Saxons of the two saints has been described above. Gerchow also observes that the inclusion of the place-references *in...brittanię insula* and *in anglia ciuitate [Wenta]na* in the (twelfth-century) additions for Bede and Æthelwold on fols 61r and 71r suggests that those additions were made outside of England; as he sees it, within England such references would have been unnecessary. The purpose of the place-references, however, is to adapt the format of the additions to that of Usuard's original text, in which each mention of a saint is generally preceded by a reference to the place where he died.

107. Ibid., pp. 250–1.

108. Ibid., p. 245.

109. Ibid., pp. 247–8. Gerchow observes that the hand responsible for most of the obits entered the names of 67 monks (not including abbots), and approximates that the original list, covering the whole year, would have included 120–30 monks. He notes that a list of Abingdon monks entered

in the *Liber uitae* of New Minster, Winchester (London, British Library, Stowe 944, fols 26v–27r), appears to indicate that in the 1020s the Abingdon community numbered some 37 monks. Assuming that the size of the community did not fluctuate violently, such a figure would suggest that a total of 120–130 for the period 954–1046/47 — a period of almost four generations, calculating at 25 years per generation — might represent something approaching a complete record of those who had died during that period.

110. For later medieval evidence of this practice, see Tolhurst, *The Monastic Breviary of Hyde Abbey*, vol. 6, p. 54.

111. On fol. 73r|6 there is an error in the Latin, with *decem & nouam* glossing *XVIIII*.

112. See above, p. 39.

113. This drypoint entry is in the same area as one of the added obits. The drypoint is subsequent to the obit, for examination under a microscope reveals that the drypoint cuts through the ink of the obit. If the added obits were indeed entered in 1046 or 1047 (see above), the lunar cue is datable after that.

114. I base this calculation on the rule for calculating the day of the moon given by Bede in ch. XXII of *De temporum ratione* (Jones, *Bedae opera de temporibus*, pp. 223–4). 21 March would have been the nineteenth day of the moon in a year in which the moon was 29 days old on 1 January. This was in the eleventh year of the cycle; see the table, ibid., p. 356.

115. See C.R. Cheney, ed., *Handbook of Dates for Students of English History*, Royal Historical Society Guides and Handbooks, 4 (London: Royal Historical Society, 1955), p. 157.

116. On the conduct of the Benedictine night office, see Tolhurst, *The Monastic Breviary of Hyde Abbey*, vol. 6, pp. 8–10 and 178–95.

117. The late thirteenth-century Abingdon calendar in Cambridge University Library Kk. 1. 22, fols 1v–7r, is edited by Francis Wormald, *English Benedictine Kalendars after A.D. 1100*, 2 vols, Henry Bradshaw Society, 77 and 81 (London: Harrison and Sons, 1939 and 1946), vol. 1, pp. 15–30.

118. Within this span occur entries assigning twelve lections to the feasts of Mary Magdalene (22 July) and Apollinaris (23 July). The commemoration of these saints by twelve lections was instituted by Abbot Faritius (1100–1117) (see Stevenson, *Chronicon monasterii de Abingdon*, vol. 2, p. 287). This provides a *terminus post quem* for the entries.

119. In the original text, the reference to St Bartholomew was wrongly included in the entry for 25 August on fol. 75r. The reference has been crossed through, and rewritten by an Anglo-Saxon hand in the outer margin of fol. 74v, alongside the entry for 24 August.

120. Cf. the entering of *cappis / in cappis* against several principal feast days

in the late thirteenth-century Abingdon calendar in Cambridge University Library Kk. 1. 22; see Wormald, *English Benedictine Kalendars after A.D. 1100*, vol. 1, pp. 19–30.

121. See Stevenson, *Chronicon monasterii de Abingdon*, vol. 2, p. 156.

122. The list may be compared with the late thirteenth-century calendar edited by Wormald, which notes the number of lections appropriate to each feast day.

123. The entry originally read *III R*. The *III* has been erased and *XII* written to its left. According to *De abbatibus Abbendoniae*, Abbot Faritius (1100–1117) instituted the commemoration of the feast of St Baltild with 12 lections (see Stevenson, *Chronicon monasterii de Abingdon*, vol. 2, p. 287). This provides a *terminus post quem* for the alteration.

124. *XII R* here occurs alongside the beginning of the Martyrology entry for 2 February, in which Cornelius is the first saint mentioned. But 2 February is the Feast of the Purification, to which, of course, the text of the Martyrology does not refer; presumably the 12 responds would have commemorated the Purification rather than Cornelius.

125. Twelfth-century addition.

126. Twelfth-century addition.

127. Because of the trimming of the outer margin, the numeral that preceded *R* has in this case been lost, so it is unclear if there would have been three or 12 responds. The commemoration was presumably for Grimbald, whose name has been added at the end of the Martyrology entry for the day.

128. Twelfth-century addition.

129. Twelfth-century addition. According to *De abbatibus Abbendoniae*, it was Abbot Faritius who instituted the commemoration of the feast of Mary Magdalene with 12 lections; see Stevenson, *Chronicon monasterii de Abingdon*, vol. 2, p. 287.

130. Twelfth-century addition. This commemoration was also introduced by Faritius; see ibid.

131. Twelfth-century addition. *.III. R* is entered at the edge of the margin, a position that indicates that it was added after the marginal addition of the phrase *gloriosi senis* to the Martyrology entry for Germanus. That phrase is in post-Conquest script.

132. Twelfth-century addition.

133. Twelfth-century addition.

134. Twelfth-century addition.

135. Twelfth-century addition.

136. Twelfth-century addition. *.III R* here occurs not in the margin, but over the reference to Taurinus on fol. 72v|17.

137. Twelfth-century addition.

138. Twelfth-century additions. Eight responds for Bartholomew, four for Ouen.

139. Twelfth-century addition.

140. Twelfth-century addition. The entry is here *.XII. R 7 A*, with *A* presumably standing for *Alleluia*.

141. Twelfth-century addition. *.III. R* here stands above, and postdates, the marginal addition to the Martyrology of a reference for St Giles (fol. 76v; Plate 2). That addition is in twelfth-century script.

142. Twelfth-century addition. *.XII R* here stands above, and appears to be in the same ink and hand as, the twelfth-century marginal addition of a reference to the ordination of Gregory. (Gregory's ordination should in fact be commemorated on 29 March. 3 September is the feast of his translation.)

143. The numeral preceding *R* has been trimmed away, but for this feast must have been *XII*.

144. Only the last two digits of the numeral remain; for this feast, the numeral must have been *XII*.

145. Most of the *X* of the numeral has been trimmed away. The commemoration was perhaps for St Jerome (mentioned at the end of the Martyrology entry for the day) rather than for the less well-known Victor and Ursus.

146. Twelfth-century addition.

147. All but the last digit of the numeral has been trimmed away; it might have been *III* or *XII*.

148. On construe marks in Anglo-Saxon manuscripts, see especially Fred C. Robinson, 'Syntactical Glosses in Latin Manuscripts of Anglo-Saxon Provenance', *Speculum* 48 (1973), 443–75, and Michael Korhammer, 'Mittelalterliche Konstruktionshilfen und altenglische Wortstellung', *Scriptorium* 34 (1980), 18–58.

149. This system occurs, for example, in the copy of the Rule of St Benedict in Tiberius A. iii and in CCCC 214, a now damaged copy of Boethius' *De consolatione Philosophiae* made perhaps at Canterbury in the late tenth or early eleventh century. For the construe marks in these manuscripts, see Henri Logeman, ed., *The Rule of St Benet, Latin and Anglo-Saxon Interlinear Version*, Early English Text Society, o.s. 90 (London: Trübner & Co., 1888), pp. xxxv–xxxviii and xli–xlii; Robinson, 'Syntactical Glosses', pp. 445–9, 451–4, 457, 459 and the two plates between pp. 454–5; and Korhammer, 'Mittelalterliche Konstruktionshilfen', pp. 34–6.

150. This system occurs in the eleventh-century Lambeth Psalter (London, Lambeth Palace Library 427). See Robinson, 'Syntactical Glosses', pp. 454–7; Korhammer, 'Mittelalterliche Konstruktionshilfen', pp. 38–9; and Patrick P. O'Neill, 'Syntactical Glosses in the Lambeth Psalter and the Reading of the Old English Interlinear Translation as Sentences', *Scriptorium* 46 (1992), 250–6.

151. This system is described by Robinson, 'Syntactical Glosses'; pp. 457–9; Korhammer, 'Mittelalterliche Konstruktionshilfen', pp. 26–9. Robinson

(p. 459) lists ten Anglo-Saxon manuscripts in which the system occurs, to which Korhammer adds a further three. Neither scholar mentions MS 57.

152. Robinson, 'Syntactical Glosses', p. 457.

153. This is the way the system is used in another manuscript of probable Abingdon provenance, the copy of Aldhelm's *De laudibus uirginitatis* in Brussels, Bibliothèque Royale 1650. See the facsimile edition by George van Langenhove, *Aldhelm's 'De Laudibus Virginitatis' with Latin and Old English Glosses: Manuscript 1650 of the Royal Library in Brussels* (Bruges: St Catherine Press, 1941).

154. Exceptions occur on fol. 107v|22, where the first type of mark occurs above a word, and on fol. 103r|9, where the second mark occurs below two words.

155. The mark below the *n* of *monachorum* is not a construe mark, but a *signe-de-renvoi* that relates to the gloss in the outer margin, where the mark is repeated.

156. See above, p. 41.

157. See above, n. 78.

3 Cambridge, Corpus Christi College 162

D.G. Scragg

Early in this century, Kenneth Sisam wrote the following:

> A few years ago, when turning over the Beowulf MS., I was surprised to observe that certain facts had escaped notice or attention. And they are worth while setting out, if only as an indication of the dangers that beset a historical study in which insufficient attention is paid to manuscript indications, often the clearest indications of time and place.[1]

His words might be an epigraph for this book as a whole. Certainly they represent one for the essay that follows, in which I seek to show how much may still be learnt from turning the pages of what may otherwise be seen as yet one more volume of Anglo-Saxon homilies.

Neil Ker[2] defines Cambridge, Corpus Christi College 162 as an ordered collection of homilies dating from the very beginning of the eleventh century, which opens with pieces for general occasions and continues with items for Sundays and feast days other than saints' days from Epiphany to Advent. It appears to be complete, with only a single leaf (following p. 382) now missing. Over half of the pieces are by Ælfric but there are many anonymous items and some unique compilations of Ælfrician and non-Ælfrician material. The manuscript has strong associations with the south-east of England, especially with St Augustine's, Canterbury.[3] On the face of it, this is a homiliary not unlike many which survive from the late Anglo-Saxon period. It is the purpose of this paper to show that this superficial impression is misleading.

THE CONTENTS OF THE MANUSCRIPT

Kenneth Sisam's masterly foundation study of the manuscript tradition of Ælfric's *Catholic Homilies*[4] showed the closeness of two versions of a Canterbury homiiiary, Oxford, Bodleian Library, Bodley 340/342 and Cambridge, Corpus Christi College 198. The first part of the latter is 'a copy, with displacements and modifications, of the series' of homilies, mainly but not exclusively by Ælfric, found in the former.[5] Since Sisam's work was published, more detailed examination of manuscripts containing homilies by Ælfric and anonymous writers has added other books to the nucleus of related manuscripts represented by Bodley 340/342 and CCCC 198. Closest to them textually is the subject of this essay, and it is with the links among these three manuscripts that we should begin.

Malcolm Godden has shown[6] that in items drawn from the *Catholic Homilies* second series, the readings of CCCC 162 (his F) are close to those in Bodley 340/342 (his D) and even closer to those in CCCC 198 (his E). I have confirmed this for the anonymous items.[7] Like CCCC 198, CCCC 162 is, in Sisam's words, a copy, with displacements and modifications, of the series of homilies found in Bodley 340/342, but in this case the displacements and modifications are more extensive. Although some of the first ten items in CCCC 162 are also found in Bodley 340/342, they do not follow the order of that manuscript. It is only with item 11 that CCCC 162 begins a clear parallel with Bodley 340/342.[8] Items 11–13 are Bodley's 15–17. CCCC 162 next has two extra items. The first is a slightly adapted version of Skeat's *Lives of Saints* XII, which in Skeat is set for Ash Wednesday but here prescribed as an alternative homily for the preceding Sunday;[9] the second is Ælfric's CH I.xi for the first Sunday in Lent. In the subsequent sequence for Lent, Bodley's five items are expanded to 12. This involves changes in two directions. The Bodley sequence includes three anonymous items which do not appear in 162, while Bodley's remaining two items (both by Ælfric) are expanded into a longer series by the inclusion of other Ælfric pieces, five of which are for Fridays in Lent which Ælfric appears to have written some time after the completion of CH II,[10] and the rest of which are items from CH I and II which whoever compiled the homiliary represented by Bodley for some reason did not include.

Subsequently, Bodley 340/342 and CCCC 162 are back in parallel with four anonymous items, in that 162's items 28–31 are Bodley's items 23–6, but whereas these are followed by Ælfric's Easter Day homily from CH I in Bodley, in 162 there appears a unique composite homily for Easter Day consisting of extracts from Ælfric's CH II Easter Day homily surrounded by anonymous passages. 162's items 33–4 are Bodley's 28–9, followed in 162 by four anonymous homilies, three for the three days of Rogationtide and the fourth for Ascension Day which follows them, all four of which I have suggested elsewhere form a block originally by one author, but one which has been adapted here by the substitution of the third in the series.[11] At this point Bodley has a series of items from CH I and II. Finally, items 39–54 correspond to Bodley's 43–7, 54–6, 58–62 and 73–4, i.e., pieces for Pentecost and the succeeding Sundays but omitting saints' days. Neither Bodley nor 162 has any of the later work by Ælfric at this point, for example the post-Pentecost homilies printed by Pope.

Sisam showed that the principal difference between the sequence in the early part of CCCC 198 and that of Bodley 340/342 is that one anonymous item in Bodley (a copy of Vercelli homily IX) was replaced by an Ælfric item (CH II.iv). This might be seen as a logical change to a late copy of the Bodley-type homiliary, with the replacement of an old-fashioned piece by a more orthodox item. But the alterations in CCCC 162 cannot be categorised in so simple a manner. Despite the substitution of Bodley's three anonymous (and tenth-century) Lenten pieces by eight Ælfric items for that season, five of which are homilies for the Fridays in Lent composed well into Ælfric's writing career,[12] contradictory evidence comes from the Rogationtide pieces, where we find CCCC 162 substituting early, anonymous items for the Bodley-type homiliary's Ælfric ones, early because two of them are again found in the Vercelli Book. Furthermore, whereas CCCC 162 increases the number of Lenten homilies by including pieces for Fridays, it reduces the number of post-Easter pieces. It could be argued that Bodley's items 34–41 were not available to the compiler of CCCC 162 if he worked from the same collection as the scribe of CCCC 198, for the latter manuscript lacks these pieces too, except that CCCC 162 includes copies of Bodley's items 35, 36 and 40 as pieces for general use in the introductory section. But at least the relationship of the three manuscripts, Bodley 340/342, CCCC 198 and CCCC 162, is now clearer. If Bodley represents a tradition in which items from Ælfric's two series of *Catholic Homilies* (plus some earlier anonymous pieces) were merged into a single chronological sequence, and CCCC 198 is an incomplete but generally faithful copy of that sequence, CCCC 162 is a more independently organised collection, its compiler utilising but at the same time extensively altering the Bodley-type homiliary. The following table lists the original items in CCCC 162, ignoring the additional final item added during the eleventh century on a blank leaf at the end, and leaving aside for the moment the introductory section of items for general use. The left-hand column lists the corresponding item number in Bodley 340/342 for pieces that the two manuscripts have in common.

Bodley 340/342	CCCC 162	Item set for	Brief Identification
15	11	Septuagesima	CH II.v
16	12	Sexagesima	CH II.vi
17	13	Quinquagesima	CH I.x
	14	Alternative for Quinquagesima	LS xii
	15	First Sunday in Lent	CH I.xi
18	16	Alternative for first Sunday in Lent	CH II.vii
	17	Friday following	Pope II

	18	Second Sunday in Lent	CH II.viii
19	19	Alternative for second Sunday in Lent	Vercelli III
	20	Friday following	Pope III
	21	Third Sunday in Lent	Pope IV, title and incipit only
	22	Friday following	Pope V
	23	Fourth Sunday in Lent	CH I.xii
	24	Friday following	Pope VI
	25	Fifth Sunday in Lent	CH II.xiii
	26	Friday following	Assmann V (by Ælfric)
	27	Palm Sunday	CH II.xiv
23	28	Alternative for Palm Sunday	Cameron B 3.2.18
24	29	Maundy Thursday	Assmann XIII
25	30	Good Friday	Vercelli I
26	31	Holy Saturday	Cameron B 3.2.25
	32	Easter Day	Cameron B 3.2.27 (+ CH II.xv)
28	33	First Sunday after Easter	CH I.xvi
29	34	Second Sunday after Easter	CH I.xvii
	35	Rogation Monday	Vercelli XIX
	36	Rogation Tuesday	Vercelli XX
	37	Rogation Wednesday	Bazire-Cross 3
	38	Ascension Day	Cameron B 3.2.45
43	39	Pentecost	CH I.xxii
44	40	Second Sunday after Pentecost	CH I.xxiii
45–6	41–2	Third Sunday after Pentecost	CH II.xxiii
47	43	Fourth Sunday after Pentecost	CH I.xxiv
54	44	Eighth Sunday after Pentecost	CH II.xxv
55	45	Ninth Sunday after Pentecost	CH II.xxvi
56	46	Eleventh Sunday after Pentecost	CH I.xxviii
58	47	Twelfth Sunday after Pentecost	CH II.xxviii
59–60	48–9	Sixteenth Sunday after Pentecost	CH II.xxxi expanded
61	50	Seventeenth Sunday after Pentecost	CH I.xxxiii
62	51–2	Twenty-first Sunday after Pentecost	CH I.xxxv
73	53	First Sunday in Advent	CH I.xxxix
74	54	Second Sunday in Advent	CH I.xl

THE COMPILATION OF THE MANUSCRIPT

Consideration of the compilation of CCCC 162 should logically begin with the opening pieces which Ker defines as eight homilies for general occasions before the chronological sequences begins with Epiphany. However, the parallels with Bodley 340/342 defined above suggest that the chronological sequence taken from the Bodley-type collection began with CCCC 162, item 11, and there is codicological evidence that item 11 does indeed represent a fresh starting point. CCCC 162 consists of 35 quires, all but one of which (Quire 3) are eights, all of regular appearance and ruled for 23 lines, and written in a single hand. The scribe occasionally rubricated letters, and the titles are in red rustic capitals with occasional use of green. In most cases, the first line of an item is in black rustic capitals, but twice the scribe opened with an elaborate green initial followed by a line of large red capitals, items 1 (where they are three lines deep) and 11 (where they are two). There are other links between items 1 and 11. Both begin on the second leaf of a quire (Quires 1 and 10), the first leaf of which is now lost, presumably left blank in each case. The loss of the first leaf of Quire 10 is now complicated by the history of the manuscript in modern times. The last two leaves of Quire 9 have also been lost, with the result that the last two words from the concluding formula of the final item *a butan ende amen* have disappeared. The manuscript is paginated in Archbishop Parker's distinctive red pencil. This sixteenth-century pagination suggests that someone — almost certainly Parker[13] — added a supply leaf (Parker's pp. 137–8) and some leaves from Cambridge, Corpus Christ College 178 (Parker's pp. 139–60) to CCCC 162 between its Quires 9 and 10. Ignoring these additions and the pagination which follows them, the quiring shows that two leaves are missing from the end of Quire 9 and one leaf from the beginning of Quire 10.

Quire 10, then, opens now almost exactly as Quire 1 does: a complete item begins on the second leaf of the quire with a distinctive opening in green and red, and in both cases the first leaf of the quire is lost, presumably blank. Quire 1 begins with a series of items for general occasions (Ker's items 1–8), and Quire 10 with a sequence broadly following that in Bodley 340/342 (Ker's items 11–54). What then about Ker's items 9 and 10, which are two Ælfric homilies for the second and third Sundays after Epiphany? These could belong either with the preceding general items, because Epiphany homilies are elsewhere prescribed alternatively as pieces for general occasions (see, for example, Bodley 340/342, items 7 and 8), or they may be part of the chronological sequence which begins in 162's item 11 with an Ælfric item for Septuagesima. Their rubric indicates the latter. But that they were written independently both of item 8 and of item 11 seems clear, for not only does item 11 open Quire 10 in the way that has been described, but items 9 and 10 are written separately on Quires 8 and 9. Quire 7 ends with one and two-thirds pages left blank after the completion of item 8. Items 9 and 10 are an afterthought, written after what are now succeeding items had been copied. It follows that the lost last two leaves of Quire 9 after item 10 were probably blank.

It is also possible that the one quire in the manuscript which is not an eight, Quire 3 with three bifolia plus a singleton, was made for the item which concludes on its final page. This is the last of the first three items in the manuscript, each from CH I but prescribed here as general pieces. The next item, a version of the Sunday letter,[14] now follows immediately, but it may be that when the Ælfric items were copied there was no intention of adding the Sunday letter and other general pieces, otherwise why not create Quire 3 as a quaternion like every other quire in the book? It is also noticeable that the singleton added to Quire 3 is inserted before the final leaf of the quire, a more vulnerable position than earlier in the quire would be but one perhaps suggested to the scribe when he realised that he needed more than the final leaf of his three bifolia to complete item 3.

Three independent blocks of writing in CCCC 162 may thus be defined, with the possibility of a fourth if the speculation about Quire 3 is accepted:

Block A.i	Quires 1–3	Ker items 1–3 for general occasions (and start of item 4)
Block A.ii	Quires 4–7	Ker items 4–8 for general occasions
Block B	Quires 8–9	Ker items 9–10 for post-Epiphany Sundays
Block C	Quires 10–35	Ker items 11–54 for Sunday and festivals from Septuagesima to Advent

IDIOSYNCRATIC READINGS OF THE MANUSCRIPT

It has now been shown that the scribe of CCCC 162 compiled an original collection, since the three blocks of quires were copied independently. His use of the Bodley-type homiliary was selective, and the late insertion of Block B shows that he was not copying any existing homiliary exactly or consecutively. He probably inserted five pieces for Fridays in Lent (Pope II, III, V and VI, and Assmann V) from a single source.[15] Furthermore, closer examination of individual items in his collection suggests that he introduced a wide range of minor adaptations of existing items. Two instances will suffice:

(a) Ker item 16, CH II.vii (Godden, l. 145): Bodley 340/342 and CCCC 198 have the erroneous reading 'Cumað ge (ge)bletsode to mines fæder rice' for the familiar Matthew 25.34 text. In CCCC 162, which all other variants would suggest was drawn from the same archetype, the scribe appears to have corrected as he wrote, for he omits 'rice', and 'to' is erased, the resultant reading 'gebletsode mines fæder' being that of the Vulgate.

(b) Ker item 19, Vercelli III (Scragg, l. 101): all manuscripts have the word 'fæsten' omitted at the beginning of a new section concerning fasting. The sense requires it, and the source has it. Again, Bodley 340/342 and CCCC 198 witness the fact that their archetype (which other variants show is the archetype for CCCC 162) omitted the word. CCCC 162 omits it also, but the main hand inserted it above the line.

The scribe of CCCC 162 is then not mechanical but is a careful copyist, conscious of the meaning of the words he wrote. Tiny alterations to sense show that he was anxious to 'improve' readings without departing radically from his copytext, as when in Vercelli homily III he inserted the word 'gelomlice' before 'rædan' in the clause 'he sceal gelomlice [God] gebiddan and rædan' (Scragg, l. 140). It is more difficult to show the scribe of CCCC 162 omitting material, but one instance should be noted. In the first of the Lenten Friday pieces, Pope II, an opening sentence in the only other surviving copy (London, British Library, Cotton Vitellius C. v) reads:

> Men þa leofestan, us lyst nu eow secgan be þam halgan godspelle þe ge gehyrdon nu rædan, þæt ge beon þe geleaffulran þurh þa boclican lare, and þe anrædran on eowrum Drihtne.

This does not appear in CCCC 162. Since there are only two surviving copies of this text, it may be that the sentence was added in Vitellius rather than omitted in the CCCC 162 manuscript, especially as similar wording appears in both manuscripts in the opening to Pope VI. But elsewhere Vitellius is slightly more reliable textually than CCCC 162.[16]

Before we ask how far he was responsible for more radical alterations, it is necessary to look at each separately. They are considered here in ascending order of length.

(a) Ker item 14, Ælfric's homily for Ash Wednesday, Skeat LS XII, has an opening paragraph which is made up of a sentence from Ælfric's conclusion (Skeat, ll. 289–92) filled out with phrases which are usually associated with Wulfstan: 'embe ure gemænan sawle þearfe ... eow is micel þearf þæt ge hyt mid micelre gymene understandon ... understande se ðe wille ... mid rihte'. The whole passage makes clearer than the opening of London, British Library, Cotton Julius E. vii, Skeat's base text, that the piece is preached on Quinquagesima, the Sunday before Ash Wednesday.[17] The Wulfstan influence is so obvious here that whoever composed the passage merits the title of a Wulfstan-imitator, and this makes CCCC 162 the earliest surviving manuscript containing work by such a person.

(b) Ker item 16, CH II.vii, has a non-Ælfrician conclusion, printed by Godden (p. 353). This short passage is heavily alliterative, and might be thought of as composed by an Ælfric imitator, but it has no features which link it with (i).

(c) Ker item 52, a pendant to a homily by Ælfric from CH I. The piece has recently been edited by Franz Wenisch.[18] Like (i) it is composite, but this time its elements are by tenth-century anonymous writers. The opening six lines in Wenisch's edition are from the same vernacular source as an eleventh-century composite homily which is based primarily on Vercelli homily IX,[19] although these lines are not in the Vercelli item. Then follows a passage containing a list of good works (ll. 8–11) which is similar to the one in Vercelli homily XIX,[20] a homily which is also in CCCC 162 (item 35). The argument that the compiler of this pendant was here thinking of the Vercelli XIX passage is given weight by the occurrence later in his piece of the phrase 'se færlice deað', which is unusual as an epithet for death of any sort, but used more appropriately a number of times in Vercelli XIX for plague. It is possible that the phrase stuck in the mind of the compiler of the pendant, especially since the rest of his piece is composed of a string of commonplace phrases which probably have no single source and may well be freely composed.

What these three adaptations of existing pieces have in common, apart from the fact that they are unique, is that they are the work of a person or persons supremely conscious of the writings of others, perhaps even of someone who may be anxious not to write anything himself which has no other written 'authority'. If they are the work of a single person, we must suspect that he has no style of his own, merely a facility in writing in the style of others. Speculation that he is the scribe of CCCC 162 must remain just that.

PARALLELS WITH OTHER MANUSCRIPTS

Although this paper began with the assumption that CCCC 162 is a copy, with displacements and modifications, of the series of homilies found in Bodley 340/342 and related manuscripts, it is clear that it is more than that. In the items which it has in common with Bodley 340/342, CCCC 162 is textually close to that manuscript (and even closer to CCCC 198), but in arrangement it is very different. It is not difficult, of course, to find homiliaries in Latin or in English which exclude sanctorale items. In the vernacular tradition, Cambridge, Corpus Christ College 303, a manuscript closely related textually to CCCC 162,[21] has two sequences of temporale homilies constituting together a (now incomplete) annual cycle, the first sequence running from the second Sunday after Epiphany to Easter and the second from Rogationtide to the twenty-first Sunday after Pentecost. But in this manuscript the two sequences are separated by a sanctorale. Thus, although there are points of comparison with CCCC 162 in the arrangement, there are also obvious points of disagreement. Perhaps a more interesting parallel is offered by Cambridge, University Library Ii. 4. 6, a collection of homilies, imperfect at the beginning, which now runs from Epiphany to the first Sunday after Pentecost, later known as Trinity Sunday.[22] This manuscript is comparable in three respects. First, as in CCCC 162, the collection excludes items for saints' days. Second, Ker argued[23] that what survive as the first three items, for the second, third and fourth Sundays after Epiphany, were added after the main part of the manuscript had been written, but by the scribe who wrote the second half of the collection. If this were so, this homiliary, as at first conceived, began with an item for Septuagesima, as CCCC 162 does from its item 11, although in both cases a decision was taken by the principal scribe(s) to add extra pieces at the beginning, including post-Epiphany items. The third point of comparison is that CUL Ii. 4. 6, like CCCC 162 but unlike any other surviving Anglo-Saxon manuscript, includes alternative pieces for Lent (in CUL Ii. 4. 6 the alternatives are for the first and fourth Sundays and Palm Sunday, as well as Easter Day; in CCCC 162 they are for the first and second Sundays and Palm Sunday as well as Quinquagesima).[24]

CUL Ii. 4. 6 has been an important manuscript for the study of Ælfric's later writings ever since Peter Clemoes saw it as the best witness of what he called TH I,[25] a set of liturgical homilies for the Proper of the Season from Christmas to Pentecost. (A later collection, called by Clemoes TH II, extends the series to the whole year.) Clemoes argued that CUL Ii. 4. 6 drew on a TH I collection issued by Ælfric after the publication of the *Lives of Saints*. Godden reinforced the view by examination of the CH II evidence, concluding that the manuscript belongs textually to a revised form of the first recension of the CH tradition.[26] But John Pope had earlier expressed doubt about the attribution of TH I (and the extended temporale sequence TH II) to Ælfric himself,[27] on the grounds that 'anyone ... would have found it convenient, in planning a Temporale for a portion of the year only, to limit it to festivals of which the date is governed by Easter'. The argument turns on the interpretation of the 'addition' of items before Septuagesima. It is possible to see the two scribes of the manuscript writing in blocks, with what survive as the opening items (Ker's additions) being the last of the first block. But the only evidence for such an arrangement is that Godden maintains[28] that CH II.iv (now the first item in the manuscript) shows the same textual affinity as items from Septuagesima on. Since items 2 and 3 (which, with 1, constitute Ker's additions) do not, the evidence is slight.[29] As the compilation of CCCC 162 shows, items may be added at the beginning (as 162's items 1–3 clearly were) with the same textual affinities as those later in the manuscript without invalidating the point that they are indeed additions.

There is no question of the CCCC 162 homiliary being one authorised by Ælfric. Its inclusion of non-Ælfrician pieces precludes that, and enough has been said above of its archetypes and of the way in which is was compiled to show that it cannot be an Ælfrician creation. But before the addition of early items, it was a collection assembled by someone interested in creating one beginning at Septuagesima, when the countdown to Easter begins, and therefore any further considerations of the extent of the collection in (and lying behind) CUL Ii. 4. 6 should take CCCC 162 into account. Indeed there are other links between CCCC 162 and CUL Ii. 4. 6. Although the latter is a Winchester manuscript, it would appear to draw on a south-eastern archetype, and it has some additions and glosses in common with CCCC 162.[30] Neither CCCC 162 nor the archetype of CUL Ii. 4 6 is directly dependent upon the other, but that the two were in one place (probably Canterbury or Rochester) is likely. What is significant for CCCC 162 in all this, therefore, is that as a manuscript it provides evidence of a move, probably in Canterbury, towards the provision of a temporale sequence beginning at Septuagesima (such as is witnessed in at least one later manuscript) at the very end of the tenth century or at the latest in the early years of the eleventh. But the compiler of CCCC 162, working without benefit of materials that were to be used in the archetype of CUL Ii. 4. 6, had to draw on anonymous homilies and composite pieces as well as such Ælfrician items as had reached Canterbury by the end of the millennium.

CONCLUSIONS

CCCC 162 offers a valuable insight into the creation of a vernacular homiliary in the post-reform period. It is clearly a carefully constructed temporale, and would appear to draw in all the alternative items the compiler could find for the period up to Easter. Almost everything in CH I and II suitable for a temporale sequence was included and sanctorale items excluded. Its compiler even seems to have gone back to CH I and II for extra Lenten pieces which had not been included in the original rearrangement of CH I and II into a single annual cycle. The compiler also included the pieces for Lenten Fridays at chronologically appropriate points, something which no other surviving manuscript does. We can deduce something of its composition from the additions made after the original organisation had been decided upon. We can see that its scribe copied in a thinking fashion, altering and adjusting his material in minute ways as he wrote, as well in the larger context of the content of the manuscript as a whole. Study of what he did brings us to the possibility of conclusions about why he did what he did, and this may in turn ultimately bring us closer to that most elusive aspect of all surviving Anglo-Saxon writings, the audience.

NOTES

I am grateful to Timothy Graham and Joyce Hill for help of various kinds in the compilation of material for this article, although responsibility for its conclusions is entirely mine. My thanks are due too to the Master and Fellows of Corpus Christi College for allowing me access to the manuscript.

1. "The Beowulf Manuscript', *Modern Language Review* 11 (1916), 335–7, at p. 335; repr. in his *Studies in the History of Old English Literature* (Oxford: Clarendon Press, 1953; repr. 1962), pp. 61–4, at p. 61.
2. N.R. Ker, *Catalogue of Manuscripts Containing Anglo-Saxon* (Oxford: Clarendon Press, 1957; repr. with supplement 1990), item 38, pp. 51–6.
3. See ibid., p. 56; John C. Pope, ed., *Homilies of Ælfric: A Supplementary Collection*, 2 vols, Early English Text Society, o.s. 259–60 (London: Oxford University Press, 1967–1968), pp. 23–4; Malcolm Godden, ed., *Ælfric's Catholic Homilies: The Second Series*, Early English Text Society, s.s. 5 (London: Oxford University Press, 1979), p. xxii and references; and D.G. Scragg, ed., *The Vercelli Homilies and Related Texts*, Early English Text Society, o.s. 300 (Oxford: Oxford University Press, 1992), pp. xxviii–xxix.
4. Kenneth Sisam, 'MSS. Bodley 340 and 342: Ælfric's *Catholic Homilies*', *Review of English Studies* 7 (1931), 7–22, 8 (1932), 51–68, 9 (1933), 1–12; repr. in his *Studies in the History of Old English Literature*, pp. 148–98.
5. Ibid., p. 155. Further details of the organisation of CCCC 198 may be found in my 'The Homilies of the Blickling Manuscript', in *Learning and Literature in Anglo-Saxon England: Studies Presented to Peter Clemoes on the Occasion of His Sixty-Fifth Birthday*, ed. Michael Lapidge and Helmut Gneuss (Cambridge: Cambridge University Press, 1985), pp. 299–316.
6. Godden, ed., *Ælfric's Catholic Homilies: The Second Series*, p. xxxiii.
7. Scragg, ed., *The Vercelli Homilies and Related Texts*, MS G, p. xxviii and n. 2.
8. I ignore the parallels with CCCC 198, even though this is a closer manuscript textually, because CCCC 198 breaks off at item 37 (= CCCC 162, item 42, Bodley 340/342, item 46). See my 'The Homilies of the Blickling Manuscript'.
9. Walter, W. Skeat, ed., *Ælfric's Lives of Saints, Being a Set of Sermons on Saints' Days Formerly Observed by the English Church*, Early English Text Society, o.s. 76, 82, 94, 114 (Oxford: Oxford University Press, 1881–1900; repr. in two vols in 1966). P.A.M. Clemoes ('The Chronology of Ælfric's Works', in *The Anglo-Saxons: Studies in some Aspects of their History and Culture Presented to Bruce Dickins*, ed. Peter Clemoes [London: Bowes & Bowes, 1959], pp. 212–47, at p. 221) argues that the text of CCCC 162 in this item is 'of an earlier type' than that of London, British Library, Cotton Julius E. vii, Skeat's base manuscript. The prescription for Ash Wednesday occurs in the rubric of Julius and of

Cambridge, Corpus Christi College 302, but not in CCCC 162 or CCCC 303. Joyce Hill has pointed out to me that the rhetoric of the opening of the piece in Julius E. vii implies that it was not necessarily intended for delivery on the Wednesday, but earlier than that.

10. See Clemoes, 'The Chronology of Ælfric's Works, p. 221; Pope, ed., *Homilies of Ælfric*, pp. 23 and 226–7.

11. See my 'An Old English Homilist of Archbishop Dunstan's Day', in *Words, Texts and Manuscripts: Studies in Anglo-Saxon Culture Presented to Helmut Gneuss on the Occasion of his Sixty-Fifth Birthday*, ed. Michael Korhammer, with the assistance of Karl Reichl and Hans Sauer (Cambridge: D.S. Brewer, 1992), pp. 181–92.

12. Clemoes ('The Chronology of Ælfric's Works', p. 221) argues that all the Ælfric items in CCCC 162 not in CH I and II were composed before his *Lives* set, including Skeat XII and XII. But they were clearly composed *after* he had completed CH I and II.

13. See R.I. Page, *Matthew Parker and His Books: Sandars Lectures in Bibliography Delivered on 14, 16, and 18 May 1990 at the University of Cambridge* (Kalamazoo: Medieval Institute Publications; The Research Group on Manuscript Evidence, The Parker Library, Corpus Christi College, Cambridge, 1993), pp. 53–5. Timothy Graham in a private communication reports that he is sure that Parker was responsible for the transference of leaves from CCCC 178 to 162, and I trust his judgment.

14. A.S. Napier, 'An Old English Homily on the Observance of Sunday', in *An English Miscellany Presented to Dr. Furnivall in Honour of His Seventy-Fifth Birthday*, ed. W.P. Ker and A.S. Napier (Oxford: Clarendon Press, 1901; repr. New York and London: Benjamin Blom, Inc., 1969), pp. 355–62.

15. See Pope, ed., *Homilies of Ælfric*, pp. 226–7.

16. Ibid., p. 227.

17. As Joyce Hill has pointed out to me privately, the rubric in Julius E. vii, 'In Caput Ieiunii', is for the subject, not the day of preaching.

18. Franz Wenisch, '*Nu bidde we eow for Godes lufon*: a Hitherto Unpublished Old English Homiletic Text in CCCC 162', in Korhammer, ed., *Words, Texts and Manuscripts*, pp. 43–52.

19. See Scragg, ed., *The Vercelli Homilies and Related Texts*, homily IX.L, p. 161, ll. 13–17.

20. Ibid., homily XIX, ll. 62–6; cf. also ll. 161–3.

21. For the latest analysis of the relationship of CCCC 162 and CCCC 303, see ibid. (where the two manuscripts are denoted G and H respectively), esp. pp. 312–13 and references.

22. Clemoes ('The Chronology of Ælfric's Works', p. 229) notes that this Sunday constituted 'the climax of the liturgical celebrations which since Christmas had commemorated the chief events in Christ's life and the

descent of the Holy Spirit'.

23. Ker, *Catalogue of Manuscripts Containing Anglo-Saxon*, pp. 31–5.

24. London, British Library, Cotton Faustina A. ix, and CCCC 302 are manuscripts closely related to CUL Ii. 4. 6, and consequently they too have some of the same parallels with CCCC 162; see Pope, ed., *Homilies of Ælfric*, pp. 48–52, Godden ed., *Ælfric's Catholic Homilies: The Second Series*, pp. xlvii–li. However, both are imperfect and late witnesses and the parallels are disregarded here.

25. 'The Chronology of Ælfric's Works', pp. 227–30. TH = Temporale Homilies.

26. Godden, ed., *Ælfric's Catholic Homilies: The Second Series*, pp. xlvi and lxxxvi–lxxxviii.

27. Pope, ed., *Homilies of Ælfric*, pp. 47–8.

28. See Godden, ed., *Ælfric's Catholic Homilies: The Second Series*, pp. xxxvi–xxxvii.

29. Even if we accept that the scribes were writing in blocks, the fact that one of them chose to begin his stint with Septuagesima, before the preceding items were written, is itself significant.

30. See Godden, ed., *Ælfric's Catholic Homilies: The Second Series*, p. xlvii and references.

4 The Prefatory Matter of London, British Library, Cotton Vitellius E. xviii

Phillip Pulsiano

With the exception of the collection of psalms in London, British Library, Royal 1 E. viii (Bible; late tenth century), and Florence, Biblioteca Laurenziana, Amiatino 1 (Bible; early eighth century), the texts of the psalms found in the surviving 24 psalters written in England in the eighth to twelfth centuries,[1] in the six psalters written on the Continent or in Ireland but brought to England in the tenth and eleventh centuries,[2] and in the so-called 'Portiforium of Wulstan' (Cambridge, Corpus Christi College 391, *c.* 1065), all circulated as separate books divorced from the larger context of the Bible.[3] Generally, the books were comprised of three main parts: prefatory matter, the collection of 150 psalms, and canticles (found in 23 manuscripts).[4] Thirteen of the manuscripts also add the supernumerary Psalm 151.[5] The prefatory texts in these psalters vary considerably and clearly reflect both different traditions and strata of additions. The prefatory matter in London, British Library, Cotton Vespasian A. i, for example, contains, among its numerous items, *Epistola Damasi* (fol. 4r), *Origio psalmorum* (fols 4v–5r), a text common among continental psalters, but found in only two other Insular psalters (London, British Library, Royal 2 B. v, fol. 7rv, and London, British Library, Cotton Tiberius C. vi, fol. 19rv), an explanation of *Diapsalma*, various texts on the interpretation of *Alleluia* and *Gloria*, and the like; a comparable collection of texts is found in Cotton Tiberius C. vi, fols 19r–21r. London, British Library, Arundel 60, by contrast, offers none of these texts, but includes instead, for example, a lunarium for blood-letting (*Ad sanguinem minuendum*, fol. 1), tables treating the ages of the moon for lunations of 30 and 29 days (fols 8v–9r), tables for calculating the limits of Septuagesima, Quadragesima, Easter, and Rogation (fol. 9v), along with one of the most common features found in the psalters, a calendar (fols 2r–7v). The collection of prefatory texts in London, British Library, Cotton Vitellius E. xviii offers still another miscellany of texts, one that includes, among other items, a mixture of Latin and Old English texts treating rules for finding Septuagesima, lucky and unlucky days, a tract on embolismalic days, notes on concurrents and epacts, prohibitions on blood-letting, unlucky days for childbirth and blood-letting, charms to protect against theft, discover theft, protect cattle, or promote crops, medicine for cattle with lung disease or for sheep, directions and diagrams pertaining to the *Sphera Apulei*, and directions for secret writing.[6] As modern readers of the codices containing the psalms, we tend to bring to them certain prejudices: these seemingly featureless, homogenous, perhaps monotonous books are to be mined for glosses, or their illustrations and initials disembodied for comparison with other manuscripts, with the calendars published in one place, the Old English items in the prefatory collections dislodged from their contexts and scattered among various journals while the Latin texts remain virtually ignored, and the texts of the psalms and canticles reserved for separate publication when glossed in Old English. What is lost in this process of scholarly dismemberment is the immediate manuscript context of the psalms, a context that can potentially inform our understanding of how these codices and, more particularly, how the psalms were regarded and understood by individual readers or within a larger literate community.[7]

CONTENTS

The prefatory matter of Cotton Vitellius E. xviii stands uniquely among the psalters written or owned in England. In order to assess both its status and its filiations, a detailed listing of the contents of fols 2r–16v follows:[8]

fol. 1rv	Blank except for pressmark.
fols 2v–7v	Calendar.[9]
fol. 8r	Verses on the limits of Easter: 'Nonus aprilis Norunt quinos....Quindene *con*stant Tribus adeptis'. The manuscript does not include the verses on the limits of Quadragesima ('Octone martis kalende quinque....Pridie nonas martis in ternis'). It is possible that they were originally contained on a lost preceding folio (see note 8), on which may also have been entered in a bottom register the Pachomius legend, for which see C. W. Jones, 'A Legend of St. Pachomius,' *Speculum* 18 (1943), 198–210; see also S. J. Crawford, *Byrhtferth's Manual*, EETS, o.s. 177 (London: Oxford University Press), 1929; repr. 1966, pp. 151–5. For parallels among the psalters, see Corpus Christi College 391, pp. 16–7 (with the legend on p. 16); Arundel 60, fol. 10r; Arundel 155, fols 9v–10r (with a representation of the Pachomius legend in the upper arch); Galba A. xviii, fol. 15rv; Tiberius C. vi, fols 3v–4r (with the legend on fol.

4r); Salisbury 150, fol. 1r (with the legend on fol. 10r); Reg. lat. 12, fol. 15r (with the legend on fol. 14v).[10]

fol. 8r — Calculation of Advent: '[Q]uicumq*ue* aduentum d*omi*ni celebrare desiderat....et absq*ue* ullo errore p*ro* certo ualebit'.

For parallels among the psalters, see Arundel 60, fols 10r; Tiberius C. vi, fol. 3v; Vat. Reg. lat. 12, fol. 20r.[11]

fol. 8r — Limits of Septuagesima, Quadragesima, Easter, Rogation, and Pentecost: '[V]bicumq*ue* inueneris .x.^{mam} lunam....[Et] sic sine errore inuenies'.

For parallels among the psalters, see Arundel 60, fols 9v; Tiberius C. vi, fol. 4r; Vat. Reg. lat. 12, fol. 20v.[12]

fol. 8v — Easter table in six columns.[13]

fol. 9r|1–6 — Rules for calculating Septuagesima: 'Gif þu [wille] witan mid gesceade þ*æt* gemære termen septuagessimalis....⁊ man ne singð leng þ*æt* godes lof .all*elui*an. ær þære [ea]stertide'.[14]

Parallel in Caligula A. xv, fol. 131r; Latin parallel in Tiberius C. i, fol. 2r.

fol. 9r|7–17 — Determining the lunar cycle: '[Gif þ]u wille witan hu eald se mona beo nu todæg on twelf monþu*m*....þeah þu wille to hundteontigum wintru*m* fare bisextus swa he fare oððe ænig oþer getæl'.[15]

Parallels in Caligula A. xv, fol. 131r; Corpus Christi College 422, p. 47.

fol. 9r|17–26 — **De diebus malis cuiusque mensis** '[T]weigen dagas syndon on æghwilcu*m* monðe ....⁊ se þreotteoða [b]utan ælcan tweon swa hit bið gewislice gyme se þe wille'.[16]

fols 9v–12r — Easter tables for the years 1031–1145.[17]

fol. 11v — Latin number names and, for most, equivalents in Roman numerals (written below the table).

fols 12r–13r|15 — **INCIPIT EMBOLISMUS** '[I]n primo igit*ur* anno emb*olismi* in ogd*oade* .iii.^{o} sunt epacte .xxii....In kł sept*embris* non .iiii. s*ecundu*m compotum sed .v. p*ropt*er saltum'.[18]

For parallels among the psalters, see Salisbury 150, fol. 11rv.

fol. 13r|16–21 — Calculation of concurrents and epacts: 'Gif þu nite hwilc concurrent beo on geare. Sec georne hwilce dæg beo .ii. kł. | apr*ilis*. Gif hit bið sunnandæge ðone biþ concurrent .i. Gif hit biþ monandæg | þonne biþ concurrent .ii. And swa fela daga swa bið agan on ðære wucan. | Ealswa fela concurrenta þu scealt habban þi geare. And swa fela nihta | swa se mona bið on .xi. kł. aprilis. And swa fela epacta þu scealt hab|ban þi geare'.[19]

Parallels in Caligula A. xv, fol. 131r; Titus D. xxvii, fol. 55r (= Henel's Type 2).

fol. 13r|22–27 Determination of feast limits: 'In [i]anuarius ofer .xvi. kł. februarii loca hwær þu habbe .x. nihta ealdn[e] monan. | on þone Sunnandæg ofer þ*æt* beluc alleluian. And on februariu[s] | ofer .vii. idus loca hwær þu finde twegra nihta ealdne monan . Þon[ne] | ofer þ*æt* on þonne sunnandæg biþ halgan dæg. On martius ofer xii [kł. apr*ilis*] | find fywertina nihta eal[d]ne monan. On þone sunnandæg of[er þæt he swa] | eald biþ þ*æt* biþ easter dæg'.[20]

Parallels in Corpus Christi College 422, pp. 42–3; Caligula A. xv, fols 131r; Titus D. xxvii, fol. 54v; Harley 3271, fols 91v–92r.

fol. 13r|28–38 Prohibition on blood-letting in the dog days: 'Eahtatina nihtu*m* ær hlafmæssan gangeð se styrra up....þa hw[ile]' (final line partly lost).[21]

fol. 13v Lunar table.

fol. 14r Easter table in six columns.

fol. 14v Explanation of the Sphere of Pythagoras with diagram: [ ]**ere** | '[Ratio spere pitagore p]hilosophi qua*m* appollogius descripsit....et sine errore*m* respicies q*u*icu*m*q*ue* inuenere uolueris | finit. Amen'.

fol. 15v|1–5 Lucky days for childbirth: '[Þ]ry dagas syndon on twelf monðum....feawa manna syndon þe þas dagas cunnon'.[22]

Parallels in Corpus Christi College 391, p. 718; Caligula A. xv, fol. 131r.

fol. 15r|6–15 Unlucky days for blood-letting: 'Find eft þry dagas on twelf monðum þa syndon swiðe unhalwende [mon]|num oððe nytenum blod to forlætenne oððe drenc to drincanne þ*æt* is se | æftemesta monandæig on aprilis. ær he gange of tune 7 se forma monan|dæg on agustus monðe 7 se æftemesta monan-dæg on decembres monðe | ær he gange of tune | se þe on þam þrim monandagum mannum oððe | nytenan blod forlæteð. ær feowerteoðan dæge he sceal swyltan. oððe | he ne gebideð þæs seofeðan dæges. 7 gif he drenc drincð to læcecræfte | ær fiftyne dagan he sceal swyltan. 7 gif hwilc man ac[enned biþ on] | þysum þrim dagum. he sceal swyltan yfelan deaðe 7 se ðe et[eð gose]|flæsc on þysum þrim dagum he sceal swyltan ær feowertugum dag[um]'.[23]

Parallel in Corpus Christi College, 391, p. 718 and 721 (to *monandæg*).

fol. 15r|16–15v|5 Unlucky days for blood-letting: 'þa ealdan læcas gesettan on ledebocum *þæt* on ælcum monðe beoð æf[re] | twegen dagas ....ac wise menn hit afund[en] þurh þone halgan gast swa swa him dihte god'.[24]

Parallels in Caligula A. xv, fol. 130v; Harley 3271, fols 90v–91r.

fol. 15v|6–8 Protection of bees against theft: '[ ]e mæder cið on þinre hyfe. þon*ne* | ne asponð nan man þine beon. ne hi ma[n] ne mæg forstelan þa hwile þe | se cið on þære hyfe bið'.[25]

fol. 15v|8–12 Directions for writing St Columkill's circle: **Ƿis is s*an*c*te* columcille circul** | 'Writ þysne circul mid þinnes cnifes orde....*þæt* he beo eall under eorðan. butan þam gewritenan'.[26]

With accompanying diagram below text (see below).

fol. 15v|13–18 Directions for writing a charm to discover theft: 'þonne þe ma[n] hwæt forstele | awrit þis swigende. 7 do on þinne | wynstran scó under þinu*m* | hó. þonne gelacsaxt þu hit | sona'.[27]

fol. 15v|19–23 Medicine for cattle with lung disease: '[Gif] hryþeru beon on lungen coðon....[Deus misereatu]r n*ost*ri 7 Exsurgat d*eu*s 7 Quicumq*ue* uult'.[28]

fol. 15v|22–25 Medicine for sheep: 'Gi[f] | sceap si on yl[o]n.... *þæt* heom cymð to bote'.[29]

fol. 15v|25–26 Charm to protect cattle: 'Ƿis is þinan yrfe to bote | [ ] ymb þin yrfe ælce æfen him to helpe. AGIOS. AGIOS. AGIOS'.[30]

fols 15v|27–16r|8 Charm for crops: '[ ] lange sticcan feðerecgede. ⁊ writ on ægðerne sticcan | [o]n ælcere ecge an pater n*oste*r oð ende...' **Þis is þeo bletsung þærto.** | 'Ut surices garbas non noceant | [h]as preces super garbas dicis & non dicto eos suspendis hiersolimam | ciuitate. ubi surices nec habitent. nec habent potestatem. nec grana collligent. nec triticum congaudent.' **Þis is seo oðer bletsung.** | '[D]*omi*ne d*eu*s om*n*ip*oten*s qui fecisti cęlum et terram. tu benedicis fructum istum | in nomine patris & filii & sp*iritu*s *sanc*ti. amen. ⁊ Pater n*oste*r'.[31]

fol. 16r|8–15 **[DE] UITA UEL DE MORTE** | 'Spera apulei platonici de uita uel de morte uel de om*n*ibus negotiis...Ratio in sanitate hominis'.

Accompanied by diagram, with numbers and numerical equivalents in left column. For parallels, see discussion of the *Sphera Apulei* below.

fol. 16r|16–18 Three Latin lines (ending lost), written below the diagram and partly glossed in Old English, pertaining to the *Sphera Apulei*:

to sunnandæge monan dæge
'[S]i domincus dies fuerit adde .xii. si lune dies
to tiwersdæge to
fuerit | adde .xvii. Si martis dies adde .xv. si dies
wodnesdæge to þunres dæge to frige
mercuiri adde | xxv Si iouis dies .x. Si ueneris
dæge to sæters dæge
dies .xv. Si saturnus d[ies]....'[32]

fol. 16v|1–5 Riddle: 'Nys þks frfgfn syllkc þknc to rædfnnf...⁊ mine bearn syndon geworden [m]ilnes fæder modor'.[33]

fol. 16v|6–25 Explanations of secret writing: 'AEIOU. a^b e^f i^k o^p u^x | Ðis is quinq*ue* uocales. mid þysum fif stafum man mæg writan swa hwæt | swa he wile. hit is lytel cræft. ac þeah man mæg dwelian manega [m]en | mid. ægðer ge ware. ge unware:— A^B F_E K_I O^P U^X— | [O]mnkum knkmkcprxm sxprxm dpmknbbtxr....[C]xnnb mbgf þx brædbn. hwæt þks mbgf bfpn. kc wfnf þæt hkt nks fð rædf' [etc.].[34]

See Plate 12 and discussion below.

fol. 17r|1a–19a Originally blank, now containing a later prayer: 'Svs[ci]*pere* digneris *domine* *deus*'.

fol. 17r|20a–17v Series of petitions, in a late hand, addressed to the Virgin Mary: '[kyrieleys]on. chr*iste*leyso*n*. kyrieleyson audi nos'.

DISCUSSION

In commenting upon the prefatory matter in one of the introductory chapters to their bibliography, *Old English Prose of Secular Learning*, Stephanie Hollis and Michael Wright suggest a focus to the miscellany of texts found in the psalter: 'Like the charms and prognostics in this manuscript, the recipes suggest that farming played a significant part in the lives of the users of the manuscript.'[35] The comment, although perhaps made in passing, misses the mark on a number of counts. First, it is difficult to imagine a religious community (of which Vitellius E. xviii is a product) for which farming was not a significant concern. Second, these texts form part of a larger structure to the prefatory matter, which can be somewhat artifically divided into a number of related sections: (1) computistical texts, (2) charms, medicines, and recipes, (3) prognosticative texts (with overlap in the other sections), and (4) secret writing. A third and more important objection to the comment resides in not taking account of the type of book in which this collection of texts is found, namely (and most obviously) a psalter.

Psalms and prayers, particularly the *Pater Noster* and *Credo*, offered an important link between religious practices and what we might call today popular superstition and 'home remedies.' In British Library, Cotton Tiberius A. iii, fol. 59rv, and Cambridge, Corpus Christi College 391 (the *Portiforium of Saint Wulstan*), pp. 617–8, the Cross is invoked in a charm/prayer against the deliberations of an enemy, requiring the recitation of both prayers and psalms to ensure protection:

> 7 sing þonne þas sealmas oþ ende. D*omi*ne d*eu*s me*us* Usquequo d*omi*ne. Exaudi d*omi*ne iustitia*m* mea*m*. kyriel*eison*. chr*ist*eleison. kyrriel*eison*. pater n*oste*r. P*er* signu*m* s*anct*e crucis de inimicis m*e*is. Lib*era* nos *deus* m*eus*. Adoramus te chr*iste*.

And further:

> And sing þisne sealm oþ ende. Sing hine aþenedum earmum swa þu oftust mæge: Ad te d*omi*ne leuaui. kyrriel*eison*. chr*i*ste*leison*. Pater n*ost*er. 7 cweþ þas preces. hoc signu*m* crucis erit in cęlo cum d*omi*n*us* ad iudicandu*m* uenerit. p*er* signu*m*. Omnis terra. D*omi*ne exaudi oratione*m*.[36]

The psalms to be recited include Pss. 7 (Domine Deus meus), 12 (Usquequo Domine), 16 (Exaudi Domine iustitiam), and 24 (Ad te Domine leuaui). Each of these psalms offers a prayer for help against the hostility of enemies, for justice against foes, and for divine support. As such, they are entirely appropriate petitions within the context of the charm/prayer. Analogously, and within the liturgical sphere, the 'Missal of Robert of Jumièges,' for example, records a 'Missa pro infirmis' (with directions in Old English), throughout which various psalms and psalm-verses are signalled for recitation, including (in order of appearance) the incipit *Circumdederunt me*, which, although occurring twelve times in the psalms, occurs verse-initially in four psalms (17.5, 87.18, 114.3, and 117.12), of which 17.5 (Dolores inferni circumdederunt me, 'the sorrows of hell have surrounded me') and 114.3 (Circumdederunt me dolores mortis, 'the sorrows of death have surrounded me') are appropriate to a mass for the infirm, 17 (Diligam te Domine), 6.3 (Conturbata sunt omnia ossa mea), 50, 55, or 56 (Miserere mei Deus), 6 (Domine ne in furore tuo; *Gallicanum* version), 31 (Beati quorum), 37 (Domine ne in furore tuo .II.), 40 (Beatus qui intelligit), 49 (Deus deorum), 50 (Miserere mei Deus secundum), 85 (Inclina Domine aurem tuam), 90 (Qui habitat), and 102 (Benedic anima mea Domino .I.).[37] Each of the psalms is appropriate to an *ordo* for the visitation of the sick. The opening verses of Ps. 17, for instance, describe (vv. 2–7) the extreme peril of the speaker followed (vv. 8–20) by an exposé of the manner by which the Lord doled out retribution and rescued the speaker (v. 17, Misit de summo et accepit me). Ps. 85 likewise presents the poor and wretched (inops et pauper) speaker as he calls upon the Lord for protection and rescue: 'Custodi animam meam, quoniam sanctus sum: saluum fac seruum tuum.' And while Ps. 90 also sends forth a call for protection, Ps. 102 stands as a hymn in praise and recognition the Lord's mercy; this is, fittingly, the last of the psalms to be recited in the *ordo*, after which begins a sequence of anointings. The *ordo* exhibits a definite structure, within which the psalms play an important role as they punctuate, in effect, the curative process.

The medicine for cattle with lung disease in Vitellius E. xviii, fol. 15v/19–23, operates within this context of the use of psalms to effect cures:

> [Gif] hryþeru beon on lungen coðon |
> [ ]tan hylle. 7 bærn to axan on middan sumeres mæssel[dæ]g [. do]
> þærto hali wæter. 7 geot on heora muð on middan | [sumeres mæ]sse
> mergen. 7 sing þas þry sealmas þær ofer. | [Deus misereatu]r n*ost*ri.
> 7 Exsurgat d*eus* 7 Quicumq*ue* uult.

Although it is not clear, given the partially destroyed text, what precisely is to be burned to ashes, the charm/remedy clearly indicates a type of ritual to be followed, including specified days, holy water, and recitation of psalms.

The psalms here are Pss. 66 (or Ps. 50, 'Miserere mei,' if Cook's reconstruction is correct) and 67, accompanied by the Athanasian Creed. Ps. 66 offers a harvest song of praise for the blessing bestowed by God through the fruitfulness of the earth (v. 7 terra dedit fructum suum, 'the earth gave her fruit'), with the implied petition that such fertility will continue. Ps. 67 takes as its central theme God's victory over his enemies (v. 2 Exsurgat Deus, et dissipentur inimici eius, et fugiant qui oderunt eum, a facie eius, 'Let God arise, and let his enemies be scattered, and let those who hate him flee from his face'), within which v. 16 may explain why the Old English has as its locus a hill: 'Mons Dei, mons pinguis; mons coagulatus, mons pinguis' (Mountain of God, a fertile mountain; a swelling mountain, a fertile mountain). Finally, the *Quicumque vult* begins with a firm statement on the relationship betwen health and faith: 'Quicumque uult saluus esse ante omnia opus est ut teneat catholicam fidem' (Whoever desires to be whole, before all things he must hold the universal faith). If we accept, instead, Cook's reconstruction of the first incipit as that to Ps. 50, the import and underlying theme remains unchanged. Psalm 50, an important penitential psalm, contains verses appropriate to effecting a cure, whether of the soul or cattle with lung disease; for example: v. 9 'Asperges me hyssopo, et mundabor: lauabis me, et super niuem dealabor' (Purify me with hyssop, that I may be clean; wash me that I may be whiter than snow), v. 12 'Cor mundum crea in me Deus: et spiritum rectum innoua in uisceribus meis' (Create a clean heart in me, O God; and a right spirit renew in my breast). Although the psalm verses are construed literally in the context of the charm/remedy, linking the renewal of the right spirit within the breast with ridding disease from the lungs, their invocation in this context accords with practices found broadly within Anglo-Saxon culture, as when in the Old English martyrology for the feast day of St Tiburtius (11 August), we read that if the saint 'song his credan oððe pater*noste*r on untru*m*ne mon, he wæs sona hal.'[38] The prayer that heals the soul also finds ready application in a petition to heal the body or to promote or protect crops, as in the blessings on fols 15v|27–16r|8, the first of which requires that the *Pater noster* (or most likely an abbreviated incipit or the '*Pater noster* letters') be inscribed on a stick.

ST COLUMKILL'S CIRCLE AND THE SPHERA APULEI

This same impetus toward locating a link between the divine power and secular commonplace governs, in a very direct way, the entire miscellany of prefatory texts. St Columkill's circle (fol. 15v) would seem to figure, even if obscurely, within this context. The text preceding the circle gives unambiguous instructions on how to prepare the circle, but offers little by way of explaining the purposes for which it was to be used: 'Writ þysne circul mid þinnes cnifes orde on anum mealan stan 7 sleah ænne stacan on middan þam ymbhagan 7 lete þane stan on uppan þam stacan *þæt* he beo eall under eorðan butan þam gewritenan.' Charles Singer offers an account from Columkill's life written in 1532 by Manus O'Donnell in which Ethne, Columkill's mother, is told by a youth in shining garb of a flagstone in a lake which she is to bring to a certain place and upon which she would give birth.[39] In view of the text concerning bees written within the circle in Vitellius E. xviii, Singer adds that the 'stake was presumably to prevent the stone from sinking and the stone thus laid was used for charming bees' (pp. 361–2). Precisely what connection bees have with the Columkill legend, however, is never specified, and it more than likely that the text in Vitellius E. xviii reflects a corrupted conflation of texts. A rendering of the text and illustration follows (damaged portions indicated):

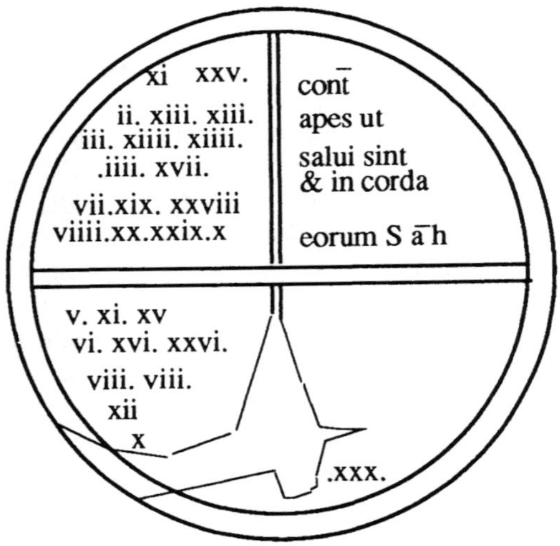

The text preceding the illustration in the manuscript presents a fragment of a charm to guard against the theft of bees: '[ ]e mædder cið on þinre hyfe. þon*ne* ne asponð nan man þine beon. hi ma[n] ne mæg forstelan þa hwile þe se cið on þære hyfe bið.' How precisely St Columkill's charm is connected with the *Sphera Apulei* remains unclear; perhaps there is no real connection whatsoever. The inscription in the circle begins with the words 'con*tra* apes' (no other expansion for the abbreviated first word has been suggested, although it may be a mistranslation of Old English *wiþ*), and the entire inscription, in fact, seems rather to be a rubric to a charm, itself unilluminated by the cryptic *S ā h*. What the directions indicate to be inscribed may refer to the circle itself and not the text. Most likely the exemplar provided the directions and the rubric, but did not contain the illustration, which was then readily supplied using the *Sphera Apulei*. Its presentation as an encoded text, at one level open to booklearned readers (who can read the directions pertaining to the sphere elsewhere in the codex and comprehend its function), and at another moving beyond this level to lore (the Columkill folk-story) and further encoding that makes sense only to those who are familiar with its meaning (S ā h), makes St Columkill's circle a complex (if nonetheless ineffectual) and arcane text, one that discloses its function (a circle to protect bees) at the same moment that it moves into obscurity.

One cannot hope to reconstruct the course of transmisison of this text, how it came to be associated with the sphere of life and death, or how this prognosticative text, in turn, came to be associated with St Columkill, but it is certain that corruption took place until it finally reached its present and obscure form. But for the scribe of Vitellius E. xviii, it may have meant something, perhaps not directly, but at least as bound within the larger context of bees, prognosticative circles, protective charms, and, appropriately, psalms. The logic throughout in the presentation of texts here and elsewhere in this preliminary matter is associative. It is relatively easy to imagine a mind moving from calculations of feasts, to prohibitions on certains days, to the most opportune moments for childbirth, to unlucky days, to charms and medicines, to prognosticative diagrams, and to secret writing, for they are all linked as they blur the boundaries between secular and divine, between what can be observed and potentially manipulated within this world and what pertains to the control of the divine. To sing 'Agios, agios, agios' to one's cattle each evening, or to inscribe a stick with the *Pater noster* may have been no less meaningful in Anglo-Saxon England than is for some today the ritual of marking the forehead with ashes on Ash Wednesday or the crossing of candles over the throat on St Blaise's feastday — or no more meaningful than the formulaic sayings on modern Christmas cards or the uttering of 'God bless you' after a sneeze. To some extent, the form of the ritual is all; what it means or how it works stands as less important to know.

We are on more certain ground with regard to the *Sphera Apulei*, which, apart from St Columkill's Circle, appears two other times in the manuscript at fols 14v and 16r. The Sphere of Life and Death was employed as a prognosticative device to determine the outcome of an illness. A circle, or in some manuscripts a diamond shape, was horizontally bisected into equal halves, the upper half representing Vita, the lower Mors. In each section were written numerals, accompanied by their letter equivalents set in a band along the outer ring of the circle or in one or more separate columns outside the diagram. In some Anglo-Saxon manuscripts, the figures of Vita and

Mors are shown each holding a scroll containing the numerals, thus supplanting the commonplace sphere. In the depiction of the sphere in Cotton Vitellius E. xviii, fol. 16r (Plate 11), the numerical equivalents of the individual's name are added together along with the age of the moon and divided by 30; the resulting number is then located in either the Vita section or the Mors section, thus revealing the outcome. The text follows:

> [De] **uita uel de morte** | Spera apulei platonici de uita uel de morte uel de om*n*ibus negotiis | & quiquid inquirere uolueris. sic computabis per om*n*es litteras. ut puta | de nomine ę gri. Adde luna*m*, quota fuerit die. qua decubuerit & quotiens | potueris diuide per triginta. & quicquid superauerit, reuerteris | ad organiolum infra scriptum. & si superiori conuenerit parti nu|merus, uitalis erit; si autem inferiori conuenerit, mortis prę sagium | est; sic ętiam & de omnib*us* negotiis. Ratio in sanitate hominis.[40]

Among Anglo-Saxon manuscripts (or manuscripts owned in Anglo-Saxon England), versions of the *Sphera Apulei* can be found in British Library, Harley 3667, fol. 4v, an elaborately arranged leaf depicting the sphere accompanied by the figures of Vita and Mors below and numerical equivalents of letters in the left column; British Library, Cotton Tiberius C. i, fol. 7v, which contains two spheres along with text from a tradition different than that from which the explanation in Vitellius E. xviii stems; British Library, Cotton Tiberius C. vi, fol. 6r, which contains the figures of Vita and Mors drawn in a fashion similar to those in another manuscript, Oxford, Bodleian Library, Bodley 579, fol. 50r (the *Leofric Missal*); British Library, Cotton Caligula A. xv, fol. 125v, a carefully executed leaf containing a sphere marked out with Greek words, their transliteration, and Latin translations, clearly related to the Sphere of Apuleius in Oxford, St John's College 17 (*Byrhtferth's Manual*), fol. 8r, and having text similar to that in Vitellius E. xviii.[41]

For what purposes was the sphere used? Singer, in his comments on the *Leofric Missal*, notes that the sphere 'is attached to a venesection text and an apparatus for fixing the date of Church festivals'.[42] The folios immediately before and after that which contains the sphere in Vitellius E. xviii contain a prohibition on blood-letting during the dog-days (fol. 13r) and two texts on unlucky days for blood-letting (fol. 15r). It is thus possible that the sphere was used to very practical ends within the monastic community to determine, after additional lunar calculations had been made, whether or not a particular time was propitious for venesection. There is no evidence that Vitellius E. xviii was used outside the monastic confines, although it is conceivable that the practical knowledge recorded in the codex would have had some currency within local communities or that its administration would have been aided by lay brothers, and most certainly so were the sphere used, as Singer suggests, in determining whether or not to administer extreme unction to the sick (p. 351), a sacrament that, according to Church dogma, can lead to a restoration of bodily health if it be expedient to the salvation of the soul.[43] The intersection of secular knowledge and divine operation here and elsewhere within the prefatory matter at once provides a view of beliefs and practices and, given the relative frequency with which such prognosticative texts, charms, and remedies occur in other manuscripts, a sense, although at best still vague, of how commonplace and thus how embedded these beliefs and practices were within at least the monastic circle and possibly within the lay community as well. In brief, these texts yield information, if obliquely and hesitantly, about a stratum of Anglo-Saxon culture that can easily be overlooked when manuscript context and filiations are ignored.

OCCULTE SCRIBENDI MODUS

Secret or encoded writing, whether through the use of letter substitution, combinations of dots and strokes, or runic letters seems to have been largely confined to riddles, curative formulas, and charms, although names of scribes and accompanying notes are also found encoded. Riddle 36 in the Exeter Book, for example, uses letter substitution in the line 'monn.h.w.m.wiif. m.x.l.kf wf.hors. qxxs…', where (imperfectly) encoded Latin translations follow the Old English words; thus *monn h*[*p*]*m*[*p*] (> *homo*), *wiif mulie*[*r*], and *hors equus*.[44] Cambridge, Trinity College, B.16.3, containing Hrabanus Maurus' *De laudibus sanctae crucis*, records on fol. *1r the following cryptogram, using simple vowel substitution: bstcbpkbt:·: ktfpr:m:·bpfrp:txf (ast capiat uite premia perpetue).[45] At fol. 17v in Vitellius E. xiii opposite the added petitions to the Virgin Mary is written 'St:f·n:·:*s* :d: mxxxxnxcxxxxx*s*' (Stefanus ede monacus). The encoded riddle in Vitellius E. xviii at fol. 16v|1–5 is also found in Oxford, Bodleian Library, Bodley 572 (2026), fol. 40r (a Cornish or Welsh manuscript, later at St Augustine's, Canterbury), along with an encoded version of part of the last line of the text on secret writing found in Vitellius E. xviii, 'cunna nu m[a]ga ðu arædan hwæt þis mage beon ic wene þæt hit nis na eð ræde.'[46] The text on fol. 16v in Vitellius E. xviii is unusual both because of its inclusion in a psalter (no other psalter contains such a text) and because it offers an extended explanation of encoding (Plate 12). A transcription of the text is given below:

> A. E. I. O. U. a^{b} e^{f} i^{k} o^{p} u^{x} — | Đis is quinq*ue* uocales. mid þysum fif stafum man mæg writan swa hwæt | swa he wile. hit is lytel cræft. ac þeah man mæg dwelian manega [m]en | mid. ægðer ge ware. ge unware :— A^{B} ^{F}E I^{K} O^{P} U^{X} — | [P]mnkum knkmkcprxm sxprxm dpmknbbktxr.

> | B 7 : thf·g: d::m::·s m·x :-ll:- :·nt:rpr:t·t::r :— | Q≡ııı- in =ı r≡=mıııı n-b-nt s·c=rd≡t=s m≡stııır≡ı l=gıııs — | Item de litteris notarium *id est* .v. uocales. a e i o u. reliquuntur pro una|quaq*ue* ab equetori littera. ut unaquaq*ue* alfabeti littera uocalem | consonante sequente in loco uocalis deducitur & sic scribitur notarium | & ita probatur. kn npmknf dk̄ sxmmk. BMFN :— | [P]btfr npstfr qxk fs kn cflks sbnctkfkcftxr npmfn txxm bdxfnkbd | rfgnxm txxm. Fkbd xplxntbs txb skcxt kn cflp st kn tfrrb. fbnfm | npstrxm cptkdkbnxm db npbks hpdkf. Et dkmkttf npbks dfbktb | Omnfs gfntfs plbxdktf mbnkbxs. Aliter unus apex 7 npstrb :— | pro una .A. sic scribitur. Et due. pro .E. Et tres. pro .I. Et quatuor. | pro .O. Et .E. pro .U. Ita probatur. :·n n::m:-n: d̄:· s:·:mm:- Et pro una | A .x. Et due .xx. pro .E. Et tres .xxx. pro .I. Et reliq*ua*. Ita probatur | xxxn nxxxxmxxxnxx dx̄ xx sxxxxxmmxxx ·:— | [C]xnnb mbgf þx brædbn. hwæt þks mbgf bfpn. kc wfnf þæt hkt nks fðrædf | Ælxxnfıı≡ fxxm-rt· dııræ cð·=ðxıınxxn :—[47]

The encoded passages read: (1) Omnium inimicorum suorum dominabitur; (2) Betheage domus max illi interpretatur; (3) Quia in ea ruminabant sacerdotes misteria legis; (4) Pater noster qui es in celis sanctificetur nomen tuum aduenied [> aduenist] regnum tuum. Fiad [> fiat] uoluntas tuas sicut in celis st [> et] in terra. eanem [> panem] nostrum cotidianum da nobis hodie. Et dimitte nobis debita. Omnes gentes plaudite manibus; (5) in nomine d‹e›i summi; (6) in nomine d‹e›i summi; (7) Cunna mage þu arædan. hwæt þis mage beon. ic wene þæt hit nis eð ræde.... The remainder of this final encoded line merits extended discussion.

Two references to the psalms are included in the text on encoded writing. The first reference is drawn from Ps. 9.26(5): [P]mnkum knkmkcprxm sxprxm dpmknbktxr (= Omnium inimicorum suorum dominabitur). The second comes at the end of a partial text of the *Pater noster* and is drawn from Ps. 46.2: Omnfs gfntfs plbxdktf mbnkbxs (= Omnes gentes plaudite manibus). While instructive in how to encode, the text also playfully challenges the reader, and the second excerpt from the psalms might be construed as applauding the reader for having succeeded this far in deciphering the text. But the passage continues, once again explaining the rules of vowel substitution, and providing still more lines to decode, first :·n n::m:-n: d̄:· s:·:mm: (= in nomine dei summe), then followed by the same line encoded differently: xxxn nxxxxmxxxnxx dx̄xx sxxxxxmmxxx. At this point, the reader, having repeatedly been instructed and having successfully decoded the lines at every turn, would confidently continue to the next encoded line, this time written in Old English: [C]xnnb mbgf þx brædbn. hwæt þks mbgf bfpn. kc wfnf þæt hkt nks fð rædf (= Cunna mage þu arædan hwæt þis mage beon; ic wene þæt hit nis eð ræde). But mounting confidence is quickly scotched with the final line: Ælxxnfıı≡ fxxm-rt· dııræ cð·=ðxıınxxn. An Anglo-Saxon reader may well have voiced resignation much as Humfrey Wanley did in his 1705 catalogue: 'Qui hanc lineam explicare poterit, mihi Oedipus erit.'[48] The encoded line, however, does have a solution, and one that has important ramifications since it reveals the name of the author (or, perhaps better, compiler) of the *Vitellius Psalter*.

ÆLFWINE AND THE VITELLIUS PSALTER

The encoded final line reads Ælxxnfıı≡ fxxm-rt· dııræ cð·=ðxıınxxn (omitting the end punctuation :—) and can be transliterated as follows: Æluunfei emuuart· deræ cðeðuenen. Rearrangement of the letters in this cryptogram reveals the solution to the puzzle: Ælfuuine me uurat. ræde ðu ðe cenne (Ælfwine wrote me. Read you who might be able).[49] British Library, Cotton Titus D. xxvii, fol. 13v, records a ciphered note containing the name of the scribe Ælsinus (Ælsige): 'Frbtfr hxmkllimus ft mpnbchxs ſlsknxs mf scrkpskt skt kllk lpngb sblxs. Bm··n ſlfƿkno mpnbchp aeqxf dfcbnp cpmpptxm kstxm ppsskdtp .ł mf ppsskdft. Bmfn', which uses a combination of letters and dots for vowels, thus 'Frater humillimus et monachus ælsinus me scripsit sit illi longa salus. Amen. ælfwino monacho aeqeo decano compotum istum possideo ł me possidet. Amen.'[50] Ælsinus has been identified as the main scribe of the *Liber vitae* of New Minster (London, British Library, Stowe 944) and the second part of Cambridge, Trinity College, R. 15. 32 containing a calendar and computus. Ælfwine became abbot of New Minster in 1031 or 1032.

As Ker notes, the calendar of Vitellius E. xviii is like those in other New Minster manuscripts, although he remarks that the added twelfth-century litanies 'suggest the cathedral priory rather than New Minster.'[51] The view agrees with that of Francis Wormald, who states that 'early in its history it crossed the road to the Cathedral (Old Minster).'[52] Wormald dates the calendar (and hence the psalter) to *c.* 1060, which the psalter's editor, James L. Rosier, accepted. Ker dates the manuscript to 's. xi med.' (i.e., 1040–1160). Wildhagen provides a *terminus a quo* of 1012 and a *terminus ad quem* of 1080. In an appendix, he also quotes the assessment of J.P. Gilson, who notes that a cross in the tables 'appears to indicate the date of [the calendar's] composition as between the years 1060 and 1087; the cross standing at the top of the column which contains the solar cycle.'[53] As Wildhagen was relying on photographs, however, he could not confirm whether the cross was written in the original hand or added later. Kenneth Sisam, noting that the *Vitellius*, *Arundel* and *Tiberius* psalters form a close group, assigns it to the period 1050–1075.[54] While there appears to be general consensus about a mid-eleventh-century date for the psalter, it is a dating that would seem to be based on inherited claims and little evidence. The dating of the manuscript to the mid-eleventh century, however, might be questioned. T.A.M. Bishop remarks that the hand of fols 20r–68r (Scribe B) of Titus D. xxvi 'closely resembles that of the calendar' in Vitellius E. xviii.[55] Ker, in addition, notes the resemblance of the hand of Scribe B to that of London, British Library, Additional 34890.[56] In her edition of 'Ælfwine's Prayerbook,' Günzel reiterates their findings and provides detailed tables showing the distribution of hands in Titus D. xxvii and xxvi.[57]

Two questions emerge with regard to the *Vitellius Psalter*: Why would the name 'Ælfwine' be written in the psalter giving his status as scribe, and, given the later date assigned to the psalter, why would the prefatory matter include Easter tables beginning in the year 1031?[58] To these questions can be added the matter of the similarity of the hands in the psalter and Titus D. xxvii and xxvi. A hypothetical interpretation of the evidence might suggest that the psalter was written in *c*. 1031, about the time of Ælfwine's appointment as abbot. But could Ælfwine also have been the scribe of the prefatory matter of the psalter? The encoded final line would seem to suggest as much, and to do so rather directly: 'Ælfwine wrote me.' The possibility that Ælfwine was a trained scribe should not be dismissed out of hand. In *Medieval Illuminators and Their Methods of Work*, J.J.G. Alexander notes that St Dunstan was described by his biographer 'as skilled in "making a picture and forming letters".' Both Osmund, Bishop of Salisbury from 1078–1099, and Mannius, Abbot of Evesham from 1044–1066, to note but two of Alexander's examples, are described as skilled in writing and illumination.[59] Might Ælfwine have possessed such skills as well? If Titus D. xxvi and xxvii were written in 1029, as Günzel maintains, or between 1023 and 1031, as Simon Keynes argues,[60] and if Vitellius E. xviii was written in *c*. 1031 or shortly thereafter, it would not be difficult to explain any slight variations in the script of both manuscripts. The implications, of course, are that Ælfwine (Scribe B), prior to his becoming abbot, also participated in the writing of Titus D. xxvii and xxvi.

The contents of the manuscripts in question may provide supporting evidence of their close affiliation through Ælfwine. The text on concurrents and epacts in Vitellius E. xviii, fol. 13r|16–21, finds its exact parallel in Titus D. xxvii, fol. 55r; that on determining feast limits on fol. 13r|22–27 appears in Titus D. xxvii at fol. 54v. The text in Titus D. xxvii shows a potentially significant error, reading 'On martius ofer .xii. kal. find…' where 'aprilis' should follow '.xii. kal.' The text in Vitellius E. xviii also shows this omission, but given that the section in which 'aprilis' would occur is destroyed in the manuscript (outer edge), no determination can be made as to whether or not the manuscript showed a similar omission. The Old English text on lucky days for childbirth, fol. 15v|1–5 finds its Latin parallel in Titus D. xxvi, fol. 4rv:

Vitellius E. xviii: [Þ]ry dagas syndon on twelf monðum mid þrim ni[ht]um o[n þam ne bið] nan wif accened ac swa hwilc wæpman swa on ðam dagum ace[ned bið ne] forealdað his lichama næfre on eorðan ær domes dæge, þ*æt* is an [ðæra] daga on æfteweardan decembre 7 tweigen on foreweardan ia[nuarii]; feawma manna syndon þe þas dagas cunnon.	Titus D. xxvii: Tres dies sunt in anno cum totidem noctibus, ut fertur, in quibus mulier numquam nascitur, et uir qui natus fuerit in ipsis numquam corpus illus putredine soluetur usque ad diem iudicii, id est nouissimus de thebet et duo primi de sabath.[61]

Another Old English text in Vitellius E. xviii, fol. 15r|6–15, on critical Mondays during which bloodletting and the eating of fowl, for example, should be avoided, finds its parallel in a Latin version in Titus D. xxvi, fols 3v–4r, although the Old English text is more generous in allowing 40 days during which death will occur, while the Latin text offers 15. The text ultimately derives from pseudo-Bede, *De minutione sanguinis, siue de phlebotomia* (PL 90: cols 960–1):

Vitellius E. xviii: Find eft þry dagas on twelf monðum þa syndon swiðe unhalwende [mon]|num oððe nytenum blod to forlætenne oððe drenc to drincanne þ*æt* is se | æftemesta monandæig on aprilis. ær he gange of tune 7 se forma monan|dæg on agustus monðe 7 se æftemesta monandæg on decembres monðe | ær he gange of tune | se þe on þam monandagum mann*um* oððe | nytenan blod forlæteð. ær feowerteoðan dæge he sceal swyltan. oððe | he ne gebideð þæs seofeðan dæges. 7 gif he drenc drincð to læcecræfte | ær fiftyne dagan he sceal swyltan. 7 gif hwilc man ac[enned biþ on] | þysum þrim dagum. he sceal swyltan yfelan deaðe 7 se	Titus D. xxvi: Dies enim aegyptiaci, in quibus nulliusmodi nex per ulla necessitate non licet hominem nec pecus sanguinem minuere. Isti trest dies per omnia cauende sunt. Id est .viii. kal. aprilis, illo die lunis, intrante agusto, illa dies lune similiter, exeunte decembrio, illa dies lune. Cum multa diligentia obseruande sunt, quia omnia uena plena sunt. Qui istis tribus diebus hominem inciderit aut pecus, statim aut die tertio moriturus erit, aut vii.man diem non pertingit. Et si potionem acceperit, ante .xv. dies moritur, et si masculus aut femina his diebus nati fuerint, mala morte morientur, et si de auca in ipsis diebus manducauerit, ante .xv. dies moritur.[62]

> ðe et[eð] [gose]|flæsc on þysum
> þrim dag*um* he sceal swyltan ær
> feowertug*um* dag[um].

The text on the calculation of Advent in Vitellius E. xviii, fol. 8r, has its parallel in Titus D. xxvii, fol. 25r, although the text stands as a commonplace in Anglo-Saxon manuscripts. Much the same can be said of the text on the calculation of Septuagesima, Quadragesima, Easter, and Rogation in Vitellius E. xviii, fol. 8r, which is roughly paralleled by the text in Titus D. xxvii, fol. 13r. Even more commonplace are the verses on Easter in Vitellius E. xviii, fol. 8r, and Titus D. xxvii, fol. 11r. Those on the limits of Quadragesima are wanting in Vitellius, although their absence can be attributed to a lost leaf preceding fol. 8. General correspondences can be seen in the lists of unlucky days (Vitellius E. xviii, fol. 9r|17–26 and Titus D. xxvi, fol. 5r). The manuscripts also contain multiple texts on bloodletting (e.g., Vitellius E. xviii, fols 15r|6–15, 15r|16–15v|5, 13r|28–32; Titus D. xxvii, fol. 22rv, Titus D. xxvi, fols 3v–4r, 6rv). Also among the more general correspondences, Titus D. xxvi, fol. 79v, contains a Latin charm for discovering theft followed by a series of magical (and meaningless) letters; that in Vitellius E. xviii, fol. 15v|13–18, although different from that in Titus D. xxvi, nevertheless adds to the sense of a general relationship that obtains between these manuscripts, as does the inclusion of a medical recipe to cure boils at fol. 17r.

If an argument can be sustained in favour of Ælfwine, abbot of the New Minster, as the scribe of the prefatory matter and the Old English gloss of Vitellius E. xviii, and if he is indeed 'Scribe B' of Titus D. xxvii and xxvi, working in close collaboration with his scribe Ælsinus, we receive intimations of a rudimentary portrait of the controlling mind behind these works, one for whom prayer and religious devotion moved in tandem with an understanding of computistical texts and for whom the preservation and transmission of that knowledge formed important concerns, especially as a reflection of his position within the monastic community.

Yet, such a tidy conclusion, attractive as it indeed appears, must ultimately be rejected, for it is undermined by evidence found in the paschal table on fol. 13v. The table is similar to those found, for example, in Oxford, Bodleian Library, Douce 296, fol. 8r, and Bodley 572, fol. 40v, and, as E.W.B. Nicholson has determined, was calculated for the years 836–1367. In discussing Bodley 572, Nicholson called attention to a diagonal stroke in the box containing the letter *e* for the year 981. He writes: 'Now my experience is that the writer of every such key put some little mark — *e.g.*, a dot, a stroke, a tag to a letter (once even the word *hic*) — to show the point which coincided with the date at which he was copying it.'[63] The cross at the head of the ninth column of letters in the table in Vitellius E. xviii, as Gilson (see above) noted, would seem to confirm a date of composition between 1060 and 1087, provided that the cross was written by the original scribe, which appears to be the case: the cross, as a result of the Ashburnham House fire of 1731, has now a slightly violet tint, which can be seen as well in the headings on the opposite folio. Furthermore, although the cross does not mark a letter, as in Bodley 572 or in British Library, Arundel 60, fol. 10v, where in the first column the letter *h* is followed by a distinct cross also appearing throughout the calendar, in the third row directly below the cross in Vitellius E. xviii above the letter *h* written in black ink stands a small dot, also in black ink. The dot appears to be original, and would thus mark the date of the psalter as 1062. The similarities of the hand responsible for the calendar in Vitellius E. xviii are not exact enough to suggest that they are to be identified as that of Scribe B of Titus D. xxvii and xxvi; any such similarities might better be explained as a type of 'house style' of the scriptorium. That we are dealing here not with an original composition by Ælfwine but with a transmitted text in Vitellius E. xviii is further evidenced by the simple copying errors in the encoded text: in the partial *Pater noster*, *adueniat* is rendered as *inueniad*, *fiat* as *fiad*, *et* as *st* and *panem* as *eanem*.

CONCLUSION

The general arrangement of the texts comprising the prefatory matter leads a reader through a process of gradually narrowing and linked horizons, from a calendar and calculations of feasts and cycles, to the application of those calculations in concrete terms (childirth, bloodletting), to medicines and charms, and concluding with the text on secret writing. The perspective of the reader progressively becomes more localised, more circumscribed as abstract concepts such as embolismalic days give way to the perhaps more mundane sphere inhabited by bees, cattle, and crops. In broad perspective, the texts begin by elucidating mysteries and end by instructing how to encode secrets. There is practical knowledge here that is at once bound to the divine, a rustic superstition enriched and made potent through the efficacy of God's power. Punctuating the texts are incipits and extracts from the psalms, drawing one to consider the connection between the commonplace and the divine. A reader coming to the end of the prefatory matter — perhaps unsuccessfully grappling with the encoded final line — and turning the (originally) blank fol. 17rv surely must have felt the impact of the ornate, visually complex initial *B* of the *Beatus uir* page with its interlined text that, very literally, translates the divine Word. The closed language of the encoded text yields to the more accessible language of psalms, the first translating the commonplace into the mysterious and obscure, the second translating the scriptural word for ready consumption by a booklearned audience.

The particular blend of texts as preliminary matter to a psalter displays a certain focus and an overarching sense of organisation. The temptation may certainly be to dismiss the collection as arbitrary, misleading one to search for unity where none exists. But one is thus faced with explaining why such attention is accorded this collection of texts that comprises at least two quires of the mauscript and that stands prominently at the beginning of a psalter.[64] Assessed in terms of other manuscripts produced at Winchester, such as London, British Library, Cotton Titus D. xxvii + xxvi, the compilaton may not appear particularly unusual. The manuscript contains a calendar, computistical texts and tables, prognostic, Ælfric's *De temporibus anni*, prayers, offices, a collectar, a litany, and various other texts. It does not contain, by contrast, such texts as the *Sphera Apulei*, charms, or medicines; and while it contains some encoded text, this does not compare with the extended explanation of secret writing in the psalter. The texts of 'Ælfwine's Prayerbook' situate themselves in ways different from those in the *Vitellius Psalter*, finding a core more linked to *computistica* and natural phenomena (through the inclusion of Ælfric's text) than the more associative collection in the psalter. Like 'Ælfwine's Prayerbook', however, the collection of texts in the *Vitellius Psalter* speaks in some way — perhaps in an unmeasurable and still obscure way — to the broader literate culture that produced these and other texts.

That the psalter is to be dated 1060 X 1062 seems certain. While the appearance of Ælfwine's name does not bear on the psalter's date of composition, it does, along with the similarities among a number of the texts in Vitellius E. xviii and Titus D. xxviii and xxvi, associate the psalter with Ælfwine's abbacy, the texts in Vitellius E. xviii, of course, having been culled from one or more exemplars. The identification of Ælfwine's connection to Vitellius E. xviii thus gives the psalter a local habitation and a name. The text as it has been transmitted, then, may well in effect reflect two periods in the history of its composition separated by an interval of at the most *c*. 30 years (the commencement of Ælfwine's abbacy) and at the least three to five years (his death is recorded in Titus D. xxvii as 24 November 1057).[65] Perhaps in some direct ways, then, Ælfwine had a hand in selecting the texts that, through transmission, came to be included in this codex.

While the precise circumstances of composition and path of transmission of the texts in Vitellus E. xviii may never fully be recovered, what remains clear, above all, from study of the prefatory matter of the psalter is that such texts, particularly as they stand within their manuscript contexts, merit close study and may lead to a clearer understanding not only of their more immediate connections (here with Ælfwine), but also of how these manuscripts were regarded and understood and how ultimately mistaken it is to disembody texts from the larger framework of the codices that contain them and the communities that produced them.

NOTES

1. *Psalters glossed in Old English*: (A) London, British Library, Cotton Vespasian A. 1 ('Vespasian Psalter'); (B) Oxford, Bodleian Library, Junius 27 (5139) ('Junius Psalter'); (C) Cambridge, University Library, Ff. 1. 23 ('Cambridge Psalter'); (D) London, British Library, Royal 2. B. v ('Regius Psalter'); (E) Cambridge, Trinity College, R. 17. 1 (987) ('Eadwine Psalter'); (F) London, British Library, Stowe 2 ('Stowe Psalter'); (G) London, British Library, Cotton Vitellius E. xviii ('Vitellius Psalter'); (H) London, British Library, Cotton Tiberius C. vi ('Tiberius Psalter'); (I) London, Lambeth Palace 427 ('Lambeth Psalter'); (J) London, British Library, Arundel 60 ('Arundel Psalter'); (K) Salisbury, Cathedral Library, 150 ('Salisbury Psalter'); (L) London, British Library, Additional 37518 ('Bosworth Psalter'); (M) New York, Pierpont Morgan Library, M. 776 ('Blickling Psalter'); (O) Paris, Bibliothèque Nationale, lat. 8846 (called the 'Paris Psalter' by art historians). *Unglossed Psalters*: (β) Berlin, Deutsche Staatsbibliothek, Hamilton 553 ('Salaberga Psalter'); (λ) London, British Library, Arundel 155 ('Eadui Psalter'); (ν) London, British Library, Harley 603 ('Harley Psalter'); (ξ) London, British Library, Harley 863; (o) London, British Library, Harley 2904 ('Ramsey Psalter'); (ρ) Oxford, Bodleian Library, Douce 296 ('Crowland Psalter'); (σ) Oxford, Bodleian Library, Laud lat. 81 (768); (P) Paris, Bibliothèque Nationale, lat. 8824 (called the 'Paris Psalter' by Anglo-Saxonists); (υ) Rome, Vatican City, Biblioteca Apostolicam Reg. lat. 12 ('Bury Psalter'); (φ) Rouen, Bibliothèque Municipale, 231 (A. 44). Arabic sigla are those standardly used in the field, with the exception of O, which is introduced here; Greek sigla are those assigned in my collective edition of the psalters (in progress).
2. (δ) Cambridge, Corpus Christi College 272 ('Achadeus Psalter'); (ζ) Cambridge, Corpus Christi College 411; (θ) Cambridge, St John's College, 59 (C9) ('Southampton Psalter'); (μ) London, British Library, Cotton Galba A. xviiii ('Athelstan Psalter'); (χ) Salisbury, Cathedral Library, 180; (ψ) Utrecht, Universiteitsbibliotheek, 32 (Script. eccl. 484) ('Utrecht Psalter').
3. One might well assume that this was the situation also with the psalters that are extant as fragments: (α) Basel, Universitätsbibliothek N. I. 2; (γ) Cambridge, University Library, Ff. 5. 27, f. i; (η) Cambridge, Magdalene College, Pepys 2981 (N^1) Cambridge, Pembroke College, 312, C. nos 1 and 2 + (N^2) Haarlem, Statsbibliotheek, 168 V 4; (κ) Durham, Cathedral Muniments, Misc. Charter 5670; (ω) Worcester, Cathedral Library, F. 173, fol. 1*.
4. The psalters containing canticles are ACDEFGIJKLP δζλμνορσυφχψ in addition to Cambridge, Corpus Christ College 391. Typically, the psalters

were accompanied by 15 canticles (as in CEGIJK δζμνορυφχψ in addition to Cambridge, Corpus Christ College, MS 391); λ includes all of the canticles, but removes three of them to a section after a series of prayers; A includes nine canticles in the original hand, with another two canticles added in an eleventh-century hand; L contains 12 canticles; F breaks off incompletely in the thirteenth canticle, and likely contained all 15 originally; σ and P each contain 12 canticles. All manuscripts containing the canticles have the same order for the first six, after which the order varies, particularly in the placement of the eighth to tenth canticle.

5. Psalm 151 is found in AEGKL ζμνουχ, Cambridge, Corpus Christi College 391 and London, British Library, Royal 1. E. viii.

6. See N.R. Ker, *Catalogue of Manuscripts Containing Anglo-Saxon* (Oxford: Clarendon Press, 1957), p. 301; James L. Rosier, ed., *The Vitellius Psalter, Edited from British Museum MS Cotton Vitellius E. xviii*, Cornell Studies in English, 42 (Ithaca: Cornell University Press, 1962), p. xviii. Rosier claims that the Latin text of the psalms and the Old English gloss are in the same hand; Ker, however, states that, although the hands are contemporary, they are 'probably not the same.'

7. On the importance of manuscript context, see Fred C. Robinson, 'Old English Literature in Its Most Immediate Context', *Old English Literature in Context: Ten Essays*, ed. John D. Niles (Woodbridge: D.S. Brewer; Totowa, New Jersey: Rowman and Littlefield, 1980), pp. 11–29; see, more recently, Fred C. Robinson, '"The Rewards of Piety": Two Old English Poems in Their Manuscript Context', *Hermeneutics and Medieval Culture*, ed. Patrick J. Gallacher and Helen Damico (New York: State University of New York Press, 1989), pp. 193–200; Graham D. Caie, 'Text and Context in Editing Old English: The Case of the Poetry in Cambridge, Corpus Christi College 201', *The Editing of Old English: Papers from the 1990 Manchester Conference*, ed. D.G. Scragg and Paul E. Szarmach (Woodbridge: D.S. Brewer, 1994), pp. 155–62; and Sarah Larratt Keefer, 'Respecting the Book: Editing Old English Liturgical Poems in Their Manuscripts', *Florilegium* 11 (1992), 32–52.

8. Old English texts that have been collated but not printed are given in full. Manuscript capitalisation and punctuation are retained. Line endings are indicated by a horizontal bar. The arrangement of the prefatory leaves has changed variously since the time of the restoration of the manuscript under Frederic Madden's supervision in 1842. The record of this early foliation is the subject of a study being prepared in conjunction with Andrew Prescott. At the front of the manuscript as presently bound stand two modern paper leaves, the first of which details the changes in the arrangement when the manuscript was rebound in 1954. According to the note, fols 8–17 'were rearranged partly as proposed by Henricj Henel' in his *Studien zum altenglischen Computus*, Beiträge zur Englischen

Philologie (Leipzig: Bernhard Tauchnitz, 1934; repr. New York: Johnson Reprint, 1967), pp. 26–8, n. 78, and 'on the basis of information given by N.R. Ker, Esq.' The old foliation is then given as follows: fols 1–7, 8, 9v, 9r, 10–12, 15, 14, 13, 16, 17v, 17r; the new foliation is set out as fols 1–7, several leaves lost, 8, one leaf lost, 9r, 9v, 10–12, 13, 14, 15, 16, 17r, 17v. For a description and microfiche reproduction of the manuscript see Phillip Pulsiano, *Psalters I*, Anglo-Saxon Manuscripts in Microfiche Facsimile, 2; Medieval and Renaissance Texts and Studies, 158 (Binghamton: Medieval and Renaissance Texts and Studies, 1994).

9. Edited by R.T. Hampson, *Medii Ævi Kalendarium, or Dates, Charters, and Customs of the Middle Ages; with Kalendars from the Tenth to the Fifteenth Century; and an Alphabetical Digest of Obsolete Names of Days; Forming a Glossary of the Dates of the Middle Ages; with Tables and Other Aids for Ascertaining Dates*, 2 vols (London: Henry Kent Causton, 1841), vol. 1, pp. 422–33; Karl Wildhagen, 'Das Kalendarium der Handschrift Vitellius E XVIII', *Texte und Forschungen zur englischen Kulturgeschichte: Festgabe für Felix Liebermann zum 20. Juli 1921*, ed. Heinrich Boehmer et al. (Halle: Niemeyer, 1921), pp. 68–118; Francis Wormald, ed., *English Kalenders before A.D. 1100*, Henry Bradshaw Society, 72 (London: Henry Bradshaw Society, 1934; repr. Woodbridge: The Boydell Press, 1988), pp. 156–67. See also J.B.L. Tolhurst, 'An Examination of Two Anglo-Saxon Manuscripts of the Winchester School: the Missal of Robert of Jumièges, and the Benedictional of St. Æthelwold', *Archaeologia* 83 (1933), pp. 27–44; N.J. Morgan, 'Notes on the Post-Conquest Calendar, Litany and Martyrology of the Cathedral Priory of Winchester with a Consideration of the Winchester Diocese Calendars of the Pre-Sarum Period', in Alan Borg and Andrew Martindale, eds., *The Vanishing Past: Studies of Medieval Art, Liturgy and Metrology presented to Christopher Hohler*, B.A.R. International Series, 111 (Oxford: B. A. R., 1981), pp. 133–71.

10. For additional parallels, see Beate Günzel, ed., *Ælfwine's Prayerbook (London, British Library, Cotton Titus D. xxvi + xxvii)*, Henry Bradshaw Society, 108 (London: Henry Bradshaw Society, 1993), p. 198, nos. 7 and 8.

11. For additional parallels, see Günzel, ed., *Ælfwine's Prayerbook*, p. 200, no. 31; Günzel omits the text in Tiberius C. vi.

12. For additional parallels, see Günzel, ed., *Ælfwine's Prayerbook*, p. 199, no. 11. Günzel errs in citing a parallel text from Salisbury 150, fol. 9v, and also in omitting the text in Tiberius C. vi. See also Henel, *Studien zum altenglischen Computus*, pp. 24–5.

13. See F.K. Ginzel, *Handbuch der mathematischen und technischen Chronologie*, 3 vols (Leipzig: J.C. Hinrichs, 1906–14), vol. 3, pp. 228, 247–51, and Günzel, ed., *Ælfwine's Prayerbook*, pp. 24–5.

14. Transcribed by Francis Tate in London, British Library, Cotton Julius C. ii, fol. 68v; edited by Henel, *Studien zum altenglischen Computus*, p. 44, with the version in Caligula A. xv and Latin parallel in Tiberius C. i.
15. Transcribed by Francis Tate in London, British Library, Cotton Julius C. ii, fol. 68v; edited by Henel, *Studien zum altenglischen Computus*, pp. 55–6, with the version in Corpus Christi College 422.
16. Edited by Max Förster, 'Die altenglischen Verseichnisse von Glücks- und Unglückstagen', *Studies in English Philology: A Miscellany in Honor of Frederick Klaeber*, ed. Kamp Malone and Martin B. Ruud (Minneapolis: The University of Minnesota Press, 1929), pp. 258–77, at pp. 261–4. The text in Caligula A. xv was edited by Rev. Thomas Oswald Cockayne, *Leechdoms, Wortcunning and Starcraft of Early England, Being a Collection of Documents, for the Most Part Never before Printed, Illustrating the History of Science in this Country before the Norman Conquest*, 3 vols, Rolls Series, 35 (London: Her Majesty's Stationery Office, 1864–66; repr. London: The Holland Press, Ltd, 1961; repr. Wiesbaden: Kraus Reprint, Ltd, 1965), vol. 3, p. 168 (with translation, p. 169; the Old English text is recorded as appearing on fol. 126r). At the bottom of fol. 9r in Vitellius E. xviii are added two late items: (1) a charm, written in a 12th/13th-century hand, bearing the incipit 'p*ro* febre'; (2) a listing of religious houses in confraternity (13th/14th century), the latter noted by Walter de Gray Birch, *Liber Vitae: Register and Martyrology of New Minster and Hyde Abbey Winchester* (London: Warren & Son, 1892), p. 49n: 'The Cotton MS. Vitellius E. xviii, belonged to a religious house which may be now identified with St. Swithin's, Winchester, by the sequence of places being preserved in it exactly as in the Winchester Cartulary...which was leagued by conventions with Peterborough, Worcester, Gloucester, Reading, Tewksbury, Chertsy, Burton, Ely, Abingdon, Glastonbury, Lewes, St. Albans, Durham, Merton, Malmesbury, Bury, Westminster, Wherwell, Romsey, Bec, and Battle'; also printed in 'On Two Anglo-Saxon Manuscripts in the British Museum', *Transactions of the Royal Society of Literature of the United Kingdom*, 2nd ed., ser. 11 (1878), p. 491 (repr. Nedeln and Liechtenstein: Kraus Reprint, 1970). The listings are contained in the cartulary in London, British Library, Additional 29436, fols 44v and 45r. I am grateful to Simon Keynes for this last reference.
17. See Ginzel, *Handbuch*, vol. 3, pp. 228, 247–51; Günzel, ed., *Ælfwine's Prayerbook*, pp. 24–5, for parallels, pp. 199–200, no. 16.
18. Cf. PL 90: 822 *Manfredi embolismorum ratio.*
19. Henel (*Studien zum altenglischen Computus*) prints the text from Titus D. xxvii, collated with those in Caligula A. xv and Vitellius E. xviii. Henzel's 'Type 1' text, which shows variations after the formula for calculating from a Monday, is found in Harley 3271, fol. 92r, and Corpus

Christi College 422, p. 47, both of which are printed by Henel (p. 49). See Günzel, ed., *Ælfwine's Prayerbook*, p. 200, no. 39; Günzel conflates the two types of texts in her note on the parallels and cites the text on epacts in Corpus Christi College 422, p. 28, but not the text on concurrents on p. 47.

20. Henel (*Studien zum altenglischen Computus*, pp. 40–3) prints the text from Harley 3271, with variants recorded from the other manuscripts. This text is labelled 'Type 1' by Henel. A variant version is found in Corpus Christi College 422, p. 46, and is printed by Henel, pp. 42–3. Under 'Type 2,' Henel presents the text found in Vitellius E. xviii, fol. 9v ([Gif þ]u wille witan hu eald se mona beo nu todæg on twelf monþ*um*). In noting parallels to Titus D. xxvii, fol. 54v, Günzel (*Ælfwine's Prayerbook*, p. 200, no. 38) conflates manuscript references to both types in the notes, even though the version in Titus is of 'Type 1'. Günzel also refers to Henel's having printed all of the texts, where collated is more accurate for all except the base text for 'Type 1'.

21. Edited by Heinrich Henel, 'Altenglischer Mönchsaberglaude', *Englische Studien* 69 (1934–35), 329–49, at p. 331. Latin parallels are found in Titus D. xxvi, fol. 4v, and Harley 3271, fols 123v–124r.

22. Edited by Henel, 'Altenglischer Mönchsaberglaube', pp. 346–7, with variants from the two other Old English versions. Förster ('Die altenglischen Verseichnisse von Glücks- und Unglückstagen', pp. 259–61) edits the versions in Caligula A. xv and Corpus Christi College 391. Förster (p. 261) prints Latin parallels from Titus D. xxvi, fol. 4v, and Royal 12 C. xii, fol. 87r, both of which have their source in pseudo-Bede, *De natiuitate infantium* (PL 90: 960), as well as a Middle English version from Oxford, Bodleian Library, Ashmole 1438, fol. 50r (p. 261, n. 1). Förster does not note the text in Vitellius E. xviii.

23. Edited by Förster, 'Die altenglischen Verseichnisse von Glücks- und Unglückstagen', pp. 273–4. As more can be read in the manuscript than Förster records, the text here is presented in full. A different tradition of texts on the *Dies Agyptiaci* is represented by Harley 585, fol. 190rv, and Vitellius C. iii, fol. 20rv; these are printed by Förster, pp. 271–3.

24. Edited by Förster, 'Die altenglischen Verseichnisse von Glücks- und Unglückstagen', pp. 265–70, in parallel with the version in Caligula A. xv. In the final line of his transcription, Förster emends the reading 'halgan gast' in Vitellius to 'halgan wisdom' following the version in Caligula A. xv (also the reading in Harley 3271). Henel, 'Altenglischer Mönchsaberglaube', pp. 336–8, edits the version in Harley 3271, with variants from Caligula A. xv and Vitellius E. xviii. Cockayne, *Leechdoms, Wortcunning and Starcraft*, vol. 3, pp. 152–5 prints the text in Harley 3271 with a facing-page translation. The text in Harley 3271 is arranged differently than in the two other versions, with Förster's sections III–V

coming before sections I–II. Latin parallels are found in Titus D. xvii, fols 22r–23r, and Harley 3271, fols 120v–121r and 122rv (printed by Henel, 'Altenglischer Mönchsaberglaude', pp. 339–41; see Günzel, *Ælfwine's Prayerbook*, p. 31 and no. 18 [text]); the text has its source in pseudo-Bede, *De minutione sanguinis siue de phlebotomia* (PL 90: 960).

25. Edited, with translation, by Cockayne, *Leechdoms, Wortcunning and Starcraft*, vol. 1, p. 397.

26. Edited, with translation, by Cockayne, *Leechdoms, Wortcunning and Starcraft*, vol. 1, p. 395, with accompanying diagram; Max Förster, 'Beiträge zur mittelalterlichen Volkskunde. VIII', *Archiv fur das Studium der neuren Sprachen und Litteraturen* 129 (1912), 16–49, at p. 48; Charles Singer, *From Magic to Medicine: Essays on the Scientific Twilight* (New York: Boni and Liveright, 1928), pp. 160–1, with edition, translation, and accompanying diagram; G. Storms, *Anglo-Saxon Magic* (The Hague: Martinus Nijhoff, 1948; repr. Folcroft, PA: Folcroft Library Editions, 1975), p. 309, with translation and accompanying diagram; Felix Grendon, 'The Anglo-Saxon Charms', *The Journal of American Folk-Lore* 22 (1909), 105–237, at pp. 204–5, with translation and accompanying diagram. Förster was the first to recognize that the diagram pertains to the *Sphera Apulei* (see below).

27. Edited, with translation, by Cockayne, *Leechdoms, Wortcunning and Starcraft*, vol. 1, p. 396, with accompanying diagram; Storms, *Anglo-Saxon Magic*, p. 311, with translation and accompanying diagram; Grendon, 'The Anglo-Saxon Charms', pp. 206–7, with translation and accompanying diagram.

28. Edited, with translation, by Cockayne, *Leechdoms, Wortcunning and Starcraft*, vol. 1, pp. 388–9. Cockayne identifies 'Miserere nostri' as the incipit to Ps. 51 [i.e., 50], but the incipit for this psalm is 'Miserere mei,' as also for Pss. 55 and 56. No psalm begins with 'Miserere nostri.' The incipit is possibily to be read as '[Deus misereatu]r nostri,' Ps. 66. 'Exsurgat deus,' which Cockayne miswrites as 'Exurgat dominus,' is the incipit to Ps. 67; 'Quicumque uult' (the Athanasian Creed) typically appears as the last canticle in the psalters.

29. Edited, with translation, by Cockayne, *Leechdoms, Wortcunning and Starcraft*, vol. 1, pp. 388–9. Cockayne reads the beginning as 'Gif sceap sionyl on,' to which he appends a note: 'Of uncertain signification.'

30. Edited by Ker, *Catalogue of Manuscripts Containing Anglo-Saxon*, item 224, art. p, p. 300; Storms, *Anglo-Saxon Magic*, p. 287 (no. 50), with translation; Cockayne, *Leechdoms, Wortcunninĝ and Starcraft*, vol. 1, pp. 386–7, with translation. Ker rightly takes the charm as ending at 'Agios', while both Cockayne and Storms (following Cockayne) record the charm as continuing for another four lines and ending with 'ofer þam oðrum sticc[a]n', the last line on fol. 15v. Fols 15v|27–16r|8, however, form a

separate charm for crops. The two items are printed in full by Ker.

31. Edited by Ker, *Catalogue of Manuscripts Containing Anglo-Saxon*, no. 224, art. q, p. 300. Storms, *Anglo-Saxon Magic*, p. 287 (no. 50, lines 4–7 of his edition only, ending at 'oðrum sticc[an]', the last line of fol. 15v), with translation; Cockayne, *Leechdoms, Wortcunning and Starcraft*, vol. 1, pp. 386–7, lines 3–7 of his edition only, ending at 'oðrum sticc[an]'; Both Cockayne and Storms link this section with the charm to protect cattle on fol. 15v|25–26. The remainder of the charm (for crops) is divided by Cockayne into two other sections; see vol. 3, pp. 234–5 (editing fol. 16r|1–3, ending at 'þæs berenes') and vol. 3, pp. 238–9 (editing fol. 16r|6–8, ending at 'Pater noster'), with translations. Storms does not edit these sections.

32. Edited by Förster, 'Beiträge zur mittelalterlichen Volkskunde. VIII', p. 47; a few letters more can be read in the last line than Förster records, and so the full text is given here. A stray 'vi.' is visible at the bottom of the leaf.

33. Edited by Max Förster, 'Ein altenglisches Prosa-Rätsel', *Archiv für das Studien der neueren Sprachen und Litteraturen* 115 (1905), 392–3; see also his 'Die Lösung des altenglische Prosarätsels', *Archiv für das Studien der neueren Sprachen und Litteraturen* 116 (1906), 367–71; 'Nochmals ae. *fregen* "Frage"', *Archiv für das Studien der neueren Sprachen und Litteraturen* 135 (1916), 399–401.

34. Edited by Humfrey Wanley, *Antiquæ literaturæ septentrionalis liber alter. Librorum* Vett. *Septentriolanium qui in* Angliæ *Bibliothecis extant, nec non multorum* Vett. *Codd. Septentrionalium alibi extantium Catalogus Historico-Criticus, cum totius Thesauri Linguarum Septentrionalium sex Indicibus* (Oxford: Sheldonian Theatre, 1705), p. 223. The text is also mentioned and partly quoted by Walter de Gray Birch, 'On Two Anglo-Saxon Manuscripts in the British Museum', *Transactions of the Royal Society of Literature of the United Kingdom*, 2nd ser., 11 (1970), 463–512, at p. 503.

35. Annotated Bibliographies of Old and Middle English Literature, 4 (Cambridge: D.S. Brewer, 1992), p. 328.

36. Phillip Pulsiano, 'British Library, Cotton Tiberius A. iii, fol. 59rv: An Unrecorded Charm in the Form of an Address to the Cross', *ANQ* n.s. 4.1 (January 1991), 3–5; Dom Anselm Hughes, ed., *The Portiforium of Saint Wulstan (Corpus Christi College, Cambridge MS. 391)*, Henry Bradshaw Society, 89 and 90 (London: Henry Bradshaw Society, 1980, 1985), vol. 2, p. 24; Julius Zupitza, 'Kreuzzauber', *Archiv für das Studium der neueren Sprachen und Literaturen* 88 (1892), 364–5.

37. H.A. Wilson, ed., *The Missal of Robert of Jumièges*, Henry Bradshaw Society, 11 (London, 1896; repr. Woodbridge: The Henry Bradshaw Society; The Boydell Press, 1994), pp. 286–95.

38. George Herzfeld, ed., *An Old English Martyrology. Re-edited from*

Manuscripts in the Libraries of the British Museum and of Corpus Christi College, Cambridge, Early English Text Society, o.s. 116 (London: Kegan Paul, Trench, Trübner & Co., 1900), p. 144; Günter Kotzer, ed., *Das altenglische Martyrologium*, Bayerische Akademie der Wissenschaften, Philosophisch-Historische Klasse, Abhandlungen, Neue Folge, 88/2 (Munich: Bayerische Akademie der Wissenschaften, 1981), vol. 2, pp. 177–8.

39. Charles Singer, 'Early English Medicine and Magic', *Proceedings of the British Academy* 9 (1920), 341–74.

40. The text appearing below the diagram, given above from fol. 16r|16–18, forms a continuation of the passage.

41. Unlike the Circle of Petrosius in St John's College 17, fol. 8r, that in Caligula A. xv adds Latin transliterations and translations of the Greek terms; for mention and diagram, see Singer, *From Magic to Science*, pp. 166–7. For additional manuscripts containing representations of the Sphere of Life and Death, see [Ernest] Wickersheimer, 'Figures médico-astrologiques des IXe, Xe, et XIe siècles', *Janus* 19 (1914), 157–77 (Paris, Bibliothèque Nationale nouv. acq. lat. 1616, fol. 7v, Bibliothèque Nationale lat. 8663, fol. 57v, Orléans 276, p. 129, along with Bibliothèque Nationale nouv. acq. lat. 1616, fol. 14r, and London, British Library, Laon 407, fol. 136v, both containing the so-called 'Tetragonus subjectus'); Charles Singer, *From Science to Magic*, pp. 144–6, 160–2 (Paris, Bibliothèque Nationale lat. 11411, fol. 99r, Oxford, Bodleian Library, Bodley 579, fol. 50r [mistakenly given as Bodley 718]); Henry E. Sigerist, 'The *Sphere of Life and Death* in Early Medieval Manuscripts', *Bulletin of the History of Medicine* 11 (1942), 292–303 (Sankt Gallen, Stiftsbibliothek 752, p. 82, Vercelli, Biblioteca Capitolare CLXXVII (Arab. 42), fol. 143r, Florence, Biblioteca Laurenziana, Plut. lxxiii. 23 [incomplete]); Lynn Thorndike, *A History of Magic and Experimental Medicine During the First Thirteen Centuries of Our Era* (New York: Columbia University Press, 1923; repr. 1947), vol. 1, pp. 692–4 [Appendix I], where 24 manuscripts are listed); Linda Ehrsam Voigts, 'The Latin and Middle English Prose Texts on the Sphere of Life and Death in Harley 3719', *Chaucer Review* 21.2 (1986), 291–305 (Middle English text, but useful for discussion of the sphere generally; discusses, e.g., Bodley 579, Tiberius C. vi); Robert Deshman, 'The Leofric Missal and tenth-century English art', *Anglo-Saxon England* 6 (1977), 145–73, at pp. 166–8 (Bodley 579, Tiberius C. vi); see also Lynn Thordike and Pearl Kibre, *A Catalogue of Incipits of Mediaeval Scientific Writings in Latin* (Cambridge, MA: The Mediaeval Academy of America, 1937), pp. 108 (*sub* Collige per numerum) and 700 (*sub* Sphera Apulei). Adelheid Heimann, in 'Three Illustrations from the Bury St. Edmund's Psalter and Their Prototypes' (*Journal of the Warburg and Courtauld Institutes* 21

(1966), 39–46), treats the sphere in Bodley 579. See also Peter S. Baker and Michael Lapidge, eds., *Byrhtferth's Enchiridion*, Early English Text Society, s.s. 15 (Oxford: Oxford University Press, 1995), p. 427, where the sphere in St John's College 17 is mentioned, along with Harley 3017, fol. 58r, Biblioteca Apostolica Vaticana, Ross. lat. 247, fol. 52v, and Vat. Urb. lat. 290, fol. 2r. A sixteenth-century representation of the sphere is found in British Library, Sloane 416, fol. 105r, which also contains (fol. 155r) another interesting text, 'Occulte scribendi modus'.

The text in Caligula A. xv reads: 'Spera apulei platonici de uita et morte uel de omnibus ergotis et quicquid inquirere uolueris. sic computabis per omnes litteras et puta de nomine egri. Addis lunam quota fuerit die qua de cuberit et quotiens potuerit diuide per xxx. et quicquid superauerit reuerteris ad organiolus infra scriptum. et si superiora conuenerit parti numerus iota erit. Si inferiori parti conuenerit moritusus erit. Sic et de omnibus negotus aut causis requires. Si dies dominicus fuerit .xiii. Si lune .xviii. Si martis .xv. Si mercurius .xx. [a third 'x' erased]. Si iouis .xi. Si ueneris .xv. Si saturnus .xxvi.'. The manuscript also contains the poem commonly accompanying the sphere: 'Collige per numeros quicquid cupis esse probandum | Iunge simul nomen feriam lunamque diei | Collectamque una summam partere trigenos | Quodque superfuerit rotulus discernet utesque | Quod retinet uitę nec noti et mortis imago', and closing with 'Si supra fuerit uiuet morietur et infra.' The poem is also found in Tiberius C. vi and Bodley 579, but is wanting in Vitellius E. xviii. The lines in Vitellius E. xviii written below the sphere (fol. 16r|16–18) clearly act as an aid in determining the correct calculation, which involves adding together the numbers of the name of the individual, the moon, and the weekday. See Voigts, 'The Latin Verse and Middle English Prose Texts on the Sphere of Life and Death in Harley 3719', esp. pp. 297–8 and 301.

42. Singer, 'Early English Medicine and Magic', p. 350.

43. See Rev. Adrian Jerome Kilker, *Extreme Unction: A Canonical Treatise Containing also a Consideration of the Dogmatic, Historical and Liturgical Aspects of the Sacrament* (St. Louis and London: B. Herder Book Co., 1927), pp. 35–8.

44. George Philip Krapp and Elliott Van Kirk Dobbie, eds., *The Exeter Book*, Anglo-Saxon Poetic Records, 3 (New York: Columbia University Press, London: Routledge and Kegan Paul, 1936), p. 198; for notes and discussion of the emendations, see p. 341. Designated Riddle 34 in Craig Williamson, ed., *The Old English Riddles of the Exeter Book* (Chapel Hill: University of North Carolina Press, 1977), pp. 89 (text), 248–52 (notes). Designated Riddle 36 by Bernard J. Muir, ed., *The Exeter Anthology of Old English Poetry: An Edition of Exeter Dean and Chapter MS 3501* (Exeter: University of Exeter Press, 1994), vol. 1, pp. 313–4 (text), vol. 2, pp. 620–1 (notes). For a brief comment on encoded writing, see Bernard

Bischoff, *Latin Palaeography: Antiquity & the Middle Ages*, translated by Dáibhí Ó. Cróinín and David Ganz (Cambridge: Cambridge University Press, 1990), pp. 177–8.

45. See Simon Keynes, *Anglo-Saxon Manuscripts in Trinity College. Old English Newsletter*, Subsidia, 18 (Binghamton: CEMERS, 1992), p. 13.

46. Both printed by Ker, *Catalogue of Manuscripts Containing Anglo-Saxon*, item 313, p. 377 (transliterated). Earlier printed by Max Förster, 'Nachmals ae. *fregen* "Frage"', p. 400. The encoded text in Bodley 572 reads: c:.:nn. n:.: m.g ð:.: aræd.n hwæt þ:.s m.g: b:on kc w:n: ꝥ h:.t nis n. :ð ræd: Is ðks frfgfn sfllkc þkngc tp rædfnf.

47. Printed in *Antiquae literaturae septentrionalis liber alter*, p. 225. The reading 'ruminabant' (r≡=mııı n-b-nt) is partly drawn from Wanley; a tear in the leaf resulted in the loss of the *u*, with only two of five strokes showing. Sections of the text were reprinted by George Hickes in his *Grammatica Anglo-Saxonica* (Oxford: Sheldonian Theatre, 1711, pp. 41–2); the entire volume has been published in facsimile, with a brief prefatory note by R.C. Alston, as volume 256 in the series English Linguistics 1500–1800 (Menston: The Scolar Press, 1970). The encoding, at its simplest level, employs different methods of vowel substitution. For example, b = a, f = e, k = i, p = o and u = x; or x = a, xx = e, xxx = i, xxxx = o and xxxxx = u; or · = a, : = e, :· = i, :: = o and :·: = u; a similar system of bars may also be used. Complexity comes in the combination of systems; for example, xxx= may be read as *ie* (taken separately) or *u* (taken in combination).

48. *Antiquæ literaturæ septentrionalis liber alter*, p. 223.

49. I must express my thanks to Carl Berkhout, who, within a mere couple of days in London in June 1995, independently solved the cryptogram and was thus able to confirm my transcription.

50. Günzel, ed., *Ælfwine's Prayerbook*, pp. 109 (text), 70–1 (discussion). For the transcription, however, I refer to the manuscript, from which Günzel's text differs slightly. An encoded word also appears at. fol. 85v at the end of an Office for the Virgin Mary: SKCFKBT (with *I* written above both *K*'s and *A* above *B*), thus SIC FIAT (Günzel, p. 136).

51. *Catalogue of Manuscripts Containing Anglo-Saxon*, item 224, p. 301.

52. *English Kalendars Before A.D. 1100*, p. vi; see p. 155 for dating. See also N. J. Morgan, 'Notes on the Post-Conquest Calendar, Litany and Martyrology of the Cathedral Priory of Winchester with a Consideration of Winchester Diocese Calendars of the Pre-Sarum Period' (note 9 above): 'The original calendar may represent the pre-Conquest text of the New Minster (later to become Hyde Abbey) but by comparison with post-Conquest texts there are several feasts particularly characteristic of the Cathedral Priory' (p. 134). Morgan advances the hypothesis that 'the calendar represents the pre-Conquest text of the Cathedral (the date of the

manuscript may in fact be shortly after the Conquest)' (p. 161, n. 11). Karl Wildhagen's edition and study of the calendar remains essential to any discussion ('Das Kalendarium der Handschrift Vitellius E XVIII') (see note 9 above).

53. 'Das Kalendarium der Handschrift Vitellius E XVIII', p. 73 for dating and pp. 117–8 for appendix.
54. *The Salisbury Psalter*, p. 58, § 116.
55. *English Caroline Minuscule*, Oxford Palaeographical Handbooks (Oxford: Clarendon Press, 1971), no. 26, p. 23.
56. *Catalogue of Manuscripts Containing Anglo-Saxon*, item 202, p. 266.
57. *Ælfwine's Prayerbook*, pp. 6–11.
58. The tables begin on fol. 8v. Because of damage to the manuscript, the Roman numerals begin with 1034, but counting back through the parallel columns to the right makes certain that 1031 is the first year entered into the column.
59. Jonathan J.G. Alexander, *Medieval Illuminators and Their Methods of Work* (New Haven and London: Yale University Press, 1992), p. 10.
60. I am deeply grateful to Simon Keynes for generously allowing me to read sections of the introduction to his edition of London, British Library, Stowe 944, the *Liber Vitae* of New Minster, in advance of its publication and for numerous exchanges about a variety of matters centering on Ælfwine. The facsimile has now appeared in print: *The Liber Vitae of the New Minster and Hyde Abbey Winchester, British Library Stowe 994, together wiith Leaves from British Library Cotton Vespasian A. viii and British Library Cotton Titus D. xxvii*, Ealy English Manuscripts in Facsimile (Copenhagen: Rosenkilde and Bagger, 1996); see in particular pp. 66–8 and 111ff. The significance of this manuscript with respect to Ælfwine and the relationship between the illustrations in the *Liber Vitae* and those in 'Ælfwine's Prayerbook' are given extended discussion by Dr Keynes, and there is reason to believe that Ælfwine was also the artist of the prayerbook (see p. 113).
61. *Ælfwine's Prayerbook*, p. 145, no. 57.
62. *Ælfwine's Prayerbook*, p. 144, no. 56.
63. E.W.B. Nicholson, *Early Bodleian Music: Introduction to the Study of Some of the Oldest Latin Musical Manuscripts in the Bodleian Library, Oxford* (London: Oxford University Press, 1901), p. xxvii and pl. xv. David N. Dumville (*Liturgy and the Ecclesiastical History of Late Anglo-Saxon England: Four Studies* [Woodbridge: The Boydell Press, 1992]) notes that alongside the year 1022 in the Easter table in Cambridge, University Library Kk. 5. 32 'are found prickings which may indicate that that was the next Easter: the manuscript may therefore have been written between Easter 1021 and Easter 1022' (p. 52). He also notes (p. 52) two red dots at the year 1061 in the paschal tables of Cambridge, Corpus

Christi College 9, which thus provides the likely date for the codex.

64. The manuscript suffered severe damage in the Asburnham House fire of 1731, and probably an equal amount of damage through attempts at reparation (hence the slashes at the edges in order to flatten out the leaves); the leaves are mounted separately in paper frames, and it is impossible to ascertain the quiring.

65. See *Ælfwine's Prayerbook*, p. 2.

5 The Conybeare-Madden Collation of Thorkelin's *Beowulf*

Kevin S. Kiernan

In 1817 John Josias Conybeare, Rawlinson Professor of Anglo-Saxon at Oxford University from 1808–1812, and Professor of Poetry thereafter, was presented with G.J. Thorkelin's 1815 first edition of *Beowulf* by his brother, William. It may seem like a fine gift today, but by his own account it led to three years of tedium between 1817–1821, when he arduously compiled the first detailed account of the *Beowulf* manuscript after the Thorkelin transcripts by collating the edition with the original manuscript in the British Museum. William paid more than once for the gift, moreover, for John Conybeare prepared selections from *Beowulf* and his long collation for the press by 1821, but then never got around to correcting all the proof sheets before his death in 1824. It was left for William to publish his brother's *Illustrations of Anglo-Saxon Poetry* in 1826. Whitney F. Bolton bought 'The Conybeare Copy of Thorkelin' to our attention after he found the book in a Philadelphia bookstore and convincingly demonstrated in a preliminary analysis that, for the most accurate account of Conybeare's readings, it was necessary to use it, rather than the posthumously published, and forever badly proofread, *Illustrations*.[1]

Recognising that the book warranted a full-blown study to assess the value of the collation, Bolton mentioned in his article that he would 'happily grant access to the Conybeare copy of [Thorkelin's edition] to any qualified person who seeks it.'[2] I borrowed the book in the early 1980s and transcribed Conybeare's collations for a planned diplomatic edition of *Beowulf*, but had to postpone these plans in 1984, after J.R. Hall discovered at Harvard University a more revealing collation (Houghton 28286.24.3*), evolving directly from Conybeare's, by Sir Frederic Madden.[3] After I transcribed the Madden collation in 1984, however, the advent of digital technology vitiated a diplomatic edition. Both of these collations are now part of the Electronic *Beowulf* image archive, giving scholars access in full-colour facsimiles to both the first edition and the first revealing collations of the state of the *Beowulf* manuscript before the 1845 restoration binding both preserved and concealed the damaged edges.[4]

An intriguing relationship underlying the history of Conybeare's collation flourished in the last six months of his life between Conybeare and the young Frederic Madden, who became an employee of the British Museum in

1828 and later was its long-time Keeper of Manuscripts (1837–1866). According to Madden's diary in Oxford, Bodleian Library, MS Eng. hist. C. 145, Conybeare first struck up this friendship on Saturday, 17 January 1824, when he came for a visit, Madden says, '& asked me to accompany him into Bath, as like myself, from too sedentary a habit, he has been obliged to have recourse to the waters' (38).[5] Conybeare's library, he discovered, housed 'every volume in Saxon literature that had ever been published, except for a few pages of a Saxon homily, which he had not got' (41). One of the books he borrowed that first night was Elizabeth Elstob's *The Rudiments of Grammar for the English-Saxon Tongue* (1715), the first Old English grammar written in English (44).[6] He later recorded in his diary that he was determined to learn all he could about 'the Saxon language' from Conybeare, the former Professor of Anglo-Saxon at Oxford (49).

Before the first day was done, Conybeare divulged that 'he had been for some time engaged in completing for the press an abstract & specimens in blank verse of a very curious Saxon poem relative to the Danes, preserved among the Cotton MSS. and published in 4to. 1815. by Thorkelin.'[7] He also told his new friend that day about his collation with the *Beowulf* manuscript, and even showed him 'the numerous corrections he had made, not only of the Saxon, but of Thorlekin's Latin translation' (42–3). Although Madden does not say so in his journal, there is some reason to think that Conybeare might have tried to engage Madden at this time to proofread for him. Without such motivation it seems pointlessly self-deprecatory that Conybeare would at their first meeting admit that 'he had sent his MS. to the press in 1821, but had not yet reviewed above eight proof sheets!' Madden's exclamation mark shows his own surprise at the disclosure. 'This is a proof of Mr C's indolence,' he writes, 'the only fault among all his merits, that is often observed' (42–3).[8] Madden's strictures seem unfair. The year Madden met him, Conybeare delivered the Bampton lectures at Oxford and published a volume on the interpretation of Scripture; at about the same time he was publishing fairly widely on chemistry and geology; and he had earned a reputation for scrupulously attending to his clerical duties in Bath Easton. Why, then, would Conybeare open himself so quickly to Madden's disapproval?

Under the circumstances it is not too far-fetched to imagine that Conybeare, apparently busy with other wide-ranging projects, befriended Madden at this time for the express purpose of hiring him to undertake the proofreading for him. If this was Conybeare's plan, it is less surprising to learn in the entry for 20 January 1824, three days after their first meeting, that Conybeare had actually given the uncorrected proof sheets to Madden. 'In the evening I read over the proof sheets of the work Mr. C. has prepared for the press, and which he was good enough to lend me,' Madden writes in his journal. 'All that has been printed amounts to 64 octavo pages, (it is to be published in this form, with a few copies in 4to. to bind up with Warton) and is intitled "Ilustrations of AngloSaxon Poetry"' (69). If he was not trying to enlist an expert proofreader, it is puzzling that Conybeare should release the proof sheets to Madden at this time.

Frustrating a conclusive investigation of this possibility, Madden by 1840 had completely replaced the section of his 1824 journal covering this acquaintance with Conybeare. On page viii of the extant version he wrote:

> *Note*. This journal for 1824 [i.e., from January] to 24th April was originally written in a volume of a smaller size than I had previously used, and was subsequently, at various times *transcribed into the present volume*.
>
> *F.M. March, 1840*

There are some overt cases in the new copy where Madden has done minor editing of the original journal, as when he repeatedly changes references from 'Thorkelin', which made some sense in 1824, to 'Beowulf', which had become a recognisable name of the poem by 1840. Some relevant things happened in the intervening years. Madden took a job in the Department of Manuscripts at the British Musem in 1828; Kemble published the first English edition of the poem using the title *Beowulf* in 1833;[9] his second edition appeared in two volumes in 1835 and 1837; and Madden became Keeper of Manuscripts in 1837. Madden had a keen sense of his historical place in the British Museum, as his voluminous journals and seemingly endless notations in manuscripts clearly attest.

Short of finding the original 1824 journal or related information in his or Conybeare's papers, we can do no more than speculate about the curious circumstances surrounding Madden's pre-publication access to Conybeare's collations in both print and manuscript forms. We do know from his journal, however, that on 27 January 1824, 10 days after learning about the 'very curious Saxon poem' at Conybeare's house, Madden sent for his own copy of Thorkelin to help him learn Old English. He certainly had more ambitious plans for the volume, moreover, for he sent for an unbound copy, which he planned to 'interleave, and add my own notes, and collate with the orig(inal) MS.—Mr. Conybeare has done this already but I should not like to ask him for his copy' (85). The next day, however, when he learned that Madden had sent for his own copy of Thorkelin, 'Mr C. immediately offered to lend me *his own copy*, with permission to transcribe his MS notes and corrections, with his collation of the text with the Cotton. MS.' (87). What is going on here? First Conybeare gives Madden his proof sheets of the *Illustrations*, containing his uncorrected collation. Then he gives him his copy of Thorkelin's *Beowulf* with the original collation, the essential source material he needs to proofread the uncorrected sheets. Are we to believe that

Conybeare was more interested in giving Madden everything he needed to duplicate Conybeare's collation than in proofreading and preparing for the press the *Illustrations*? It is far more credible that Madden in his 1840 replacement of the 1824 journal excised or revised some of the story behind Conybeare's otherwise extraordinary behaviour.

There are other gaps and inconsistencies surrounding Madden's use of Conybeare's collation. On 31 January, Madden records that he had finished translating Edward Thwaite's excerpt of George Hickes' grammar,[10] another book Conybeare loaned him, 'and shall now pursue my study of Mr. C's MSS. until the Beowulf arrives' (96). In this context 'Mr. C's MSS.' presumably refers to Conybeare's manuscript notes, corrections and collations from the interleaved copy of Thorkelin, which Conybeare had just given him permission to transcribe.

But the situation is not so straightforward. We learn from the journal on 10 February that 'The copy of Thorkelin's Beowulf I sent for in sheets, is sold, so I have now ordered the bound copy from Bohn, at 1.4.0.' (110). It is surprising to find that Madden purchased a bound copy, because his own *interleaved* collation of Thorkelin survives in the Houghton Library at Harvard.[11] This volume unequivocally shows that he went to the considerable trouble and expense of unbinding the new book, interleaving it and rebinding it. Madden's rebound interleaved copy includes a transcription of Conybeare's collation as well as his own collation, which augments and corrects Conybeare's work. There is convincing reason to believe, however, that the rebinding was done after he transcribed Conybeare's notes and did the first phase of his own collation. In the first place, it is unlikely in the extreme that he was able to have the new copy interleaved and rebound in two weeks. Yet on 24 February he writes 'In the evening [I] began to copy Conybeare's MS. notes from his interleaved copy of Beowulf, which he had sent' (143). Moreover, he copied all of Conybeare's collation and recorded most of his own on the printed pages, rather than on the interleaves. For Madden's collations to be of any value, it is of course necessary to distinguish between his copy of Conybeare's notes and his own independent observations of the state of the manuscript.

Continuing the transcription in the evening of 27 February, Madden soon acknowledged to himself, at any rate, his larger plans for *Beowulf*. 'I should like much to publish a new edition with corrections', he writes, 'accompanied by an English version and Notes' (145). These ambitions would explain why he had the edition interleaved sometime after he finished copying Conybeare's collation and beginning his own. According to his diary, it takes him two weeks, from 24 February to 1 March, to finish transcribing Conybeare's notes. On 3 March, he records, he 'called on Mr Conybeare and returned Thorkelin's Beowulf' (146–7). Conybeare was not at home when he called, however, and we hear no more about Conybeare in

Madden's journals until Conybeare's death in June.

Madden learned of Conybeare's death on 15 June 1824, according to the next volume of his journal in Oxford, Bodleian Library, MS Eng. hist. C. 146 (30). Then he did not lose any time in pursuing his plans for an edition of *Beowulf*. Two days later at the British Museum he sent for the *Beowulf* manuscript, referring to it as Vespasian rather than Vitellius A. xv, but otherwise leaving no doubt that he was sending for *Beowulf*, 'which I have not before had an opportunity of looking at' (30).[12] He begins his collation with the manuscript on 21 June 1824, less than a week after hearing of Conybeare's death. 'Notwithstanding Conybeare's having gone *three* times over it', Madden immediately observes, 'he has omitted to notice a quantity of errors, & has added a few himself' (32).

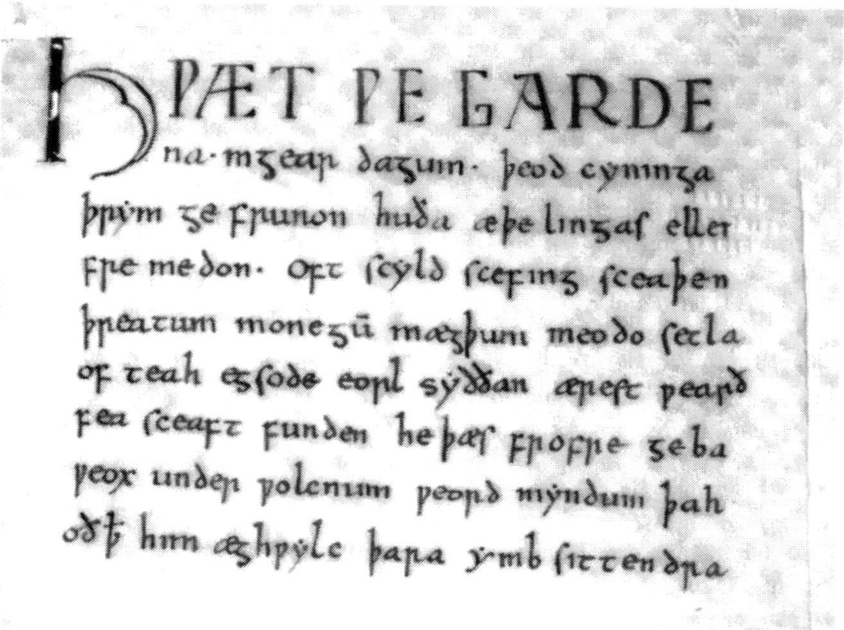

Two days later he mentions 'tak[in]g facsimiles fr[o]m t[he] MS. of Beowulf, & ... continuing the collation of it.' One of these facsimiles is a careful tracing of the first page of *Beowulf* to line recto 9, which is now the first page of Madden's collation.[13] He adds rather ruthlessly, 'Now Conybeare is dead I am at perfect liberty to publish it in any way I please', and goes on to imagine using 'some such title as this. "Remains of metrical Romances, written in the Dano-Saxon dialect, and now for the first time published with an English transl[atio]n, copious illustrations, & critical observations. A literal *Latin* version is annexed"' (34).

The next day, 24 June, he spent the whole day collating, and continues to disparage Conybeare's collation. 'There are a prodigious number of errors overlooked by Conybeare', he says, '& even names spelt wrong, as *AEgthreow*, all through the poem, for *Ecgthreow* [sic], which he has not noticed!' (34-5). His own misspelling of the name Ecgtheow may serve as fair warning to proud collators everywhere. When he finished his collating on 30 July, Madden boasts, 'I completed today my collation of *Beowulf*, & what poor Conybeare called "Tædium trienne" has not occupied me (even at 1/2 an hour at a time) more than *two months*.' Mocking Conybeare's 'Tædium Trienne', Madden copied the comment at the end of his own and then added, 'Tædium quator hebdomadum'.

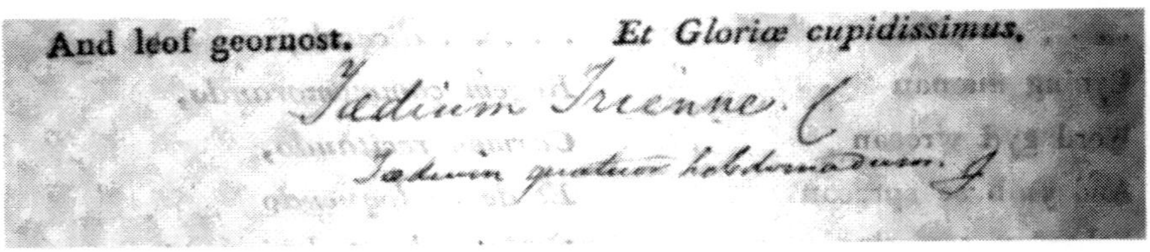

He goes on to say that 'I am confident enough to assert that I have not overlooked a single letter, mark, erasure, or abbreviation, & have now the text *precisely as it stands in the MS*., which Conybeare, partly from haste, & want of care, & partly from not being able to read the MS. left in a very corrupt state, notwithstanding all his emendations of Thorkelin's wretched transcript' (59). Madden's work is not perfect, needless to say. Even his careful tracing of the opening nine lines of the manuscript contains a *d* for an *ð* in *weorð* in line 8.

There are, to be sure, many more mistakes and omissions in Conybeare's collation. But there are as well some important details that Madden's later work cannot supersede. Conybeare, for example, lets us know that two leaves in the *Beowulf* manuscript were still out of place when he collated, as he duly notes on the interleaves facing pages 9 and 61, for fol. 147A(131), and pages 187 and 231, for fol. 189A(197).[14]

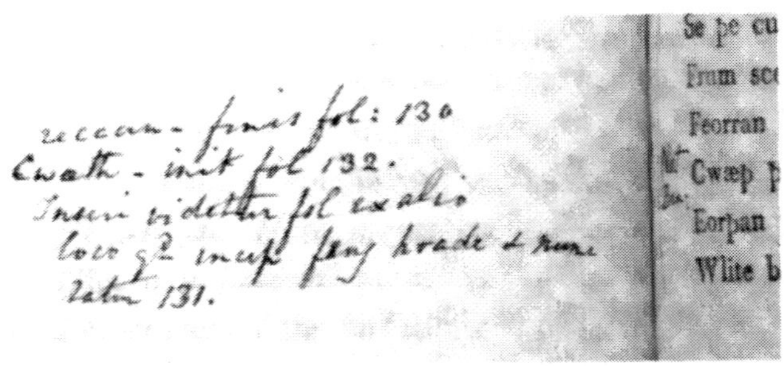

A striking example of the superiority of Madden's collation over Conybeare's can be seen in his restoration by facsimile of what appeared to be a lost reading from the edge of the manuscript. On fol. 180r|16 (verse line 2268), the crumbled edge now ends with the letters *hwe*. Thorlekin A recorded the meaningless form *hweir*, whereas Thorkelin B by haplography unfortunately skipped over this section. In his edition, Thorkelin therefore printed A's *hweir*, which Conybeare in his collation accepted as the manuscript reading. Modern editors conjecturally restore the word as *hwe(arf)*, on the palaeographically sound assumption that the *i* was in fact a minim forming the *ea* ligature. At some stage in his collating Madden provided a facsimile on the interleaf that not only shows *hwear* but also a following descender, virtually confirming the editorial restoration.

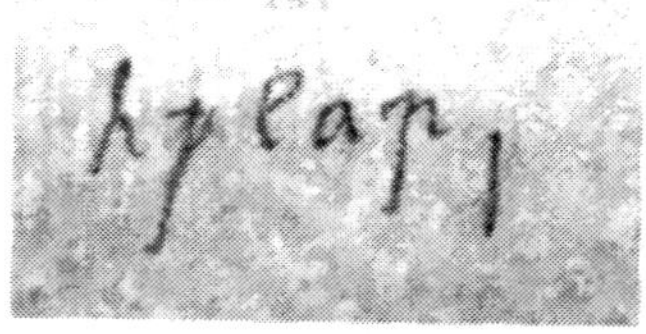

While Madden's collation is undoubtedly much more accurate than Conybeare's, it is not, as we have already seen, 'the text *precisely as it stands in the MS*'. Its accuracy, moreover, was achieved in large part because it was done in the immediate context of Conybeare's collation. Madden's gloating at Conybeare's expense seems particularly unseemly, in view of the special access he was given to Conybeare's copy of Thorkelin and to the uncorrected proof sheets of his *Illustrations of Anglo-Saxon Poetry*. Even in the unlikely event that Conybeare did not expressly ask him to proofread for him, the question lingers why Madden, the quintessential collator with the relevant materials in hand, did not undertake the task out of friendship, reciprocity, curiosity or duty. Instead, on 39 July 1826, when Conybeare's brother William presents him with a copy of the posthumous book, Madden rather ironically dismisses it as 'very *faulty*, as I have before had occasion to prove — but I have not got my own collated copy at hand, to point out the errors' (460).

An enduring value of Conybeare's original collation in his copy of Thorkelin is that it shows, by Conybeare's practice of under-pointing lost letters, the considerable amount of deterioration along the damaged edges of the manuscript in the time between the Thorkelin transcripts and his collation. By the same means Madden's collation records further deterioration after Conybeare, and often shows in addition, as Madden rightly says, the letters Conybeare indicates were lost are in fact still there in the manuscript. Thinking that Hall's comprehensive study of the collations was imminent in

1986, I confined myself to a few general remarks along these lines in *The Thorkelin Transcripts of Beowulf*:

> In his 1817 collation of the MS with Thorkelin's 1815 first edition of the poem, J.J. Conybeare made dots beneath letters he could no longer see in the MS. By his testimony well over 900 letters Thorkelin records were gone from the edges by the time of the collation. However, the collation is not entirely reliable, for Conybeare failed to make dots beneath letters that are palpably conjectural restorations in Thorkelin's edition. For example, both transcripts show that the bottom corner of 195r was gone when they were made (A has *laðm* and B has *laðn* for r20, both have *gry* for r21); yet in his edition Thorkelin reads *laðne* and *gryre*, and Conybeare passes over both conjectural restorations without marking them. A more accurate collation made by Sir Frederic Madden in 1824, recently discovered by J.R. Hall in the Houghton Library at Harvard, shows far more deterioriation than Conybeare noted.[15]

With the facsimile one can see that Thorkelin in fact printed '*laþ*....' (225), and that Conybeare in his collation added *ne* over the first two dots.

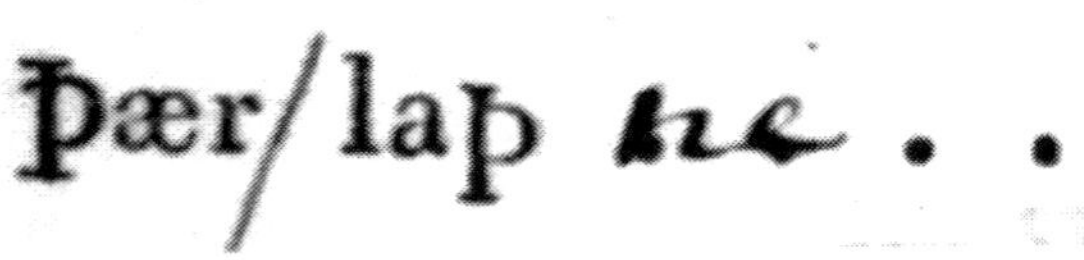

Far from showing that Conybeare failed to mark a conjectural restoration by Thorkelin, the case shows Conybeare restoring a reading overlooked by both A and B. Following Conybeare, Madden in his copy of Thorkelin added the letters *ne* within the line, crossed out Thorkelin's dots, and noted 'nulla lacuna. F[rederic].' It appears, then, that a very shrunken *e*-head still survived at the edge of the vellum as late as 1824. At the same time, Madden underpointed the *-re* in *gryre*, showing simultaneous deterioration. While Conybeare's collation is to some extent superseded by Madden's more meticulous work, one cannot properly assess the evidential value of Madden's collation without understanding its relation to Conybeare's.

The pivotal importance of these closely related collations can be usefully illustrated by reference to the readings in the damaged parts of the manuscript that are preserved by Thorkelin B alone. In *The Thorkelin Transcripts of Beowulf* (hereafter TTB), I came to the conclusion that it was often impossible to judge the authority of these readings in Thorkelin B, because of Thorkelin's practice of editing, both as he transcribed and after he no longer had access to the manuscript. To illustrate the potential for uncertainty I listed a number of readings from the damaged edges where

Thorkelin might have introduced intelligent editorial restorations, even if the manuscript was no longer intact. 'Anyone with a rudimentary knowlege of Old English', I argued,

> could have supplied the missing letters in *wed(e)ra* 139v1, *(þ)a* 140v6, *(hw)ær* 147A(131)v1, *(h)is* 147A(131)v3, *hi(l)de* 163r3, *col(l)en* 169v4, *(s)iððan* 173v1, *(on) ende* 174v3, *guð(um)* 178r12, *(o)n* 178v8, *(b)am* 178v11, *byrnend(e)* 180r19, *(win)trum* 180v3, *on (þære) westenne* 181r2–3, *meowla(n)* 193r17, *wundu(r)* 195r14, and *hæfd(e)* 198r19.[16]

In fact, *hi(l)de* 163r3 does not really belong in this list. B is indeed the sole authority for *l*, but A records *hib-* (not *hid-*, as Zupitza says[17]), confirming that a letter survived at the edge of the manuscript. A's reading actually helps confirm B, if we assume that A mistook the curved bottom of *l*, probably distorted by heat, for the bow of a *b*.

The sigla I use in the following are Thk with page numbers (e.g., Thk 10–11) for references to Thorkelin's 1815 edition; A and B for the Thorkelin transcripts (1787 and *c.* 1790 respectively); CT for Conybeare's collation in his interleaved copy of Thorkelin (*c.* 1817–1819, i.e., '*trienne*'); and MT for Madden's collation in his interleaved copy of Thorkelin (1824, perhaps with later additions, especially on the interleaves). To facilitate reference to my collations in TTB, which the following notes augment and supersede, I use the same format, giving manuscript folio and verse lines, followed by the number of readings for which we are dependent on A or B. Round brackets show readings derived from A (often supported by B); square brackets distinguish 84 readings dependent on B alone.

RESTORATION AND COLLATIONS REVISITED

Fol. 132rv, verse lines 113a–134b: (A 11, B 2):

gi/[ga](nta)s r20–v1; Thk 11, 'gigantas'. CT underlines, and writes 'gi…is', drawing a minim before *s* that looks like the right side of *a*.

MT carefully copies Conybeare, and then later, using the manuscript, copies above it the remnant from the verso, this time with a much better Caroline *s*.

B's excellent conjectural restoration is not based on the manuscript. Written in a much later hand, both the conjectural -[ga] and the *-ntas* v1, the latter confirmed by A, are on the wrong page in B, following *gi-* r20.

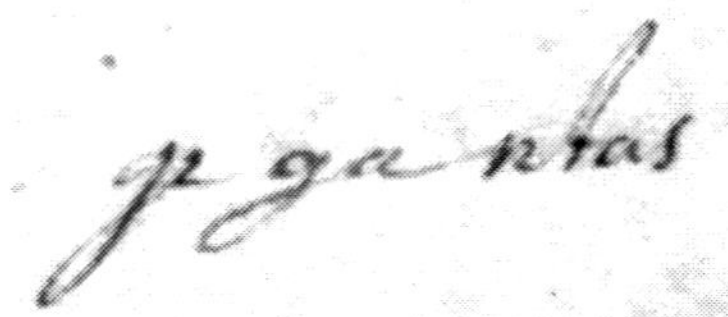

As this case illustrates, we must be doubly careful about accepting B's readings, because Thorkelin's conjectural restorations are sometimes extremely persuasive and almost certainly correct. CT treats the sequence *gi...is* as if it all came on the verso, while MT separates the letters with an open bracket where the page changes and places a 'b' in the margin to mark the verso.

Fol. 139r, verse lines 401b–423a: (A 9, B 2):

hea[rd] r2; Thk 33, 'Heard'. CT accepts the whole word, but MT points *d*. A omitted by haplography r2-3 from *heorotes* (eye-skipping to *heoðe* in the next line). No reason to doubt B.

Fol. 139v, verse lines 423a–444b: (A 10, B 1):

(wed)[e]ra 1; Thk 34, 'Wedera'. CT points the *d*, whereas MT points *W* (the *w* was apparently lost between A and B, because B added it later, presumably from A). A's *wedra* is an attested variant spelling, but the fact that Madden points only *W* indicates that *-ede-* still existed when he collated and that B's unsyncopated spelling is therefore correct.

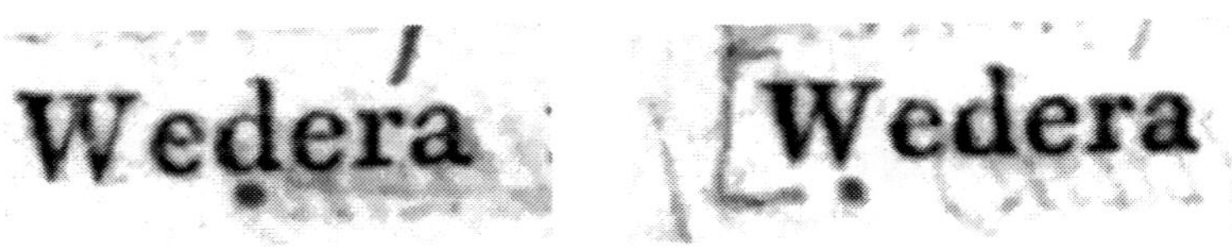

Fol. 140v, verse lines 464b–486a: (A 5, B 1):

[þ]a 6; Thk 38 'þa'. CT accepts the whole word, but MT points *þ*. The agreement between AB is illusory, because A did not copy the line and B himself supplied it in A later. There is no reason to think that B wrote (as he often does) *þ* for *ð*, however, because the descender of what is presumably *þ* still survives.

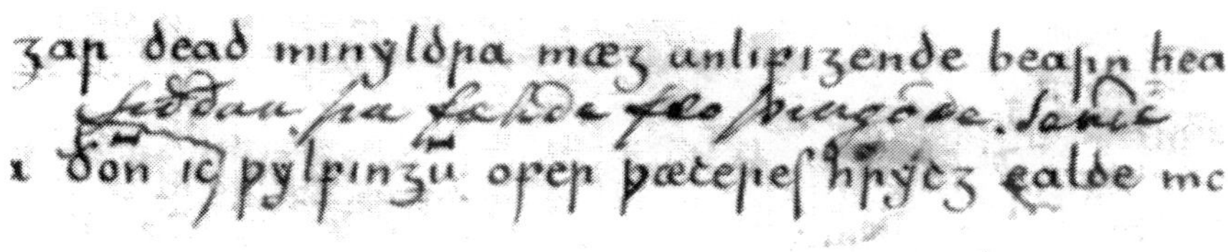

Fol. 147A(131)v, verse lines 762b–782b: (A 9, B 3):

[hw](ær) 1; Thk 59, 'Hwær'. CT accepts the whole word, but MT points every letter and confirms the word was gone in his transcript facing pages 9–10, where he thought the misplaced leaf belonged. A has …*ær*, leaving open other possibilities for conjectural restorations (e.g., *ðær*).

[h]is 3; Thk 59, 'his'. MT points *h* (and his transcription has '..s'). It may be an intelligent conjectural restoration in B; A omitted the word, perhaps because *h* was already gone and the remainder obviously fragmentary.

Fol. 148r, verse lines 827a–849a: (A 14, B 1):

h[r..] 8; Thk 65, 'hrægl'. CT and MT point 'rægel'. *hrof* seems inevitable if B's *r* is reliable.

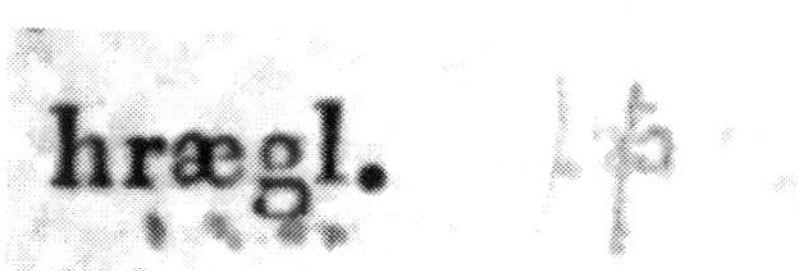

Fol. 151v, verse lines 986b–1009a: (A 2, B 1):

[h]ilde 1; Thk 76, 'hilde'. A skipped this word, because it was a dittographic error in the manuscript (see fol. 151r|20). MT writes in the word and notes that 'Hilde is repeated'.

Fol. 160v, verse lines 1377a–1398b: (A 6, B 1):

Ecgþeo-[w]es 7–8; Thk 105, 'AEgþeowes'. CT accepts the spelling (including AE for Ec), whereas MT crosses out 'AE' and writes 'ec'. Forms without *w* are attested for both *Ecgþeow* and *Ongenþeow*, but not in the first scribe's part of the manuscript. B's *w* may be an easy conjectural restoration of a proper name, but there is no reason to reject his restoration.

Fol. 161v, verse lines 1423–1448a: (A 17, B 1):

[f...] 2; Thk 108 'fughton'. CT and MT cross out *g* and point the rest of the word. Given its position, *f* is likely to be a conjecture, based on the alliteration.

Fol. 169v, verse lines 1802b–1826a: (A 33, B 5 or 7):

[ða c]om or perhaps **[ða com]** 1; Thk 136, 'Coman' (abandoning B). CT and MT point the whole word. Faint traces of what appear to be *-om* (B) or *-m* remain on an angle of the vellum, but there is room for continued conjecture, too.

[f](ar)ene 3; Thk 136, 'farene'. CT and MT point *fa*, but there is no reason to doubt B here.

col-[l](en)-(f)erhð 3–4; Thk 136, 'collen ferþ'. CT and MT point *len*. MT provides a corroborating transcript, 'cuma col.... ferhð sic MS'. But there is no evident reason to doubt B's *l*.

Fol. 173v, verse lines 1978b–1999: (B 1):

[s]iððan 1; Thk 149, 'Iþþan' (based on A's *..iððan*, rather than B's *syððan*). CT and MT have '..Iþþan', but CT writes '/Syð. Q[uære]?' in the margin, and MT similarly notes 'yððan MS. evidently syththan. F'. The remaining traces, however, support A: CT and MT mistake, in my opinion, the vestiges of uncial *s* (cf. *s* in *secean* v11) for the dot and left side of *y*, and the *i* (disfigured by a tiny hole) for the hair-stroke of *y*. B's *syððan* is an intelligent conjectural restoration.

Fol. 174r, verse lines 2000–2019a: (A 20, B 6):

hige[lac] 1; Thk 150, 'Higelac'. CT and MT point *lac*, which B wrote in later over dots. A leaves a space here. B most likely made a conjectural restoration, based on his knowledge of the proper name, Higelac. There are other possibilties, such as the adjective *higerof*, 'brave-minded', which also fits the context ('lord Higelac' or 'brave-minded lord').

hwy(l)[ce..](...) 2; Thk 150, 'hwylce / ....' (A *hwyle*, followed by a blank space; B *hwylce*..). CT and MT add two dots after *hwylce* and CT crosses out Thk's line of dots and writes 'nihil deficit'. Disagreeing, MT later writes *on* or *or* (copying an Insular *r*, if so) on these dots and notes, 'Forte litera des[un]t. F'. Modern editors, following Thorpe, conjecture that five letters, *orleg-*, were lost after *hwylc*, an emendation of both A and B.

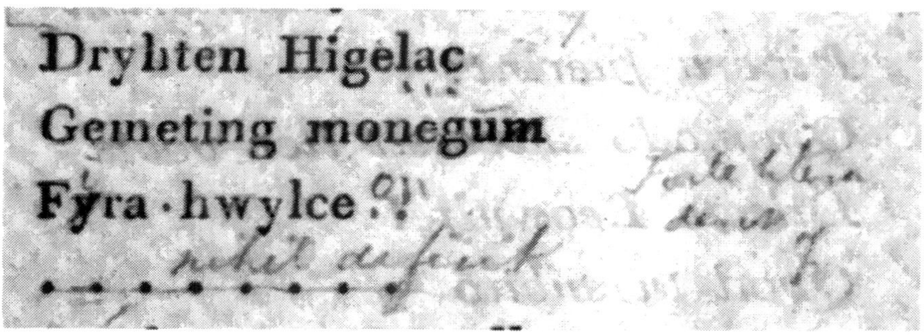

(fæ)[r] 9; Thk 151, 'Fær' (A fæ..., B fer..). CT and MT point the whole word.[18] There is room and reason for other conjectures.

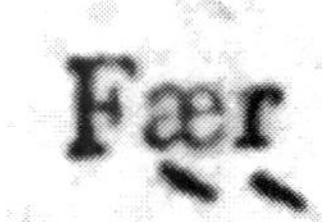

Fol. 174v, verse lines 2019a–2041b: (A 20, B 3):

[...u](gu)ðe 2; Thk 151, 'guþe' (rejecting B). Ignoring *þ* for *ð*, both CT and MT accept Thk's emendation of B, strongly suggesting that the first *u* as well as what was presumably a *d* were then gone.

[on] 3; Thk 152, 'on'. CT accepts the whole word, but MT points *o*. B may have provided an intelligent conjectural restoration; A first wrote what looks like an *e*, apparently beginning to write *ende*, the next word in the line, but then smudged out the letter and left a blank before *ende*.

Fol. 175r, verse lines 2041b-2062a: (A 28, B 8):

g(e)[nam] 1; Thk 153, 'genam'. CT points *nam*, and writes in the margin, 'vid./ m. u nu/'. MT writes, 'mi MS. It is mi or nu. F. I think t[he] latter.' B changed *ge m.* to *genam.* later.

gri(m)[me] 2; Thk 153, 'grim...'. CT and MT accept the fragmentary reading. B added *me* later, apparently as a conjectural restoration.[19] Here and elsewhere, Thorkelin treats B as an unreliable witness.

mec(e) [c] 6; Thk 153, 'mece'. CT accepts the whole word, but MT points second *e*. B's lonely '*c*' is presumably an error, the start of *g* from the beginning of the next line. Once again, Thorkelin ignores the testimony of B.

Fol. 177r, verse lines 2127b–2146b: (A 22, B 7):

fæð[rungu] 1 Thk 159, 'fædrunga / Þær under' (*Þær un-* a conjectural restoration linking the end of line 1 with the following *-der* r2). CT and MT both point *-unga / Þær un-*. B's *ungu* were written later on original dots and are probably spurious.[20] The final letter in B is *u*, not *a* (the top is open, at any rate).

hroðg[ar..] 2; Thk 'Hroþgare'. CT accepts the whole word, but MT points *are*. It is possible that the edge of the manuscript was already gone, and B simply restored the proper name. Thorkelin in his edition supplied a dative ending, which all editors accept, but a genitive is another possibility.[21]

Fol. 178r, verse lines 2166b–2185: (A 34, B 6):

re[n...] 2; Thk 162, 'Deaþre'. CT and MT accept, seeing nothing following *re*. The *n* in B was written in another ink, and without any corroboration from A is to that extent suspect. Thorkelin rejected it in his edition.

(b)[eal]dode 11–12, Thk 163 'beal dode'. CT and MT point *eal*, which B wrote later. If they are conjectural, B provides an excellent restoration.

gu(ð)[um] 12; Thk 163, 'gudum'. CT and MT point *dum*, but MT also crosses *d* to *ð*, leaving it uncertain whether or not the letter was still there. Assuming the reading is authentic, it is likely that B expanded the *u*-macron abbreviation to *um*.

Fol. 178v, verse lines 2186–2207a: (A 22, B 5):

[dri]hten 1; Thk 163, 'Drihten'. CT and MT both point *Dri.*

B added these letters and altered an original *n* to *h*. much later with a shakey hand and a different ink, when he no longer had access to the manuscript.

I have elsewhere used this reading as an instance of how Thorkelin sometimes makes B an edition-in-progress, rather than an objective transcription.[22] If one is trying to determine the state of the manuscript when he copied, his practice of editing while transcribing is especially dangerous, because his conjectural restorations, as in this case, are sometimes almost certainly right, except for the spelling. It is presumably for this reason that in his edition Thk frequently accords more authority to A than to B, his own transcript. As I point out in TTB, elsewhere the second scribe invariably uses the spelling *dryhten*, not *drihten*.

[o](n) 8; Thk 164, 'On'. CT accepts the whole word, but MT points *On.* A *.n*, B *on*; even without B, *on* would remain an inevitable restoration in the context. Dependence on B is for *o* (TTB, p. 145), and not *on* (TTB, p. 80).

[b](a)m 11; Thk 164, 'bam'. CT points *ba*, MT only *b*. If *b* was also gone when B copied, as his original reading *..m* suggests, he would have been able to make the later conjectural restoration with *...am* (confirmed by A) and the following *samod*.

Fol. 180r, verse lines 2252b–2274: (A 19, B 1):

byrnend[e] 19; Thk 170, no reading (following A, who commits a haplographic error). CT notes on the facing interleaf, 'opene standun fethe byrnende beorgas seceð omissa apud Thorkelin'. Thus CT independently corroborates B, who knew enough Old English to supply the *e* with or without the manuscript. MT copies CT, correcting *standun* to *standan*, *fethe* to *sethe*, and *beorgas* to *biorgas*. It is remarkable that Thorkelin gives more authority to A than to B here.

Fol. 180v, verse lines 2275-2296a: (A 11, B 8):

[bearn] 1; Thk 170, 'bearn'. CT accepts the whole word, while MT points every letter. The vestiges support B and CT, but the alliterative pattern suggests *h* for *b* (perhaps *hearm*, 'injury, harm'). Zupitza's restoration, *hord*, is not supported by the spacing or the traces, but all modern editors accept it.

[win]trum 3; Thk 170, 'wintrum'. CT accepts the whole word, but MT points *win*. Madden comments on the first three lines, 'the whole of these lines nearly obliterated', but beside Thk's 'Hic lacuna incidit, qvæ XV versibus respondet absentibus', he says, 'nulla lacuna except[in]g 3 illeg[ible] letters want[in]g'.[23] For the last two fairly legible letters, *ðy sel*, which B omitted, Madden (belying his claim that everything is exactly as it is in the manuscript) has *ðl læ.?*.

Ne byþ him wihte ð Non est illi creatura.
Hic lacuna incidit, qvæ XV versibus respondet absentibus.

[Conybeare]

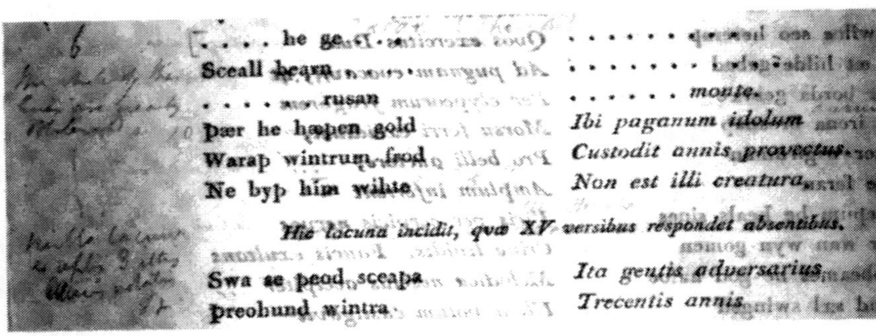
. . . . he ge. . . .
Sceall hearn . . . .
. . . . rusan . . . . . . monte.
Þær he hæþen gold Ibi paganum idolum
Waraþ wintrum frod Custodit annis provectus.
Ne byþ him wihte Non est illi creatura
Hic lacuna incidit, qvæ XV versibus respondet absentibus.
Swa se þeod sceaþa Ita gentis adversarius
Þreohund wintra Trecentis annis

[Madden]

Fol. 181r, verse lines 2296–2315b: (A 25, B 4)

[þære] 2; Thk 171, 'þære'. CT accepts the whole word, but MT points 'ære'. Although some of the left side of the bow and the descender of what B says is *þ* remains, there is not enough to confirm *þ* over, say, *wynn* or *f*. Moreover, B's feminine demonstrative *þære* is apparently a conjectural restoration, which most modern editors have accepted as authoritative. The expected form in poetry with the following *westenne* is *þam*.[24]

Fol. 182v, verse lines 2361b-2384a: (A 9, B 2):

[.on] 3, Thk 176, omits (following A rather than B). CT writes an ellipsis of three dots, MT three dots followed by *n*. No apparent reason to question B here.

Fol. 189A(197)r, verse lines 2655b–2681: (A 34, B 3):

nio(s)[nan] 13; Thk 199, 'niosnian'. CT and MT both point *snian*. B has *nan* on dots, and may be based on A. With square-topped *a*, the sequence of minims in *mosum* (A) resolves to the presumed correct form, *niosian*.

Fol. 189r, verse lines 2705a–2731a: (A 27, B 1):

beal(onið)[i] 8; Thk 202, 'Bealo niþ' (cf. A *nið*). CT accepts the whole word, but MT puts a point after it and notes, 'a letter gone after nith. F[rederic]'. Thus MT supports B where Thorkelin does not. The minim B records may be the left side of the *e* editors conjecturally restore.

Fol. 193r, verse lines 2909b-2937a: (A 24, B 1):

meowl(a)[n] 17, Thk 217, 'meowla' (following A). CT and MT point *a*, note 'ita M[S]'. The left side of *a* remains on the edge of the vellum. There is no reason to doubt B's reading.

Fol. 194r, verse lines 2964a–2990a: (A 2, B 1):

he[d..] 20, Thk 221, '............./....' (following A). CT crosses out the first line of dots, and he supplies *he* on the first two dots of the second line. MT copies CT, but also adds in the line what remained of the ascender of *d*; later, when the book was interleaved, he made a facsimile on the facing page by copying MS *bær he* and the top of *d* or *ð*, as in the manuscript now, except for the bottom of *e*. The height of the ascender indicates that B miscopied *d* for *ð*, but there is no vestige of a hair-stroke.

Fol. 195r, verse lines 3015b–3041a: (B 1):

wundu[r] 14; Thk 225, 'Wundur'. CT accepts the whole word, but MT points *s*, more than half of which still survives on the edge. The fact that A omits the *r* suggests that it was already fragmentary and that B conjecturally restored it.

Fol. 198r, verse lines 3121b-2150a: (A 13, b 7):

[syfone] 1; Thk 231, 'Syf one'. CT points *one* as does MT; Madden later (judging by the different types of underdotting) indicates that *syf* was also gone, but much of it can still be pieced together.

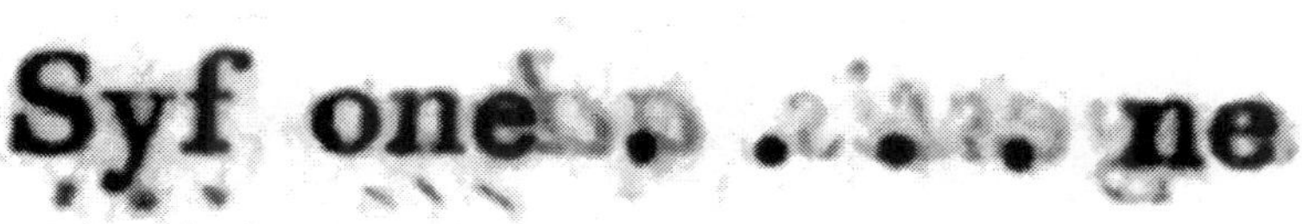

In fact, after the book was interleaved, Madden provided a detailed facsimile on the interleaf, which shows, corroborating B and the manuscript now, what appears to be the top and bottom of high *s* and the bottom of *f*. His facsimile also shows the top of *s* in *somne*, the next word.

hæfd[**e**] 19; Thk 233, 'hæfde'. A omits the *e* and B adds it later, opening the possibility that it was gone when B copied, and that it may be his conjectural restoration. CT does not underpoint the *e*, but MT does.

Fol. 198v, verse lines 3150b–3182 (A 11, B 4):

[**bi**]**ð** 17; Thk 235, 'biþ'. CT and MT point *bi*, but MT provides a facsimile on facing interleaf that shows the tops of *b* and *i* still visible in the manuscript.

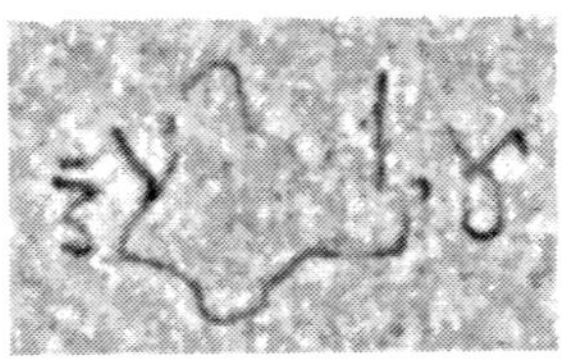

freog[**en**] 18; Thk 235, 'freo gen'. CT accepts the whole word, but MT corrects *gen* to the *g*-macron abbreviation for *ge*. The faulty expansion in B is a typical feature of his edition-in-progress.

NOTES

1. *English Studies* 55 (1974), 97–107. The colophons are on p. 236 and the facing leaf. In the colophons Conybeare makes clear that he started the collation in 1817 and continued the work in 1818 and 1819. When he finished collating, he wrote 'Tædium Trienne. C.' on the last page.
2. Ibid., p. 98.
3. Hall is preparing a comprehensive study of nineteenth-century collations,

'Early Scholars and the *Beowulf* Manuscript', which he expects to complete by the year 2000.

4. When asked if we might digitise the Conybeare collation for the Electronic *Beowulf* in 1994, Whitney Bolton promptly donated the book to the British Library to expedite our work. The Houghton Library at Harvard allowed us to begin digitising the Madden collation in 1994, and to bring the British Library camera to Harvard in 1996 to complete the work. All of these materials will be published on CD-ROM in 1998 by British Library Publications and the University of Michigan Press.
5. For the first extensive discussion using these diaries, see Robert W. and Gretchen P. Ackerman, *Sir Frederic Madden: A Biographical Sketch and Bibliography* (New York: Garland Publishing, Inc., 1979). The entire collation is listed there as 'Diary of Sir Frederic Madden, 1819–73, 43 vols., Bod. MSS. Engl. hist. c. 140–82' (p. 73).
6. English Linguistics, 1500–1800 (A Collection of Facsimile Reprints), no. 57 (Menston: Scolar Press, 1968).
7. After the poem was given its now customary name, Madden inserted *Beowulf* preceding 'a very curious poem relative to the Danes' (p. 42). His changes to his original journal in the surviving 1840 version are further discussed below.
8. Primary sources of his biography in the *Dictionary of National Biography*, vol. 4, are the Royal Society's *Catalogue of Scientific Papers* and the Geological Society's *Transactions* (p. 986). For other short accounts of Conybeare, see Hans Aarsleff, *The Study of Language in England* (Princeton: Princeton University Press, 1967), pp. 175–6, and Georgian R. Tashjian, 'Richard Rawlinson and the Anglo-Saxon Professorship at Oxford', in Georgian R. Tashjian, et al., *Richard Rawlinson: A Tercentenary Memorial* (Kalamazoo: New Issues Press, Western Michigan University, 1990), pp. 83–98.
9. John M. Kemble, ed., *The Anglo-Saxon Poems of Beowulf, The Travellers Song, and the Battle of Finnes-burh* (London: William Pickering, 1833).
10. *Grammatica Anglo-Saxonica, ex Hickesiano Thesauro Excerpta* (1711), English Linguistics, 1500-1800, no. 256 (Menston: Scolar Press, 1970). The journal shows that Madden began translating on 21 January. Hall has found this translation, too, in the Medlicot Collection. See 'William G. Medlicot (1816-1883): An American Book Collector and His Collection', *Harvard Library Bulletin*, n.s. 1.1 (1990), 13–46, at p. 39.
11. See J.R. Hall, 'Some Additional Books at Harvard Annotated by Sir Frederic Madden', *Notes & Queries* 32 (1985), 313–15.
12. Here, and the next day, when he made a detailed description of the manuscript, Madden refers to it as Vespasian A. xv, instead of Vitellius A. xv. See Kiernan, 'Madden, Thorkelin, and MS Vitellius/Vespasian A XV', *The Library*, 6th ser., 8.2 (1986), 127–32.

13. Other facsimiles, meticulous drawings rather than tracings, survive on the interleaves, as illustrated below. There may be other tracings among Madden's papers. They would be worth looking for, judging by the one that we have now.
14. See Kiernan, *Beowulf and the Beowulf Manuscript*, 2nd ed. (London and Ann Arbor: British Library Publications and University of Michigan Press, 1996), pp. 137–8, n. 47.
15. *The Thorkelin Transcripts of* Beowulf, Anglistica, 25 (Copenhagen: Rosenkilde and Bagger, 1986), p. 150, n. 46.
16. Ibid., p. 145
17. Julius Zupitza, *Beowulf: Reproduced in Facsimile from the Unique Manuscript British Museum MS. Cotton Vitellius A. xv*, Early English Text Society, o.s., 77 (London: Oxford University Press, 1882); 2nd ed. containing new reproduction of the manuscript and introduction by Norman David, Early English Text Society, o.s., 245 (London: Oxford University Press, 1959; repr. 1981).
18. Fr. Klaeber emends to *f(acne)* and credits Kemble, rather than Thorkelin, for *fær*. *Beowulf and the Fight at Finnsburg*, 3rd ed. (Boston: D.C. Heath and Company, 1950), p. 75 n.
19. The *grim sefa* of the editions, emending *me* to *se* and combining it with *fa* in the next line, should be regarded as a conjectural restoration, based solely on Kemble, who freely changed manuscript readings even in his collation.
20. See my discussion of later readings on dots in TTB, p. 138: '...when dots are written over, it may only mean that Thorkelin...later made a conjectural restoration of a reading lost before he copied the manuscript.' I did not attempt to treat this uncertain area exhaustively, as I say: 'A few examples of his use of dots will show how unreliable they can be.'
21. In TTB (pp. 78, 145) I mistakenly give *hroðg(are)* instead of *hroðg(ar)* as the possibly restored reading. It is correctly given as *Hrodgar..* in my collations, however (p. 79).
22. TTB, p. 144.
23. Here Thorkelin again accords more trust and greater authority to A than to his own transcript. Faced with their deliberate erasure, A left lines 1–3 blank, whereas B tried to transcribe them.
24. See TTB, p. 145. George Jack mistakenly changes *þam* to *þæm*, which the second scribe never uses; see *Beowulf: A Student Edition* (New York: Oxford University Press, 1994), line 2298 note. J.R. Hall discusses the reading at length in '*Beowulf* 2298a: *on þ[ā] westenne*', *Notes and Queries* 43.3 (1996), 254–7. I am grateful to Hall for carefully reading a draft of this essay and helping me avoid some mistakes and clarify some possible misunderstandings. Illustrations reproduced by permission of the British Library Board, the Danish Royal Library and the Houghton Library.

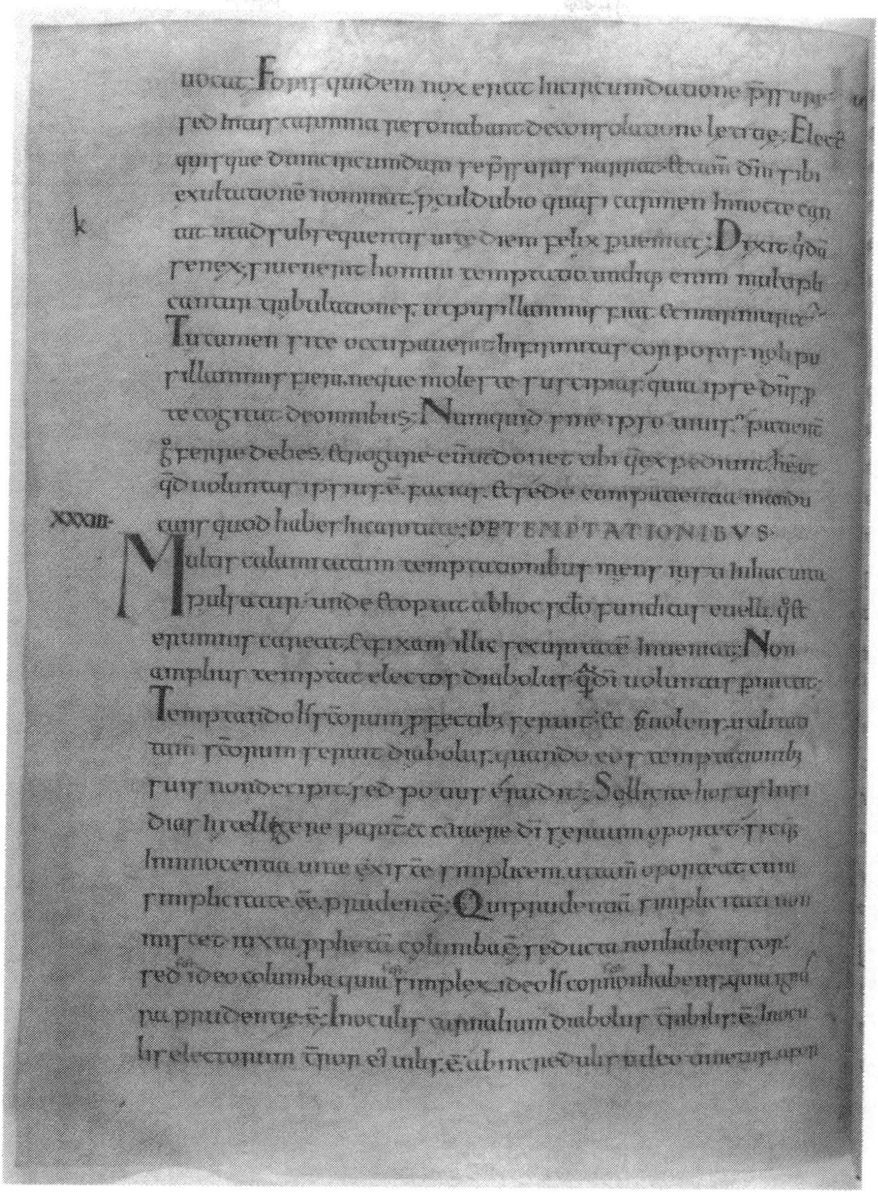

Plate 1. Cambridge, Corpus Christi College 57, fol. 124v. Portion of text from chapters XXXII–XXXIII of Smaragdus' *Diadema monachorum*. A human face is sketched within the initial 'Q' in line 23. Reproduced by permission of the Master and Fellows of Corpus Christi College, Cambridge.

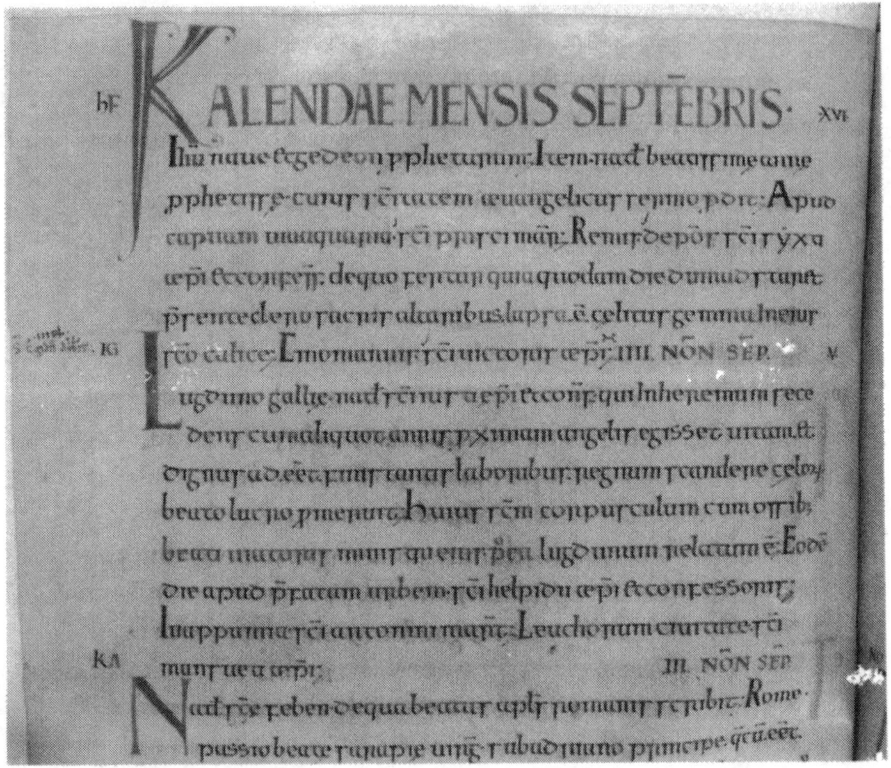

Plate 2. Cambridge, Corpus Christi College 57, fol. 76v (detail). Martyrology entries for 1–2 September. In the margins alongside the beginning of each entry are the appropriate lunar letter, Dominical letter and Golden Number. Added above the marginal reference to St Giles is a note indicating that his feast day is to include 12 responds. Reproduced by permission of the Master and Fellows of Corpus Christi College, Cambridge.

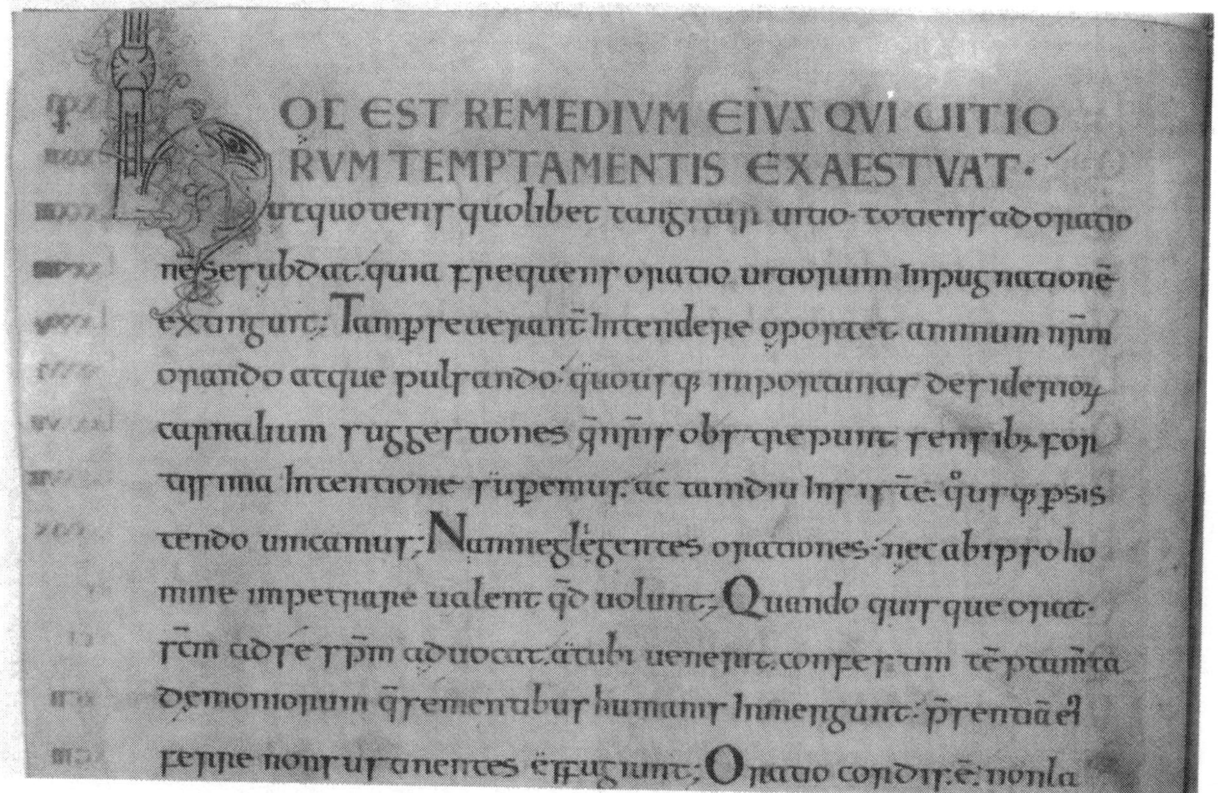

Plate 3. Cambridge, Corpus Christi College 57, fol. 97v (detail). Opening of Smaragdus' *Diadema monachorum*, with Type IIb initial. Construe marks are entered below or above several words in the text. Reproduced by permission of the Master and Fellows of Corpus Christi College, Cambridge.

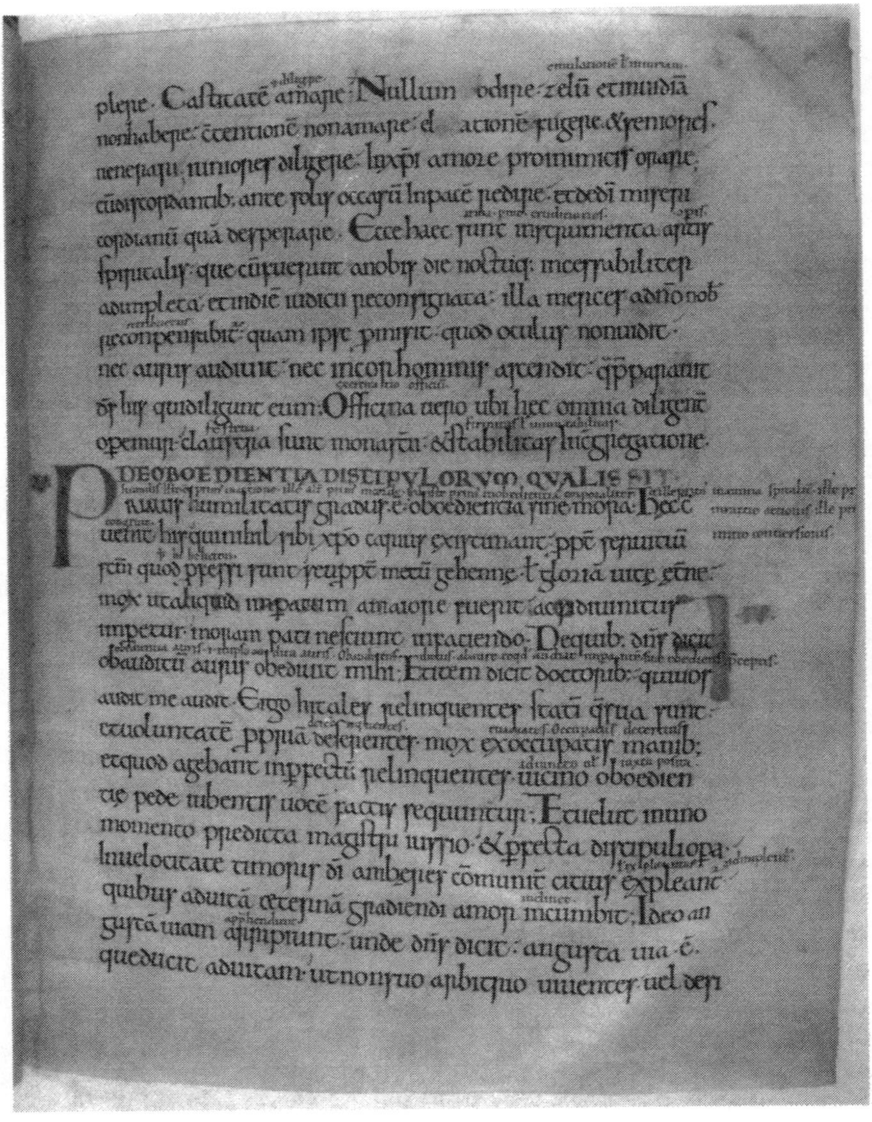

Plate 4. Cambridge, Corpus Christi College 57, fol. 8r. Replacement leaf, written in a hybrid minuscule that attempts to imitate the original Square minuscule script of the manuscript. The interlinear Latin glosses belong to the same set of glosses to the Rule of St Benedict as do those on the original leaves. Reproduced by permission of the Master and Fellows of Corpus Christi College, Cambridge.

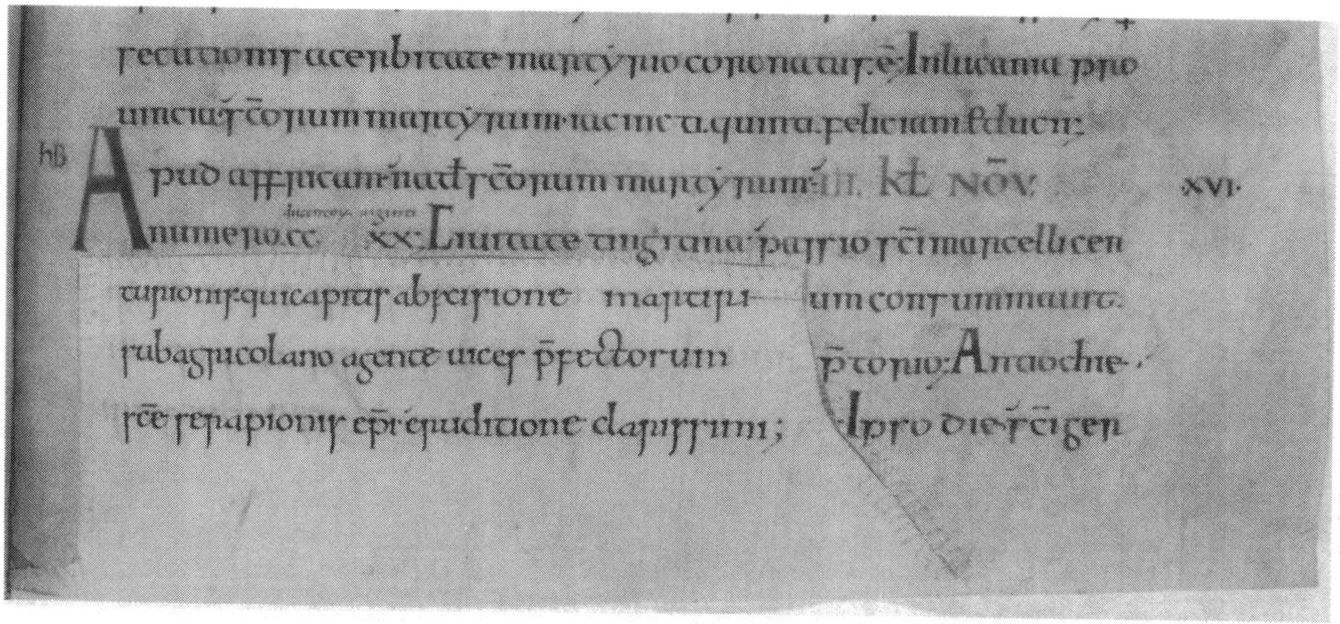

Plate 5. Cambridge, Corpus Christi College 57, fol. 85r (detail). At the bottom of the page is a replacement patch whose script imitates the original Square minuscule. Reproduced by permission of the Master and Fellows of Corpus Christi College, Cambridge.

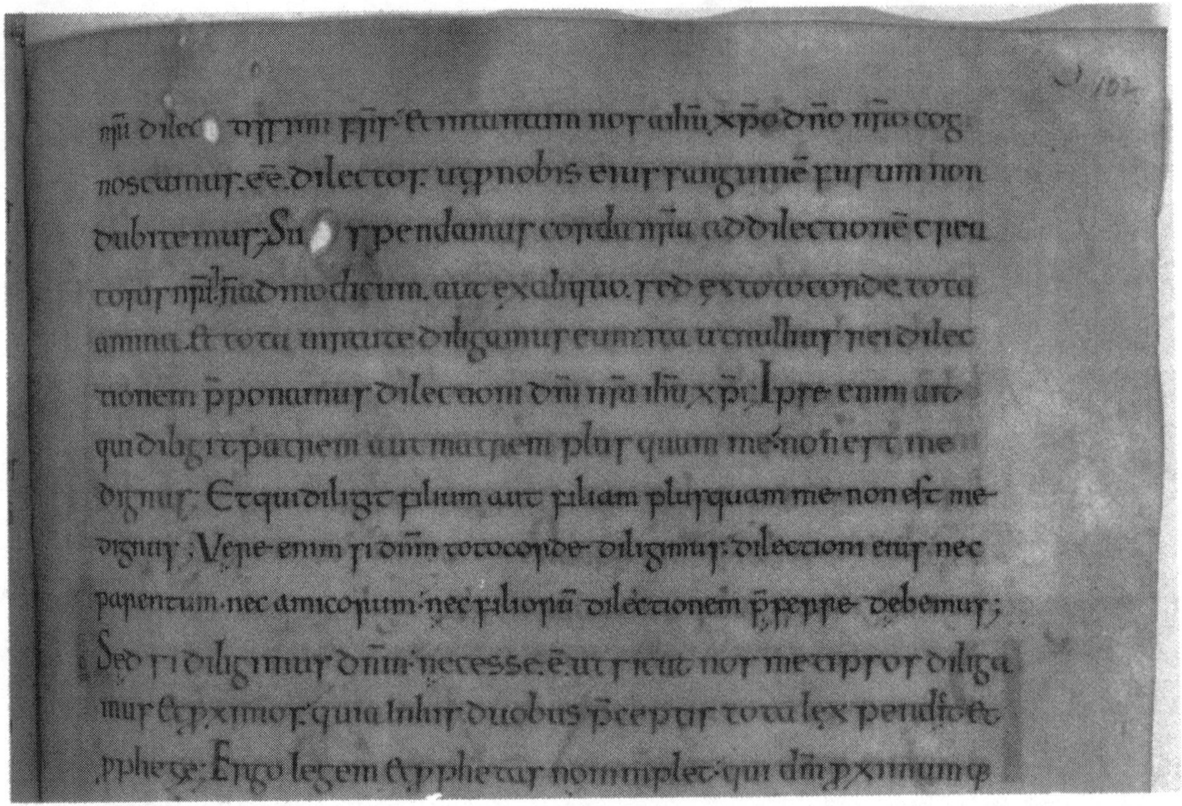

Plate 6. Cambridge, Corpus Christi College 57, fol. 102r (detail). Portion of chapter IV of Smaragdus' *Diadema monachorum*. Lines 9–10 and most of line 8 have been erased and rewritten in imitative script. Note the presence of construe marks under some words of the rewritten text. Reproduced by permission of the Master and Fellows of Corpus Christi College, Cambridge.

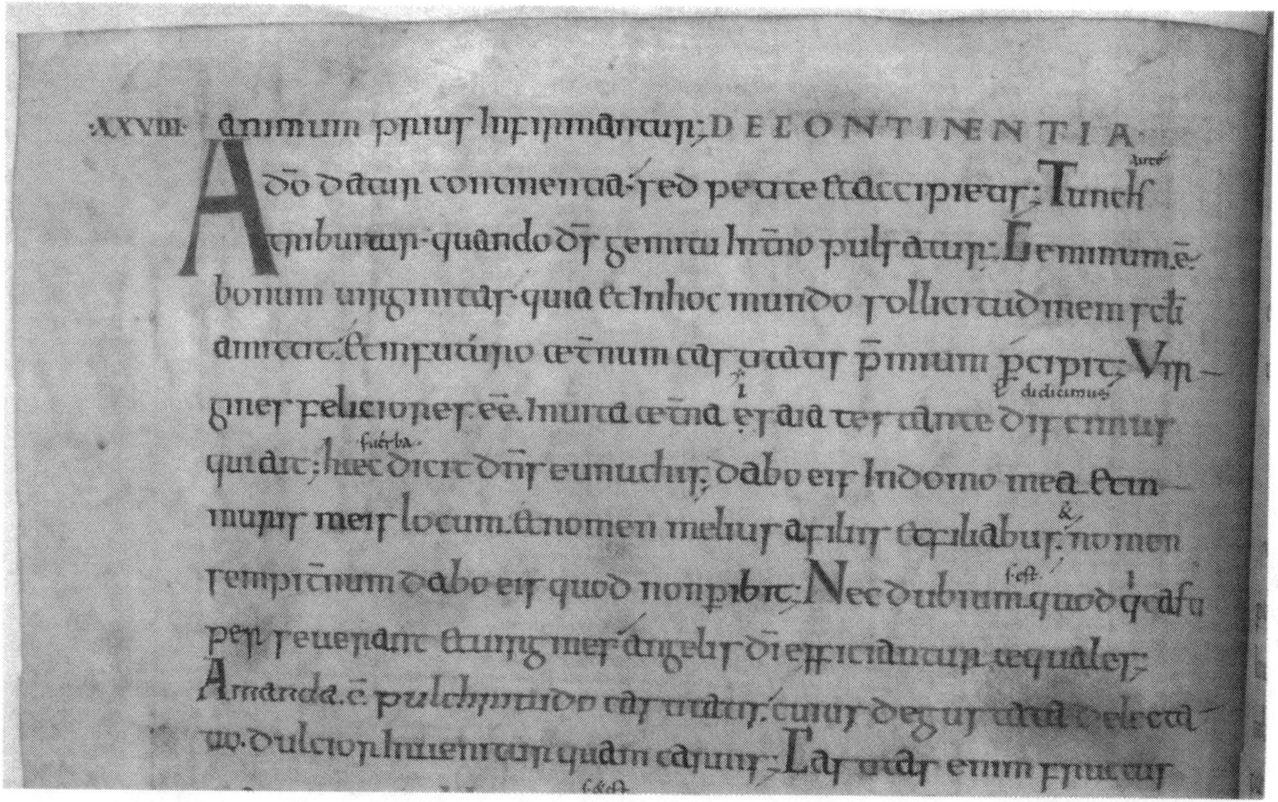

Plate 7. Cambridge, Corpus Christi College 57, fol. 121v (detail). Portion of chapter XXVIII of the *Diadema monachorum*. Several letters of the original script, notably all the occurrences of flat-topped 'a', have been adjusted by a later hand. Reproduced by permission of the Master and Fellows of Corpus Christi College, Cambridge.

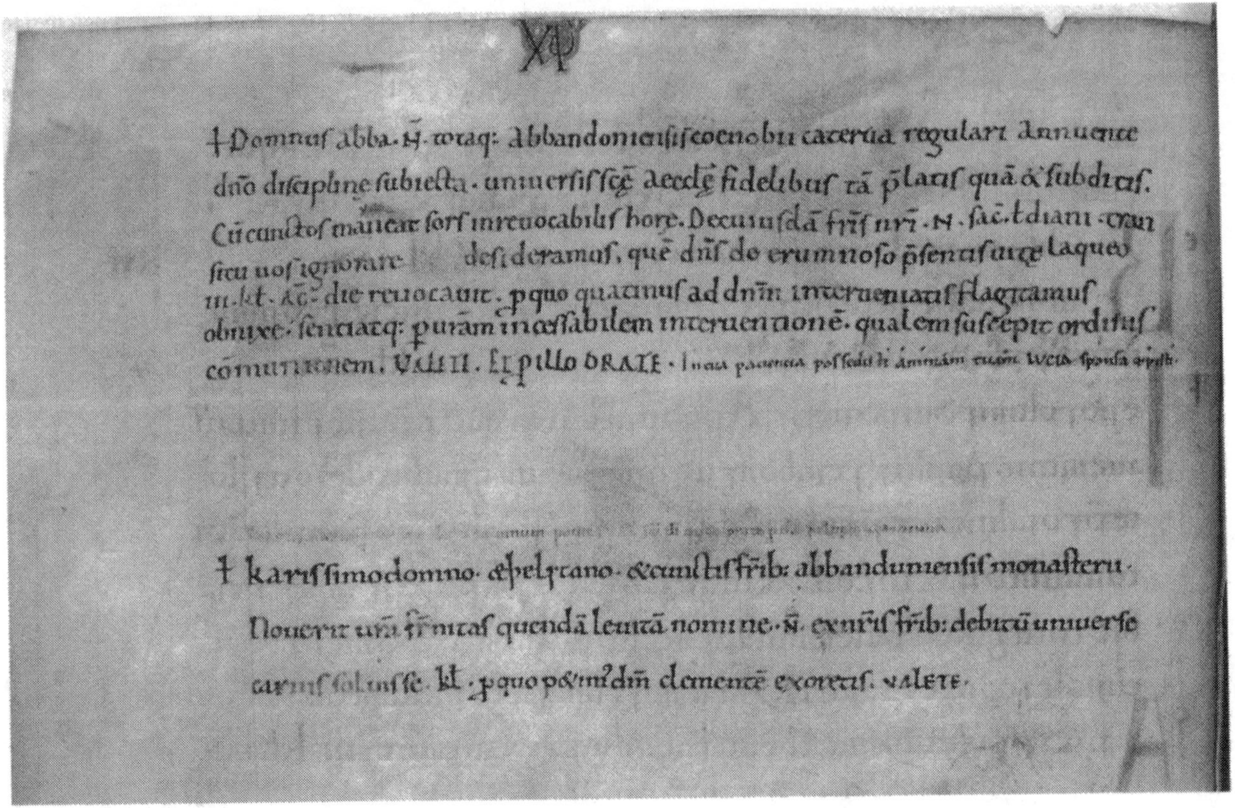

Plate 8. Cambridge, Corpus Christi College 57, fol. 94v (detail). Added formulae for announcing the death of a member of the Abingdon community, and for announcing to Abbot Æthelstan and the Abingdon brethren the death of a member of another community. Reproduced by permission of the Master and Fellows of Corpus Christi College, Cambridge.

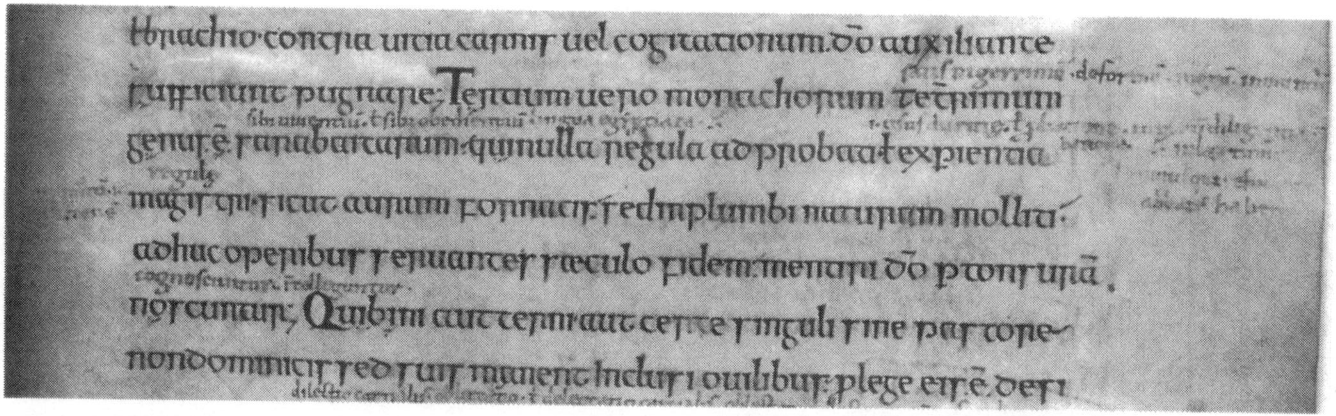

Plate 9. Cambridge, Corpus Christi College 57, fol. 5r (detail). Portion of chapter I of the Rule of St Benedict, showing interlinear and marginal glossing, and construe marks. Reproduced by permission of the Master and Fellows of Corpus Christi College, Cambridge.

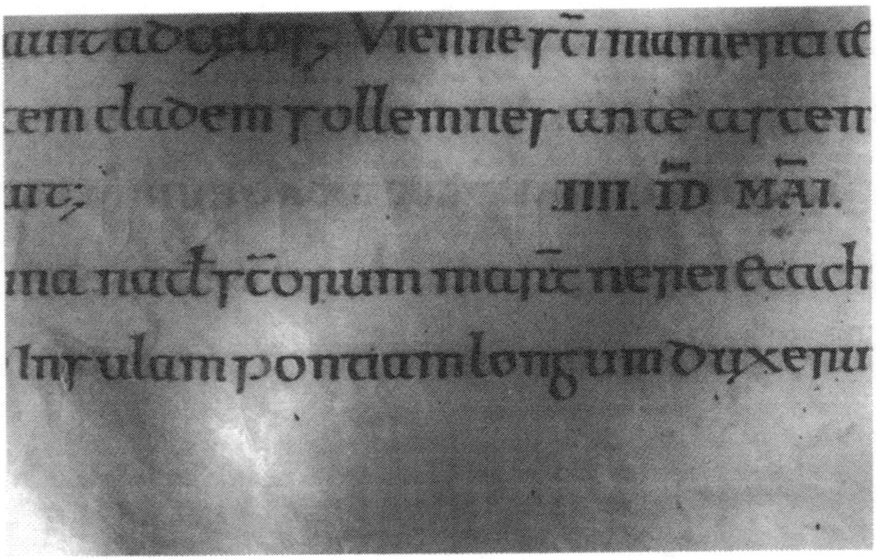

Plate 10. Cambridge, Corpus Christi College 57, fol. 58v (detail). The bottom three lines show the beginning of the Martyrology entry for 12 May. To the left of the date '.IIII. ID MAI.' is the drypoint cue 'luna XXIIII'. Reproduced by permission of the Master and Fellows of Corpus Christi College, Cambridge.

Plate 11. London, British Library, Cotton Vitellius E. xviii, fol. 16r, *Sphera Apulei*. Reproduced by permission of the British Library.

Plate 12. London, British Library, Cotton Vitellius E. xviii, fol. 16v, explanation of secret writing, with show-through of the *Sphera Apulei* from fol. 16r. Reproduced by permission of the British Library.

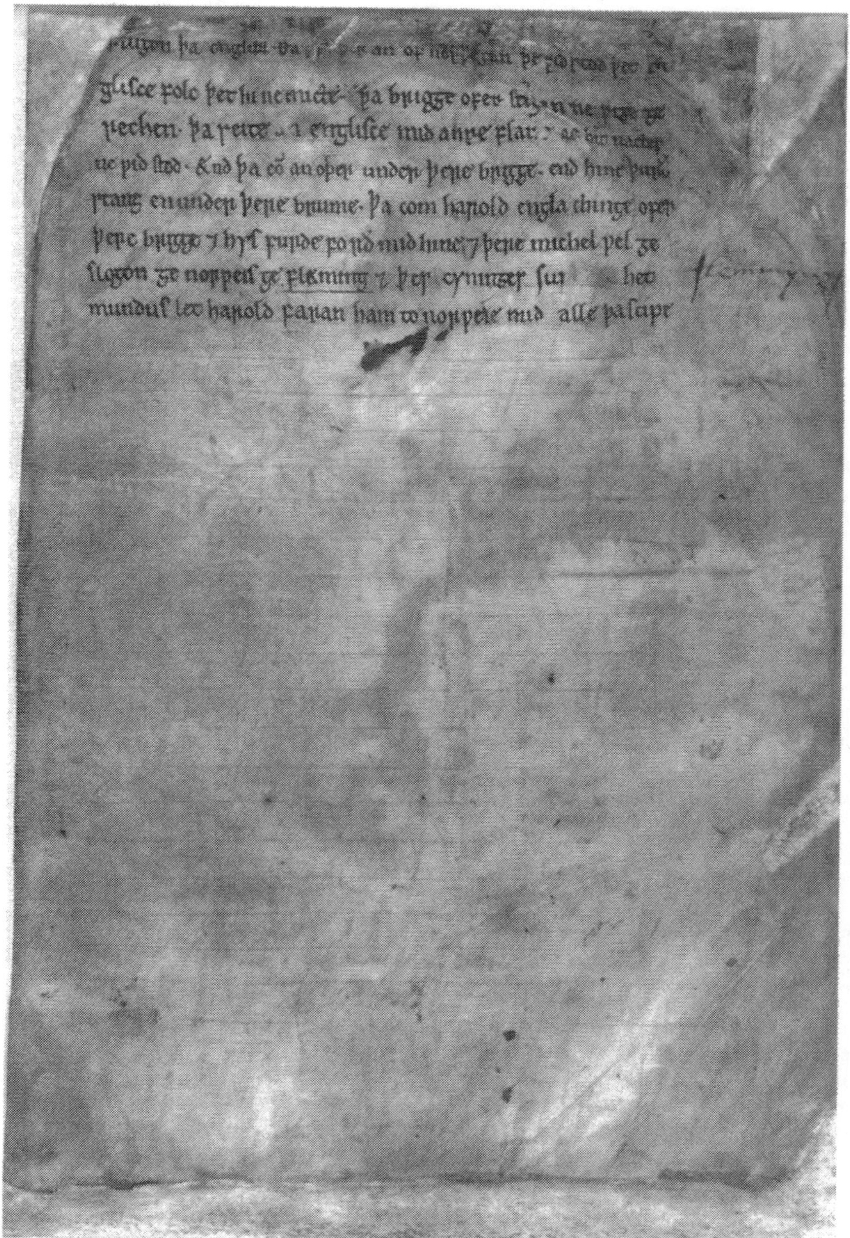

Plate 13. London, British Library, Cotton Tiberius B. i, fol. 164r. Reproduced by permission of the British Library.

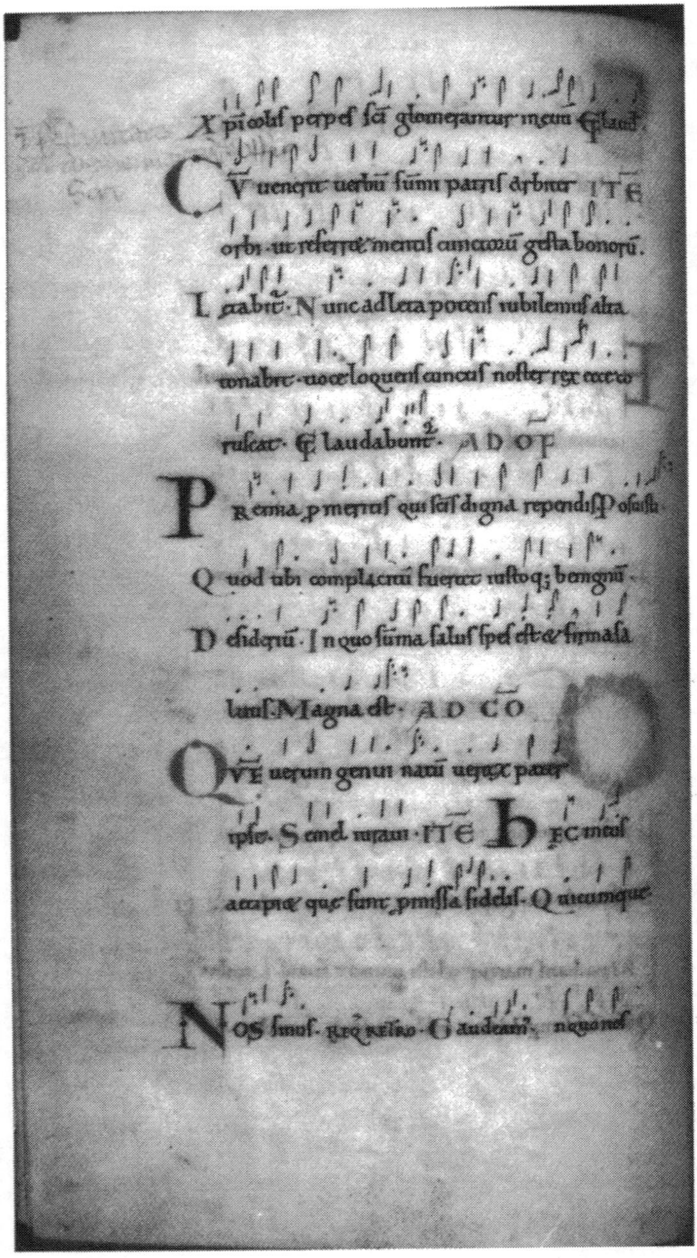

Plate 14. London, British Library, Cotton Caligula A. xiv, fol. 33v. Reproduced by permission of the British Library.

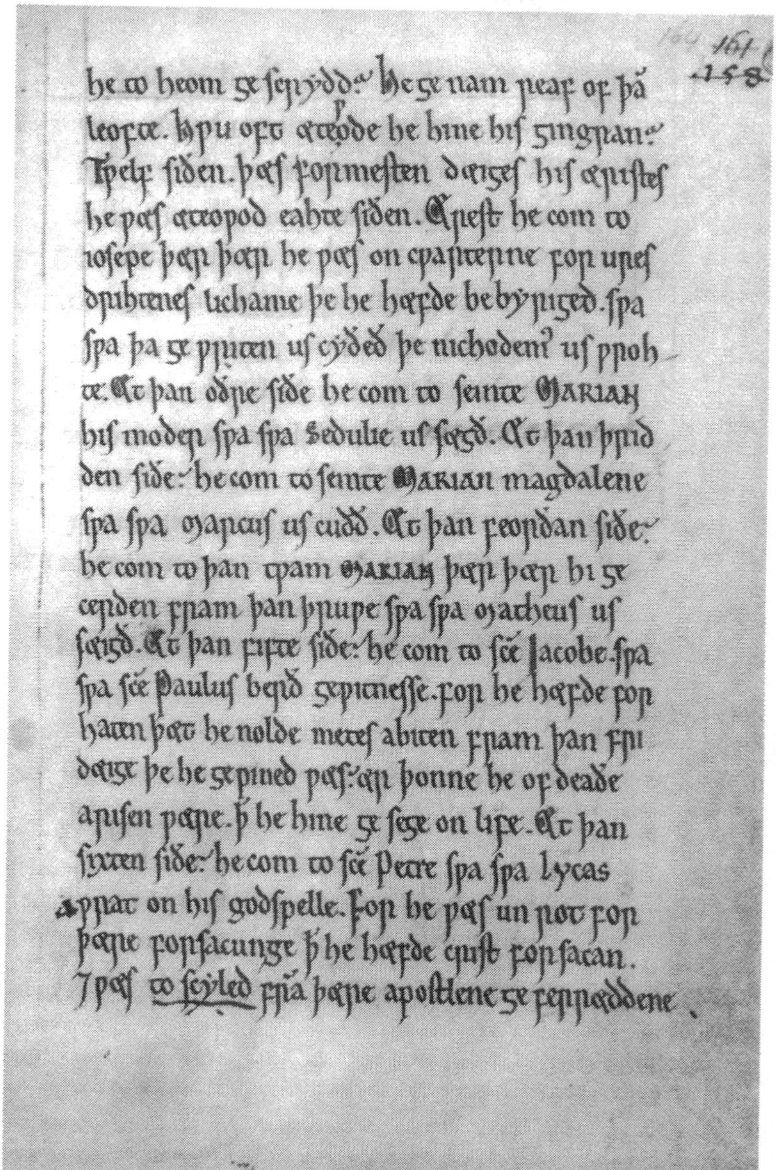

he to heom ge scrydde. He ge nam reaf of þā
leofte. Hu oft ætywode he hine his gingran.
Twelf siðen. Þæs formesten dæiges his æristes
he wæs ætywod eahte siðen. Ærest he com to
iosepe þær þær he wæs on cwarterne for ures
drihtenes lichame þe he hæfde bebyriged. swa
swa þa ge writen us cyðeð þe nichodemus wroh
te. Æt þan oðre siðe he com to seinte MARIAN
his moder swa swa Sedulie us sægð. Æt þan þrid
den siðe. he com to seinte MARIAN magdalene
swa swa Marcus us cuðð. Æt þan feorðan siðe.
he com to þan twam MARIAN þær þær hi ge
wenden fram þan þruwe swa swa Matheus us
sægd. Æt þan fifte siðe. he com to sce Iacobe. swa
swa sce Paulus bereð gewitnesse. for he hæfde for
haten þæt he nolde metes abiten fram þan fri
dæige þe he gepined wæs. ær þonne he of deade
arisen wære. þ he hine ge sege on life. Æt þan
sixten siðe. he com to sce Petre swa swa Lucas
awrat on his godspelle. For he wæs un wrot for
þere forsacunge þ he hæfde crist forsacan.
⁊ wæs to scyled fram þere apostlene ge ferrædene.

Plate 15. London, British Library, Cotton Vespasian D. xiv, fol. 164r. Part of the Old English translation of Honorius Augustodunensis' *Elucidarium*, copied by the third scribe (C), showing the use of both Caroline and Insular forms of *g* (e.g., line 2 'gingran'). Reproduced by permission of the British Library.

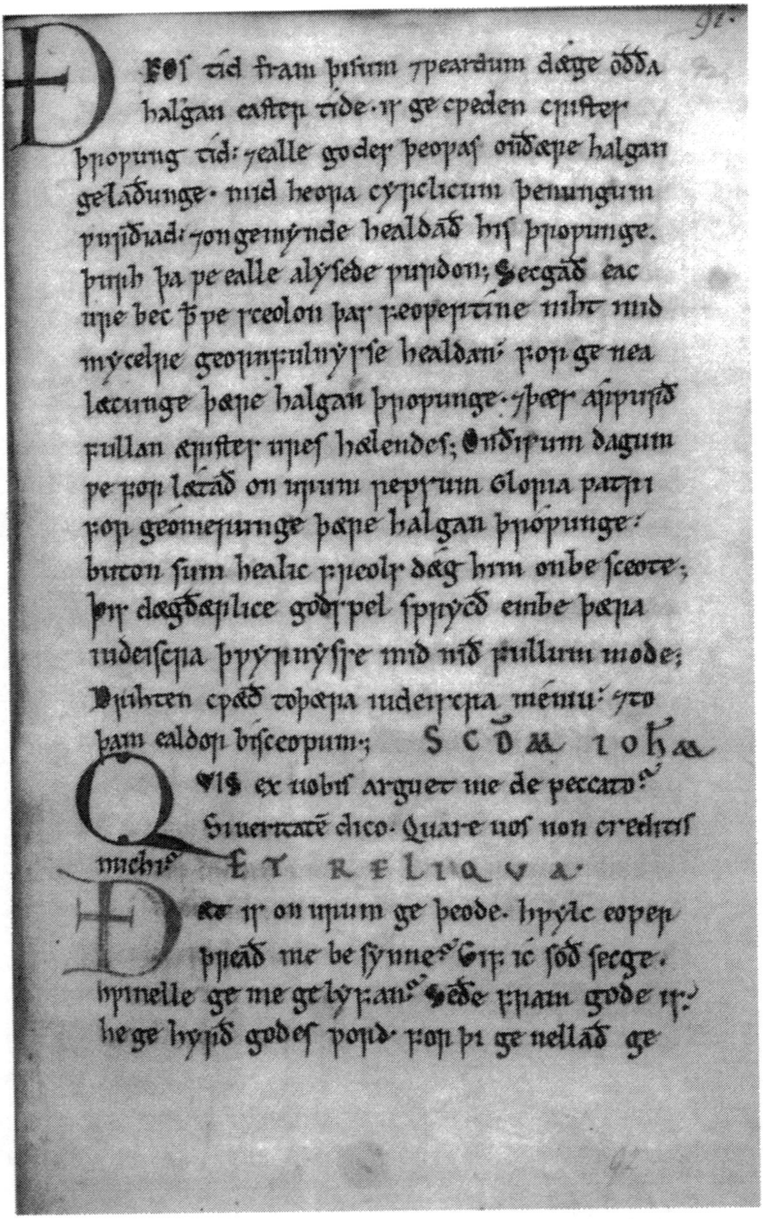

Plate 16. London, British Library, Cotton Faustina A. ix, fol. 92r. Part of Ælfric's *Dominica V in quadregesima*, showing the use of the Caroline form of *g*. Reproduced by permission of the British Library.

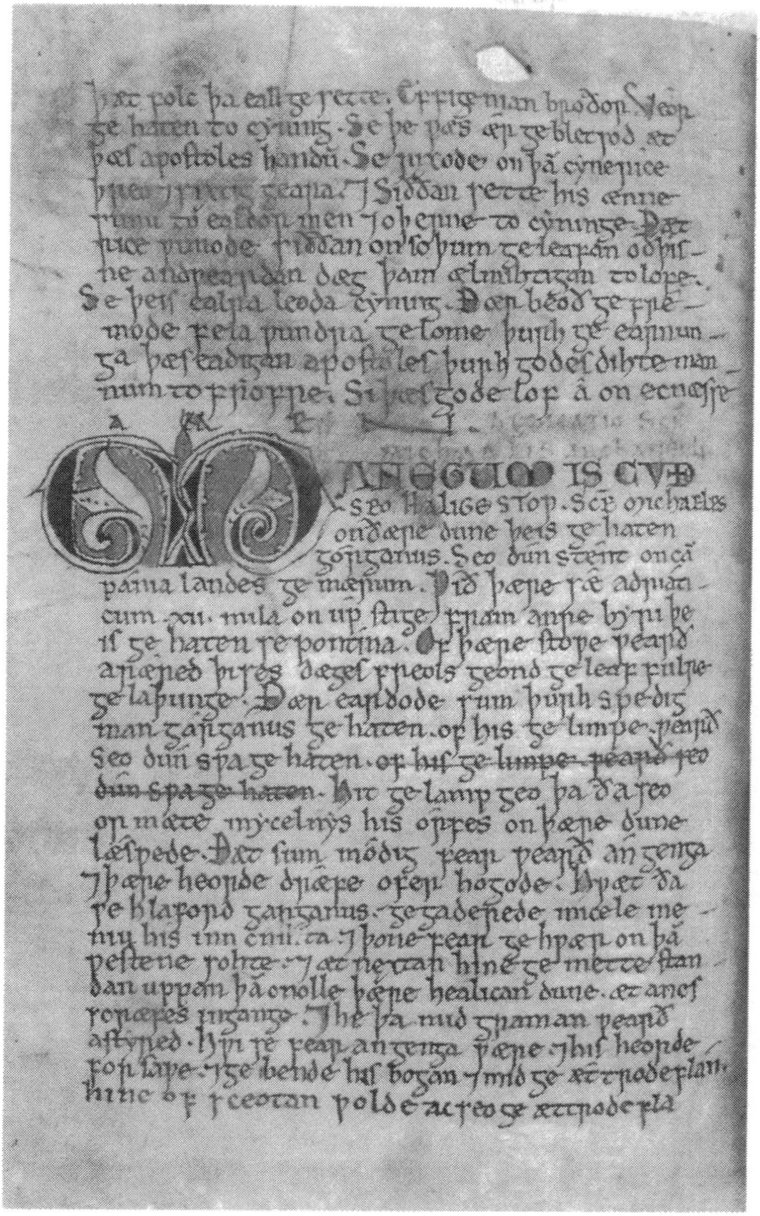

Plate 17. Cambridge, Corpus Christi College 367, Part II, fol. 27v, showing the opening of Ælfric's *Dedicatio sancti Michaelis archangeli*. Reproduced by permission of the Master and Fellows of Corpus Christi College, Cambridge.

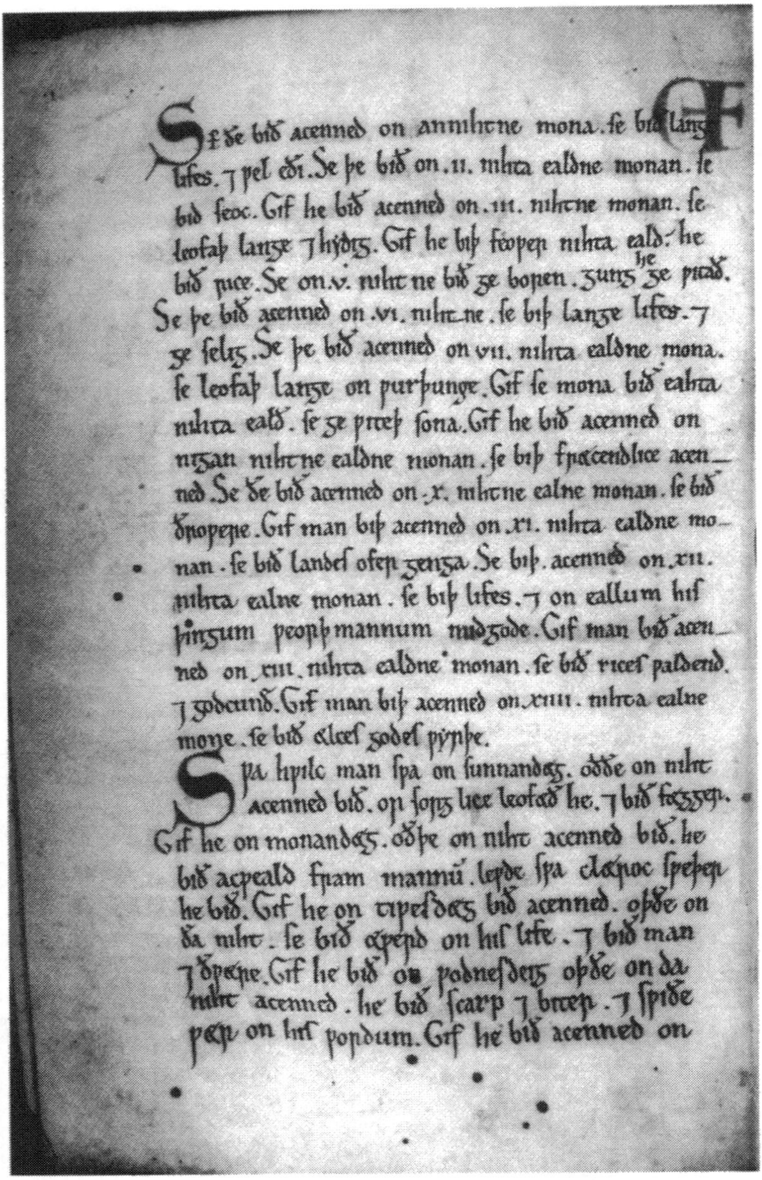

Plate 18. Oxford, Bodleian Library, Hatton 115, fol. 148v. Contains two prognostications concerning the significance of the age of the moon at childbirth and the significance of the days of the week at childbirth. Reproduced by permission of the Trustees of the Bodleian Library.

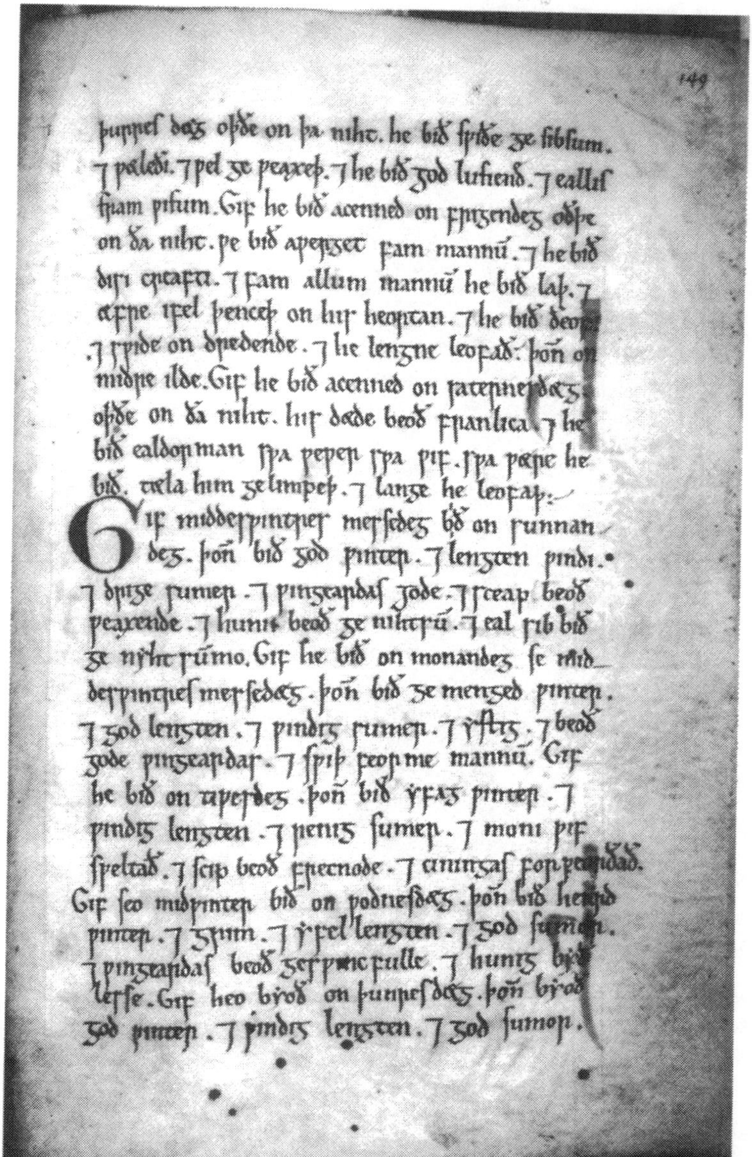

Plate 19. Oxford, Bodleian Library, Hatton 115, fol. 149v. Contains prognostications concerning the significance of the age of the days of the week at childbirth and the significance of the days of the week on which Christmas falls. Reproduced by permission of the Trustees of the Bodleian Library.

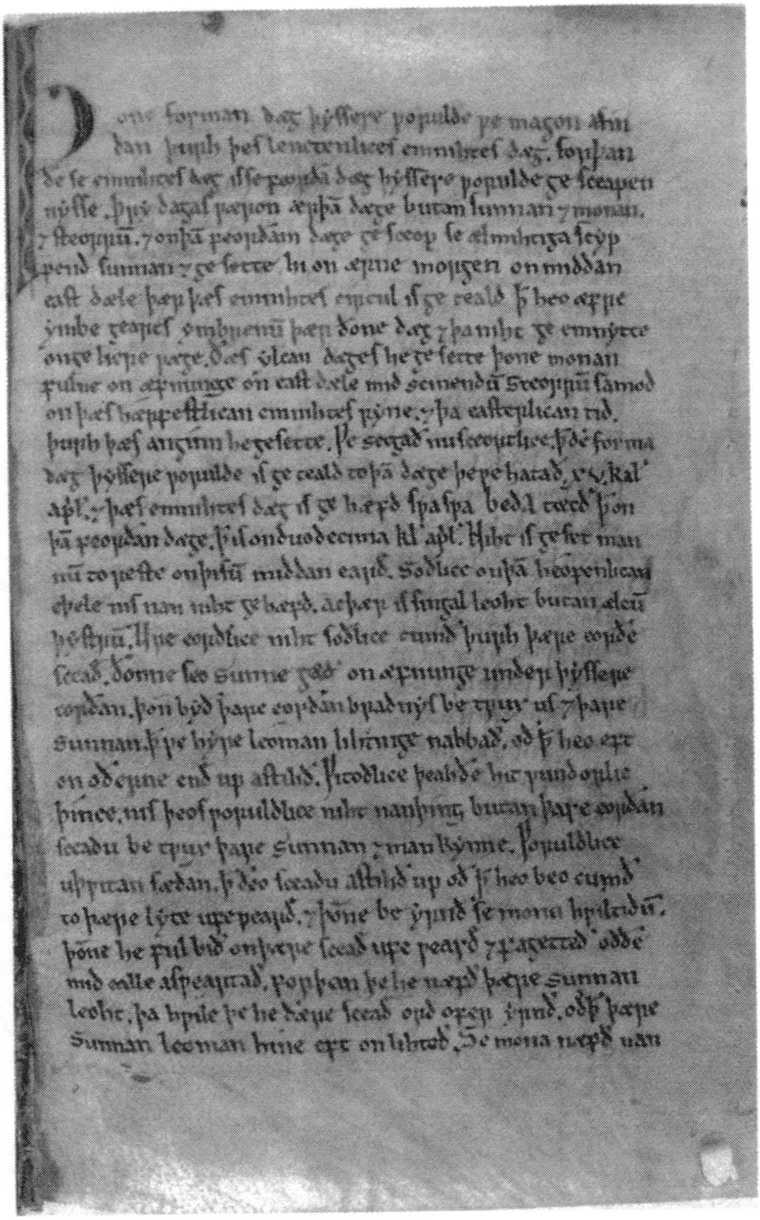

Plate 20. Cambridge, Corpus Christi College 367, Part II, fol. 1r. Shows the opening of Ælfric's translation of Bede's *De temporibus*. Reproduced by permission of the Master and Fellows of Corpus Christi College, Cambridge.

6 Reading the C-Text: The After-Lives of London, British Library, Cotton Tiberius B. i

Katherine O'Brien O'Keeffe

At the far end of the display case for select manuscripts of chronicles in the British Library, the case containing, among other manuscripts, Cotton Tiberius B. i, is a highly unusual 'history'.[1] It is, in a manner of speaking, a chronicle, whose entries are on long, thin strips of parchment a few millimetres wide. Each strip of parchment is written back and front with the sparest of entries from unconnected years. The strips of text are gathered at one end, but unlike folio leaves of a conventional book gathered at a spine, these leaves are gathered at a handle, creating not a book so much as a whip. Its shaft of wood is spindled and painted, and the strips themselves, written in green and red inks, are painted at the ends in a metallic colour now much faded. This ornamented object is at once *chronicon* and *flagellum*, whose 'pages' of history are the sinuous tongues of a lash. What was its use? One could hardly flog a satisfactory penitence with such a medium. If one could, it would not be for long — the mutual writing of object on body, body on object (where any blood from a well-inscribed body would soon obscure the penitential text) would be self-cancelling. That it is an object for meditation is more likely.

This text-scourge first and foremost was meant to be read, though it must be admitted that any reading is complicated by the construction of the text. Since the strips were written on both sides, technically their notations could have been read with equal meaning with the flagellum right side up or upside down. But in the complexity of that act of reading, we are forced to acknowledge the crucial significance of the textual medium. If the text-scourge is a history, its narrative can only be 'read' as the punishment of time visited on living bodies, a history materialised in the shape of its own significance. To 'read' the text is to acknowledge a specific action of history upon one. If the text-scourge is, conversely, a flagellum, it is one whose promise of punishment is inexorably real, if metonymic, as time inevitably inscribes the bodies of those handling the whip. This reading of the flagellum, in so far as it is a reading less of text than of object, is easily accommodated by its location in the case. The flagellum was, perhaps always, a curiosity, a collectible, because the text of the chronicle it embodies was always secondary to the body of the object itself. What is 'read' in the flagellum is its physique.

This meditation on function prompted by the late-medieval curiosity, Additional 16280, focuses attention usefully on a central concern of this essay, the after-lives of one of its companions in the case, Tiberius B. i. This essay concerns itself primarily with the manuscript at three moments in time: in the monastic library in the twelfth century, perhaps at Abingdon; in the sixteenth century on the desk first of Robert Talbot and then of John Leland; and, finally, in its current residence in a display case of the British Library. My focus is on questions of use and what the accretive traces of its users may tell us of the life of the manuscript before and in the age of mechanical reproduction.

PRESENT STATE AND POSSIBLE BEGINNINGS

British Library, Cotton Tiberius B. i contains four Old English texts: the *Orosius*,[2] *Menologium*,[3] *Maxims II*[4] and the C-text of the Anglo-Saxon Chronicle.[5] The collation of fols 3–165 of the manuscript is as follows: 1–11^{8}, 12^{8} + one leaf after 8, 13^{10} + one leaf after 9, 14^{1} (a singleton now attached to the following quire), 15–20^{8}, 21^{4}, 22^{2}. The final bifolium of the manuscript, containing just eight lines of text supplied to the Chronicle, was added in the later twelfth century and testifies to the use of the manuscript a century after the C-text was copied. That the manuscript is a composite is indicated by the dating of its two parts: the text of the *Orosius* (Quires 1–14) is dated by N.R. Ker to xi^{1}; he dates Quires 15–21 to xi med.[6] Of immediate interest is the evidence for the joining of the two parts of the manuscript. Since it is a Cotton manuscript, it would be easy to suppose that the marriage of the two parts was made by Cotton himself, given his weakness for synthetic volumes.[7] But the antiquarian use of the manuscript in the sixteenth century makes it clear that the manuscript was already a unit when Cotton acquired it.[8]

Patrick Conner has recently argued that the first three texts in Tiberius B. i can be read as 'supplements to the collected annals of English history', and he regards *Orosius* as having been added later to the Chronicle material.[9] There are, I believe, some codicological indications that the order of assembly is precisely the reverse, that the Chronicle material was not just combined with the already completed *Orosius*, but was designed to be added to it. At present the outer measurements of the volume are *c.* 195 mm. wide by 280 mm. high. Some trimming by the binders has clearly been done, since at several points Talbot's annotations have been cropped away.[10] The *Orosius* shows two sets of measurements, indicating that its layout was reconceived during copying. The first 34 folios are ruled for 25 lines, 152 mm. wide (from the outer bounding lines) by 215 mm. high. Fol. 35r and following are ruled for 27 lines, and at this point the measurements of the writing grid change to 145 mm. wide (from the outer bounding lines) by 220 mm. high.[11] As the collation above indicates, *Orosius* was regularly quired for eight leaves until Quire 12, which adds a singleton after 8, and Quire 13, a quire of 10 with an added singleton after 9. The fourteenth and final quire of the *Orosius* is a singleton (fol. 111), and as it is in the same, fourth hand whose stint started at fol. 45r|4, it is unlikely to be a supply leaf. The text of the *Orosius* is complete on fol. 111v|21, ending with Book 6, chapter 38 (misnumbered 36). The rest of the page is blank. The singleton, then (even if it had once been a bifolium designed as a wrapper and then cut when the Chronicle texts were added), suggests that the copyist of the *Orosius* did not envision adding other texts to his book.[12]

While the average height of the writing area for the second grid of the *Orosius* is 220 mm., the height of the grid on fol. 111 is 213 mm. The following Quire 15 contains the Chronicle texts, *Menologium* and *Maxims*, as well as the beginning of the C-text. While the writing grid of the entire quire is ruled consistently to be 145/146 mm. wide, the outer two sheets of the quire are ruled for a length of 212 or 213 mm., although its inner two sheets are ruled for 218 or 220 mm. That is, the outer sheets of Quire 15 match precisely the ruling grid for the last folio of the *Orosius*, and the inner sheets match the measurements for the ruling grid of *Orosius* Quires 5–13. If one were to argue that Quire 15 had been ruled and left blank by the last scribe of the *Orosius*, it would be hard to explain the singleton, now Quire 14, unless it had originally been part of the present Quire 15 (= a hypothetical 15^{10}), ruled in the early eleventh century and left blank. Such a hypothesis would also have to explain why the inner eight leaves of the hypothetical Quire 15 were arranged hair facing hair and flesh facing flesh (as the rest of the Chronicle texts), when the preceding five quires of the *Orosius* were arranged in the Insular manner. Also to be explained would be the anomalous resulting quire HHFHFHFHFF.[13]

If, on the other hand, the quire was added by scribe 1 of the Chronicle texts, then it appears as if the grid of the later material was designed to complement the already existing *Orosius* to which the Chronicle matter was to be added.[14] With the exception of Quire 17, whose writing grid measures 149 mm. by 220 mm., and the supply Quire 22, whose ruling is anomalous, the measurements of the writing grid for the annal entries of the C-text are 145 mm. by 220 mm., a grid less than ideal for the layout of the Chronicle.[15] The layout of the *Orosius* provided wide outer margins but narrower margins at the binding, and it could pose problems even for the *Orosius*, as the heavy compression of numbers in the chapter headings for Book 6 (on fols 96r and 97r) attest.[16] This layout, with its ruled column for capitals (7–8 mm. wide at each side of the writing grid) suited the *Menologium* and *Maxims*, their texts written straightforwardly in long lines, but was only superficially suited to the common layout of the Chronicle, which had to accommodate annal years preceding each 'fruitful' entry. In marked contrast is the layout for the 'common stock' of the Chronicle in the A-text, where the columns for annal number, initial capital and text are carefully marked with vertical bounding lines and the horizontal rulings are extended across into the annal number column.[17] Had the C-text followed the practice of the closely-related B-text, it would have used its wide outer margins for the annal numbers, shifting the location of the annal numbers from left to right of the first line of an entry, depending on whether the entry was on the verso or the recto.[18] That it does not normally adopt this expedient, even when the narrower recto margins necessitated severe compression of longer annal numbers, suggests a perceived pressure to follow a visually consistent layout. When that uniformity gives way in the entries after the year 1000, the degree of inconsistency may be an index of changing circumstances at the scriptorium after mid-century.

Without this understanding of the physical state of the manuscript it would be easy to miss the connection between the earlier text of *Orosius* and the *Menologium*, *Maxims* and Chronicle. As I read the physique of the book, the three texts forming the Chronicle matter were selected to be added to the *Orosius* to create a book of histories — one containing world history (Tiberius B. i alone has the heading 'Her onginneð seo boc þe man Orosius nemneð' for the Old English translation), chronology and English history.[19] Such a goal accounts for the effort to make a fit between the end of *Orosius* and the beginning of the Chronicle texts and the formatting of the Chronicle text in the frame of the earlier work. This reading of the body of the C-text and of the *Orosius*, by focusing on the book as a product of a process of accretion, views the presence of the C-text in what is now known as Cotton Tiberius B. i as an outcome of a reading of the *Orosius*, a reading which prompted a particular response and use.[20] But the Chronicle itself, apart from the process of being written, is subject, in turn, to reading and use which affect the body of the text.

The manuscript has suffered from wetting (especially towards the back of the manuscript), presumably one of the consequences of the 1731 fire at Ashburnam House. Manuscripts rescued from the fire were dried under less than ideal circumstances; not only are a number of folios stained from the top of the page, several folios at the end show some shrinkage, and the penultimate quire of four was reassembled incorrectly.[21] Tiberius B. i saw a bit of good luck in 1865, however. Preservation records indicate that the manuscript was repaired and rebound in March 1839 and again in 1865.[22] It thus narrowly escaped the disastrous fire in the bindery on 10 July 1865, in which those manuscripts out for binding and not secured in the shop's iron safe were incinerated,[23] among them the doubly unfortunate Tiberius B. xi.[24] The results of the nineteenth- and twentieth-century conservation efforts for Tiberius B. i documented in the British Library records and visible on the body of the manuscript itself, are readily obvious. Not immediately obvious as such, however, is another arguable effort at conservation, undertaken in the later twelfth century. This effort speaks to the use of the manuscript nearly a century after it was first assembled.

THE SENSE OF AN ENDING

In its present binding, Quire 22 (= fols 164–165, a bifolium) is sewn onto its own paper binding strip, as is every other quire in the book. Although the inner rulings of the Chronicle text to the end (fol. 162v) are 130 mm. wide, the last bifolium is ruled for 126 mm. (see Plate 13), though maintaining the wide outer margin in the eleventh-century text. The bifolium was ruled at one go through the hair side, fols 164v–165r, and its measurement and preparation indicate that this bifolium was not 'original' to the Chronicle manuscript. On fol. 164r a twelfth-century hand continues the record of the events of 1066 broken off in the middle of the account of the battle of Stamford Bridge (the end of the now out-of-order fol. 162v). I offer below a diplomatic transcription of the continuation:[25]

> flugon[1] þa englisa[2] Đa[3] wes[4] þer an of norwegan þe wiðstod[5] þet en
> glisce[6] folc þet hi ne micte[7] þa brigge ofer stigan[8] ne sige ge
> rechen. þa[9] seite an[10] englisce mid anre flan(e)[11] ac hit nactes
> ne widstod. ænd[12] þa cō an oþer under þere brigge. end hine þur`u´[13]
> stang en under þere brunie. Þa[14] com harold engla chinge ofer
> þere brigge 7 hys furde forð mid hine 7 þere michel wel ge
> slogon ge norweis ge flæming 7 þes cyninges [15]su ..... het
> mundus[15] let harold faran ham to norweie mid alle þa scipe

Textual notes:

1. The top stroke of 'f' and top of 'l' are lost in a fold at the corner of the page. As with the earlier pages, fol. 164r has suffered from wetting and the top line shows shrinkage.
2. The last two letters are difficult to decipher. Especially problematic is the tall 's', since its shoulder attaches below the top of the ascender, making it resemble the beginning of an 'r', though written above the line of writing. Compare 'r' in 'oþer' (l. 4). Plummer and Onions print 'Englisca' without comment. Dickens notes the error.[26]
3. The crossbar of the capital 'ð' crosses both ascender and bow-stroke.
4. A slight tear in the vellum between wyn and 'e' is now covered over with repair tape. There is no evidence that there was an 'æ' rather than 'e'. Compare 'ænd' (l. 4) and 'flæming' (l. 7).

5. The cross stroke on 'ð' is now barely visible. Nowell (Additional 43704, fol. 107v) transcribes 'wiðstod'. Dickins and Conner read 'widstod'.
6. The head of the first 'e' is faded. The two-chambered 'g' is made 'Insular' by the drawing of a flat line to remake the head. Compare the following 'brigge' (l. 2) where the first 'g' is two-chambered.
7. Following 'micte' is a mark, probably a smeared point. After this a stroke the width of a minim has been erased. There are now four light brown points above, connecting 'micte' and 'þa'.
8. The 'a' is now partially obscured in a crease in the vellum. The bottom left of its bow and the top of its back are visible.
9. Plummer prints 'Ða'.
10. The bottom of the bow of 'a' is visible and the lower part of its back. The second stroke of 'n' is readable. Traces of the outline of each letter are just visible.
11. The top of the tongue, top of the head stroke, and a bit of the bottom of 'e' are visible. The second stroke of 'n' is partially flaked or rubbed off. Onions prints 'flame' in error.
12. With the 'æ' shaped like an ampersand. Compare 'flæming'.
13. A straight-shouldered 'u' has been added above the line as a correction. The following attempt at a letter form is unclear, perhaps the first head stroke of a 'g' subsequently abandoned. Compare the stroke curved to the right at the baseline beginning the body of flat-topped 'g' in 'brigge' (l. 6). Dickins reads 'þurð'.
14. With a capital 'þ'.
15...15. su..... A second minim has been erased and remains of a third minim are visible. Ultraviolet examination shows two erased minims after the present 'su‹n›' but not three. After this there was an 'e', preceding 'het' and before that an ascender, probably for 'þ'. Plummer prints 'sunu Hetmundus' noting part erasure of 'sunu'.[27] Conner likewise prints 'sunu Hetmundus'.

In his continuation of the C-text's entry for 1066, the scribe attempts the characteristic Insular forms throughout, though they are not his metier: his flat-topped 'g' is actually a 't' with a reversed tail. Despite his efforts, two-chambered 'g' steps in (see l. 2), and the first of these is corrected by adding a clumsy, flat head. The shape of 'a' is the standard twelfth-century development of Caroline 'a'.[28] The letter 'f' is a compromise of twelfth-century and Insular elements, with a bit of a descender and a cross-bar slightly above the line of writing. The letter 'r' too reflects compromise. The standard twelfth-century 'r' (see 'ofer' l. 2) is given a longer tail and an extended shoulder which is sharply broken. The angled back of 'd' is successfully Insular. The scribe uses both tall and low 's', and manages to keep wyn and thorn distinct. The ungainly shape of 'æ' (only used twice) is substantially that of an ampersand. The Insular sign for 'and' is used throughout. The 'y' is symmetrical and has a tapered ascender. Ascenders on 'þ', 'h', 'l' and 'b' are ticked to the right. The shoulder of 'h' is turned in slightly to the left.

The orthography of fol. 164r shows typical early Middle English spellings with relatively conservative treatment of inflectional endings.[29] The following breakdown illustrates the distinctive features of the supplement.

Vowels in accented syllables:

1. a or o before nasals
   The scribe generally prefers *a* before nasals: *flan(e)*, *stang*, *ham* but *com*.
2. OE æ, e, ea
   The scribe uses *æ* and *e* interchangeably: *wes*, *þer*, *þet*, *ænd*, *end*, *flæming*, *gerechen*, *wel* (for OE *wæl*). He writes *seite* for OE *sceat* (see MED *s.v. shēten*).
3. OE i/y
   Both *i* and *y* appear: *hi*, *hit*, *hys*, *hine*, *brigge* (but fol. 162v = *brycge*), *chinge*, *cyninges*. (Fol. 162v shows several spellings: *cyng*, *cynning*, *cyningc*, *cyning*; the word is spelled *cingc*, *cing* on fol. 162r.)
4. *u* for OE *y* appears in *brunie*, *furde* (cf. fol. 162v *fyrde*). On *brunie* see Onions, p. 506.

Consonants:

1. OE c, ċ
   The scribe represented OE *ċ* as *ch*: *michel*, *gerechen* (= OE *miċel*, *geræċan*), but mistakenly adds 'h' to the stop 'c' (*chinge* [with redundant 'e'] but elsewhere *cyninges*).[30]
2. OE g, ġ
   Where elsewhere in early Middle English scribes may use Caroline and Insular 'g' to distinguish voiced stop and voiced spirant, the three instances of Caroline 'g' in the supplement (the second corrected to flat-topped 'g') appear accidental. (Compare *flugon* [Insular 'g'], *englisa* [Caroline 'g'], *englisce* [l. 2, Caroline 'g' corrected to Insular], *brigge* [one of each].)
   gg for cg: *brigge*.
   i/g: OE *Norwegan* (nom. *Norwege*): *Norwegan* (dat. pl.), *norweis* (?for acc. pl.), *norweie* (?for dat. sg.).
3. OE h
   In OE where 'h' represents a velar spirant, the scribe substitutes 'c': *micte*, *nactes*.
4. OE sc

Englisce (twice), *scipe*, but also: *englisa* (for OE *englisce*), *seite* (for OE *sceat*).[31]

Accidence:

A substantial number of OE inflectional endings are preserved:

nouns: *folc*, *brigge* (acc. sg. fem.), *flane* (dat. sg. fem.), *furde*, *cyninges*, *engla*

adjectives: *anre*, *englisce* (nom. sg. nt.)

demonstratives: *þa* (acc. sg. fem.), *þere* (dat. sg. fem.)

verbs: *flugon* (pret. 3 pl. indic.), *geslogon* (pret. 3 pl. indic.), *oferstigan* (inf.), *faran* (inf.), but *gerechen* (inf.).

errors: with scribal 'e': *englisce* (nom. sg. masc. for OE *englisc*), *þere* (for OE *þær*), *chinge* (for OE *cyning*), *seite* (for OE *sceat*). *Englisa* (for OE *englisce*) may reflect the spelling of (and the scribe's misunderstanding of) *englisca* (gen. pl.) immediately preceding on the last line of fol. 162v.

Additionally, at two points the scribe shows *mid* governing the accusative — 'mid hine' (l. 6) and 'mid alle þa scipe' (l. 8) — rather than the dative ('mid anre flane' [l. 3]).[32] The mixture of forms discussed above suggests but cannot prove that the scribe was copying from late Old English rather than adding something new in his own twelfth-century dialect. The accidence of the passage suggests as well that he was relatively careful about preserving the inflectional endings of Old English; note, for example, *flugon*, *norwegan*, *oferstigan*, *geslogon*, *faran*. Further investigation of the inclusion of the supplement will require examination of evidence for the story in the twelfth century.

To understand the context of the supplement, in terms of both the narrative which it continues and the circumstances of its inclusion in Tiberius B. i, it would be useful to take up the account of the Battle of Stamford Bridge a few lines before the end of fol. 162v (what was previously the last page of the eleventh-century quire before the current fol. 164r) in order to present a readable text.[33]

Ða co*m* Harold Engla cyning heom ongean on unwaran begeondan þære brycge, 7 hi þær togædere fengon 7 swyðe heardlice lange on dæg feohtende wæron. 7 þær wæs Harold cyning of Norwegan 7 Tostig eorl ofslagen 7 ungerim folces mid heo*m* ægðer ge Normana ge Englisca. 7 þa Normen l flugon þa Englis‹c›a. Ða wes þer an of Norwegan þe wiðstod þet Englisce folc þet hi ne micte þa brigge oferstigan ne sige gerechen. Þa seite an Englisce mid anre flane ac hit nactes ne widstod ænd þa com an oþer under þere brigge end hine þurustang en under þere brunie. Þa com Harold Engla chinge ofer þere brigge 7 hys furde forð mid hine 7 þere michel wel geslogon ge Norweis ge Flæming 7 þes cyninges su‹nu þe› het 'Mundus'[34] let Harold faran ham to Norweie mid alle þa scipe.

Then Harold, king of the English, moved against them by surprise beyond the bridge, and they clashed together there and were fighting very hard long into the day. And Harold, king of the Norwegians, and Earl Tostig were slain there and a countless number of people with them, both of Norwegians and English. And the Norwegians fled the English. There was one of the Norwegians who opposed the English people so that they might neither cross the bridge nor gain victory. Then an Englishman shot with an arrow, but it did not avail, and then another came under the bridge and stabbed him underneath his byrnie. Then Harold king of the English came over the bridge and his army with him, and they slaughtered a great many, both Norwegian and Fleming. And Harold let the king's son, called 'Mundus', travel home to Norway with all his ships.

None of the other versions of the Anglo-Saxon Chronicle contains a story even remotely similar. The E-text has the shortest version of the battle, noting the deaths of the Norwegian king and Earl Tostig and commenting that Harold prevailed valiantly.[35] The D-text shares some detail with C on the surprise attack, the lengthy fight with heavy casualties on both sides, the deaths of Harold Fairhair and Tostig and the flight of the Norwegians, but makes no mention of the solitary defender of the bridge.[36] Interestingly, Henry of Huntington offers an account very close to that in C:

Quod audiens, Haraldus rex Anglorum cum manu ualida obuiauit eis apud Steinfordesbrige. Pugna igitur incepta est qua grauior non fuerat. Coeuntes namque a summo mane usque ad meridiem, cum horribiliter ruentes utrimque perseuerarent, numerus maximus Anglorum Norwagenses cedere, sed non fugere, compulit. Vltra flumen igitur repulsi, uiuis supra mortuos transeuntibus, magnanimiter restiterunt. Quidam uero Norwagensis, fama dignus eterna, super pontem restitit, et plus quadraginta uiris Anglorum securi cedens electa, usque ad nonam diei horam omnem exercitum Anglorum detinuit solus. Vsquequo quidam nauim ingressus per foramina pontis, in celandis eum percussit iaculo. Transientes igitur Angli Haraldum regem et Tosti ceciderunt, et totam Norwagensium aciem uel armis strauerunt uel igne deprehensos combusserunt.[37]

Hearing this, Harold, king of the English, came to meet them with a strong force at Stamford Bridge. Battle was begun, which could not have been more severe. Engaging from first light until noon, although they

> persisted attacking horribly on both sides, the great number of the English forced the Norwegians to yield but not to flee. Pushed therefore beyond the river, with the living trampling the bodies of the dead, they held out with spirit. Indeed, a certain Norwegian, worthy of everlasting fame, remained on the bridge, and felling more than 40 of the English men with his chosen ax, all the way up to the ninth hour of the day held back the entire army of the English. Finally, someone having gone in by boat struck him through the gaps in the bridge with a spear to the private parts. Crossing the bridge, then, the English army killed Harold the king and Tostig, and they destroyed the Norwegian army by arms or incinerated those overtaken by fire.

Henry began working on the *Historia Anglorum* (that version extending to 1129) sometime before 1133, and would ultimately bring the narrative to 1154.[38] He certainly made use of some version of the E-text, and Plummer notes that he had to have used the C-text for particular information not obtainable in other versions: among these the unincorporated Mercian Register (including the entry for 921 not in B), a shared error with C ('Cantwarabyrig' for 'Cantwic') and the story of Stamford Bridge.[39] But his use of the Stamford Bridge story is problematic. While Plummer maintains that Henry took the story from C, he argues: 'This is not only peculiar to C, but is in the very nature of the case unique, for it was evidently written down from oral tradition long after the event in very broken Saxon' (though conceding in a note that Henry might have gotten the story independently from oral tradition).

Plummer assumes that this little account in itself is later than the C-text, added to make up for an apparent loss at the end of the C-text proper. The difficulty with this assumption is that Ker dates the supplement on fol. 164r to xii², a dating which makes it likely that the copying of the supplementary C-text *followed* rather than preceded Henry of Huntingdon's history. And unless we are willing to argue that the supplementary text in C is a back translation from the *Historia Anglorum* (which while possible is not probable) we must conclude that when Henry of Huntingdon saw the C-text, this little story was part of the text.

How are we to understand the twelfth-century scribe's efforts? The production of the Insular letter forms surely took considerable concentration, and the labour taken for *g* and *r* particularly indicate that. What then justified the effort? The use of Insular letters suggests an effort to supplement the damaged end in a harmonious manner, producing the later script-equivalent of the layout adjustment made a century earlier at fol. 112. The entry ends without punctuation eight lines into a bifolium, and we will never know if the scribe anticipated further additions. In the sense that this late twelfth-century addition is an act of conservation it also embodies a particular kind of historical awareness. By this I mean that the supplied sheet attempts a script consonant with what precedes and yet the orthography shows the intrusion of the linguistic change of, perhaps, a hundred years. It is this changed orthography which keeps the supplied material from being antiquarian. The letter forms are conserved to produce a perceived visual harmony, but the altered orthography suggests that in one sense, at least, the text still lived.

MEANS AND ENDS

We move in time to the manuscript's life in the hands of sixteenth-century antiquaries. The manuscript was in the possession of a number of individuals immediately after the dissolution of the monasteries: Robert Recorde,[40] Robert Talbot, John Leland, John Joscelyn,[41] Robert Nowell[42] and William Bowyer, from whom Robert Cotton[43] acquired it, though none of these had a greater impress on the manuscript than Robert Talbot.[44] Talbot's glossing of the manuscript is highly text-dependent. His annotation of the *Orosius* shows an interesting mixture of lexical glosses and glosses on place-names, and he has clearly worked against a copy of the Latin text. His glossing is done primarily in Latin, though occasionally in English, depending on the type of gloss. Although the glosses are episodic, Talbot avails himself of both margins and interlinear spaces for his annotations. With the exception of the Old English additional chapter on the Voyage of Ohthere and Wulfstan, where his glossing is predominantly geographic, Talbot's primary interest in glossing the Old English *Orosius* is lexical. The reverse, however, is true for the C-text of the Chronicle.

The simplest Chronicle glosses are identifications of individuals: for the entry '⁊ sc̄e Æþeldrið forðferde' Talbot writes in the right-hand margin: 'for Audreye' (fol. 123r). In the story of Hengest and Horsa, 'Wyrtgeorne' is glossed 'Vortygeorn*us*' (fol. 118r). Despite the confused spacing of the words on fol. 119r|2–3, Talbot recognises the name in the phrase 'an brit to lafe' ('[not] one Briton left') and glosses with the Latin 'Bryto'. There is the occasional lexical gloss, e.g., *bocstafas* glossed in the right margin 'literas', *dic* glossed 'fossa' (both fol. 117r), but *werede* glossed in English 'well manned' (fol. 127r). Some phrases are glossed in Latin, though whether because they were perceived to be particularly hard or particularly translatable is unclear. For example, '⁊ Oswald his onfeng' is correctly glossed above 'eu*m* suscepit' (fol. 121v). In 'Her Cantware geþyngedon wið Ine ⁊ him gesealdon', etc. (fol. 123v), *geþyngedon* is glossed above as 'feceru*n*t pacem'.

In terms of sheer quantity, however, the greatest amount of glossing is devoted to places and place-names. Talbot's obsession is the identification of English place-names with either their Latin or, more frequently, English equivalents. There are towns: 'Her gesæt Theodorus arcebisceop sinoð on Hæðfelda' glossed '*scilicet* Hatfylde' (fol. 123r); 'nemned Portes | muþa' glossed 'Portesmouth' (fol. 119r), and rivers: 'Her Kenwealh gefeaht æt Bradanforda be Afene' glossed in the right hand margin 'Avon flu*men*', and islands: '⁊ Wihtgare Wihte ealand' glossed 'Wyoht'. Examples could be multiplied, since the glossing extends throughout the text of the Chronicle. Code switching abounds. Though the language of the gloss is Latin, the place-names are generally in English: thus '*scilicet* Hatfylde' and 'Avon *flumen*'.

Talbot's pursuit of place-names in the C-text of the Chronicle is an act of identification and of appropriation. Its scholarly identification (with its Latin apparatus) works to reclaim history in a forgotten language — one which tantalisingly was and was not Talbot's own. As such it endeavours to overcome the work of 500 years, to undo the strangeness of the past. But at the same time, its appropriation of those places is a practical abridgment of history, an implicit claim that the old, quaintly-named town or river, identified by its modern English name, is identical with the modern place. Such identification makes possible a variety of reclamations, as will be illustrated in a moment by Leland's use of Talbot and of the manuscript he borrows from him. But for the moment I am particularly interested in the significance of Talbot's actual use of the manuscript and the intimacy of it. Quite simply, he used it familiarly; he wrote all over it in his own hand in various inks, not in an imitation of 'Saxon' script. To be sure, his use of the manuscript was no act of reverence, though at the same time it was no act of contempt. (For contempt one only need think of the fate of the countless manuscript leaves sent to the binders to make pastedowns or to the butchers to wrap meat pies.) It is, however, a use which, in its familiarity, acknowledges the continuing tie of text with the body of the manuscript.

Leland's use of the manuscript he borrows from Talbot is the mirror image of Talbot's use. Talbot's glossing is a record of investigation and translation. By contrast, Leland uses the history as part of his project to render the English countryside clear, identifiable and controllable for Henry VIII:

> Wherfore after that I had perpendid the honest and profitable studies of these historiographes, I was totally enflammid with a love to see thoroughly al those partes of this your opulente and ample reaulme, that I had redde of yn the aforesaid writers: yn so muche that al my other occupations intermittid I have so travelid yn yowr dominions booth by the se costes and the midle partes, sparing nother labor nor costes, by the space of these vi. yeres paste, that there is almoste nother cape, nor bay, haven, creke or peere, river or confluence of rivers, breches, waschis, lakes, meres, fenny waters, montaynes, valleis, mores,

> hethes, forestes, [*chases*], wooddes, cities, burges, castelles, principale manor placis, monasteries, and colleges, but I have seene them; and notid yn so doing a hole worlde of thinges very memorable.[45]

Impelled by the names in the histories, as Howard Marchitello notes in his study of the politics of sixteenth-century English maps, Leland 'seems to have been driven mad beneath the accumulated weight of his empirical data, and his life work thereby left uncompleted at his death'.[46]

In his use of the manuscript, and of Talbot, in the service of Henry's surveillance of England, recorded in the *Collectanea*, Leland reverses the process of Talbot's glossing, and he lists instead the lemmata, i.e., the 'original' names, only occasionally providing Talbot's glosses for them.[47] But the *Collectanea* found its way into print some two centuries later, when Thomas Hearne published Leland in 1715.[48] The eighteenth-century printed outcome of Talbot's glossing is three and a half pages of double newspaper-style columns listing the now disembodied places, arranged in the order of their occurrence in the manuscript, but incomprehensible without the manuscript as a map to their weird geography, or, more accurately, to their weird mapping of space upon time. By this I mean that the evocation of locations ('Exanceastre', 'Snotingahamme', 'Tame', 'Gypeswic', etc.) has no rational geographic order. The only spatial clue to this ordering is the manuscript itself; without it we get the epitome of a decontextualised literacy — a pure list. But even so, the manuscript is still essential to the meaning of this now encrypted list. The list's claim to authenticity is established by the italicised title at the head of the first page of place-names: 'Owte of an old saxon Booke caullid of summe the old Englisch Historie'. This 'old Englisch Historie' becomes the absent warrant for the truth claims of the list. Decontextualised and printed though they are, the names are 'true' because their origin is both a history and an old, English book. The now absent body of the book ensures the integrity of the text. This useful separation, permitted and encouraged by the accessibility of print, brings us to the present moment of our book.

ENDGAMES

When the manuscript ceased to be used in a familiar way, it did not, obviously, cease to exist, though its function altered. Apart, of course, from the catastrophic fire in 1731, since the time of its inclusion in Cotton's library the manuscript seems to have enjoyed a quiet history of transcription and consultation.[49] But its current state of conservation and exhibition in an age of infinite reproducibility invites a reading of its new uses. Indeed, given its arrangements for the texts, the museum case asks us to consider the C-text and the flagellum as members of the same class of objects. The present arrangement of chronicle manuscripts in the exhibition case in the Manuscripts Saloon of the British Library dates to 1983, when Andrew Prescott reworked the chronicle cases for the permanent exhibition.[50] And while both Additional 16280 and Tiberius B. i each had earlier independent stints on exhibition, this was their first collocation. The flagellum went on exhibit shortly after its purchase in 1846, as part of the first exhibition of manuscripts in the Saloon, timed to coincide with the Great Exhibition of 1851. The compartment in which it was displayed contained a number of sixteenth-century religious books, several presentation volumes of Tudor monarchs, all in original, sumptuous bindings; the flagellum was exhibited next to another curious object, a 'Manual of Prayers, in German.... In the original leather binding, with brass bosses and corners, to which is attached a leathern thong and knob, for the purpose of suspending it from the girdle'.[51] The presence of the manual and the flagellum in the case along with the other texts in their gorgeous bindings suggests a multiple function for the textual objects on exhibition. They are curiosities, testimonies to sixteenth-century piety, markers of historical difference. And surrounding the case were signs of empire: to the right was the 'Oriental Table' and against the wainscot various documents were exhibited, among them the Bull of Innocent III, granting England and Ireland in fee to King John. The flagellum remained on display until 1878.[52]

No manuscript of the Anglo-Saxon Chronicle was exhibited either in 1851 or 1859. It would not be until 1887 when Edward Maunde Thompson arranged an exhibit to illustrate English palaeography, placing Tiberius B. i alongside the *Beowulf* manuscript (Cotton Vitellius A. xv). There it remained, even though in 1895 a separate display on the 'Chronicles of England' had been added. The exhibited manuscript in this display was the D-text, Cotton Tiberius B. iv. At the time the palaeographical exhibit was dismantled in the 1950s and 1960s, Tiberius B. i replaced Tiberius B. iv in the Chronicles case. When Prescott reconceived the Chronicles case in 1983, he included the flagellum both for the intrinsic interest of the object and as a tribute to the Madden/Bond displays of 1851–1878.[53] His interesting and thought-provoking juxtaposition of flagellum and chronicle prompts questions on the manuscript's function in the age of reproduction.

At the time when the flagellum was on exhibition, the Chronicle was in the heyday of its nineteenth-century editions. Thorpe offered his two-volume synoptic edition in 1861, and Earle's edition, languishing in the press for eight years, was finally published in 1865, to be redone at the end of the century in Plummer's masterful edition.[54] When the Chronicle is effectively disembodied, that is, when its text is reproduced for use, its body goes on display. In a sense, the manuscript on exhibition presents itself as a curious object: it is oddly written, very old, very rare; for these reasons and others, its value is both obvious and elusive. That value is pointedly addressed in

Walter Benjamin's meditation on the work of art affected by the means of mechanical reproduction.

In his extended commentary on 'The Work of Art in the Age of Mechanical Reproduction', Benjamin considers the crisis of the art object brought on by its almost infinite reproducibility.[55] For Benjamin, this crisis is most acutely manifest in the question of authenticity. Since he argues that the presence of the original is prerequisite to authenticity,[56] reproductions dilute, precisely because they cannot copy the history of the object:

> The authenticity of a thing is the essence of all that is transmissible from its beginning, ranging from its substantive duration to its testimony to the history which it has experienced. Since the historical testimony rests on the authenticity, the former, too, is jeopardized by reproduction when substantive duration ceases to matter. And what is really jeopardized when the historical testimony is affected is the authenticity of the object.[57]

This authenticity thus includes everything that has happened to the object: cracks, chips, blots, changes in venue, changes in owners. In forefronting presence as the crucial attribute of authenticity, Benjamin places authenticity outside reproducibility. Subject to mechanical reproduction, the original does not maintain its authority. As Benjamin points out, photography can improve the 'readability' of the object in question, and photographic reproduction enables the original to meet the beholder half-way. In this sense, Benjamin anticipates the effects of photographic technology on modern manuscript use, the most impressive of which is digital photography. But with the advantages of reproducibility, there is loss: the quality of presence is depreciated, and authenticity is interfered with.[58] While Benjamin concerns himself with the art object and the art of film, he dismisses the mechanical reproduction of writing in a clause: 'print is merely a special, though particularly important, case.'[59] But the fate of the manuscript in the age of reproduction is more complex than Benjamin allows, and any question about its mode of existence is indexed by print culture's habitual separation of text from manuscript body and complementary apprehension of the manuscript as textual object.

As items in a collection, the flagellum and the chronicle are, in a sense, both objects for meditation. But in a more analytical frame, and given the bifurcation between object and content that Hearne's edition of the *Collectanea* epitomises, the museum case suggests that in our age, Tiberius B. i has come to function in at least two ways as a fetish. From an anthropological perspective, a fetish is simply an object endowed with extraordinary powers. When Marx appropriates the notion of fetish, he applies it to the commodity rendered an object when abstracted from the labour which produced it. In an enlightening approach to collections, Susan Stewart combines anthropological, psychoanalytic and Marxist approaches to interpret the collected object as fetish:

> The fetishized object must have a reference point within the system of the exchange economy.... The further the object is removed from use value, the more abstract it becomes and the more multivocal is its referentiality. The dialectic between hand and eye, possession and transcendence, which motivates the fetish, is dependent upon this abstraction. Thus, just as we say that in its qualities of eclecticism and transcendence the collection can serve as a metaphor for the individual personality, so the collection can also serve as a metaphor for the *social* relations of an exchange economy.[60]

For our object-at-hand, the rarity of the manuscript generates an economic value in terms of its collection, but that same rarity, its uniqueness in Benjamin's terms, is warrant not only for its authority within the collection, but the authority of the printed versions of it. Such authority depends on the complete separation of text (or content) from manuscript. The bifurcation of text and object begun with the advent of print, and its prospect of infinite reproducibility, saw the C-text move from familiar object (in the eleventh, twelfth and even sixteenth centuries) to become the manuscript guarantor of authentic versions of it. We can manipulate the text infinitely in print and electronically precisely because it has been removed from its body and its body now rests in the case. This process is the reverse of Benjamin's description of the fate of the art object — reproduction for him meant simple second-order copies. Our editions do not duplicate; they remake and rewrite, and may do so because their truth warrant is always the object in the case.

Hence the aspect of fetish: in the case, Cotton Tiberius B. i cannot be read. There it is transformed into a sign of a book, not a book itself. In the case, it becomes a *sign* of history and in that sign resides its authenticity. As such, it is more like the flagellum than a book, for the flagellum functions as a sign of shaped time rather than as a conventional history. The exhibition of Tiberius B. i merely marks the formalisation of the modern separation of book from textual body. When Tiberius B. i is removed to the Students' Room its practical use changes: there it is re-placed into the scene of reading. But its authenticity as exhibition object accompanies it — one may still touch but not write. The action of history on Tiberius B. i, in the way that Benjamin argues the art object has a history, now becomes surreptitious and accidental. *Our* writing on the manuscript reverts to the primitive, limited to the body oils our fingers deposit on the membrane as a byproduct of turning the pages.

In the age of electronic reproduction the manuscript remains the object of final appeal in matters of textual dispute. Indeed, coincident with the increased manipulability of the text in various electronic editing formats has come an increased interest in accounting for and interpreting the minutia of manuscript evidence. The British Library's Initiatives for Access, which has now come to an end, was at the forefront in experimenting with digitised manuscripts, and the forthcoming CD ROM of the Electronic *Beowulf* is the happy outcome. If digitised manuscripts will mark the access of the future, that fate for Tiberius B. i will spell one further, useful development in Cotton's concept of a national collection. And the distance between body and text will be the distance between the case and the ether. To make this observation is not to long for the healing of the text/body split; that would be useless nostalgia. But if the presence of Tiberius B. i in the case is symptom of a certain death of the object, in that death and transfiguration it becomes a sign of a different sort from the flagellum of history at the other end of the case.[61]

NOTES

1. London, British Library, Additional 16280. The flagellum was acquired in 1846. See the *Catalogue of Additions to the Manuscripts in the British Museum in the Years 1846–47* (London: Trustees of the British Museum, 1864, repr. 1964), p. 174. See also p. 151 below.
2. Janet Bately, ed., *The Old English Orosius*, Early English Text Society, s.s. 6 (London: Oxford University Press, 1980).
3. Elliott Van Kirk Dobbie, ed., *The Anglo-Saxon Minor Poems*, Anglo-Saxon Poetic Records, 6 (New York: Columbia University Press, 1942), pp. 49–55, 170–4.
4. Ibid., pp. 55–7, 174–6.
5. Harry August Rositzke, ed., *The C-Text of the Old English Chronicles*, Beiträge zur Englischen Philologie, 34 (Bochum-Langendreer: Heinrich Pöppinghaus, 1940; repr. New York: Johnson Reprint, 1967). I am currently preparing an edition of the C-text for The Anglo-Saxon Chronicle: A Collaborative Edition, general editor, Simon Keynes.
6. N.R. Ker, *Catalogue of Manuscripts Containing Anglo-Saxon* (Oxford: Clarendon Press, 1957; resissued with supplement 1990), item 191.
7. See Colin G.C. Tite, *The Manuscript Library of Sir Robert Cotton*, The Panizzi Lectures (London: The British Library, 1994), pp. 45–7, 104–6.
8. Notations at fols 154v and 158r of London, British Library, Harley 6018 (the 1621 Catalogue) indicate that Tiberius B. i was one of four books Cotton obtained from Robert Bowyer, Keeper of the Records in the Tower. Robert Talbot (d. 1558) extensively annotated the book. (See C.E. Wright, 'The Dispersal of the Monastic Libraries and the Beginnings of Anglo-Saxon Studies: Matthew Parker and his Circle, a Preliminary

Study', *Transactions of the Cambridge Bibliographical Society* 3 [1951], 208–37.) Elsewhere, Wright identifies as Talbot's the hand of the note across the top of Tiberius B. i, fol. 3r ('Robert Talbot and Domitian A. ix', *Medium Ævum* 6 [1937], 170–1). Nowell's Chronicle transcripts in London, British Library, Additional 43704 (dated 1565) contain on fols 94r–107v extracts from the C-text. On fol. 1r of the same notebook, he makes an extract beginning 'Julius se Cæsar for on bryttanie *þæt* igland', and which he identifies as 'Ex Orosio in Anglicu*m* traducto ab Elfredo rege ut putatur'. The entry is almost certainly taken from the *Orosius* in Tiberius B. i, fol. 92r. On transcripts of the *Orosius* from Tiberius B. i, see Bately, *The Old English Orosius*, p. xxv, n. 2.

9. Patrick W. Conner, ed., *The Abingdon Chronicle, A.D. 956-1066*, The Anglo-Saxon Chronicle: A Collaborative Edition, 10 (Cambridge: D.S. Brewer, 1996), p. xix. Conner makes this suggestion as part of an extended argument about the origin of the manuscript at the refounded Abingdon Abbey.

10. See Tite, *The Manuscript Library of Sir Robert Cotton*, p. 48, on Cotton's disregard for antiquarian annotations. Loss from the edges of the manuscript seems not to have ended with Cotton's binders. Charles Plummer gives the full reading of an annotation by Talbot written across the top margin of fol. 118v (perhaps taken from Earle), but at present almost all of its top line is cut off. See Charles Plummer, ed., *Two of the Saxon Chronicles Parallel*, with a bibliographical note by Dorothy Whitelock, 2 vols (Oxford: Clarendon Press, 1892–1899, repr. Oxford: Oxford University Press, 1952), vol. 2, §21, and note to *an.* 457.

11. This shift does not coincide precisely with a new hand; the hand changed at fol. 34v|13.

12. The recto of fol. 111 is, not surprisingly, the hair side, and its orientation suggests that it was not part of a wrapper. The manner of preparing the quires in the *Orosius* changes at Quire 8. The first seven quires are arranged in the standard continental practice, but Quires 8 through 13 are arranged in the older manner where hair meets flesh: HHHHFFFF. The eleventh-century quires of the Chronicle are so arranged that hair meets hair and flesh meets flesh, but the twelfth-century supplement is at present arranged FH.

13. See note 11 above.

14. Neither hypothesis satisfactorily accounts for the presence of the slightly longer grids on the two inner leaves in the present Quire 15. But whether the present Quire 15 was originally ruled with the *Orosius* and then actually used a generation later, or whether it was ruled and added afterwards, the consequences are the same, that the writing grid for the *Orosius* determined that for the Chronicle texts.

15. See Janet Bately, 'Manuscript Layout and the Anglo-Saxon Chronicle',

Bulletin of the John Rylands University Library of Manchester 70 (1988), 21–43.

16. Though not for the list of chapter headings for Book 5 (fol. 83rv). The scribe is the same for both lists.

17. See Janet M. Bately, ed., *The Anglo-Saxon Chronicle, MS A*, The Anglo-Saxon Chronicle: A Collaborative Edition, 3 (Cambridge: D.S. Brewer, 1986), pp. xlvi–lxii, esp. p. li. See also the early folios in the facsimile of the Parker Chronicle (Robin Flower and Hugh Smith, eds., *The Parker Chronicle and Laws [Corpus Christi College, Cambridge, MS. 173]*, Early English Text Society, o.s. 208 [London: Oxford University Press, 1941 for 1937], esp. fols 7v and 8r). Individual rulings for annal years in Tiberius B. i were made by the rubricator in the process of copying. I am indebted to Timothy Graham for confirming this for me.

18. See Bately, 'Manuscript Layout and the Anglo-Saxon Chronicle', p. 28. Simon Taylor, ed., *The Anglo-Saxon Chronicle, MS B*, The Anglo-Saxon Chronicle: A Collaborative Edition, 4 (Cambridge: D.S. Brewer, 1983), p. xvii, reports the measurements of the writing grid in London, British Library, Cotton Tiberius A. vi as follows: 'The written space occupies *ca* 155 x 120 mm., and is ruled for twenty-three long lines, per page; it has double vertical bounding-lines, 8 mm. apart, on each side of the page.' The C-text deviates from its own regular practice at several points; I discuss these in my forthcoming edition.

19. In its versified mnemonic for feast days, the *Menologium* memorialises liturgical time. Its beginning of the cycle with Christ's birth ('Crist wæs acennyd') recapitulates the impulse to orient Anglo-Saxon history similarly in the opening lines of the C- and B-text 'Ær Cristes geflæscnesse...'.

20. Plummer, ed., *Two of the Saxon Chronicles Parallel*, vol. 2, p. xxx, is uncertain 'whether it [the Chronicle] and the Orosius originally belonged together or not'.

21. The correct order of the final leaves should be fols 159, 161, 163, 160, 162, 164. In Additional 43704, fols 94r–107v, Nowell makes extracts from a number of entries from the C-text of the Chronicle, at several points supplementing them from D. His entry for 1065 is supplemented from D, from which he presumably supplied the missing 'Mlxv', although he leaves a blank space for the annal number for the 1066 entry. Nowell copied the C-entries in order, leaving a half page blank in agreement with the end of the entry for 1056 (fol. 163v). Nowell's apparent ease in tracking down the entries suggests that the pages were in the right order in the sixteenth century. Similarly, the order of place-names in Leland's *Collectanea* shows that the leaves were in correct order. (London, British Library, Julius C. vi, fols 99v-100v; *Joannis Lelandi Antiquarii de Rebus Britannicis Collectanea*, ed. Thomas Hearne, 2nd ed., 6 vols [London:

Benjamin White, 1774; repr. Westmead, Farnborough: Gregg International Publ., 1970], vol. 4, pp. 124–5).

22. London, British Library, Additional 62577, *List of Cottonian MSS with the Progress made in repairing, binding, and inlaying of the collection. From the year 1839*. The manuscript was bound again in January 1957.

23. For the definitive account of the fate of the Cotton Collection after the fire see now Andrew Prescott, '"Their Present Miserable State of Cremation": The Restoration of the Cotton Library', in *Sir Robert Cotton and his Collections*, ed. C.J. Wright (in press). I am grateful to Dr Prescott for making the manuscript of this study available to me.

24. See Ker, *Catalogue of Manuscripts Containing Anglo-Saxon*, item 195.

25. There have been several presentations of the supplement. Plummer edits and prints the supplement in italics (*Two of the Saxon Chronicles Parallel*, vol. 1, p. 198); C.T. Onions, 'Some Early Middle-English Spellings', *Modern Language Review* 4 (1908–1909), 505-7, at p. 505, prints a text with some misreadings. Conner edits it as part of the Abingdon Chronicle (*The Abingdon Chronicle, A.D. 956-1066*, p. 39). I indicate my differences at various points in the textual notes below.

26. Bruce Dickins, 'The Late Addition to *ASC 1066*', *Proceedings of the Leeds Philosophical and Literary Society*, Literary and Historical Section 5.1 (1938), 148–9, at p. 148.

27. Dickins, ibid., p. 148, reporting an ultra-violet reading by C.E. Wright, would read '⁊ þes cyninges sunu þe het mundus let harold faran ham...'.

28. On the development of the mid-twelfth-century hand see N.R. Ker, *English Manuscripts in the Century After the Norman Conquest* (Oxford: Clarendon Press, 1960), pp. 34–9.

29. See C.T. Onions, 'Some Early Middle-English Spellings', p. 505. For specific Anglo-Norman orthographic features, see notes 30 and 31 below.

30. M.K. Pope, *From Latin to Modern French with Especial Consideration of Anglo-Norman* (Manchester: Manchester University Press, 1934), notes that the use of the digraph 'ch' to represent /k/ before /i/ and /e/ is a feature of early Anglo-Norman manuscripts. See §1209 and §694. I am grateful to Maureen B.M. Boulton for this reference.

31. On the interchange in Anglo-Norman among the symbols 's', 'z', 'c' and 'sc' see ibid., §1231.

32. On the use of the accusative in Old English as an Anglian symptom see Bruce Mitchell, *Old English Syntax*, 2 vols (Oxford: Blackwell, 1985), vol. 1, §1195, and for its use in Middle English see Susan Irvine, ed., *Old English Homilies from MS Bodley 343*, Early English Text Society, o.s. 302 (Oxford: Oxford University Press, 1993), p. lxxii, and Cecily Clark, ed., *The Peterborough Chronicle 1070–1154*, 2nd ed. (Oxford: Clarendon Press, 1970), p. liv.

33. Joscelyn ends his extract from the C-text for 1066 (annotation, Tiberius

B. iv, fol. 79v) with Harold's journey to Sandwich and assembly of his fleet in the summer of 1066.

34. This reading follows the suggestion of Bruce Dickins, 'The Late Addition to *ASC 1066*', p. 148, although my account of the erasure differs somewhat from his.

35. For the E-text of the Chronicle, see Plummer, *Two of the Saxon Chronicles Parallel*, vol. 1.

36. For the D-text, see now G.P. Cubbin, ed., *The Anglo-Saxon Chronicle, MS D*, The Anglo-Saxon Chronicle: A Collaborative Edition, 6 (Cambridge: D.S. Brewer, 1996).

37. Diana Greenway, ed. and trans., *Henry, Archdeacon of Huntingdon: 'Historia Anglorum'. The History of the English People* (Oxford: Clarendon Press, 1996), pp. 386-88. My translation. William of Malmesbury also mentions the story: William Stubbs, ed., *Willelmi Malmesbiriensis Monachi de Gestis Regum Anglorum Libri Quinque*, 2 vols, Rolls Series (London: Eyre and Spottiswoode, 1887–1889), vol. 1, p. 281. 'Haroldus, nuntio accepto, cuntis viribus regni eo contendit: pugna ingens commissa, utrisque gentibus extrema vi nitentibus. Angli, superiorem manum nacti, Noricos in fugam egerunt: sed tantorum et tot virorum victoriam, quod forsitan posteritas difficile credat, unus Noricus multa hora interpolavit; siquidem, in ingressu pontis qui Stantfordbrigge dicitur consistens, uno et altero et pluribus nostræ partis interemptis, omnes a transitu arcuit. Invitatus ad deditionem, ut tanti roboris homo largam clementiam Anglorum experiretur, invitantes ridebat; subinde, rugato vultu increpitans, imbecillis animi homines esse qui nequirent uni resistere. Nemine itaque proprius accedente, quod inconsultum æstimarent cum illo cominus congredi qui salutis omne viaticum desperatus effunderet, unus ex collateralibus regis jaculum ferreum in eum eminus vibrat; quo ille, dum gloriabundus proludit, ipsa securitate incautior, terebratus, victoriam Anglis concessit. Continuo enim libero transitu exercitus trajectus, Noricos palantes a tergo cecidit'. According to Antonia Grandsen, William used a 'lost' chronicle (*Historical Writing in England c. 550 to c. 1307*, 2 vols [Ithaca: Cornell University Press, 1974], vol. 1, p. 178, n. 96). She dates the *Gesta regum* to 1125 (p. 168) with revisions made between 1135 and 1143. On William's borrowing of annals from the Anglo-Saxon Chronicle see *Gesta regum*, Book 1, cap. xx.

Compare also Florence (John) of Worcester's account: 'Verum quinto post hæc die, id est, VII. kal. Octobris [25 Sept.], feria secunda, rex Anglorum Haroldus, multis millibus pugnatorum, armis bellicis instructorum, Eboracum veniens, et Norreganis in loco qui Stanford-brycge dicitur occurrens, in ore gladii regem Haraldum comitemque Tostium, cum majori parte sui exercitus, occidit, ac plenam victoriam, licet acerrime pugnatum fuisset, habuit. Filium autem ejus Olavum, et comitem de Orcada insula, Paulum nomine, qui ad naves custodiendas cum exercitus parte fuerant dimissi, acceptis prius ab eis obsidibus et sacramentis, cum xx. navibus et reliquiis exercitus, in patriam redire libere permisit' (Benjamin Thorpe, ed., *Florentii Wigorniensis Monachi Chronicon ex Chronicis, ad adventu Hengesti et Horsi in Britanniam usque ad annum M.C.XII*, 2 vols [London: English Historical Society, 1848–1849, vol. 1, pp. 226–7).

While William has the story of the Norwegian holding off the English army, he does not include the crucial detail of the stab beneath the byrnie, recounting, instead, that the valiant Norwegian was pierced by a spear thrown 'from a distance'. Florence's account lacks the anonymous Norwegian altogether.

38. For an authoritative account of the versions see Greenway, ed. and trans., *Henry, Archdeacon of Huntingdon: 'Historia Anglorum'*, pp. lxvi–lxxvii. For an evaluation of Henry as historian see James Campbell, *Essays in Anglo-Saxon History* (London: Hambledon Press, 1986), pp. 212–13.

39. Plummer (*Two of the Saxon Chronicles Parallel*) traces Henry's use of information from the E-text to version η (see vol. 2, p. lvi; on his use of the C-text see vol. 2, p. lvii). Henry himself lists in his Prologue the many sources he used to compile his history: 'Bede uenerabilis ecclesiasticam qua potui secutus historiam, nonnulla etiam ex aliis excerpens auctoribus, inde cronica in antiquis reseruata librariis compilans, usque nostrum ad auditum et uisum preterita representaui' (*Historia Anglorum*, p. 6) ['I followed Venerable Bede's Ecclesiastical History as far as I was able, excerpting not a little from other authors, whence, ransacking chronicles preserved in ancient libraries, I have recorded the past up until the things we have heard and seen']. Greenway (*Henry, Archdeacon of Huntingdon: 'Historia Anglorum'*) prefers to think that Henry of Huntingdon used not C but a C-type version (p. xciii) and excludes the story of Stamford Bridge from consideration because it post-dates Henry. Yet the possibility of the story's preexisting the supplement is precisely what is in question here. The story of Stamford Bridge is in the earliest version of the *Historia Anglorum*.

40. In *The Whetstone of Witte, Which is the Seconde Parte of Arithmetike: Containyng the Extraction of Rootes: The Cossike Practise, with the Rule of Equation: and the Woorkes of Surde Nombers* (London, 1557), sig. a. iii^{r-v}, Recorde mentions the voyage of Ohthere 'in auncient recorde of the old Saxon tonge'. There are only two surviving copies of the Old English *Orosius*, that in Tiberius B. i and the early tenth-century manuscript London, British Library, Additional 47967 (the Lauderdale or Tollemache manuscript). The Lauderdale manuscript, however, is defective at the section of the account where Ohthere identifies himself as being from Halgoland; at present this account is on supply leaves of the seventeenth

century (see Bately, ed., *The Old English Orosius*, p. xxii, n. 2, and D.S. Brewer, 'Sixteenth, Seventeenth and Eighteenth Century References to the Voyage of Ohthere [Ohtheriana IV]', *Anglia* 71 [1952–1953], 202-11). Angelika Lutz ('Das Studium der Angelsächsischen Chronik im 16. Jahrhundert: Nowell und Joscelyn', *Anglia* 100 [1982], 301-56, at p. 301, n. 1) discusses Recorde's extracts from the C-text of the Chronicle in Cambridge, Corpus Christi College 138. Recorde did not himself, however, annotate the manuscript. I am indebted to Timothy Graham for drawing my attention to Recorde's comment.

41. Joscelyn glosses and collates the D-text, Cotton Tiberius B. iv, from manuscripts A, B, C and E. See Lutz, 'Das Studium der Angelsächsichen Chronik', pp. 343–56, for Joscelyn's use of the C-text.

42. On Nowell's use of the C-text see especially Lutz, ibid., pp. 324–30. See also Robin Flower, 'Laurence Nowell and the Discovery of England in Tudor Times', *Proceedings of the British Academy* 21 (1935), 47–73, esp. pp. 59–62, for Nowell's study of place-names and maps; and Brewer, 'Sixteenth, Seventeenth and Eighteenth Century References to the Voyage of Ohthere [Ohtheriana IV]', pp. 202–11.

43. On Cotton's acquisition see Harley 6018, fol. 154v (1621 Catalogue). For William Somner's later use of Tiberius B. i see Angelika Lutz, 'Zur Entstehungsgeschichte von William Somners *Dictionarium Saxonico-Latino-Anglicum*', *Anglia* 106 (1988), 1–25, at pp. 7–15.

44. On Talbot's use of the manuscript see note 8 above. Wright identified Talbot as the author of the note at the top of Tiberius B. i, fol. 3r: 'Rex alfred*us* orosium interpretat*us* e*st* boetiu*m* *et* beda*m* de histori*a* eccl*esias*tica' ('Robert Talbot and Domitian A. ix', pp. 170–1). Talbot's note is transcribed by Leland in Cotton Julius C. vi, fol. 99v|15–16. For an important account of Talbot's practices of annotation and ownership of manuscripts see Timothy Graham, 'Robert Talbot's "Old Saxonice Bede": Cambridge University Library MS Kk. 3. 18 and the "Alphabetum Norwagicum" of British Library, Cotton MS Domitian A. IX', *Books and Collectors 1200–1700: Essays Presented to Andrew Watson*, ed. James P. Carley and Colin G.C. Tite (London: British Library Publications, 1997), pp. 295–316.

45. *The Itinerary of John Leland in or About the Years 1535–43*, ed. Lucy Toulmin Smith, 5 vols (London: George Bell and Sons, 1907–1910), vol. 1, pp. xl–xli.

46. Howard Marchitello, 'Political Maps: The Production of Cartography and Chorography in Early Modern England', *Cultural Artifacts and the Production of Meaning: The Page, the Image, and the Body*, ed. Margaret J.M. Ezell and Katherine O'Brien O'Keeffe (Ann Arbor: University of Michigan Press, 1994), pp. 13–40, at p. 24.

47. For a comparison of Leland's knowledge of Old English with that of

Talbot, see Graham, 'Robert Talbot's "Old Saxonice Bede": Cambridge University Library MS Kk. 3. 18 and the "Alphabetum Norwagicum" of British Library, Cotton MS Domitian A. IX', p. 295 and n. 3.

48. See note 21 above.

49. Somner used it for his *Dictionary*. See Bately, ed., *The Old English Orosius*, p. xxv, n. 2, on the use of Tiberius B. i for transcripts and editions of the *Orosius*. After Talbot, alteration of the manuscript was slight. There appear to be pencil annotations in an unidentified seventeenth-century (?) hand (fol. 11v, left margin: 'Otcheri perip[l]us tempore | Alfredi' with a *signe de renvoi* to the end of the Ohthere section, fol. 15r). In a private communication, Andrew Prescott identifies the pressmark VIII F on fol. 1 as a Montague House pressmark (in use from about 1810–1827). The manuscript was foliated in ink by Joseph Planta and refoliated in pencil in 1884. See also J. Ingram, ed., *The Saxon Chronicle* (London: Longman, Hurst, Rees, Orme and Brown, 1823), pp. xxii–xxiii, who first collated the C-text for a 'modern' edition.

50. I am indebted to Dr Andrew Prescott, Curator, Department of Manuscripts, British Library, for the details of the history of the display for both Additional 16280 and Tiberius B. i.

51. *List of Autograph Letters, Original Charters, Great Seals and Manuscripts exhibited to the Public in the Department of Manuscripts* (London: Trustees of the British Museum, 1851), pp. 33–4.

52. In the display of 1859, the flagellum was set out in a case illustrating ornamental bindings (see ibid.).

53. Personal communication from Andrew Prescott. For Madden's tireless work with the Cotton Collection, see Prescott, '"Their Present Miserable State of Cremation": The Restoration of the Cotton Library'.

54. For an account of the history of editing the Chronicle see Plummer, ed., *Two of the Saxon Chronicles Parallel*, vol. 2, pp. cxxvii–cxxxvii.

55. Walter Benjamin, *Illuminations: Essays and Reflections*, ed. Hannah Arendt, trans. Harry Zohn (New York: Schocken Books, 1968), pp. 217–51.

56. Ibid., p. 220.

57. Ibid., p. 221.

58. Ibid., p. 221.

59. Ibid., p. 219.

60. Susan Stewart, *On Longing: Narratives of the Miniature, the Gigantic, the Souvenir, the Collection* (Baltimore and London: The Johns Hopkins University Press, 1984), pp. 163–4.

61. It is a pleasure to acknowledge the generous support for this research from the Institute for Scholarship in the Liberal Arts, College of Arts and Letters, University of Notre Dame.

7 Lay Literacy in Anglo-Saxon England and the Development of the Chirograph

Kathryn A. Lowe

INTRODUCTION

Few subjects have aroused such interest of late as the study of historical literacy. It is still a comparatively new area of research and has greatly expanded since the end of the last century, when apparently only 30 studies had been published on the subject in English. By 1970 the number had multiplied to over 4000,[1] and 11 years later the mass of secondary literature on the subject prompted the publication of *Literacy in History: An Interdisciplinary Research Bibliography*.[2]

The study of early English medieval literacy in particular has followed much the same pattern. Virtually nothing was published on the subject until 1977, when Patrick Wormald published his influential article, 'The Uses of Literacy in Anglo-Saxon England and its Neighbours'.[3] Since then various studies have appeared, culminating in the 1990 publication of essays by Simon Keynes and Susan Kelly in *The Uses of Literacy in Early Mediaeval Europe*, edited by Rosamond McKitterick.[4] The later medieval period has been comprehensively treated in Michael Clanchy's *From Memory to Written Record: England 1066–1307*.[5] The appearance of both of these books in paperback (Clanchy's is now in its second edition) testifies to the popularity of the topic, which is increasingly being studied as a separate subject in universities.[6]

Wormald's conclusions are unequivocally stated: '[T]he traditional view of restricted literacy is substantially valid for the whole early English period'; 'we do not find conclusive evidence of a 'take-off' of literacy in post-Alfredian England.'[7] His views are summarised and endorsed by Clanchy: 'It seems unlikely that England was governed by a bureaucracy using documents in its routine procedures before 1066.'[8] Keynes' study of royal government in the later Anglo-Saxon period surveys the same material, but reaches entirely different conclusions:

> [R]oyal government in the tenth and eleventh centuries depended to a very considerable extent on the use of the written word, and...late Anglo-Saxon society was well accustomed to such manifestations of

'pragmatic literacy'.

> [T]he taxi-run for the 'take-off' of literacy began many years before 1066.[9]

To an extent, of course, Wormald's article suffers from its age. Significant contributions to the subject of Anglo-Saxon history have been made since his paper was published in 1977, most notably Keynes' own work on royal diplomas,[10] which may have led him to modify some of his statements. However, there is a fundamental lack of agreement running through their argument which derives from the decision to reject or accept certain kinds of material as evidence for the extent of the use of the written word during the period. Wormald crucially discounts the evidence supplied by vernacular texts:

> [W]e cannot deduce a widespread ability to read anything from the fact that names of owners or makers were sometimes engraved upon Anglo-Saxon coins, weapons or memorials; or a generally high standard of lay culture from the fact that there were documents in the vernacular.
>
> [T]he rise of written English proves nothing about lay literacy.[11]

In contrast, Kelly, surveying the earlier period, highlights their significance: '[T]he implications of the use of the vernacular in formal and informal documents are issues of the greatest importance.'[12] In order to understand the reasons behind these different approaches, it is necessary to consider the theoretical framework adopted by each scholar. This can be seen to affect not only the questions asked of the material, but also the nature of the evidence admitted.

GOODY AND STREET: THE 'AUTONOMOUS' AND 'IDEOLOGICAL' APPROACHES TO LITERACY

Interest in the subject of medieval literacy seems to have arisen from the publication of a number of popular studies on anthropological investigation, tempting historians and sociologists to apply such finds in an examination of historical literacy. One article, 'The Consequences of Literacy', by Jack Goody and Ian Watt, proved to be highly influential in these non-anthropological circles.[13] In their paper, Goody and Watt implied that their conclusions about the nature and effects of literacy in classical Greece held good for literacy in all societies. They asserted that alphabetic literacy engenders a distinction between myth and history and the development of 'objective' history; that in non-literate societies, history is reinterpreted by the present, whereas in literate societies current philosophy is influenced by selected cultural traditions. They further claimed that writing objectifies words; that literate societies have an interest in exact time-sequences and time-keeping devices; and that literacy develops logic (context-free thought, analytic thought, teleological and rational thought, development of syllogisms), detachment and individualisation of experience. They described those societies which do not display these characteristics fully as having 'restricted' (or 'conditional') literacy. By this catalogue, Goody and Watt showed their fundamental belief in the 'great divide' theory, that is, that simpler societies lack certain cognitive skills that more complex societies possess. However, they asserted that the acquisition of such skills is concomitant upon the acquisition of literacy, replacing earlier theories of the 'great divide' which had variously considered the absence or presence of these cognitive characteristics to constitute the difference between wild/domesticated, concrete/scientific or pre-logical/logical societies. This view had earlier been formulated by Talcott Parsons, who contended that the difference between 'archaic' and 'advanced intermediate' societies is the difference between 'craft' and fuller upper-class literacy.[14] By far the most influential proponent of the 'great divide' theory has been Walter Ong, whose views have been most accessibly expressed in *Orality and Literacy: The Technologizing of the Word*.[15]

The attraction of Goody and Watt's ideas to historians of literacy is obvious, for if one accepts their hypothesis that certain cognitive processes can only be developed through the acquisition of literacy, then the absence of such characteristics in a given culture would indicate a lack of literacy on a significant scale in that society. This was the approach adopted by Wormald, who referred enthusiastically to their work as 'exciting'. His underlying reliance on their philosophy led to the attempt in his article to find a standard of literacy comparable with that of other cultures, what he termed a *civilization de l'écrit*:

> If we are to describe early English society as literate in a sense that would satisfy the ancient, or later medieval, historian, we must show that the proportion of laymen able to read at least a vernacular writ or poem was socially, if not statistically, significant.[16]

He also chose to devote a comparatively large amount of space to Continental parallels, arguing that 'early English society was exposed to most of the same pressures as the rest of barbarian Europe, and a preliminary consideration of the continental and insular background...should give us some indication of what to expect in England.'[17] In his eagerness for comparative study and subsequent generalisations Wormald demonstrated his reliance on Goody and Watt, as did his choice of the term 'restricted' in his concluding remarks: 'the traditional view of restricted literacy is substantially valid for the whole early English period.'[18]

Goody and Watt's assertions have had considerable effect, and many writers have adopted or developed their theories or assumptions without questioning their validity. However, they were not everywhere received uncritically. In the same volume of essays in which 'The Consequences of Literacy' appeared, Kathleen Gough, failing to find the effects of literacy as outlined by Goody and Watt in her case-study of the north Indian state of Kĕrala, and obviously unwilling to attribute everything to the notion of 'restricted' literacy, cogently argued that literacy is an enabling rather than a causal factor.[19] She contended that literacy *permitted* large-scale organisation, critical accumulation, storage and retrieval of knowledge, systematic use of logic, pursuit of science and the elaboration of the arts, but did not by itself *cause* them. She noted that the literate community in Kĕrala, by and large, did not produce any significant literature. Neither did they choose to use their literacy to investigate the world through scientific methods, or to record historical events, as one might have been led to expect from Goody and Watt. The adults in the lower castes used their literacy instead for recording land transfers, tenures and mortgages, accounts for reading and transmitting book crafts. In other words, they used literacy in a way which suited the needs of their society. Her work, together with that of Roger Schofield (who argued in the same collection of papers that the structure of education largely determines the nature of literacy), began to move towards a realisation that literacy cannot and should not be treated as a separate technology, independent of culture and ideology.[20]

Goody and Watt's theories were refined by Goody himself in a later work, *The Domestication of the Savage Mind*.[21] Here he recognised that the title of his earlier article, 'The Consequences of Literacy', was itself ill-chosen and would have been better called 'The Implications of Literacy'. He continued, however, to assert his fundamental belief in the 'great divide' theory, and further developed the hypothesis that such cognitive changes may be described as changes in the mode of communication, and that it is literacy that constitutes the 'great divide' between them. This theory was intended to supersede all earlier explanations of the 'great divide'. However, he acknowledged that such dichotomous treatment is simplistic and does not take into account the complexities of human development. But he continued to assert that the theory itself was both still tenable and preferable to other explanations:

> In drawing attention to the significance of this factor, I attempt to avoid the conceptual slush into which one flounders when such differences are attributed either to 'culture' (who denies it, but what does it mean?) or to a vague, descriptive division.[22]

This passage contains a criticism of those who seek to attribute differences in cognitive processes to differences in culture, and implicitly, of those who regard literacy itself as inseparable from culture, although Goody himself had moved to at least partial acceptance of this view in *Domestication*. These opposing theories have been most forcefully developed by Brian Street in his books, *Literacy in Theory and Practice* and *Social Literacies*.[23] Street described the view of literacy espoused by Goody and Watt as 'autonomous':

> The exponents of an 'autonomous' model of literacy conceptualise literacy in technical terms, treating it as independent of social context, an autonomous variable whose consequence for society and cognition can be derived from its intrinsic character.[24]

Opposed to this is the 'ideological' standpoint, upheld by Street himself. This theory claims that the meaning of literacy depends on its social institutions, that literacy is already firmly embedded in an ideology, and cannot be isolated:

> The ideological model...does not attempt to deny technical skill or the cognitive aspects of reading and writing, but rather understands them as they are encapsulated within cultural wholes and within structures of power. In that sense the 'ideological' model subsumes rather than excludes the work undertaken within the 'autonomous' model.[25]

The terms 'autonomous' and 'ideological' appear to have attained popular currency, and have been adopted by many anthropologists, sociologists and linguists working on literacy.[26]

Street showed that Goody and Watt's so-called 'inherent' qualities of literacy were merely conventions of literate practice in a particular society, and that their article relied far too heavily on the model of classical Greece, to which their understanding of the 'consequences' of literacy applied. Many of their earlier arguments were shown by Street to be naive. Historians are themselves a product of their own ideologies and so inevitably reinterpret history in terms of the present, whether part of a literate society or not. Writing can never be said to objectify words, because the author of those very words is again a product of an ideology. Non-literate cultures are no less intrinsically 'logical' than their literate counterparts. Earlier texts had confused logic with explicitness. With these distinctions stripped away, it becomes less clear that the watershed in terms of intellectual and aesthetic development between 'archaic intermediate' and 'advanced intermediate' societies described by Parsons can be said to exist at all.

PRESENT WORK

It is Street's 'ideological' approach to the study of literacy which was the framework adopted — consciously or unconsciously — by the authors of the articles contained in *The Uses of Literacy in Early Mediaeval Europe*.[27] This framework allowed literacy to be examined in its historical and social context, in terms of the institutions of the particular society. In short, it permitted Keynes and Kelly to admit a large body of evidence not available to Wormald working within the 'autonomous' model of literacy. Instead of having to impose preconditions for literacy and society, they could examine the ways in which the written word was used in Anglo-Saxon society.

It may appear unnecessary, or at least rather unfair, to criticise an article which was written so long ago and which has clearly been superseded by more recent work. Indeed, it would be so, were it not for the fact that Wormald's conclusions are still accepted as substantially valid in more popular circles. Clanchy's *From Memory to Written Record: England 1066–1307*, for example, has been praised by Street, and, more recently, by McKitterick, as representative of the 'ideological' approach to literacy. The book demonstrated that literacy is dependent on social institutions for its development. In it, Clanchy discussed the various uses of literacy during the post-Conquest period, describing the making of records, the varieties of writings and the gradual acceptance of written records for practical purposes among lay people. He cogently argued that a shift from a reliance on oral to literate modes has to take place, that a 'literate mentality' has to be created, before literacy can spread.

As the subtitle of his book suggests, however, Clanchy is only peripherally interested in the Anglo-Saxon period, and much of his discussion of literacy in the centuries leading up to the Conquest is of an introductory nature. In this opening chapter, he acknowledges the help of Wormald, both at that time colleagues at Glasgow University. The synthesis of Wormald's arguments leads to Clanchy's inevitable conclusion that 'it seems unlikely that England was governed by a bureaucracy using documents in its routine procedures before 1066.' The section is not revised in the second edition of the book in 1993, despite the publication of McKitterick's collection of essays some three years earlier.

Clanchy's conclusions have been adopted by Goody himself in his 1986 work, *The Logic of Writing and the Organization of Society*. His section on the expansion of writing and law in medieval England uses Clanchy's summary of the pre-Conquest situation and is markedly less cautious in its wording:

> Under the Anglo-Saxons, writing was employed for charters and for some other legal and administrative purposes. But with the Norman

> Conquest there was a quantum jump in its application.[28]

Goody's book appears to have been issued simultaneously in hardback and soft covers, thus targeted at (and presumably attaining) an audience far wider and more general than could possibly have been reached by Wormald's article and by Clanchy's monograph. The irony, of course, is that Goody is essentially using a conclusion based on his own outmoded theory that he himself had later reworked.

The medieval period clearly holds a fascination for studies of modern literacy, and Clanchy's research is employed in many recent inquiries into the subject. Street, for example, discusses Clanchy's findings in an attempt to show how 'the acquisition of literacy has to do with deeper aspects of ideology, culture and even epistemology, rather than just being an empirical matter of extending "skills" and "knowledge"'[29] and cites the situation in medieval England as an example of 'colonial' literacy. In doing so, he shows his reliance on Clanchy's restatement of Wormald's thesis:

> There are a number of ways in which the acquisition of literacy affects a society. *For social groups with virtually no prior exposure to literacy* it is likely that the dominant feature of acquisition will not be so much the consequence of literacy *per se* but the impact of the culture on the bearers of that literacy. By definition, literacy is being transferred from a different culture, so that those receiving it will be more conscious of the nature and power of that culture than of the mere technical aspects of reading and writing.[30]

He goes on to summarise Clanchy's opening chapter as a 'description of how the Normans introduced literacy in medieval England', and asserts 'What had given written texts legitimacy in the pre-Norman period had been their association with Christian proof.'[31] In reality, however, the medieval example may not prove such a paradigm of 'colonial' literacy that Street suggests. Once again, we find Wormald's view dominating current scholarly opinion about the use and extent of literacy in Anglo-Saxon England, despite the developments in research both at the general theoretical and subject-specific level.

KELLY, KEYNES AND THE ROLE OF WRITING IN GOVERNMENT

The ideological approach used by the authors of *The Uses of Literacy in Early Mediaeval Europe* allowed Keynes and Kelly to turn the focus from an unproductive search for a *civilization de l'écrit* based on classical and European models towards the study of charters and the role that writing played in government and in society. In her examination of lay use of the written word in the early Anglo-Saxon period, Kelly plotted the development of the Anglo-Saxon charter from its disputed origins and essentially ecclesiastical nature into an instrument of interest and use to the layman. An important development, as she noted, was the appearance from the ninth century of vernacular documents such as writs, leases and wills alongside the Latin diploma.[32]

Keynes concentrated on the later part of the Anglo-Saxon period, demonstrating that, contrary to existing scholarly opinion, the routine procedures of the late Anglo-Saxon period made extensive use of the written word. Together, Keynes' and Kelly's work showed that it is better to see the spread of literacy in the thirteenth and fourteenth centuries as stemming from a process that had already begun in Anglo-Saxon England, rather than as a purely post-Conquest phenomenon.

The evidence for writing in Anglo-Saxon government is supplied by the large number of diplomas issued during the period. How these diplomas should be interpreted is, of course, a matter of debate. When it comes to the question of lay literacy in the pre-Conquest period, the evidence is less tangible. We have, for example, a number of vernacular wills issued by laymen. However, these owe their preservation to their major beneficiaries — ecclesiastical institutions — to whose obvious advantage it was to produce and preserve the texts in the first place. It is clear that the simple existence of these documents alone is unlikely to convince the sceptic of the degree of lay interest in the written record, Wormald for one: 'we cannot deduce...a generally high standard of lay culture from the fact that there were documents in the vernacular.'[33] We instead need to look for signs of Clanchy's 'literate mentality' in this earlier period, indications that the layman was actively interested in written documentation and the benefits that it could bring.

In the final part of this article, I briefly rehearse some of the well-known instances of lay enthusiasm for the written document and their corresponding appreciation of the benefits that possession of such charters could bring. I conclude by examining the form and function of a particular type of document which, I believe, presents us with our best evidence for the growth of a literate mentality amongst the Anglo-Saxons: the chirograph.

ANGLO-SAXON LAY SOCIETY AND THE DEVELOPMENT OF THE CHIROGRAPH

Keynes completed his survey of the later Anglo-Saxon period by considering the role of the written document in wider society. He discusses several lawsuits involving laymen where possession of the diplomas relating to the estate in question appears critical. As he observes, one of the most interesting cases involves the appropriation of the title-deeds to an estate by the kinsmen of its previous owner. The lack of title-deeds to the estate was thought by the Church to put it at a significant disadvantage. The account of the lawsuit is preserved in the *Libellus Æthelwoldi*, a mid-twelfth-century chronicle from Ely which is believed to stem from a lost vernacular work dating from the late tenth century. The *Libellus Æthelwoldi* was in turn used by the compiler of the better-known *Liber Eliensis*.

> Tulerunt tamen graviter episcopus et abbas, quod Aluuoldus et alii cognati Eadrici cyrographa de Havekestune et de Neuuetun habebant. Per hoc enim metuebant sibi quandoque calumpnias ac dolos oriri.

> But the bishop and abbot considered it a serious matter that Ælfwold and the other kinsmen of Eadric were in possession of the charters to Hauxton and Newton. On this account they feared that claims and trickeries could arise at some time.[34]

The value placed by ecclesiastics on the written document, after all their own innovation, is perhaps unsurprising. However, the resolution of the dispute suggests that one layman at least was an assiduous collector of charters and was fully aware of their value:

> Tunc abbas et omnis cetus fratrum accesserunt et petierunt ab eo, ut pro amore Dei sancteque Æðeldryðæ predicta cyrographa ad opus ecclesie sue ab Aluuoldo fratre Ædrici emeret. Et dixerunt se daturos eidem Aluuoldo pro illis cyrographis cyrographum unum de Ramesia et de Sprouuintune, quod est in Eastsexe, quo cyrographo multum indiguit, et insuper promiserunt ei .xxx. aureos.

> Then the abbot and whole congregation of brothers approached him and asked him, for the love of God and St Æthelthryth, to buy those charters from Ælfwold brother of Eadric for the work of their church. And they said that they would give Ælfwold for the charters a charter for Ramsey and Sproughton in Essex, a charter he greatly wanted, and they promised him thirty mancuses as well.

As Keynes points out, there is no suggestion that Ælfwold could read, or even understand, the Latin of these diplomas, but the vernacular boundary clause and vernacular endorsements would have supplied him with all the information he needed. These innovations in themselves must have promoted the increased acceptance of the written word. Hooke notes that boundary clauses appear from the seventh and eighth centuries. Early examples are generally simple affairs naming only a few features along the boundaries of the estate, but become increasingly sophisticated as the period progresses.[35]

The problem here, of course, is that the majority of charters do not survive in contemporary form. In these instances it is impossible to say whether the boundary clause formed an integral part of the original text or was a later addition to it. Indeed, the earliest contemporary single-sheet charter containing Latin bounds is datable to AD 732.[36] There is a single example of an eighth-century single-sheet charter containing a boundary clause in English (S 59, AD 770), but the use of the vernacular does not appear to have become popular until after the middle of the following century.

It is also interesting that several charters survive which serve to replace lost ones: two tenth-century diplomas (S 367, S 371) note that they have been produced for a layman, Æthelfrith *dux*, whose archives were destroyed by fire:

> Contigit quod ÆÐELFRIÐ O duci omnes hereditarii libri ignis vastatione conbusti perierunt; Tali igitur necessitate cogente prædictus dux rogavit EADƿEARDUM regem. ÆÐELREDUM quoque et ÆÐ ELFLEDAM qui tunc principatum et potestatem gentis Merciorum sub prædicto rege tenerunt. Omnes etiam senatores Mer`ciorum´ ut ei consentirent et licentiam darent alios libros rescribendi;
>
> Tunc illi unianimiter omnes devota mente consenserunt ut alii ei libri scriberentur eodem modo quo et priores scripti erant In quantum eos memoriter recordari potuisset.[37]

> It befell Ealdorman Æthelheah that all his charters of inheritance were destroyed, consumed by the ravaging fire. Accordingly, the aforesaid ealdorman, impelled by such necessity, petitioned King Edward, and also Æthelred and Æthelflæd, who then held rulership and power over the race of the Mercians under the aforesaid king as well as to all the leading men of the Mercians that they should give their consent and permission for rewriting other charters for himself.
>
> Then they all with devoted mind unanimously gave their consent that other charters should be written for him in the same terms as the earlier ones had been, in so far as he could relate them from memory.[38]

Charters such as these, where laymen feel the need to replace lost title-deeds, indicate a keen understanding of the potential value of the written record.

A further indication that the importance of the written word was appreciated as evidence is found in the development of the chirograph. A chirograph is the name given to a document which was written out in duplicate, triplicate or very occasionally quadruplicate on a single sheet of membrane. It was cut into its separate portions after the word 'CYROGRAPHVM' (or equivalent) had been written across the line of the cut(s).[39] Later in the Middle Ages the cut became a wavy or indented one, hence its common name of indenture. The attraction of this form of document to the illiterate is obvious, for one can easily check that one part matches the other by lining up the part and counterpart. Although chirographs are found from the west of Germany (from the tenth century) and from France (from the eleventh century), it seems that the form was an Insular innovation.[40]

Chirographs seem to have been almost exclusively reserved for recording contracts between parties: wills, leases and accounts of agreements concerning the exchange of land were commonly recorded in this manner. Dispute settlements were also often produced as chirographs. I have found 64 examples of charters dating from the pre-Conquest period which show evidence of having been produced in chirographic form.[41] They are listed in the Appendix below. These charters either survive as portions of chirographs or in later cartulary copies that state that more than one copy has been produced in what I term a 'marker' clause. These clauses tend to follow the basic formula: 'There are three of these documents. Foundation *x* has one, foundation *y* has the second, *z* (the lessee, testator, interested party) the third.'

The preservation of a single-sheet portion is no guarantee that the charter is either genuine or original. S 312 and S 313 (nos 6, 7), for example, are versions of the same royal grant to Winchester (one in English, one in Latin), purporting to date to AD 854.[42] Both survive as portions of chirographs. S 313, however, is written throughout in a script of the mid-eleventh century. S 312 is believed to have been forged at the same time, although its single-sheet text only survives in a fifteenth-century copy. Bizarrely, the will of Leofwine (1522, no. 24), which survives as the lower portion of a chirograph dated AD 998, appears entirely genuine in every respect, but its script seems to be of the mid-eleventh century.[43]

There are references in other texts to other documents which are no longer extant, but which appear to have been produced in chirographic form. One such narrative from the *Libellus Æthelwoldi* describes the making of a chirograph:

> Tunc Brihnotus abbas testamentum huius Siferdi coram uxore et coram filia sua coramque omnibus supramemoratis fecit scribi in tribus cyrographis coramque cunctis fecit recitari lectumque fecit incidi unamque partem cyrographi retinuit Siuerdus, alteram autem dedit abbati, tertiam vero misit statim per prefatum Brihtelmum Æieluuino alderman, qui tunc temporis deiebat in Ely, et petiit ab eo, ut suum testamentum ita stare concessisset quomodo abbas illud scripserat et ordinaverat apud Lindune coram predictorum testimonio virorum. Cum itaque Aieluuinus alderman hoc audisset et cyrographum vidisset, remisit illico ad eum Wlnothum de Stouue cum Brihtelmo sciscitatusque

> est ab eo quid aut quomodo vellet de testamento suo. Qui mox per eosdem renuntiavit ei sic suum testamentum absque omni contradictione vel mutatione se velle stare, sicuti prefatus abbas illud in cyrographo posuerat. Quod ut Aieluuinus alderman audivit, totum concessit ut staret, sicuti ipse Siverhtus testatus erat.
>
> Then Abbot Brythnoth arranged for the will of Siferth to be written down in a tripartite chirograph, in the presence of his wife and daughter and all the people mentioned above, and had it read out before them all. When it was read, he had it cut, and Siferth kept one part of the chirograph, giving the second part to the abbot. The third part he sent at once by the aforesaid Byrhthelm to Ealdorman Æthelwine, who at that time was dwelling at Ely, and asked him to allow his will to stand, just as the abbot had written it and set it down at Linden in the witness of the aforementioned men. And when Ealdorman Æthelwine heard this and saw the chirograph, he sent Wulfnoth of Stowe back there to him with Byrhthelm and asked him what it was he wanted concerning his will. He [Siferth] soon reported back to him [Æthelwine] through them [Wulfnoth and Byrhthelm] just that he wanted his will to stand free from challenge or alteration, just as the aforesaid abbot had set it down in the chirograph. When Ealdorman Æthelwine heard this, he granted that it should stand in its entirety, just as Siferth had made it.[44]

The whole process is described in unusual detail. More unusual still is the preservation of such a lengthy narrative in a chronicle.[45] Generally, the *Libellus Æthelwoldi* contains little more than a bald summary of the relevant contents of a will. For example: 'Æthelstanus, filius Manne, dum moreretur, dedit sancte Ætheldreðe c acras in Walde.'[46] This particular summary is especially pertinent, as another Latin account of this will survives from Ramsey Abbey. This version describes not only the testator's bequests to both foundations, but also includes details of his extensive provision of property to his family with instructions concerning the manumission of thirty slaves. A report of the dispute immediately follows the version of the will:

> Post obitum igitur ejusdem Æthelstani, uxor ipsius, parentum inducta suggestione, huic testationi omnino contradixit, conventionem quandam excogitatam prætendens quam, ut dicebat, inter se habuerant ipsa et vir ejus dum adhuc viveret.[47]
>
> And so after the death of the same Æthelstan, his wife, at the instigation of her parents, completely disputed this will, on the pretext of a certain contrived agreement which she said that she and her husband

had made between them while he was still alive.[48]

Although a settlement was reached, witnessed and recorded, it was evidently considered prudent to retain a more comprehensive account of the will in the Ramsey archives. It may well be that the preservation of this level of detail in the Siferth episode could similarly have been born out of a necessity to guard against the possibility of future litigation over property bequeathed by the testator. It may well be that several chirographs owe their preservation to legal disputes in this way. Three chirographs explicitly record disputes or their settlements (S 1454, no. 21, S 1460, no. 27, S 1472, no. 51) and there is evidence that a further two (S 1376, no. 18, S 1423, no. 33) which appear to be straightforward leases could also represent the outcome of settlements.

It is highly probable that many chirographs have not survived, for of the 31 which still survive as portions only about one-third additionally contain a marker clause.[49] We therefore know of the majority only through the accident of survival in their chirographic form. When one considers the high attrition rate of single-sheet charters in general (less than one-fifth of the surviving number of charters dating from the Anglo-Saxon period are extant in contemporary form), it is clear that we have lost considerable numbers of this form of document. We do not have a single example of a surviving part and counterpart: again, suggestive of the proportion of chirographs which have been lost.[50]

Occasionally, post-Conquest scribes render the marker clauses of vernacular charters when summarising their content into Latin. The abstracts of the wills of Wulfgifu (S 1810, no. 22, from Ramsey) and of Leofflæd (S 1520, no. 39, from Ely), for example, mention that their copy-texts were originally produced in triplicate although the vernacular texts no longer survive: 'Hec scripto tripliciter consignantur. Unum est apud Ely, aliud in thesauris regis, tertium Leofleda habet.'[51] It is probable, however, that this type of information was often omitted: the various Latin summaries of the bequest of Thurstan (S 1530, nos 45, 46), for example, give no indication that the document was produced as a chirograph, despite the presence of a marker clause in the surviving portion from the same archive.[52] The Latin version of S 1425, no. 57, a lease, similarly omits the marker clause from its vernacular text. This Old English version, preserved in a seventeenth-century transcript of a lost cartulary from St Albans, has only recently been brought to light in a discovery which must rate among the most exciting for years.[53]

Sometimes scribes appear to have included additional information about their charters as a postscript to their copies: S 1387, no. 32 (AD 1016 x 1020), for example, survives both in single-sheet form, copied in the third quarter of the eleventh century onto the dorse of another charter, and in a thirteenth-century charter roll. The latter ends 'And þisses iþrites (*for* iwrites) ídoua (*for* icloua) is on cridíamtone. mid hure elder boken', information which is omitted from the single-sheet copy.[54] The transcription error of 'ídoua' for 'icloua' indicates that the thirteenth-century scribe was unfamiliar with the noun and did not add the statement himself. Its omission from the single-sheet copy suggests that the lease was originally a portion of a chirograph without a marker clause. It seems that the Crediton portion was used by the eleventh-century copyist and its counterpart (subsequently annotated) by the thirteenth-century scribe, either directly or indirectly.

We owe our knowledge of several chirographs to the observant nature of some early editors. S 1273 (no. 8), S 1283 (no. 9) and S 1459 (no. 29), for example, were copied by the antiquary John Smith in the eighteenth century, but the collection of 25 Worcester single-sheet documents of which they were a part was lost in a fire of 1752. Fortunately, Smith noted the fact that S 1283 and S 1459 were portions of chirographs: 'Inferiori parte hujus cartæ sunt semilitteræ hujus vocis, viz., Cyrographum', '*Ad imam Pag. vox* (cyrographum) *dimidiata*', and in his catalogue Wanley described S 1273 as '*Superiori parte Cartæ cernuntur semi-literæ vocum* CYROGRAPHVM ALHƿINI EP̄. 7 ÆÐELƿvLfI. DvCis.'[55] Of these three, only S 1459 contains a marker clause. There is no indication in either of the other texts as transcribed that more than one copy was produced of each charter.

The earliest chirographs unsurprisingly show the greatest degree of variation in form. The earliest example is a cartulary copy of a statement made before the synod of *Aclea*, datable to AD 804 (S 1187, no. 1), in which a layman, Æthelric, announces his intention to bequeath land. Copies of the declaration are to be retained by two of his friends and bishop Aldwulf of Lichfield:

> Si aliter fiat ut non opto aliquis homo contendat contra libros meos vel hereditatem indigne tunc habet Aldƿulfus episcopus in Licetfelda istius cartulæ comparem et amici necessarii mei et fidelissimi alias. id est. Eadbyr`h´t Eadgaring. 7 Æðelheh Esning. ad confirmationem hujus rei.[56]

> If it shall happen otherwise — as I hope it will not — that any man contends dishonourably against my title-deeds and inheritance, then Bishop Eadwulf has in Lichfield the duplicate of this charter, and my close and most faithful friends have others, namely Eadberht, son of Edgar, and Æthelheah, son of Esne, in confirmation of this matter.[57]

The formulation of the marker clause is unusual because it specifies that copies are to go to two of Æthelric's most trusted friends, rather than (as is usual) stipulating that a copy is to be retained by the testator and by one or more interested foundations. We know that Æthelric's disposition of the minster at Westbury-on-Trym was subject to dispute and we may perhaps attribute the preservation of the marker clause both in this cartulary version and in a short version preserved in another Worcester cartulary to the legal wrangling surrounding the bequest.

More useful for the purposes of evaluating developments in form are those chirographs which survive in contemporary single-sheet form. The earliest surviving portion (S 1270, no. 4), a lease by Bishop Cuthwulf of Hereford of uncertain provenance, is datable to the middle of the ninth century. However, its status is questionable. It survives in single-sheet form in a script now believed to be 'probably contemporary' with its date.[58] The upper half of the word 'continetur' occurs on the lower right-hand edge of the parchment.[59] Although both the legend and its placement are unique (all other portions have their legend spread across the width of the membrane), two of the other early portions do exhibit a degree of variation in their legends, which might support the inclusion of S 1270 amongst their number.[60] The earliest unproblematic portion is S 221, no. 10 (AD 901), a royal grant of land to the community of Much Wenlock. Before that there is evidence that a further two chirographs now lost (S 1273, no. 8, S 1283, no. 9) were originally issued as portions and survived as such into the eighteenth century. Two other early examples, a record of an agreement between Archbishop Ceolnoth and kings Ecgberht and Æthelwulf at Kingston (S 1438, no. 3, AD 838) and the will of Badanoth Beotting (S 1510, no. 45, datable to AD 845 x 852), each mention that two copies of the transaction are to be made:

> Duasque scripturas per omnia consimiles hujus reconciliationis conscribere statuimus. alteram habeat archiepiscopus cum telligraphis ecclesiæ Christi. alteram Ecgberht et Aetheluulf reges cum hereditatis eorum scripturis.[61]

> We have ordered two copies of this agreement completely alike in all respects to be drawn up. One the archbishop is to keep with the charters of Christ Church, the other kings Ecgberht and Æthelwulf with the records of their inheritance.

> ðonne is min willa ðæt ðissa gewriota sien twa gelice, oðer habben higon mid boecum oðer mine ærfeweardas heora dei.[62]

However, neither charter appears to have been produced in the form of a chirograph. It is inadvisable to place much emphasis on just two examples given the uncertainties and limitations of palaeographical dating. However, it is interesting that none of the ten surviving chirograph portions produced before the end of the tenth century contain marker clauses in addition to their distinctive physical form. It may be that early chirographs were produced either as portions of chirographs or included marker clauses (hence their survival in cartularies), but that these features did not appear in combination. The surprisingly high ratio (12:7) of portion types to marker-clause types as preserved in cartulary texts in those charters produced before the end of the tenth century suggests their superior popularity during this early period, especially when one considers the considerably more limited chances of survival of this type. The more consistent use of marker clauses from the eleventh century onwards strikes me as a significant one, for it suggests an awareness of the necessity to indicate the existence and whereabouts of further copies. The relative fortunes of these types appears as Figure 7.1 (see page 204). The graph shows that roughly equal numbers of portion-only type and combined type survive after AD 1000. The increase in the number of charters containing marker clauses in cartularies is noteworthy. Given the correspondingly sharp rise in numbers of surviving combined-type chirographs during this period, it seems likely that these cartulary marker clauses were copied from originally combined-type chirographs. The combined type therefore appears to have been the dominant form in the eleventh century, usurping the popularity of the portion-only type.

It seems that the chirograph achieved currency because of the increasing interest of the layman in the written document, and not merely because of the growth of bureaucracy in the Church; of the 31 chirographs with marker clauses that involve laymen, all but five note that the layman concerned was provided with a copy of the will, lease or agreement in question.[63] Of these five, one (S 1510) notes instead that a copy is intended for the testator's heirs, another (S 1460) for the owner of the estate (rather than the layman who brought a claim against the estate), a third (S 1187) that copies were to be given to the layman's friends. The clearest example of lay interest is afforded by S 1237 (no. 64), a grant of land by a layman, Ælfgar, *quandam comes*, to the church of Saint-Remi, Rheims, dating from AD *c*. 1061. The text mentions that two copies of the grant were to be made:

> Hoc scriptum in duabus cartis habetur divisum, quarum unam Anglicâ linguâ scriptam idem comes Algarus secum retinuit, aliam voce Latinâ dictatam sancto Remigio devotus transmisit.[64]

> This deed exists divided into two charters, of which Ælfgar kept one written in English for himself, the other in Latin he piously conveyed to Saint-Remi.

The copy intended for the layman appears to have been written in Old English because it was intended to form part of a working archive for the layman, and was not produced merely out of ecclesiastical convention. The type of document customarily made in chirographic form (the lease, the will) extensively concerned laymen: of the 64 chirographs, only 11 are of exclusively ecclesiastical or royal interest.[65] Four of these (S 281, no. 2, S 312, no. 6, S 313, no. 7, S 981, no. 34) are considered to be forgeries or at best unacceptable in their received form. A further two (S 1465, no. 37, S 1472, no. 5) involve minor clergy. One portion, S 1220, no. 28, a grant of a swine-pasture *æt Swiðrædingdænne*, concerns only laymen. Its survival is presumably attributable to the interest of the land to Christ Church. Although the identification of the estate is disputed, the archbishop of Canterbury is known to have held land T.R.E. at both possible locations.[66] We may assume that very many more chirographs involving laymen proved of no concern to the foundation responsible for their production and were not preserved by them.

It is possible to see some variation between types of document in chirographic form and archive. Well-represented foundations are Bury St Edmunds (8 chirographs), Christ Church, Canterbury (15), Old Minster, Winchester (8) and Worcester (17). All except Bury St Edmunds are large archives, containing hundreds of pre-Conquest charters; Bury St Edmunds is unusual in that almost all of its archive comprises vernacular charters, the majority of which are wills. Very few of its charters survive in contemporary form and all eight chirographs are known only from their marker clauses in cartulary copies. Christ Church, Canterbury, contains a wide variety of chirographic texts, including wills, records of disputes and agreements which are preserved in a mixture of single-sheets and later copies. Old Minster, Winchester, has only one single-sheet portion, an eleventh-century forgery of a royal grant. Worcester presents the most interesting profile. The foundation itself is well known for its outstanding series of over 100 leases, and this preponderance is reflected in its surviving 17 chirographs, 11 of which are leases. Only one of these leases contains a marker clause, S 1423, no. 33, which survives as the lower portion of a lease issued by Abbot Ælfweard of Evesham. This portion apparently came to Worcester in compliance with its marker clause, which indicates that portions were retained by Evesham, Worcester and the layman concerned. Unlike Old Minster, Winchester, it does not appear to have been customary to produce combined-type leases at Worcester. It seems significant that the archive contains no examples of contemporary single-sheet leases other than those in chirographic form. This strengthens Kelly's suggestion that it was usual to produce leases in the form of a chirograph from the tenth century, certainly at this foundation.[67] It is certainly difficult to see why some leases were produced as chirographs and others were not. Those which have survived as portions do not appear to concern unusually large pieces of land or record particularly complex arrangements. Nor do they not appear to have been produced for lessees of high rank.

Another interesting issue raised by these leases is the variation they display in language. We know, for example, that it was customary for diplomas to be produced in Latin and for writs and wills to be composed in English, but there appears to be no established tradition with leases. When we consider the 77 leases surviving from Bishop Oswald's episcopate (AD 961 x 992), for example, we find that, although boundary clauses (which occur in almost half of the leases) are always in English, the body of the leases themselves display considerable variation in language: 13% are in English, 56% are in Latin and 31% are in a mixture of English and Latin. Choice of language seems to have been an arbitrary decision, one that is not date-dependent and does not appear to have been influenced by the likely linguistic competence or status of the lessee. For example, although most (but not all) leases to ecclesiastics seem to have been issued in Latin, leases to thanes (assuming that at least a proportion of those styled *fidelis* or *minister* were of that rank) survive in both Latin, English and in combination, whereas all three of the leases issued to men styled *artifex* are in Latin without bounds. Although none of these survives in chirographic form, a parallel is the slightly later example of the lower portion of a chirograph, S 1407, no. 61, again in Latin throughout, which records the lease of two hides and a yardland to Bishop Eadred's man (*fidelis vir*), Balwine.[68] It is hard to imagine that anyone other than Balwine himself would have been the recipient of the lease's counterpart and equally hard to imagine what sense he would have been able to make of a document written entirely in Latin. There seems no rationale behind these choices: odd, when such a large number of leases was produced in a comparatively short period from a single archive. I wonder instead if one portion of the chirograph was customarily produced in Latin for the foundation and in English for the lessee. Those leases that survive in English, therefore, were originally issued to the lessee rather than the lessor and returned to the foundation either for safekeeping or on expiry of the lease. The evidence supplied by the marker clause from Saint-Remi (see above) would support this hypothesis.

It should be emphasised that I am not suggesting that the layman could read such texts, but the highly visual nature of these texts and the ease with which counterparts could be matched and checked would make them appealing and strengthen his interest in possessing documents produced in this way. Thus, a layman becomes more central to a 'literacy event' and can fully participate within it.[69] The literacy event in this instance is centred around the layman: the chirograph would either be produced for him (in the case of a will) or would directly involve him (in the case of a lease). This can be contrasted with other forms of documents issued during the period, like writs. These, as we have seen, traditionally convey administrative orders and their contents could be only of peripheral concern to the majority of laymen. There could, on the other hand, be no written document that would touch a layman or his life more nearly than his own will. For example, Thurstan, the testator of S 1531, is implicitly addressed as a thane in a writ of King Edward (S 1068), but it contents would presumably be only of passing interest to him:

> Eadward king gret Alfric biscop and alle mine þeynes on Norf' 7 on Suff' frendlike. And ic kithe ihu þat ic wille þat Vui abbot be þe minst*r*es wirðe at Seynt Eadmu*n*des biri. and alle þinge þe þer to bireth...[70]

However, the text of his will, originally produced in chirographic form, contains instructions for the disposition of property garnered over a lifetime:

> ic Þurstan Wine sune kithe alle manne ihu ic an þe þing þe me god haueð lent so longe so his wille beth.[71]

A modern analogy could perhaps be the difference between receiving a handwritten letter personally addressed and a typewritten envelope addressed 'to the owner/occupier' and delivered to every property on the street. The recipient is targeted, but not individually targeted. Documents produced in chirographic form are written in the vernacular; the layman would therefore be able to understand the text when it was read to him after being copied. This can be contrasted with the diploma, where the majority of the text is written in a language which conveys only authority and sanctity to the listener, not understanding. He could see part and counterpart cut before his eyes and would receive one portion for himself. At any later stage he could take his document to his local church to have it read. His copy would include information about the existence and whereabouts of the other parts. He would be able to vouch for their authenticity himself by matching them up with this portion without having them read. The physical form of the chirograph uniquely allows the layman to engage with a written text without the aid of an intermediary.

Any study of the growth of literacy inevitably has to describe a difficult, often slow, transition from a period in which oral transmission and the testimony of witnesses is paramount, through a stage where such evidence runs concomitant with, and is supplemented by, written documents. The Siferth will-making episode discussed above appears to reflect this intermediary period. Gradually attitudes change, and people come to appreciate, respect, accept and finally want the benefits of this new technology for themselves. It is investigation into a type of document like the chirograph, in form and function so attractive to the layman, that provides us with our best evidence that the growth of the literate mentality and change in attitude to the written document was neither confined to the

Church or the State nor, indeed, to the centuries following the Norman Conquest.

NOTES

1. John Oxenham, *Literacy, Writing, Reading and Social Organisation*, Language and Society Series (London: Routledge and Kegan Paul, 1980), p. ix.
2. Harvey J. Graff, *Literacy in History: An Interdisciplinary Research Bibliography*, Garland Reference Library for the Humanities, 254 (New York: Garland Publishing, Inc., 1981).
3. *Transactions of the Royal Historical Society*, 5th ser. (1977), 95–114.
4. Simon Keynes, 'Royal Government and the Written Word in Late Anglo-Saxon England'; Susan Kelly, 'Anglo-Saxon Lay Society and the Written Word', *The Uses of Literacy in Early Mediaeval Europe*, ed. Rosamond McKitterick (Cambridge: Cambridge University Press, 1990, repr. 1992), pp. 226–57 and 36–62 respectively.
5. London: Edward Arnold, 1979; 2nd ed., Oxford: Blackwell, 1993.
6. The Anglo-Saxon, Norse and Celtic Department in Cambridge periodically offers a special paper in the subject. About half of the Finals paper 'Medieval English Manuscripts in Context' run by the English Language department at Glasgow University is concerned with the nature and extent of literacy in the medieval period.
7. 'The Uses of Literacy in Anglo-Saxon England and its Neighbours', pp. 113 and 114 respectively.
8. *From Memory to Written Record*, p. 32.
9. 'Royal Government and the Written Word in Late Anglo-Saxon England', p. 255.
10. *The Diplomas of King Æthelred 'the Unready' 978–1016*, Cambridge Studies in Medieval Life and Thought, 13 (Cambridge: Cambridge University Press, 1980).
11. 'The Uses of Literacy in Anglo-Saxon England and its Neighbours', pp. 95 and 104 respectively.
12. 'Anglo-Saxon Lay Society and the Written Word', p. 51.
13. Jack Goody, ed., *Literacy in Traditional Societies* (Cambridge: Cambridge University Press, 1968), pp. 27–68.
14. *Societies: Evolutionary and Comparative Perspectives*, Foundations of Modern Sociology Series (Englewood Cliffs: Prentice-Hall, 1966).
15. London: Methuen and Co., Ltd., 1982.
16. 'The Uses of Literacy in Anglo-Saxon England and its Neighbours', p. 95.
17. Ibid., pp. 96–7.
18. Ibid., p. 113.
19. 'Literacy in Kērala', *Literacy in Traditional Societies*, ed. Jack Goody and

Ian Watt, pp. 132–60.

20. 'The Measurement of Literacy in Pre-Industrial England', ibid., pp. 311–25.
21. Themes in the Social Sciences (Cambridge: Cambridge University Press, 1977).
22. Ibid., p. 46.
23. *Literacy in Theory and Practice*, Cambridge Studies in Oral and Literate Culture, 9 (Cambridge: Cambridge University Press, 1984); *Social Literacies: Critical Approaches to Literacy in Development, Ethnography and Education*, Real Language Series (London and New York: Longman, 1995).
24. 'Introduction', *Cross-Cultural Approaches to Literacy*, ed. Brian Street, Cambridge Studies in Oral and Literate Culture, 23 (Cambridge: Cambridge University Press, 1993), pp. 1–21, at p. 5.
25. Ibid., p. 9.
26. David Barton, *Literacy: An Introduction to the Ecology of Written Language* (Oxford: Blackwell, 1994), pp. 59–65.
27. McKitterick's introduction to the collected papers (pp. 1–10) displays a sensitive understanding of the theoretical debates underpinning the anthropological study of literacy (pp. 4–5).
28. *The Logic of Writing and the Organization of Society*, Studies in Literacy, Family, Culture and the State (Cambridge: Cambridge University Press, 1986), p. 160.
29. *Social Literacies: Critical Approaches to Literacy in Development, Ethnography and Education*, pp. 30–1.
30. Ibid., p. 30; emphasis mine.
31. Ibid., pp. 31 and 32 respectively.
32. The use of the writ seems to have become commonplace by the late tenth century. I find it significant that a development in its function and importance can be traced from its original use as a method of conveying administrative orders to its eventual assumption of the role of the Latin diploma late in the period; see Florence E. Harmer, *Anglo-Saxon Writs*, The Ward Bequest, 10 (Manchester: Manchester University Press, 1952), p. 37.
33. 'The Uses of Literacy in Anglo-Saxon England and its Neighbours', p. 95.
34. Simon Keynes and Alan Kennedy, *Anglo-Saxon Ely: Records of Ely Abbey and its Benefactors in the Tenth and Eleventh Centuries* (Woodbridge: Boydell and Brewer, forthcoming), ch. 38. E.O. Blake, ed., *Liber Eliensis*, Royal Historical Society, Camden 3rd ser., 92 (London: Offices of the Royal Historical Society, 1962), 2.27, p. 101. Translations from the *Libellus* are those of Keynes and Kennedy, but for ease of use the Latin quotations have been taken from the *Liber Eliensis* with cross-reference to the corresponding chapter in the *Libellus*. I am most grateful

to Dr Keynes for making a draft of the *Libellus* available to me.

35. Della Hooke, *The Anglo-Saxon Landscape: The Kingdom of the Hwicce* (Manchester: Manchester University Press, 1985), pp. 52–3.

36. S 56 (AD 759), S 59 (AD 770). Anglo-Saxon charters are referred to here by their now-standard Sawyer number (P.H. Sawyer, *Anglo-Saxon Charters: An Annotated List and Bibliography*, Royal Historical Guides and Handbooks, 8 [London: Offices of the Royal Historical Society, 1968]) followed (in the case of the chirographs) by a number corresponding to its position in the Appendix to this article. A revised edition is being prepared by Dr S.E. Kelly, who has generously made a draft of the work available to the academic community.

37. S 367. Walter de Gray Birch, ed., *Cartularium Saxonicum*, 3 vols (London: Whiting and Co., 1885–1899), no. 603.

38. S.D. Keynes, 'A Charter of King Edward the Elder for Islington', *Historical Research* 66 (1993), 303–16, at pp. 310–11.

39. The most elaborate example is S 1454 (AD 990 x 992) with the legend CPILREOTGVRMAEFSVTM, which, when the letters are read alternately, gives CIROGRAFVM PLETVM EST (Keynes, 'Royal Government and the Written Word in Late Anglo-Saxon England', p. 250 n. 94).

40. Attempts to link the form back to the Roman *syngrapha* are not persuasive. See A. de Boüard, *Manuel de diplomatique française et pontificale: diplomatique générale* (Paris, Editions Auguste Picard, 1927), pp. 365–71). B. Bischoff ('Zur Frühgeschichte des mittelalterliche Chirographum', in his *Mittelalterliche Studien*, 3 vols [Stuttgart: Anton Hiersemann, 1966–1981], vol. 1, pp. 118-22) argues for an Irish origin.

41. I exclude from the discusson those charters which have survived in more than one contemporary copy if they are not in chirographic form or do not contain a marker clause noting the existence of other copies.

42. The relationship between these two charters is discussed by Keynes (*Facsimiles of Anglo-Saxon Charters*, Anglo-Saxon Charters Supplementary Volume 1 [Oxford: Oxford University Press, 1991], p. 8).

43. See ibid., p. 6.

44. S. Keynes and A. Kennedy, *Anglo-Saxon Ely: Records of Ely Abbey and its Benefactors in the Tenth and Eleventh Centuries*, ch. 12; Blake, ed., *Liber Eliensis*, 2.11, p. 87.

45. I have discussed elsewhere the various methods and priorities of chronicle scribes who had to translate and summarise vernacular documents ('The Anglo-Saxon Vernacular Will: Studies in Texts and Their Transmission', unpublished Ph.D. dissertation, University of Cambridge, 1990).

46. Keynes and Kennedy, *Anglo-Saxon Ely: Records of Ely Abbey and its Benefactors in the Tenth and Eleventh Centuries*, ch. 18; Blake, ed., *Liber Eliensis*, 2.13, p. 91.

47. W. Dunn Macray, ed., *Chronicon Abbatiae Rameseiensis*, Chronicles and

Memorials of Great Britain and Ireland during the Middle Ages (London: Longman, 1886), no. 33.

48. I should like to thank Timothy Graham for his valuable help with rendering the Latin of these charters.

49. See the note to Figure 1 for exclusions from the reckoning.

50. Clanchy notes that it is unusual even in later medieval times for more than one part of a chirograph to survive to the present day (*From Memory to Written Record*, p. 88).

51. Blake, ed., *Liber Eliensis*, 2.88, pp. 157–8. It cannot, however, be assumed that several other summaries of wills and grants (for example, S 1231, S 1493, S 1518, S 1808) from Ramsey which are described by the word 'chirographum' in their introductory rubrics were necessarily produced in this way, for the word retains a more general sense of 'document' throughout the period.

52. I discuss the relationship between the three Old English texts and four Latin versions of S 1530 in 'The Anglo-Saxon Vernacular Will: Studies in Texts and Their Transmission', pp. 66–74 and 177–9.

53. Simon Keynes, 'A Lost Cartulary of St Albans Abbey', *Anglo-Saxon England* 22 (1993), 253–79.

54. J.B. Davidson, 'On Some Ancient Documents Relating to Crediton Minster', *Report and Transactions of the Devonshire Association* 10 (1878), 237–54, at p. 240.

55. John Smith, *Historiae Ecclesiasticae gentis Anglorum libri quinque auctore, ... Beda ... una cum reliquis ejus Operibus Historicis in unum volumen Collectis* (Cambridge: Typis Academicis, 1722), pp. 722, 778; Humphrey Wanley, *Liber Veterum Septentrionalium, qui in Angliae Bibliothecis extant, nec non multorum Veterum Codicum Septentrionalium alibi extantium Catalogus Historico-Criticus, cum totius Thesauri Linguarum Septentrionalium Thesauris* (Oxford: Sheldonian Theatre, 1705), p. 302, no. 7.

56. Birch, ed., *Cartularium Saxonicum*, no. 313.

57. Dorothy Whitelock, ed., *English Historical Documents c. 500–1042*, 2nd ed. (London: Eyre Metheuen, 1979), p. 513.

58. See Keynes, 'A Lost Cartulary of St Albans Abbey', p. 3, who comments that Sawyer's date of s. x med is 'certainly too late'.

59. Keynes' alternative suggestion, that the word is an error for 'continuatur' and refers to the continuation of the text on the dorse (like a modern 'P.T.O.') has the similar disadvantage of being unparalleled and strikes me as a less preferable explanation (*Facsimiles of Anglo-Saxon Charters*, p. 3).

60. E.g., S 221, no. 10: '...ME CRUCIS +'. In the draft of her revised edition of Sawyer's *Anglo-Saxon Charters: An Annotated List and Bibliography*, no. 221, Kelly suggests that this may be for 'signum alme crucis'. It

appears that S 1273 (no. 8), now lost, orginally read 'CYROGRAPHVM ALHƿINI EP̄. ⁊ ÆÐELƿvLfI. DvCis.' which must have taken some squeezing onto the parchment.

61. Birch., ed., *Cartularium Saxonicum*, no. 421.

62. A.J. Robertson, *Anglo-Saxon Charters*, Cambridge Studies in English Legal History, 2nd ed. (Cambridge: Cambridge University Press, 1956), no. 6, p. 10, ll. 18–21.

63. S 1187 (no. 1), S 1510 (no. 5), S 1460 (no. 27), S 1459 (no. 29), S 1474 (no. 54). The number includes S 1531 (no. 49), which notes that one of the portions is destined for the testator's *hired*.

64. William Dugdale, *Monasticon Anglicanum*, ed. John Caley, Henry Ellis and Bulkeley Bandinel, 6 vols (London: Longman and Co., Lackington and Co., and Joseph Harding, 1817–1830), vol. 6.2, p. 1042 (no. 1).

65. S 281, no. 2 (AD 838), S 1483, no. 3, S 3133, no. 7 (AD 854), S 221, no. 10 (AD 901), S 1368, no. 14 (*c.* AD 964), S 1449, no. 15 (AD 964 x 979), S 981, no. 34 (AD 1016 x 1035), S 1465, no. 37 (AD 1032), S 1400, no. 42 (AD 1038 x 1050), S 1472, no. 51 (AD 1044 x 1045).

66. See Keynes, *Facsimiles of Anglo-Saxon Charters*, pp. 6–7, for discussion of the possibilities.

67. 'Anglo-Saxon Lay Society and the Written Word', p. 49.

68. Four leases are in favour of lessees styled 'man' (*fidelis homo/vir*, *hold ⁊ getriow man*). Although the status of these laymen cannot be ascertained with certainty, the term *man* is used in the laws, alongside general specification, to refer to a *ceorl*. I am grateful to Dr Carole Hough for this information.

69. Barton (*Literacy: An Introduction to the Ecology of Written Language*, p. 36) notes that the term, derived from the sociolinguistic idea of speech events, was first used in relation to literacy by A.B. Anderson, W.H. Teale and E. Estrada ('Low-Income Children's Preschool Literacy Experiences: Some Naturalistic Observations', *Quarterly Newsletter of the Laboratory of Comparative Human Cognition* 2 [1980], 59–65), who defined it as being an occasion during which a person 'attempts to comprehend graphic signs'. The notion was developed by Shirly Brice Heath, who further characterised a 'literacy event' as 'any occasion in which a piece of writing is integral to the nature of participants' interactions and their interpretive processes' ('Protean Shapes in Literacy Events: Ever-Shifting Oral and Literate Traditions', *Written Language: Exploring Orality and Literacy*, ed Deborah Tannen, Advances in Discourse Processes, 9 [Norwood: Ablex Publishing Corportion, 1982], pp. 91-117, at p. 93).

70. Harmer, ed., *Anglo-Saxon Writs*, no. 8.

71. Whitelock, *Anglo-Saxon Wills*, no. 31, p. 80, ll. 1–3.

APPENDIX

List of Chirographs

References:

Birch 1885–1899	Walter de Gray Birch, ed., *Cartularium Saxonicum*, 3 vols (London: Whiting and Co., 1885–1899).
Blake 1962	E.O. Blake, ed., *Liber Eliensis*, Royal Historical Society, Camden 3rd ser., 92 (London: Offices of the Royal Historical Society, 1962).
BM Facs.	E.A. Bond, *Facsimiles of Ancient Charters in the British Museum*, 4 vols (London: British Museum Publications, 1873–1878).
Davidson 1878	J.B. Davidson, 'On Some Ancient Documents Relating to Crediton Minster', *Report and Transactions of the Devonshire Association* 10 (1878), 237–54.
Dugdale 1817–1830	William Dugdale, *Monasticon Anglicanum*, ed. John Caley, Henry Ellis and Bulkeley Bandinel, 6 vols (London: Longman and Co., Lackington and Co., and Joseph Harding, 1817–1830).
Keynes 1993	Simon Keynes, 'A Lost Cartulary of St Albans Abbey', *Anglo-Saxon England* 22 (1993), 253–79.
Lowe 1990	Kathryn A. Lowe, 'The Anglo-Saxon Vernacular Will: Studies in Texts and Their Transmission', unpublished Ph.D. dissertation, University of Cambridge, 1990.
O'Donovan 1988	M.A. O'Donovan, ed., *Charters of Sherborne*, Anglo-Saxon Charters, 3 (Oxford: Oxford University Press, 1988).
OS Facs.	W.B. Sanders, ed., *Facsimiles of Anglo-Saxon Manuscripts*, trans. W. Basevi Sanders, 3 vols (Southampton: Ordnance Survey Office, 1878–1884).
Robertson 1956	A.J. Robertson, *Anglo-Saxon Charters*, Cambridge Studies in English Legal History, 2nd ed. (Cambridge: Cambridge University Press, 1956).
Smith 1722	John Smith, *Historiae Ecclesiasticae gentis Anglorum libri quinque auctore, ... Beda ... una cum reliquis ejus Operibus Historicis in unum volumen Collectis* (Cambridge: Typis Academicis, 1722).
Somner 1726	William Somner, *A Treatise of Gravelkind, Both Name and Thing*, 2nd ed. (London: Gyles, Woodman,

Lyon and Davis, 1726).

Stevenson 1858 Joseph Stevenson, *Chronicon Monasterii de Abingdon*, Chronicle and Memorials of Great Britain and Ireland during the Middle Ages, 2 vols (London: Longman, 1858).

Thorpe 1865 Benjamin Thorpe, ed., *Diplomatarium Anglicum Ævi Saxonici* (London: Macmillan, 1865).

Wanley 1705 Humphrey Wanley, *Liber Veterum Septentrionalium, qui in Angliae Bibliothecis extant, nec non multorum Veterum Codicum Septentrionalium alibi extantium Catalogus Historico-Criticus, cum titius Thesauri Linguarum Septentrionalium Thesaurus* (Oxford: Sheldonian Theatre, 1705).

Whitelock 1930 Dorothy Whitelock, *Anglo-Saxon Wills*, Cambridge Studies in English Legal History (Cambridge: Cambridge University Press, 1930).

1. S 1187 AD 804

Edited:	Birch 1885–1899, no. 313
Archive:	Worcester
Status:	Cartulary copy
Description:	Æthelric declares his intention to bequeath land
Language:	Latin
Issued:	Triplicate: Bishop Aldwulf, two friends
Text:	Si aliter fiat ut non opto aliquis homo contendat contra libros meos vel hereditatem indigne tunc habet Aldƿulfus episcopus in Licetfelda istius cartulæ comparem et amici necessarii mei et fidelissimi alias. id est. Eadbyr`h´t Eadgaring. ⁊ Æðelheh Esning. ad confirmationem hujus rei. Short version: Si fiet quod non opto. ut aliquis homo contra meos contenderit libros. tunc habet Aldulfus episcopus in Licetfelda. istius cartæ comparem. et amici mei fidelissimi alias. Eadberht Eadgaring. ⁊ Æþelheh Esning.

2. S 281 AD 838

Edited:	Birch 1885–1899, no. 423
Archive:	Old Minster, Winchester
Status:	Cartulary copy
Description:	Egbert, king of Wessex to see of Winchester; grant of 40 hides
Language:	Latin
Issued:	Duplicate: bishop, king
Text:	Cum hanc prænominata terra comparat ⁊ requirat. duasque

scripturas per omnia consimiles hujus reconciliationis conscribere statuimus. alteram habeat episcopus cum telligraphis ecclesie. alteram Egberht et Æðelwlf reges cum hereditatis eorum scripturis.

3. S 1438 AD 838

Edited:	Birch 1885–1899, no. 421
Archive:	Christ Church, Canterbury
Status:	Contemporary sheet
Description:	Record of agreement made at Kingston between Archbishop Ceolnoth and Kings Ecgberht and Æthelwulf concerning the recovery of land by Christ Church, Canturbury.
Language:	Latin
Issued:	Duplicate: Archbishops, kings
Text:	Duasque scripturas per omnia consimiles hujus reconciliationis conscribere statuimus. alteram habeat archiepiscopus cum telligraphis ecclesiæ Christi. alteram Ecgberht et Aetheluulf reges cum hereditatis eorum scripturis.

4. S 1270 AD 840 x 852

Manuscript:	Hereford, Dean and Chapter.
Facsimile:	Keynes 1993, no. 3
Archive:	Uncertain
Status:	Probably contemporary sheet
Description:	Bishop Cuthwulf of Hereford; lease of four hides of land to Ealdorman Ælfstan for three lives
Language:	Latin
Portion:	continetur (upper)

5. S 1510 AD 845 x 853

Edited:	Robertson 1956, no. 6
Archive:	Christ Church
Status:	Contemporary sheet
Description:	Will of Badanoth Beotting
Language:	English
Issued:	Duplicate: foundation; heirs
Text:	ðonne is min willa ðæt ðissa gewriota sien twa gelice oðer habben higon mid boecum oðer mine ærfeweardas heora dei.

6. S 312 AD 854

Facsimile:	*OS Facs.*, vol. 2, Winchester 1
Archive:	Old Minster, Winchester

Status: Single-sheet forgery, s. xv
Description: Æthelwulf to St Peter and Old Minster, Winchester; grant of 20 hides
Language: Latin
Portion: CY RO GRA PHVM (upper)

7. S 313 AD 854
Manuscript: Edinburgh, University Library, Laing Charter 18
Facsimile: Keynes 1991, no. 24
Archive: Old Minster, Winchester
Status: Forgery, s. xi
Description: Æthelwulf to St Peter and Old Minster, Winchester, grant of 20 hides
English: CYRO GRA PHVM (upper)

8. S 1273 AD 855
Edited: Smith 1722, pp. 769–70 (Birch 1885–1899, no. 490)
Archive: Worcester
Status: Sheet; lost
Description: Bishop Alhwine of Worcester to Æthelwulf, *dux*, and Wilfthryth his wife; lease of 11 hides
Language: Latin
Portion: '*Superiori parte Cartæ cernuntur semi-literæ vocum* CYROGRAPHVM ALHƿINI EP̄. 7 ÆĐELƿvLfI DvCis.' (Wanley 1705, p. 302, no. 7)

9. S 1283 AD 899 x 904
Edited: Smith 1722, pp. 771–2 (Birch 1885–1899, no. 560)
Archive: Worcester
Status: Sheet; lost
Description: Bishop Wærferth to Cyneswith; lease of 3 hides
Language: English
Portion: 'Inferiori parte hujus cartæ sunt semilitteræ hujus vocis, viz. Cyrographum' (Smith 1722, p. 722)

10. S 221 AD 901
Manuscript: British Library, Cotton Ch. viii. 27
Facsimile: *BM Facs.*, vol 3, no. 1
Archive: Much Wenlock
Status: Contemporary sheet
Description: Æthelred and Æthelflæd, rulers of Mercia, to community of Much Wenlock; grant of land
Language: Latin

Portion: ...ME CRUCIS + (upper) (? signum alme crucis)

11. S 1281 AD 904
Manuscript: British Library, Add. Ch. 19,791
Facsimile: *BM Facs.*, vol. 3, no. 2
Archive: Worcester
Status: Contemporary sheet
Description: Bishop Wærferth to Wulfsige, his reeve; lease of 1 hide for three lives
Language: English
Portion: CYROGRAPHVM (lower)

12. S 1417 AD 925 x 933
Manuscript: Winchester College, Muniment Room, Cabinet 7, Drawer 2, no. 3
Facsimile: *OS Facs.*, vol. 2, Winchester College 2
Archive: New Minster, Winchester
Status: Contemporary sheet
Description: The *familia* of New Minster, Winchester, to Alfred, *minister*, lease of 20 hides in return for money and annual rent.
Language: Latin
Portio: CY RO GRAF FVM (upper)

13. S 1506 AD 958 x 958 (?958)
Manuscript: British Library, Stowe Ch. 27
Facsimile: *OS Facs.*, vol. 3, no. 28
Archive: Christ Church
Status: Contemporary sheet
Description: Will of Æthelwyrd
Language: English
Portion: CYREGRAFFA (upper)

14. S 1368 AD *c.* 964
Edited: Birch 1885–1899, no. 1136
Archive: Worcester
Status: Cartulary copy
Description: Bishop Oswald to King Edgar, letter setting out conditions under which he grants leases
Language: Latin
Issued: Triplicate: Worcester, two bishops
Text: Harum textus epistolarum tres sunt ad pretitulationem et ad signum. una in ipsa civitate que vocatur Uuigraceaster. altera cum venerabili Dunstano archiepiscopo in Cantuaria. tertia

cum Atheluuoldo episcopo in Uuintonia civitate.

15. S 1449 AD 964 x 975

Edited: Robertson 1956, no. 49
Archive: Old Minster, Winchester
Status: Cartulary copy
Description: Record of adjustment of the boundaries between the monasteries in Winchester
Language: English
Issued: Triplicate
Text: Se þe ðis þonne awendan wylle ðe ic to sibbe ⁊ to gesehtnesse betweoh þam mynstre [g]eradigod hæbbe odðe þara ðinga þe on þissan þrim cyrografu*m* ðe on ðissu*m* þrym mynstru*m* to swytelungu*m* gesette syndon. awende hine sé eca drihten fram heofenan rice.

16. S 1326 AD 969

Manuscript: British Library, Additional Ch. 19792
Facsimile: *BM Facs.*, vol. 3, no. 28
Archive: Worcester
Status: Contemporary sheet
Description: Bishop Oswald to his kinsman Osulf *cniht*; lease for three lives
Language: English
Portion: CYROGRAVVM (upper)

17. S 1216 AD 971 x 980

Edited: Robertson 1956, no. 51 (English)
Stevenson 1858, vol. 1, p. 355 (Latin)
Archive: Abingdon
Status: Cartulary copy
Description: Ælfhere, ealdorman to Abbot Osgar, record to the sale of 20 hides
Language: Latin and English versions
Issued: Duplicate
English: ⁊ þysses gewrites geclofan nam se ealdorman Ælfhere to swytelunga.
Latin: hujus etiam scripti divisionem recepit ipse princeps jam prædictus pro ostensione.

18. S 1376 AD 975 x 978

Edited: Robertson 1956, no. 53 (English)
Archive: Old Minster, Winchester

Status: Cartulary copy
Description: Grant of 12 hides by Bishop Æthelwine and community of Old Minster to Ælfwine in exchange for 2 hides
Language: Latin and English versions
Issued: Quadruplicate: layman, Old Minster, New Minster, Nunnaminster
Text: Þonne synt ðyses gehwerfes .IIII. gewrytu to geswitulunge. an is mid Ælfwine. oðer in ealdan mynstre. þridde on niwan mynstre. feorðe on nunan mynstre.
Note: Marker clause not in Latin version

19. S 1487 AD 975 x 1016
Manuscript: British Library, Stowe Ch. 36
Facsimile: *OS Facs.*, vol. 3, no. 37
Archive: Westminster
Status: Contemporary sheet
Description: Will of Ælfhelm
Language: English
Portion: CYROGRAPHVM (lower)

20. S 1347 AD 984
Manuscript: British Library, Additional Ch. 19794
Facsimile: *BM Facs.*, vol. 3, no. 32
Archive: Worcester
Status: Contemporary sheet
Description: Archbishop Oswald to Cynelm his *minister*; lease of 2 1/2 hides for three lives
Language: Latin
Portion: CYROGRAVVM (lower)

21. S 1454 AD 990 x 992
Manuscript: British Library, Cotton Augustus ii. 15
Facsimile: *BM Facs.*, vol. 3, no. 37
Archive: Christ Church
Status: Contemporary sheet
Description: Record of a dispute between Wynflæd and Leofwine
Language: English
Portion: CPILREOTGVRMAEFSVTM (upper)

22. S 1810 AD 995 x 1001
Edited: Birch 1885–1899, no. 1059
Archive: Ramsey
Status: Cartulary copy

Description: Bequest by Wulfgifu to St Benedict's, Ramsey (incomplete)
Language: Latin
Issued: Triplicate: bishop, Ramsey, testatrix
Text: Hoc scriptum fuit in tribus partibus divisum, quarum una remansit in manibus Æthelstani episcopi, alteram mecum retinui, tertiam obtuli Ramesiam.

23. S 939 AD 995 x 999
Manuscript: Canterbury Dean and Chapter, Chart. Ant. B. 1
Facsimile: *OS Facs.*, vol. 1, no. 17
Edited: Whitelock 1930, no. 16 (2)
Archive: Christ Church
Status: Contemporary sheet
Description: King Æthelred confirms the will of Æthelric
Language: English
Issued: Triplicate: Christ Church, king's *haligdom*, widow
Text: þissa gewrita syndon þreo. an is æt Xp̄es cyrcean. oðer æt þæs cinges haligdome. þridde hæfð seo wúduwe.
Portion: CYROGRAPHVM CYROGRAPHVM (central)

24. S 1522 AD 998
Manuscript: Bodleian Library, Eng. hist. a. 2, no XII
Facsimile: Keynes 1991, no. 14
Archive: Westminster
Status: Later sheet (s. xi?)
Description: Will of Leofwine
Language: English
Portion: CHIROGRAPHUM (lower)

25. S 1534 AD *c.* 1000
Manuscript: British Library, Harley Ch. 83. A 2
Facsimile: *BM Facs.*, vol. 4, no. 42
Archive: Worcester
Status: Contemporary sheet
Description: Will of Wulfgeat
Language: English
Portion: CYROGRAFVM (lower)

26. S 1385 AD 1003 x 1016
Manuscript: British Library, Additional Ch. 19795
Facsimile: *BM Facs.*, vol. 4, no. 13
Archive: Worcester
Status: Contemporary sheet

Description: Archbishop Wulfstan to Wulfgifu, lease of 1/2 hide for three lives
Language: Latin and English bounds
Portion: CYROGRAVVM (lower)

27. S 1460 AD *c*. 1010 x 1023
Manuscript: British Library, Cotton Ch. viii. 37
Facsimile: *BM Facs*., vol. 4, no. 14
Edited: Robertson 1956, no. 83
Archive: Worcester
Status: Contemporary sheet
Description: Record of a dispute between Bishop Athelstan and Wulfstan and his son Wulfric
Language: English
Issued: Triplicate: St Mary's, Worcester, St Æthelberht's in Hereford, owner of estate
Text: Nu syndan þissa gewrita þreo. an on Wigernaceastre æt SC̄A Marian þær þæt land toherð. ⁊ oðer on Hereforda æt Sc̄e Æþelbrihte. ⁊ þridde a mid þam þe þæt land on hande stande.
Portion: CYROGRAPHVM (lower)

28. S 1220 AD 1013 x 1020
Manuscript: London and Oslo, Schøyen Collection, MS 600
Facsimile: Keynes 1991, no. 19
Archive: Christ Church
Status: Probably contemporary sheet
Description: Godwine to Leofwine the Red; grant of a swine-pasture
Language: English
Portion: + CYROGRAPFHVM (upper)

29. S 1459 AD 1014 x 1016
Edited: Smith 1722, p. 778 (Robertson 1956, no. 76)
Archive: Worcester
Status: Sheet; lost
Description: Marriage agreement concerning Wulfric and the sister of Archbishop Wulfstan
Language: English
Issued: Duplicate: archbishop, bishop
Text: Nu syndon to ðysum forƿordan tƿa geƿrita. oþer mid ðam arceb. on ƿigere ceastre. ⁊ oþer mid Aeþelstane bisc. on herforda
Portion: '*Ad imam Pag. vox* (cyrographum) *dimidiata*.' (Smith 1722, p. 778)

30. S 1503 AD 1014
Manuscript: British Library, Stowe Ch. 47
Facsimile: *OS Facs.*, vol. 1, no. 38
Archive: Christ Church
Status: Contemporary sheet
Description: Will of Ætheling Æthelstan
Language: English
Portion: CYROGRAPHVM (upper)

31. S 1461 AD 1016 x 1020
Edited: Somner 1726, pp. 195–7 (Robertson 1956, no. 77)
Archive: Christ Church
Status: Sheet; lost
Description: Marriage agreement between Godwine and Brihtric
Language: English
Issued: Triplicate: Christ Church, St Augustine's, layman
'Portion': 'an old Saxon tripartite deed or charter' (Somner 1726, pp. 76–7)
Text: 7 þyssa geƿrita synd ðreo, an is æt cristes cyrcan, oðer æt S. Augustine, ꝥ þridde hæfð Byrhtric self.

32. S 1387 AD 1016 x 1020, probably 1018
Edited: Davidson 1878, pp. 239–40
Archive: Exeter (from Crediton)
Status: Cartulary copy
Description: Bishop Eadnoth to Beorhtnoth; mortgage of a yardland
Language: English with Latin, English bounds
Portion: And þisses iþrites (*for* iwrites) ídoua (*for* icloua) is on cridíamtone. mid hure elder boken.

33. S 1423 AD 1016 x 1023
Manuscript: British Library, Additional Ch. 19796
Facsimile: *BM Facs.*, vol. 4, no. 15
Edited: Robertson 1956, no. 81
Archive: Worcester
Status: Contemporary sheet
Description: Abbot Ælfweard to Æthelmær; lease of 4 1/2 hides for three lives
Language: English
Issued: Triplicate: St Mary's, Worcester, Evesham, layman
Text: 7 þyssa gewrita synd .III. an lið on Wigracestre æt Sc̄a Marian mynstre. 7 oðer lið on Eofesha*m*me. 7 þridde hæfð Æðelmer.

Portion: CYROGRAPHVM (lower)

34. S 981 AD 1016 x 1035
Edited: Robertson 1956, no. 85 (English)
Thorpe 1865, pp. 326–7 (Latin)
Archive: Christ Church
Status: Sheet, s. xi^{ex}; spurious
Description: King Cnut to Christ Church; reversionary grant of land after death of king's priest
Language: Latin and English versions
Issued: Triplicate: Christ Church, St Augustine's, king's *haligdom*
Text: And þissera gewrita synd þreo an is innon Cristes cyrcean. 7 oðer æt sc̃e Augustine. 7 ꝥ þridde is inne mid þæs kynges haligdome.
Et horum brevium tria sunt; unum in æcclesia Christi, alterum in monasterio Sancti Augustini, et tertium in thesauro regis cum reliquiis sanctorum.

35. S 1520 AD 1017 x 1035
Edited: Blake 1962, pp. 157–8
Archive: Ely
Status: Cartulary copy
Description: Will of Leofflæd
Language: Latin
Issued: Triplicate: Ely, king's *thesaurus*, testatrix
Text: Hec scripto tripliciter consignantur. Unum est apud Ely, aliud in thesauris regis, tertium Leofleda habet.

36. S 1528 AD s. xi, probably after A.D. 1020
Edited: Whitelock 1930, no. 25
Archive: Bury St Edmunds
Status: Cartulary copy
Description: Will of Thurketel Heyng
Language: English
Issued: Triplicate: Holme, Bury, testator
Text: þise write sinden þre. and is on Holme and oþer on Byri. þridde mid Thurkitel seluen.

37. S 1465 AD 1032
Edited: Somner 1726, pp. 213–6 (Robertson 1956, no. 86)
Archive: Christ Church
Status: Lost; described by Somner as 'a copy of a Saxon charter' (1726, p. 120)

Description: Declaration of arrangements made between Eadsige, priest and Christ Church, concerning land
Language: English
Issued: Triplicate: Christ Church, St Augustine's, priest
Text: ⁊ þissa geƿrita synda .III. an is æt Cristes-cyrican, ⁊ an æt S. Augustine, ⁊ an hæfð Eadsige mid him sylfan.

38. S 1399 AD 1033 x 1038
Manuscript: British Library, Additional 19797
Facsimile: *BM Facs.*, vol. 4, no. 19
Archive: Worcester
Status: Contemporary sheet
Description: Bishop Brihtheah to Wulfmær, his cniht, lease of 2 hides for three lives
Language: English
Portion: CYROGRAPHVM (lower)

39. S 1521 AD 1035 x 1044
Edited: Whitelock 1930, no. 29
Archive: Bury St Edmunds
Status: Cartulary copy
Description: Will of Leofgifu
Language: English
Issued: Triplicate: king's *haligdom*, testatrix
Text: Nu sinden þise write þre. on is mid þise kinges halidome. and oþer at seynt Eadmunde. ⁊ þridde mid Leofgiue seluen.

40. S 1527 s. xi, probably before AD 1038
Edited: Whitelock 1930, no. 24
Archive: Bury St Edmunds
Status: Cartulary copy
Description: Will of Thurketel
Language: English
Issued: Triplicate: Bury, bishop, testator
Text: Þise write sinden þre. on is at seynt Eadmu*n*desbiri. oþer haueð þe bisscop. þridde haueð Þurketel himself.

41. S 1393 AD 1038
Manuscript: British Library, Additional Ch. 19798
Facsimile: *BM Facs.*, vol. 4, no. 22
Archive: Worcester
Status: Contemporary sheet
Description: Bishop Lyfing to Earcytel; lease of 2 hides for three lives

Language: Latin
Portion: CYROGRAPHVM (upper)

42. S 1400 AD 1038 x 1050
Manuscript: British Library, Stowe Ch. 42
Facsimile: *OS Facs.*, vol. 3, no. 43
Edited: Robertson 1956, no. 108
Archive: Christ Church
Status: Contemporary sheet
Description: Archbishop Eadsige to Christ Church; grant of land
Language: English
Issued: Duplicate: Christ Church, St Augustine's
Text: Nu synd ðissa gewrita twa. an is æt Xp̄es cyrcean. oþer æt sc̄e Augustine.
Portion: CYROGRAPHVM (lower)

43. S 1224 AD *c.* 1040
Edited: Robertson 1956, no. 92
Archive: Bury St Edmunds
Status: Cartulary copy
Description: Grant of land by Stigand in reversion to Bury St Edmunds
Language: English
Issued: St Edmunds, layman
Text: þise wrtte sínden tua. on ís bínnen seynt Eadmu*n*des birí. 7 oþer hauið Stigand.

44. S 1394 AD 1042
Manuscript: British Library, Additional Ch. 19799
Facsimile: *BM Facs.*, vol. 4, no. 23
Archive: Worcester
Status: Contemporary sheet
Description: Bishop Lyfing to his thegn Æthelric; lease of 2 hides for three years
Language: English
Portion: CYROGRAPHVM (upper)

S 1530 AD 1042 x 1043
45. (a) Canterbury Dean and Chapter, Chart. Ant. C. 70
Facsimile: *OS Facs.*, vol. 1, no. 25
Edited: Whitelock 1930, no. 30
46. (b) British Library, Cotton Augustus ii. 34
Facsimile: *BM Facs.*, vol. 4, no. 33
Edited: Lowe 1990, pp. 69–70

Archive: Christ Church
Status: Contemporary sheets
Description: Bequest of Thurstan
Language: Latin and English versions
Issued: Triplicate: Christ Church, St Augustine's, testator
Text (a): ⁊ þissera gewritu syndan þreo. an is æt xp̄es cyrcean. oþer æt sc̄e Augustine. ⁊ þridde biþ mid heom sylfan.
Text (b): ⁊ þissera geƿrita sindan þreo. an is æt xp̄es cyrcean. oðer æt sc̄e albane.* þridde mid heom sylfan.
[*Written in a later hand over 'augustine. ⁊'.]
Portion (a): CYROGRAPHVM (upper)
Portion (b): CYROGRAPHVM (upper)
Note: Marker clause not preserved in Latin versions

47. S 1468 AD 1043 x 1044
Edited: Robertson 1956, no. 97
Archive: Bury St Edmunds
Status: Cartulary copy
Description: Agreement between Æthelmær and Abbot Ufi conerning land
Language: English
Issued: Duplicate: St Edmunds, layman
Text: þise Write sínden tua on ís bínnen seynt Eadmu*n*des bírí and oþer haued Aylm*er* hymself.

48. S 1391 AD 1043 x 1044
Edited: Robertson 1956, no. 98
Archive: Old Minster, Winchester
Status: Cartulary copy
Description: Bishop Ælfwine to Osgod; lease of land for life in exchange for a piece of land
Language: English
Issued: Old Minster, bishop's charters, layman
Text: Þyssa gewrita syndon þreo. án ís on ealdan mynstre. oþer ís mid þæs bisceopes landbocan. þridde hæfð Osgod.

49. S 1531 AD 1043 x 1045
Edited: Whitelock 1930, no. 31
Archive: Bury St Edmunds
Status: Cartulary copy
Description: Will of Thurstan
Language: English
Issued: Triplicate: St Edmunds, Ely, testator's *hired*
Text: þise write sinden þre. on schal into seynt Eadmu*n*de. And on

into Ely. and on schal ben innon min owen hird.

50. S 1470 AD 1043 x 1047
Edited: Robertson 1956, no. 100
Archive: Bury St Edmunds
Status: Cartulary copy
Description: Agreement between abbey and Wulfgeat and wife over land
Language: English
Issued: Triplicate: layman, St Edmunds, Bishop Stigand
Text: þise wríte sínden þre on hauið Wlfgeat hímself. oþer ís ín seynt Eadmu*n*des birí. þride hauid Stigand bisscop.

51. S 1472 AD 1044 x 1045
Manuscript: Canterbury Dean and Chapter, Chart. Ant. A. 207
Facsimile: *OS Facs.*, vol. 1, no. 23
Edited: Robertson 1956, no. 102
Archive: Christ Church
Status: Contemporary sheet
Description: Record of settlement of dispute between Abbot Æfstan and Leofwine, priest
Language: English
Issued: Triplicate: Christ Church, St Augustine, priest
Text: nu [sin]d þisse gewrite þreo. an is æt Cristes cyricean. ⁊ oþer æt Sc̄e Augustine. ⁊ þridde hæfð Leofwine preost.
Portion: CYROGRAPHVM (upper)

52. S 1473 AD 1044 x 1048
Manuscript: British Library, Cotton Augustus ii. 35
Facsimile: *BM Facs.*, vol. 4, no. 28
Edited: Robertson 1956, no. 103
Archive: Christ Church
Status: Contemporary sheet
Description: Account of purchase of land by Godric from his sister Eadgifu
Language: English
Issued: Triplicate: Christ Church, St Augustine's, layman
Text: Nu synd þissa gewrita þreo an is æt Cristes cyricean. ⁊ oþer æt sc̄e Augustine. ⁊ þridde hæfð Godric mid him.
Portion: CYROGRAPHVM (upper)

53. S 1471 AD *c.* 1045
Manuscript: British Library, Cotton Augustus ii. 70
Facsimile *BM Facs.*, vol. 4, no. 27

Edited:	Robertson 1956, no. 101
Archive:	Christ Church
Status:	Contemporary sheet
Description:	Agreement between Archbishop Eadsige and Æthelric concerning land
Language:	English
Issued:	Triplicate: Christ Church, St Augustine's, layman
Text:	Nu synd þissa gewrita þreo. an is innan Cristes cyricean. 7 oþer æt sc̄e Augustine. 7 ꝥ þridde hæfð Ægelric mid him sylfan.
Portion:	CYROGRAPHVM CYROGRAPHVM (central)

54. S 1474 AD 1046

Edited:	O'Donovan 1988, no. 17
Archive:	Sherborne
Status:	Cartulary copy
Description:	Agreement between Bishop Ælfwold and Care concerning land
Language:	English
Issued:	Duplicate: Sherborne, Crediton
Text:	Þyssera geƿrita syndon tƿa. an ys æt Scireburnan. 7 þæt oþer æt Cridiantune. sprecaþ buta an:-

55. S 1403 AD 1047 x 1052

Edited:	Robertson 1956, no. 107
Archive:	Old Minster, Winchester
Status:	Cartulary copy
Description:	Bishop Stigand to Wulfric; lease of 2 hides, one yardland and three yardlands for two lives
Language:	English
Issued:	Triplicate: Old Minster, Wilton, layman
Text:	Þissa gewrita syndan þreo an ís on ealdan mynstre. and oþer is on Wiltune. and þridde æfed Wlfric.

56. S 1402 AD 1047 x 1053

Edited:	Robertson 1956, no. 106
Archive:	Old Minster, Winchester
Status:	Cartulary copy
Description:	Bishop Stigand to Æthelmær; lease, of 1 hide for his life and that of his son, Sæman, for sum of money
Language:	English
Issued:	Duplicate: Old Minster and layman
Text:	Þissa gewrita syndan twa an ís on ealdan mynstræ. and oþær

hæfð Æþelmær.

57. S 1425 AD 1050 x 1052

Edited:	Keynes 1993, p. 267 (part only)
Archive:	St Albans
Status:	Cartulary copy
Description:	Abbot Leofstan and St Albans Abbey to Tova, widow of Wihtric, lease for her lifetime and that of her son, of land in exchange for money and an annual render of honey
Language:	Latin and English versions
Issued:	Triplicate: St Albans, Tova and *Eowes hamme* (?Eynsham)
Text:	Đissa gewrita synt iii. An in on þam mynstre, oþer is mid þan wife, ðridde is on eowes hame.
Note:	Marker clause not in Latin version

58. S 1516 s. xi med

Edited:	Whitelock 1930, no. 33
Archive:	Bury St Edmunds
Status:	Cartulary copy
Description:	Will of Eadwine
Language:	English
Issued:	Triplicate: St Edmunds, St Benet at Holme, testator
Text:	þise write sinden þre. on is binnen at sc̄e Eadmu*n*de. an other at sc̄e Bene*dicte* on Holm. ⁊ te þridde haued Eadwine himself.

59. *OS Facs.*, vol. 2, Ilchester 5 (not listed in Sawyer) s. xi med

Manuscript:	Dorchester, Dorset Record Office, D 124
Facsimile:	*OS Facs.*, ii Ilchester 5
Archive:	Abbotsbury
Status:	Sheet; s. xi med
Description:	Tole, Orc's widow, to Abbotsbury (fragmentary)
Language:	English
Portio:	PHVM (lower)

60. S 1476 AD *c.* 1053

Edited:	Robertson 1956, no. 114
Archive:	Old Minster, Winchester
Status:	Cartulary copy
Description:	Agreement between Bishop Stigand and Wulfweard over 10 hides of land
Language:	English
Issued:	Triplicate: Old Minster, New Minster, layman
Text:	Þissæ gewrita syndon .III. an is on ealdan mynstræ. And þæt

oþær ís on niwan mynstre. And þæt þridde heafð Wulfwearð.

61. S 1407 AD ?1053
Manuscript: British Library, Additional Ch. 19800
Facsimile: *BM Facs.*, vol. 4, no. 32
Archive: Worcester
Status: Contemporary sheet
Description: Bishop Ealdred to Balwine, his man, lease of 2 hides and a yardland for three lives
Language: Latin
Portion: CYRO GRA PHVM (lower)

62. S 1478 AD 1053 x 1055
Edited: Robertson 1956, no. 115
Archive: Eynsham
Status: Cartulary copy
Description: Agreement between Bishop Wulfwig and Earl Leofric and wife about endowment of monastery
Language: English
Issued: Triplicate: king's *haligdom*, layman, bishop
Text: Nu syndon þisse gewrita .þreo. an is mid þæs kyngces haligdome. 7 oðer is mid Leofrice eorle. 7 ꝥ þridde is mid þam ƀe. on ða halgan stowe.

63. S 1405 AD 1058
Manuscript: British Library, Additional Ch. 19801
Facsimile: *BM Facs.*, vol. 4, no. 38
Archive: Worcester
Status: Contemporary sheet
Description: Bishop Ealdred to Dodda, his minister, lease of 2 hides and a yardland for life
Language: English
Portion: CYROGRAVVM (lower)

64. S 1237 AD *c.* 1061
Edited: Dugdale 1817–1830, vol. 6, p. 1042, no. 1
Archive: Saint-Remi, Rheims
Status: Cartulary copy
Description: Ælfgar, *quandam comes*, grant of land to St Remigius
Language: Latin
Issued: Duplicate: layman (English), Saint-Remi (Latin)
Text: Hoc scriptum in duabus cartis habetur divisum, quarum unam Anglicâ linguâ scriptam idem comes Algarus secum retinuit,

aliam voce Latinâ dictatam sancto Remigio devotus transmisit

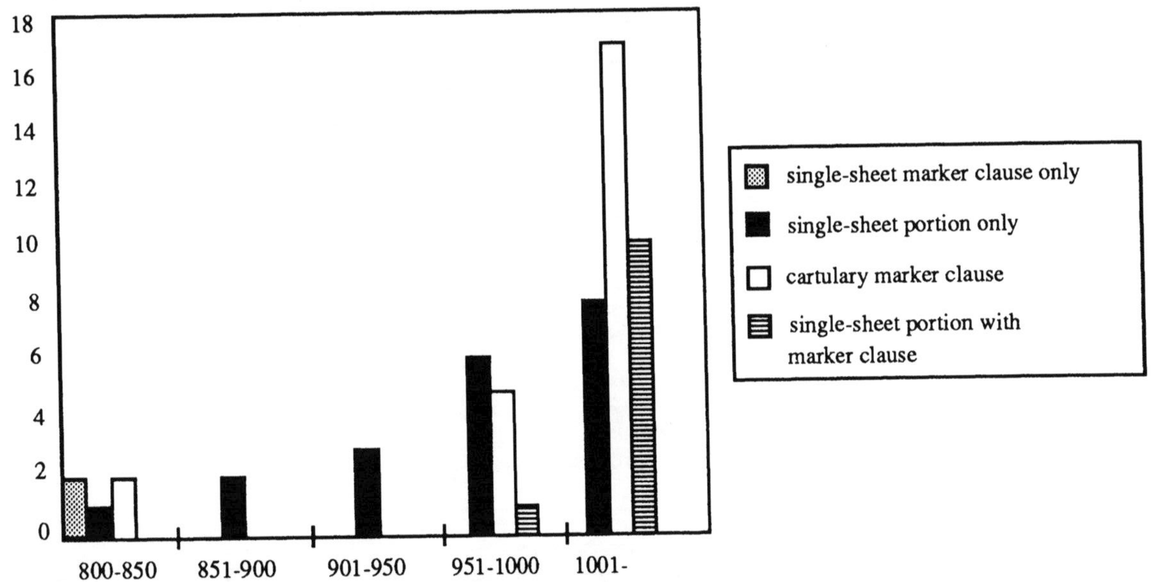

Figure 7.1. Charters are ordered by their earliest possible date of issue. Excluded from the data sheet are those charters believed to be forgeries or considered generally untrustworthy (S 312, no. 6, S 313, no. 7, S 981, no. 34), three charters which do not survive in contemporary form and whose original status cannot be ascertained (S 1522, no. 24, S 1387, no. 32, S 1465, no. 37) and the fragmentary no. 59.

8 Memorialised Readings: Manuscript Evidence for Old English Homily Composition

Mary Swan

In their examination of attitudes to textual identity in Anglo-Saxon scholarship, Allen J. Frantzen and Charles L. Venegoni state that 'it is not just through their origins, but also through their transmission, their corruption and revision in time, that texts acquire meaning'.[1] This essay's examination of the heritage of three manuscript copies of adapted and recontextualised material from Ælfric's *Catholic Homilies* (CH) shows how the meanings a text acquires through time depend on its identity and status as perceived by those who transmit it, and on the form in which it is transmitted.[2] The manuscript texts to be discussed are the late Old English Ælfric/anonymous composite homily in London, British Library, Cotton Cleopatra B. xiii, fols 44r–55v (Ker, item 144, art. 6), probably written in Exeter in the third quarter of the eleventh century;[3] and one homily which, uniquely for an Ælfric/anonymous piece, survives in two manuscript copies: Oxford, Bodleian Library, Auctarium F. 4. 32, fols 10r–18v (Ker, item 297, art. *a*), provenance unknown, from the second half of the eleventh century; and Cambridge, Corpus Christi College 303, pp. 76–82 (Ker, item 57, art. 18), probably written at Rochester in the first half of the twelfth century. These texts provide evidence for speculation about the ways in which scribes and compilers had access to material for homily composition, and for addressing the issues of authority and textuality — or rather intertextuality — in late Anglo-Saxon England.[4]

Ælfric's careful instructions for the transmission of his works are well known.[5] In the case of the reuse of the *Catholic Homilies* and their mixing with anonymous material it is clear that, in so far as we can see from the surviving evidence, Ælfric's attempt to exercise this version of authorial control was often spectacularly unsuccessful.[6] The *Catholic Homilies* survive in a very wide range of manuscripts from the late tenth to twelfth centuries, and in an even wider range of states, from whole homilies copied faithfully into manuscripts largely or wholly consisting of the series, through freestanding excerpts of sections in mixed manuscripts, to tiny snatches of material incorporated in composite pieces of unknown authorship.

Relatively little is known about the form in which compilers had access to material from the *Catholic Homilies*. None of the surviving examples of composite Ælfric/anonymous pieces names Ælfric as the author of the *Catholic Homilies* excerpts it contains, and it is important always to bear in mind the likelihood that a compiler may come into contact with, and subsequently reuse, an excerpt from a homily without ever knowing its 'original' author. Indeed, twentieth-century notions of authorial and textual identity may well tempt us to make inappropriate assumptions about the attitudes of Anglo-Saxon homily compilers both to their source-material and to the status and ownership of the composite texts they produce.[7]

The search for 'fixed', 'original' Anglo-Saxon texts drove editorial and analytical work on, and indeed determined, the homiletic canon for many years, and has resulted in the marginalisation of many later or 'variant' versions of texts. Katherine O'Brien O'Keeffe discusses the limitations of such practices with regard to Old English poetry: 'the modern, critical reflex to recover an authorial text devalues the historical significance and meaning of the actual, realised texts which show us the poem working in the world.'[8] The workings of prose texts in the world are best studied by tracing their influences, uses and reuses, and by investigating what surviving manuscript copies can reveal about how they may have been transmitted and why they may have undergone alteration.

The study of 'actual, realized texts' and their heritage of sources and influences has led recently to a reassessment of the methodology of source study. In her article, 'Working with Patristic Sources: Language and Context in Old English Homilies', Clare Lees warns of the dangers of the 'status of a source as a *fact*', and urges a revision of what she calls 'the relationship among text, source, and cultural history'.[9] Attempting to source homiletic texts should be a usefully complicated exercise with room for acknowledgment of the nuances of intertextual relationships as represented in surviving manuscripts. In working with multiple copies and manuscript versions of the *Catholic Homilies*, it is apparent that any investigation not just of the identity of possible sources for Anglo-Saxon composite homilies, but also of the possible conditions of their use, has to work with a model which reflects what is understood about attitudes to textuality in the early Middle Ages. Traditional models for source-study often imply that similarities between two texts must be the result of the author/scribe of one copying out a portion of the other from a manuscript exemplar, and that any variations between two versions must result from unconscious error at this point of copying, or from the transmission of that error through a chain of copies. Such models are the product of a print-culture mentality and a belief in 'fixed' texts which does not take account of how much more fluidly textual identity and authorship operate in the early Middle Ages. Anglo-Saxon manuscript culture does not prioritise an authorial original, but rather remakes a text and transmits its authorship to a new writer or scribe each time it is copied.

In mixing excerpts from the *Catholic Homilies* with material not by Ælfric, Ker's item 144, art. 6, item 297, art. *a* and item 57, art. 18 remake their *Catholic Homilies* source texts by recontextualising them, and take over their authorship by rephrasing and reframing them. An examination of the nature of their compilers' access and attitude to their sources is a vital element in assessing how the meaning of the *Catholic Homilies* material is changed. As already noted, we have no way of knowing in what form the compilers of articles 6, *a* and 18 had access to their *Catholic Homilies* material; the current essay aims to examine their treatment of material and ideas from the *Catholic Homilies* rather than to establish manuscript relationships. Any textual variations could, of course, be the result of something as random as scribal miscopying. A close study of how the Ælfric material in these two composites compares to surviving manuscript versions of the whole *Catholic Homilies* in question, however, provides some interesting data for speculation about textual reuse.

London, British Library, Cotton Cleopatra B. xiii, article 6, has as its rubric *dominica ante rogationum*, and centres upon the story of Jonah, which begins approximately half way through the homily and takes up over one-third of the text.[10] The homily encourages the observance of the custom of Rogationtide and stresses the importance of prayer and fasting. The main source of this homily is a version of the Jonah story very close to that preserved in Vercelli Homily XIX.[11] Paul Szarmach discusses article 6 in a comparison of three Old English versions of the Jonah story, and uses the Vercelli homily as the closest version for comparison with article 6.[12] Article 6 also makes use of CH I *In Letania Maiore*.[13] Its opening eight and a half manuscript pages are taken up with a continuous extract which corresponds, with persistent minor variations, to the opening of Vercelli XIX. Throughout this opening section of article 6, single words or short phrases are added to or omitted from the Vercelli version, and word order differs. After this the compiler begins to interweave Ælfric's *In Letania Maiore* in the most intricate ways. It is first used for a short exhortation to prayer which takes up six manuscript lines. This is lengthened in article 6 with three manuscript lines on details of prayer. The Vercelli text then recommences for 58 continuous lines, which show consistent minor differences from the Vercelli version of the same order as those described above. This is followed by an extensive block of Vercelli text augmented by a series of excerpts from *In Letania Maiore*, ranging from less than one to 11 lines, many of which begin and end in mid-sentence. Some of this sequence is reproduced below:

Art. 6, ll. 314–20:
... 7 se forswealh þone witegan 7 he wæs on him þry dagas 7 þreo niht 7 abær hyne to þam ylcan lande þe he ær to faran sceolde 7 þarut aspau ofer þære sæ staðe.

CH I, p. 246, ll. 12–14:
... and he forswealh þone witegan, and abær hine to ðam lande þe he to sceolde, and hine ðær ut-aspaw.

Vercelli XIX, ll. 129–33:
... 7 hine sona an mycel hwæll forswealh, 7 he wæs on him þry dagas 7 .iii. niht. 7 syððan, eal swa hit God wolde, seo sæ þone fisc ferede oð he com to þam ilcan eðle þe he ær on bodian sceolde, se witega, 7 hine þærut of him aspaw ofer þære sæ staðe.

The opening clause of this example from article 6, '... 7 se forswealh þone witegan', corresponds closely to the Ælfric version of the Jonah story, but the following clauses, '7 he wæs on him þry dagas 7 þreo niht', are not in the Ælfric version, and closely resemble the Vercelli version. The next section of this sequence in article 6, '7 abær hyne to þam ylcan lande þe he ær to faran sceolde 7 þarut aspau', could be either a rather close reproduction of the Ælfric text or a shortened and modified excerpt from the Vercelli version, and the final words of this excerpt from article 6, 'ofer þære sæ staðe', bear a closer resemblance to the Vercelli version than to the Ælfrician one.

Short, apparently compiler-written, phrases occasionally string together the various sourced passages in article 6, and throughout this flitting back and forth between the Ælfric and Vercelli texts, article 6 shows the addition and substitution of odd words. The narrative order of the Vercelli version is observed throughout, whereas that of the Ælfric homily is not. It is difficult to imagine how this composite text could have been comfortably produced by a compiler working from written copies of the Vercelli and Ælfric homilies, or what might prompt such fluidity of movement into and out of the Ælfric homily if access to it was gained in this way.

The composite homily preserved in Oxford, Bodleian Library, Auctarium F. 4. 32 (article *a*) and Cambridge, Corpus Christi College 303 (article 18) is, unlike the previous example, almost completely unsourced.[14] Article *a* has no manuscript rubric, although its erased first line may have given a title; article 18's manuscript rubric is *In inuentione Sancte Crucis*. Both are copies of a homily on the Finding of the True Cross. They are extremely close, showing only minor differences of vocabulary and spelling and occasionally diverging for a short phrase. Inserted into approximately the first tenth of this homily as represented by articles *a* and 18 are three short excerpts from CH II *Inventio Sanctae Crucis* which are used to amplify articles *a* and 18's description of Constantine:[15]

1a Art. *a*, ll. 6–8:
He wæs eawfæst on þeawum and arfæst on dædum, Cristenra manna fultumend and næs þeah þa gyt gefullod.

b Art. 18, p. 76, ll. 5–6:
he wæs eawfæst on þeawum ⁊ arfæst on dædum cristenre manna fultumiend ⁊ næs swa þeah þe get gefullod.

c CH II, ll. 6–7:
se wæs eawfæst on ðeawum. and arfæst on dædum. cristenra manna fultumigend. and næs ðeah gyt gefullod.

2a Art. *a*, ll. 12–15:
Þa wearð hit sona þam mæran Constantine þam kasere gecyd and he þa sone gegaderode mycele fyrde and ongæn his fiond ferde mid carfullum mode and gelome beheold wiþ heofenas weard, biddende giorne godcundne fultum

b Art. 18, p. 76, ll. 8–11:
þa wearð hit sona þan mæren constantine þam casere gecydd ⁊ he þa sona gegaderode myccle ferde ⁊ ongean his fynd ferde mid carfullum mode ⁊ gelome behyld wiþ heofenes weard biddende georne godcundne fultum.

c CH II, ll. 10–11:
Þa ferde se casere. swiðe carful mid fyrde. and gelome beheold wið heofonas weard. biddende georne godcundne fultum.

3a Art. *a*, ll. 28–31:
He awoc þa bliþelice for þære fægeran gesihðe and for þære mæran behatenan sige, and mearcode him on heafde halig rode tacen and on his guðfanan gode to wurðmynte.

b Art. 18, p. 76, ll. 19–20:
he awoc þa bliðelic for þære fægran ⁊ for þære mæran behatene sige ⁊ mærcode him þa on his heafode halig rode tacen and on his guðfanan gode to wurðmente.

c CH II, ll. 15–17:
he awoc ða bliðe. for ðære gesihðe. and for ðan behatenan sige.

and mearcode him on heafde halig rodetacn. and on his guðfanan gode to wurðmynte.

In passage 1 above, article *a* is almost identical to the Ælfric version, but shows the insertion of 'þa' between Ælfric's 'þeah' and 'gyt'. Article 18 also inserts a word, 'þe', at this point, and in addition inserts 'swa' before 'þeah'. These tiny, monosyllabic additions increase the verbal emphasis of the passage and lend it a more colloquial style by loosening its structure.

Passage 2 seems to be amplified in narrative terms in articles *a* and 18. Ælfric's succinct description of the emperor's departure with the army and his praying to heaven is lengthened in articles *a* and 18 with the addition of the emperor's name and an account of his gathering of an army and of the advance against the enemy. In increasing the length of clauses, articles *a* and 18 alter Ælfric's word order and transform the first eight words of the *Catholic Homilies* passage ('Þa ... fyrde') into a 25-word sequence. This lengthening, naming and reiteration of the sides involved in the battle all serve to make more explicit the narrative content, but do not alter it in any substantial way.

In passage 3, minor verbal additions are again made to the Ælfric text: articles *a* and 18 add 'mæran' before Ælfric's 'behatenan sige', and article 18 gives 'mærcode him þa on his heafode' for Ælfric's 'mearcode him on heafde'. As with passage 1, these differences do not alter the gist of the Ælfric narrative, but loosen its syntax and style. Although articles *a* and 18 agree in many of the alterations they make to the Ælfric passages, article 18 introduces some alterations which are not in article *a*, and so may be a later stage in the chain of transmission.

To analyse the possible reasons for the sort of textual variation seen in these examples and indeed do justice to the creative possibilities inherent in the Anglo-Saxon homiletic tradition, it is important to consider the variety of ways in which material written for delivery as a homily might be transmitted. For example, a writer such as Ælfric may compose a homily using new, 'original' material as well as material exactly replicating or echoing a range of sources and influences. This homily will then 'work in the world' in a variety of ways: by being read aloud to a congregation who will retain some of its content and, especially when they have heard it more than once, begin to store it in their memories along with other, thematically-related material, and perhaps by being recopied by a scribe for use in another location.[16] This recopying will almost certainly introduce changes to the Ælfrician text, at least at an unconscious level through scribal error, and possibly at a conscious level through the insertion of extra material from another source, or the alteration of Ælfric's phraseology or vocabulary. Such alterations to the substance of a homiletic text may be the result of a scribe working from and juxtaposing written copies of the Ælfric homily and of other texts or, since monastic scribes will have listened to many homilies as members of a congregation, and will be trained in memorisation techniques, they may alter the Ælfric homily by introducing portions of other texts which they have memorised, or indeed recopy the Ælfric homily itself from memory, introducing conscious or unconscious changes as they write. An Ælfrician homily, therefore, might undergo a chain of transmission from its composition in the late tenth century, through a series of tenth- and eleventh-century oral deliveries from written copies in church, written recopyings from written versions and written recopyings from memorised, orally-delivered versions, to written recopyings in the twelfth century from written eleventh-century versions. No complete chain of manuscript versions of such a process remains, but some surviving 'variant' copies of Ælfrician homilies, including those discussed in this essay, may be part of such a chain of transmission.

As a theoretical framework for exploring the dynamics of the operation of sources and influences, reception theory enables us to break down the hierarchy of original source/variant product. The most influential work in this area, such as that of Hans Robert Jauss, uses the model of meaning generated in the interaction between a written original text and a 'silent' reader, rather than in the author's original creative act.[17] Reception theory, then, already moves the focus of critical attention away from the author and towards the working of a text in the world, but it uses the modern concept of literature as something privately, silently received, and of its reception as a purely mental act. In the production of Anglo-Saxon homiletic literature, the situation and the possibilities are considerably more animated. Preaching lies at the intersection of oral and literate activity: the preacher reads out the text of a written document and the congregation receives it aurally and communally. If we envisage this as one possible version of the initial reception of an 'original' text — one of the *Catholic Homilies*, for example — then one possible 'hearer response', as outlined above, would be the reuse in writing or preaching of all or part of it by the preacher or by a member of the congregation.

Examination of the conditions for such textual reception and reproduction raises many questions about access to homiletic texts. Mary Carruthers' *The Book of Memory* sets out a wealth of information about medieval scholastic training in the art of *memoria* and its implications for the act of reading and the notion of authority.[18] Carruthers' observations are vital in helping us to reassess our understanding of the process behind Old English texts by taking into account the working practices and attitudes to textuality possible in an environment where skilled memorisation and reproduction of material from memory are fostered both by long-standing traditions of orally-transmitted stories and by formal training in memorisation.

Carruthers distinguishes two forms of medieval memorisation and reproduction: memoria *ad res*, the deliberate, trained storing and reproduction of the gist of a text, and *memoria ad verba*, the storing and reproduction of its precise wording.[19] In his review of *The Book of Memory*, Martin Irvine acknowledges the possibility that 'what appears to be an inaccurate citation by a medieval writer is usually a case not of failure of memory ... but of recollection *ad res* ... by its subject matter, theme or wider significance'.[20] As Irvine notes, admitting the possibility of this form of memorising means reconceiving and redefining the terms of source study. We need to allow the possibility of apparently inaccurate uses of source material being the result not of error, but of a different intellectual enterprise on the part of the users who have accessed their material from memory instead of copying from a book in front of them on the table, and whose memory storage method was never intended to be verbatim.

In his study, *Memorization in the Transmission of the Middle English Romances*, Murray McGillivray cites movement of material, transposition and inversion, omission, telescoping and amplification as potential evidence of reproduction of text from memory.[21] Although his work is with a much later group of texts, his use of an oral and written production-reception model has clear application to the Anglo-Saxon homiletic tradition. O'Brien O'Keeffe's work on the transmission of Old English verse also identifies the sort of variation which might indicate the reuse of memorised formulae. Homiletic prose, although less formally constructed than poetry, does favour formulaic modes of expression, and O'Brien O'Keeffe's statement that 'The presence of variant readings which are semantically, metrically and syntactically appropriate suggests a strong overlay of oral habits of transmission in the copying' could also be applied to our examples.[22]

The differences between articles 6, *a* and 18 and their Ælfrician source texts do not fit happily the usual default hypothesis of a scribe deliberately setting out to alter a text from a written copy. The amplification of the *Catholic Homilies* text and the use of formulaic descriptors and collocations correspond to some of the ways texts evolve through the process of memorisation and remembrance. The juxtaposition of material from texts apparently chosen for their common subject-matter shows a compiler working associatively around a theme to make a new text by selecting and compiling excerpts from existing ones chosen not for their meaning or function in the whole, 'original' text but for their suitability for their new content. This is a way of working facilitated by trained memorisation of a wide range of material.[23]

Assuming that the compiler of article 6 had access to a complete copy of CH I *In Letania Maiore*, its opening of the Jonah story and its final two-thirds have been rejected. As Szarmach states in his study, the sections from Ælfric added to the Vercelli version in article 6 'strengthen the narrative effect'.[24] It is notable that much of the didactic explanation which Ælfric provides after telling the Jonah story, and the careful logical sequence with which he links the various stages of his homily, are omitted in article 6. The ways in which Ælfric's account of the Jonah story have here been made to tally with the Vercelli version, and the very skilful working together and juxtaposing of the texts, raise the possibility that the compiler reproduced the Vercelli version either from the direct copying of a written text, or from *memoria ad verba*, and memorised and reproduced the *Catholic Homilies* material *ad res*, turning mentally to it whenever it could supply dramatic detail or useful phraseology. The decision to use Ælfric's Jonah story could at times have been triggered by its very close verbal echoes in the Vercelli version. These would jog the memory into producing appropriate parallels or continuations from the other text.[25]

The interesting slight differences amongst articles *a*, 18 and CH II *Inventio Sanctae Crucis* also show the degree of variation produced by reproduction of memorised texts. Other possible indicators of memorised material are the loosely alliterative, and therefore easily memorable, quality of much of the Ælfric material reused in articles *a* and 18; the combination of precise and expanded reproduction of the Ælfric text in articles *a* and 18's versions of passage 2; and the notion of a narrative trigger in the anonymous versions for the reproduction of memorised snatches of Ælfric's comments on Constantine.

Despite the comparison of precise verbal detail in this essay's analysis of the two composite homilies, it is not my intention to judge the likelihood of direct manuscript acquaintance between any of these composite homilies and their Ælfrician or anonymous sources. Such correspondences and variants in multiple copies of any text could be signs of memorised reproduction in some earlier version or versions rather than an indication that one surviving copy has directly deviated from another. These case studies are interesting candidates for memorised readings of Ælfric's *Catholic Homilies* because, to adapt Jean Leclercq's remarks on the reuse of scriptural texts, they perhaps show the compiler's verbal memory excited by textual echoes which can evoke allusions and whole quotations, each word hooking up to a chain of memorised references.[26] The instances in the composite homilies discussed above of many of the features McGillivray lists support the case for the value of studying so-called 'variant' manuscript texts as examples of the possible precision and fluidity of memorisation and the creativity it enables in a manuscript culture. Carruthers eloquently describes this process and what it tells us about medieval cultural mentality and textuality: 'Because it recalls signs, reminiscence is an act of interpretation, inference, investigation, and reconstruction, an act like reading.'[27]

The case studies in this essay show how much can be learned about composition technique in Anglo-Saxon England from the close study of different manuscript versions of a text. So-called 'variant' versions of texts by known authors, such as those in articles 6, *a* and 18, have until recently been ignored by editors and critics, or dismissed as late and corrupt reworkings of the 'original' texts which have for so long held the focus of critical attention. In fact, far from being of little interest, these examples of composition technique are vital witnesses to the reading of and response to Ælfric by homily compilers through a dynamic process of reception, rumination and recall. This response could be seen in Ælfric's own terms as a diminution of his authority and a failure to transmit a memorial to his body of work, as his texts are broken down and refashioned to fit the style and concerns of the anonymous homiletic tradition. Certainly, the meanings of his texts are transformed from the careful and complex expositions of biblical and hagiographical narrative and doctrine which he designed to be read in sequence and without interruption from other material, into the convenient, familiar and detachable stock of narrative snippets which compilers find useful to focus and heighten the effect of their composite homilies. I would argue, however, that the variety and frequency with which his writings are reinscribed make Ælfric a narrative authority who is not only memorised but also memorialised: stored in the mental, cultural, communal library of texts available to the compilers of Old English homilies.

NOTES

1. 'The Desire for Origins: An Archaeology of Anglo-Saxon Studies', *Style* 20 (1986), 142–56, at p. 151.
2. Ælfric had composed both series of *Catholic Homilies* by 994. Both series are edited by Benjamin Thorpe, *The Homilies of the Anglo-Saxon Church. The First Part, Containing the Sermones Catholici, or Homilies of Ælfric*, 2 vols (London: Ælfric Society, 1844–1846); the Second Series is edited by Malcolm Godden, *Ælfric's Catholic Homilies: The Second Series*, Early English Text Society, s.s. 5 (London: Oxford University Press, 1979). Throughout this essay I will refer to Thorpe's edition for the First Series of *Catholic Homilies* and to Godden's for the Second. For a survey of recopying and adaptation of the *Catholic Homilies*, see my unpublished Ph.D. thesis, 'Ælfric as Source: The Exploitation of Ælfric's *Catholic Homilies* from the Late Tenth to Twelfth Centuries' (University of Leeds, 1993).
3. N. R. Ker, *Catalogue of Manuscripts Containing Anglo-Saxon* (Oxford: Clarendon Press, 1957; repr. with supplement 1990).
4. Several recent studies of Anglo-Saxon and later medieval literature have addressed the issues of nature of textuality and, by comparison, orality, in medieval culture. Examples include Carol Braun Pasternack, *The Textuality of Old English Poetry*, Cambridge Studies in Anglo-Saxon England, 13 (Cambridge: Cambridge University Press, 1995), and A.N. Doane and

Carol Braun Pasternack, eds., *Vox intexta: Orality and Textuality in the Middle Ages* (Madison: University of Wisconsin Press, 1991). The Anglo-Saxon literature treated in these and other recent articles, however, is almost exclusively poetic; very little attention has so far been paid to the place of Old English prose in this context.

5. In the final prayer of the *Catholic Homilies*, he requests: 'Gif hwa ma awendan wille. ðonne bidde ic hine for godes lufon þæt he gesette his boc onsundron. fram ðam twam bocum ðe we awend habbað' (Godden, ed., *Catholic Homilies, The Second Series*, p. 345, ll. 7–9). In the Preface to his later collection, the *Lives of Saints*, Ælfric asks that anyone who copies the book takes care to be accurate and not to insert extra material; see Walter W. Skeat, ed., *Ælfric's Lives of Saints*, Early English Text Society, o.s., 76, 82, 94, 114 (London: Oxford University Press, 1881–1900; repr. as two volumes 1966), vol. 1, p. 6, ll. 74–6.

6. For an analysis of the variety of reuse of the *Catholic Homlies* and the ways in which the character of the texts was altered, see Swan, 'Ælfric as Source', pp. 181–97; for an example of the mixing of Ælfrician and apocryphal material in manuscripts, see Mary Clayton, *The Cult of the Virgin Mary in Anglo-Saxon England*, Cambridge Studies in Anglo-Saxon England, 2 (Cambridge: Cambridge University Press, 1990), p. 266.

7. In her 1996 Toller Lecture, 'Translating the Tradition: Manuscripts, Models and Methodologies in the Composition of Ælfric's *Catholic Homilies*' (*Bulletin of the John Rylands University Library of Manchester*, forthcoming), Joyce Hill suggests that such assumptions may have been made in the past about Ælfric's attitude to and identification of his sources. She speculates that the reason for Ælfric's failure to cite Paul the Deacon's compilation of patristic writings as a source for many of his compositions may be simply that Ælfric did not know the identity of the Carolingian compiler whose work he used, rather than a deliberate decision to name the ultimate patristic source of material instead of its immediate source. Questions of textual and authorial identity with regard to Ælfric's pastoral letters are explored by Hill in 'Ælfric, Authorial Identity and the Changing Text', in *The Editing of Old English: Papers from the 1990 Manchester Conference*, ed. D.G. Scragg and Paul E. Szarmach (Woodbridge: D.S. Brewer, 1994), pp. 177–89.

8. *Visible Song: Transitional Literacy in Old English Verse*, Cambridge Studies in Anglo-Saxon England, 4 (Cambridge: Cambridge University Press, 1990), pp. 193–4.

9. *Speaking Two Languages: Traditional Disciplines and Contemporary Theory in Medieval Studies*, ed. Allen J. Frantzen (Albany: State University of New York Press, 1991), pp. 157–80, at pp. 162 and 179 respectively.

10. The homily is edited by A.M. Luiselli Fadda, *Nuove Omelie Anglosassioni*

della Rinascenza Benedettina (Florence: Felice Le Monnier, 1977), pp. 70–99. The references to article 6 and quotations from it which follow are taken from my edition of this homily in 'Ælfric as Source', pp. 242–54.

11. D.G. Scragg, ed., *The Vercelli Homilies and Related Texts*, Early English Text Society, o.s. 300 (Oxford: Oxford University Press, 1992), pp. 315–28.

12. 'Three Versions of the Jonah Story: An Investigation of Narrative Technique in Old English Homilies', *Anglo-Saxon England* 1 (1972), 183–92.

13. In his edition of Vercelli XIX, Scragg collates with the text of CH I *In Letania Maiore*, edited by Peter Clemoes in his unpublished Ph.D. thesis, 'Ælfric's Homilies, First Series: The Text and Manuscript Tradition' (University of Cambridge, 1956). In the present essay, I refer to Thorpe's edition in *The Homilies of the Anglo-Saxon Church*, vol. 1, pp. 244–58, as this is the only complete published edition.

14. Auctarium F. 4. 32, article *a*, is edited by Mary-Catherine Bodden, *The Old English Finding of the True Cross* (Cambridge: D.S. Brewer, 1987), pp. 60–112, with collations from CCCC 303, article 18. In the discussion which follows I have not used Bodden's references to the line numbers of passages from her edition of article *a* and to Godden's edition of CH II *Inventio Sanctae Crucis*, since these contains errors and, even with the errors corrected, I identify different groups of correspondences between the anonymous and Ælfrician texts.

15. CH II *Inventio Sanctae Crucis* is edited by Godden, *Ælfric's Catholic Homilies: The Second Series*, pp. 174–6. In the examples which follow, I cite article *a* from Bodden's edition, CCCC 303, article 18, from my transcription of the manuscript, and CH II *Inventio Sanctae Crucis* from Godden's edition.

16. In the Latin preface to the First Series, Ælfric acknowledges that his work will be both read and heard when he describes it reaching the ears of readers 'legentium vel audientium' (Thorpe, ed., *The Homilies of the Anglo-Saxon Church*, vol. 1, p. 1, l. 9.

17. The work of Hans Robert Jauss, one of the major theorists in the field of reception theory, is well represented in *Toward and Aesthetic of Reception*, trans. Timothy Bahti (Minneapolis: University of Minnesota Press, 1982). For an account of the background to and influences of Jauss and other reception theorists, see Robert C. Holub, *Reception Theory: A Critical Introduction* (London and New York: Methuen, 1984). For discussion of reception theory and Anglo-Saxon studies, see Allen J. Frantzen, *Desire for Origins: New Language, Old English, and Teaching the Tradition* (New Brunswick and London: Rutgers University Press, 1990).

18. *The Book of Memory: A Study of Memory in Medieval Culture*

(Cambridge: Cambridge University Press, 1990).

19. Ibid., pp. 86–7.

20. Martine Irvine's review appeared in *Modern Philology* 90 (1993), 533–7, at p. 535.

21. Murray McGillivray, *Memorization in the Transmission of Middle English Romances*, Albert Bates Lord Studies in Oral Tradition, 5; Garland Reference Library in the Humanities, 1275 (New York and London: Garland Publishing, Inc., 1990). Another interesting study of possible manuscript and performance evidence for memorised reproduction of a Middle English text is Linda Marie Zaerr and Mary Ellen Ryder, 'Psycholinguistic Theory and Modern Performance: Memory as a Key to Variants in Medieval Texts', *Mosaic* 26.3 (1993), 21–35.

22. *Visible Song*, p. 21.

23. The uses and understanding of memory in the Middle Ages are the subjects of a number of recent publications, including James Fentress and Chris Wickham, *Social Memory* (Oxford: Blackwell, 1992); and Janet Coleman, *Ancient and Medieval Memories* (Cambridge: Cambridge University Press, 1992). For discussions and examples of medieval memory training, see Carruthers, *The Book of Memory*; J. Leclerq, *The Love of Learning and the Desire for God: A Study of Monastic Culture*, trans. C. Misrahi (New York: Fordham University Press, 1961; 3rd ed. 1982); Martin Irvine, *The Making of Textual Culture: 'Grammatica' and Literary Theory 350–1100*, Cambridge Studies in Medieval Literature, 19 (Cambridge: Cambridge University Press, 1994), pp. 214, 275 and 327; and Peter S. Baker and Michael Lapidge, eds., *Byrhtferth's Enchiridion*, Early English Text Society, s.s. 15 (Oxford: Oxford University Press, 1995), pp. lxxiv–lxxix.

24. 'Three Versions of the Jonah Story', p. 191.

25. Jean Leclercq discusses such verbal echoes in *The Love of Learning*, pp. 73–4. For visual examples of chains of memorised reference, see Carruthers, *The Book of Memory*, pp. 246–7 and pl. 28.

26. *The Love of Learning*, pp. 73–4.

27. *The Book of Memory*, p. 25.

9 An Episode in the Medieval Afterlife of the Caligula Troper

E.C. Teviotdale

Given the history of most early medieval trope manuscripts, one would expect the results of an investigation of the high medieval 'afterlife' of the Caligula Troper (London, British Library, Cotton Caligula A. xiv, fols 1–36) to be both predictable and dull. Tenth- and eleventh-century tropers are usually unpretentious manuscripts containing a cycle of tropes to selected proper chants of the Mass (introit, offertory, communion) and a section of troped ordinary chants (*Kyrie*, *Gloria*, *Sanctus*, *Agnus dei*). Corrections and additions were often made during the course of the generation or so following their original manufacture. New pieces might be written on parchment integral to the original codex, or new gatherings with additional tropes might be added to the original book, or both.[1] Occasionally, the original notation *in campo aperto* was replaced with more modern notation, but it seems that most early tropers were ignored once their notation was no longer in current use and once the singing of proper tropes had gone out of fashion (both not long after 1100). The Caligula Troper, however, is not a typical trope manuscript.

An extremely handsome volume with an ambitious programme of illumination, the Caligula Troper was never systematically corrected and has only one addition made within a generation of its original manufacture. This is all the more remarkable because the manuscript later attracted the attention of those in whose library it found itself. The work of a marginal annotator reveals an active interest in the codex and its repertoire at a time when we would more readily expect the book to have been ignored or even discarded.

The Caligula Troper is one of three tropers surviving from Anglo-Saxon England.[2] It contains tropes to the proper chants of the Mass arranged in an annual cycle, followed by a fairly extensive *commune sanctorum*. The manuscript is fragmentary in two respects: the text ends *in medias res*, and there are several lacunae within the preserved portion of the codex. Some leaves may have been excised for their miniatures, but it does not seem that all the losses resulted from the actions of a picture collector. The appearance of the text script (English Caroline minuscule) and of the musical notation (Anglo-Saxon neumes) leaves little doubt that the book was produced in England in the eleventh century. There is no true consensus among scholars regarding the localisation of the codex.[3] The book was most probably produced in the third quarter of the eleventh century, at a time before characteristically Norman handwriting had entirely supplanted native traditions, but not necessarily before the Conquest.

By the end of the twelfth century, the troper was at Worcester cathedral priory, where it was bound with a late twelfth-century troper-proser of local manufacture (fols 37–92).[4] At some time after the two music volumes were bound together, a series of annotations was made in lead point in the composite manuscript. It is difficult to judge the date of these annotations; their author was using an instrument that required more pressure in writing than the customary quill, and the letter forms are sometimes crude. They most probably belong to the thirteenth century, but it is impossible to be precise.

The lead point annotator marked 13 pieces in the outer margin of the manuscript with the annotation *Scri* (or shorter versions, *Scr*, *Sc* or *S*).[5] These annotations generally appear at the beginning of a piece. Presumably they are all short for the imperative *scribe*, and it was intended that the tropes be copied. The notations, therefore, would have been instructions to a scribe.

The annotator was also responsible for five more lengthy rubrics, four in the troper and one in the later troper-proser. Two of these indicate the assignment of pieces to particular feast days. On fol. 33v (in the section of the troper devoted to the common of a martyr), the rubric *in festivitate sancti thomae martyris officium* is followed by the usual notation *scribe*. This almost certainly was meant to prescribe the use of the trope *Cum venerit verbum* (cued to the introit *Laetabitur iustus*) for St Thomas of Canterbury (d. 1170). On fol. 67v (i.e., in the twelfth-century troper-proser), the prose *Exsulta caelum et laetare* is correctly assigned to the Nativity of John the Baptist: *Scribe Sancto Iohanne baptista*.[6]

On fol. 8r, *Ex ore infantium* (the incipit of the introit antiphon for the feast of the Holy Innocents) has been inserted between lines 14 and 15 immediately following *Dicantur igitur*, one of the pieces marked for copying by the annotator.[7] *Dicantur igitur* appears in the Caligula Troper as the last section of a *versus ante officium*, a composition sung at the beginning of Mass but not explicitly associated with the introit. The addition of the cue for the antiphon effectively transformed *Dicantur igitur* into an introductory trope to the introit. The annotator has also written *require purificatione* in the upper margin of fol. 10r. This most probably constitutes the selection of the piece at the top of the page, the introit trope *Adest alma virgo parens* (cued to *Suscepimus deus*), for the feast of the Purification, although it may be an indication that the annotator intended to mark a Purification trope in another manuscript.

On fol. 11v, the annotator has written in the upper margin (very close to the present-day edge of the page) *de sancto o...d require in natale unius confessoris*. This is a cross-reference to *Quem caeli cives*, an introit trope for the common of a confessor marked on fol. 34v. Although the annotation is difficult to see and cannot be deciphered in its entirety, there is little doubt that it was meant to prescribe the use of *Quem caeli cives* (a trope to the introit *Statuit ei*) for the feast of St Oswald of Worcester (d. 992) on 28 February; it appears in the upper margin of the page that contains the end of the feast of the Purification (2 February) and the beginning of the Annunciation (25 March) in the Anglo-Saxon manuscript.

The repertoire marked by the lead point annotator consists almost entirely of introit tropes, and the one *versus ante officium* has been fashioned into an introductory trope (see Appendix). The annotator probably also marked tropes on leaves since lost from the manuscript. Two factors speak in favour of this interpretation. One of the pieces marked by the annotator, *Quem caeli cives*, is incomplete in the manuscript as it is preserved today. It ends *in medias res* at the bottom of the page, the following page being missing from the present-day codex.[8] Furthermore, conspicuously absent from the repertoire to be copied as we now can reconstruct it is any trope for Easter, the most solemn feast of the church year. The annotator probably selected a trope or *versus ante officium* for that feast on a lost leaf (there is a lacuna at the beginning of the Easter tropes in the manuscript as it is preserved today).

It is difficult to assess exactly how large a repertoire the annotator originally identified. The 13 pieces in the Anglo-Saxon troper signalled by the notation *scribe* or by a liturgical rubric are for the following feast or ferial days: St John the Evangelist; the Holy Innocents; Christmas;[9] the Purification; the Annunciation; Monday, Tuesday and Wednesday of Easter week; St Peter; the Nativity of the Virgin; St Martin; St Thomas of Canterbury; and St Oswald of Worcester. The annotator did not mark tropes for the first Sunday in Advent, for the first two masses of Christmas day, or for St Stephen, all of which are complete in the Caligula Troper. The most likely additions to the corpus I have been able to define are a trope for Easter (as already mentioned) and tropes for Palm Sunday, Ascension, the Assumption of the Virgin and All Saints (all major feasts that begin or end in the midst of the introit tropes in the Anglo-Saxon manuscript). In any event, the corpus would have been small by comparison with the trope collections of the early Middle Ages, including that of the Caligula Troper itself. In summary, the annotator provided instructions for the copying of a modest repertoire of introit tropes and a *versus ante officium* (to be performed as an introit trope) from the Anglo-Saxon troper, as well as a prose from the later troper-proser, and he may well have known the troper in a form less fragmentary than we now have it.

The corpus of tropes defined by the annotator can only be described as eclectic. There are pieces of varying length, from a single introductory element to a five element complex. Furthermore, the tropes selected by the annotator are as stylistically diverse as is the trope genre itself. There are seven tropes in quantitative verse (either hexameters or, in one case, elegiac distichs) and one in what appear to be flawed hexameters. Four of the tropes are in prose, and one is in rhythmic verse.[10] The annotator, therefore, seems to have favoured neither verse nor prose. Nor have I been able to identify a thematic coherence among the pieces he selected.

Although he selected some English pieces (of which three may have been composed by St Æthelwold's pupil Wulfstan),[11] the annotator may not have been particularly aware of their origin. Indeed, he probably thought of all of the pieces in the troper as belonging to the Anglo-Saxon past because of their presence in an Anglo-Saxon manuscript.[12] In summary, the annotator's specific criteria for inclusion elude identification, except that he was particularly interested in introit tropes (as opposed to offertory or communion tropes) and that he limited himself to one trope per feast day.

The activities of the lead point annotator of the Caligula Troper are particularly suited to Worcester in the thirteenth century, where an interest in things Anglo-Saxon is apparent above all in the occupation of the 'tremulous hand'.[13] This figure, almost certainly a monk of the priory, is most famous for the marginal and interlinear glosses he added to many late Anglo-Saxon vernacular manuscripts.[14] His annotations, which include translations of problematic Old English words into Latin and Middle English, reflect their author's keen interest in the Anglo-Saxon language. He also copied an Old English text into an eleventh-century Latin liturgical book,[15] and he made occasional liturgical notes, usually in Latin.[16] Although most of his glosses are in ink, a large number from before his maturity are in lead point, the medium favoured by the annotator of the Caligula Troper.[17] The absolute or relative chronology of the activities of the tremulous hand and the annotator of the troper may never be established with precision. Nevertheless, we can well imagine the two men sitting side-by-side as they explored the priory's library, studying and annotating manuscripts from the late Anglo-Saxon period.

The twelfth century, when the Anglo-Saxon language as a literary medium waned in the face of Norman cultural dominance, saw both a decline in the copying of proper tropes and the introduction of notation on a four-line stave in England.[18] The repertoire of the troper must have seemed to the thirteenth-century annotator much as the Old English homilies appeared to the tremulous hand: the pieces were exotic and their notation archaic. The annotator of the Caligula Troper, however, had more than an antiquarian interest in the tropes he marked; he included liturgical assignments for the pieces, which suggests that he expected them to be sung by his contemporaries. One particularly compelling piece of evidence concerning the annotator's intentions is the assignment of *Cum venerit verbum* to the feast of St Thomas of Canterbury, a twelfth-century figure culted throughout England in the thirteenth century. The annotator was not interested in 'reconstructing' Anglo-Saxon practice; he was instead interested in the contemporary celebration of the liturgy.

The musical notation in the Anglo-Saxon troper conveys the contours but not the exact pitches of the melodies. In the absence of a continuing oral tradition, therefore, the music of the tropes would be lost to the annotator. At first sight, it seems unlikely that proper tropes continued to be sung in England during the period after they ceased to be copied into manuscripts. Nevertheless, there is evidence from the Continent for the late survival of a limited repertoire of proper tropes.[19] Furthermore, it is interesting to note that two motets on the Marian introit *Salve sancta parens* were copied (and presumably performed) at Worcester in the high Middle Ages.[20] Although it cannot be determined conclusively whether the melodies of the tropes marked by the lead point annotator of the Caligula Troper were remembered at Worcester in the thirteenth century, it seems inescapable that the annotator expected that the tropes he marked would be copied and performed.

NOTES

1. For a concise discussion of the work-a-day character of early medieval tropers, see Paul Evans, *The Early Medieval Trope Repertory of Saint Martial de Limoges*, Princeton Studies in Music, 2 (Princeton: Princeton University Press, 1970), pp. 32–5.
2. The principal studies of the Anglo-Saxon tropers are: Walter Howard Frere, *The Winchester Troper: From Manuscripts of the Xth and XIth Centuries*, Henry Bradshaw Society, 8 (London: Henry Bradshaw Society, 1894) and Alejandro Enrique Planchart, *The Repertory of Tropes at Winchester*, 2 vols (Princeton: Princeton University Press, 1977). See more recently, 'Tropers', in *The Liturgical Books of Anglo-Saxon England*, ed. Richard W. Pfaff, *Old English Newsletter*, Subsidia, 23 (Kalamazoo: Medieval Institute Publications, Western Michigan University, 1995), pp. 39–44.
3. For a summary of published opinion, see my 'The 'Hereford Troper' and Hereford', in *Medieval Art, Architecture and Archaeology at Hereford*, ed. David Whitehead, British Archaeological Association Conference Transactions, 15 (Leeds: W.S. Maney, 1995), pp. 75–81.
4. The argument is outlined in my 'Some Thoughts on the Place of Origin of the Cotton Troper', in *Cantus Planus: Papers Read at the Fourth Meeting, Pécs, Hungary, 3–8 September 1990*, ed. László Dobszay (Budapest: Hungarian Academy of Sciences, 1992), pp. 407–12.
5. Fols 7r, 8r, 9v, 12r, 15v, 16r, 17r, 23r, 26v, 29v, 33v, 34v and 67r.
6. No liturgical rubrics were supplied when the manuscript was written. Besides this annotation, one other liturgical rubric was added by a later hand, this one in ink (fol. 72v).
7. Frere (*The Winchester Troper*, p. 104) remarked the presence of this cue,

but Planchart denied it (*The Repertory of Tropes*, vol. 1, p. 235, n. 1 and vol. 2, p. 32).

8. I am assuming that the annotator meant to signal the entire trope and not just the introductory element. I see no way to confirm or refute this conjecture.

9. The annotator presumably thought of *Deus pater filium* (cued to the Christmas introit *Puer natus est*) as a Christmas piece, even though it is assigned to the Circumcision (the Christmas octave) in the Caligula Troper.

10. On the themes, language and prosody of the tropes found uniquely in the Caligula Troper, including two marked by the annotator, see Ritva Jacobsson, 'Unica in the Cotton Caligula Troper', in *Music in the Medieval English Liturgy: Plainsong & Mediaeval Music Society Centennial Essays*, ed. Susan Rankin and David Hiley (Oxford: Clarendon Press, 1993), pp. 11–45.

11. On Wulfstan of Winchester as a composer of tropes, see Michael Lapidge and Michael Winterbottom, eds., *Wulfstan of Winchester: The Life of St Æthelwold*, Oxford Medieval Texts (Oxford: Clarendon Press, 1991), pp. xxxi–xxxiv.

12. The concordances for the tropes selected by the annotator are listed in Planchart, where the texts of the tropes are edited (*The Repertory of Tropes*, vol. 2, pp. 32, 44, 103–4, 109, 112, 115–6, 128–9, 136–8, 155–6, 169–70, 175–6, 176–8 and 187). The text of *Exsulta caelum* is edited in *Analecta hymnica medii aevi* (vol. 9, ed. G.M. Dreves, pp. 181–2). I owe my knowledge of the concordance pattern for *Exsulta caelum* to David Hiley, who generously shared unpublished material.

13. On the tremulous hand, see N.R. Ker, 'The Date of the 'Tremulous' Worcester Hand', *Leeds Studies in English* 6 (1937), 28–9 (repr. in *Books, Collectors and Libraries: Studies in the Medieval Heritage*, ed. Andrew G. Watson (London: Hambledon Press, 1982), pp. 67–8); Christine Franzen, *The Tremulous Hand of Worcester: A Study of Old English in the Thirteenth Century* (Oxford: Clarendon Press, 1991). I once thought that the annotations in Caligula A. xiv might be the work of the tremulous hand himself ('Some Thoughts', p. 408, n. 9), but I am less inclined to think so now.

14. The manuscripts he annotated include eight large collections of homilies, two copies of King Alfred's Old English translation of the *Pastoral Care* of Gregory the Great (including the manuscript sent by Alfred to Worcester) and vernacular versions of Bede's *Ecclesiastical History* and Gregory's *Dialogues*. See Franzen, *The Tremulous Hand of Worcester*, pp. 29–74.

15. Cambridge, Corpus Christi College 391. This manuscript also has drypoint annotations, perhaps of the thirteenth century, indicating the liturgical assignment of some Office antiphons for the Sundays after

Pentecost. I am grateful to R.I. Page (former librarian, Corpus Christi College) for permission to examine this manuscript.

16. See, for example, the page discussed by Ker in 'The Date of the "Tremulous" Worcester Hand'.

17. Franzen, *The Tremulous Hand of Worcester*, pp. 5–28.

18. The Caligula Troper itself is the latest surviving source of proper tropes from England.

19. None of the tropes marked in the Caligula Troper, however, is present in the post-twelfth-century Continental graduals containing proper tropes. (I owe this point to Andreas Haug, who generously searched the repertoire included in his forthcoming *Musicalischer Index zum Corpus Troporum*.) Closest in time and place to the annotations in the Caligula Troper is the repertoire of proper tropes in Provins, Bibliothèque municipale 12 (24). See David Hiley, 'Provins Bibliothèque municipale 12 (24), a Thirteenth-Century Gradual with Tropes from Chartres Cathedral', in *Recherches nouvelles sur les tropes liturgiques*, ed. Wulf Arlt and Gunilla Björkvall, Studia latina Stockholmiensia, 36 (Stockholm: Almqvist & Wiksell, 1993), pp. 239–69.

20. Anselm Hughes, *Worcester Medieval Harmony of the Thirteenth and Fourteenth Centuries* (Burnham: The Plainsong and Mediaeval Music Society, 1928), pp. 62–6; Luther Dittmer, *The Worcester Fragments*, Musicological Studies and Documents, 2 ([Rome]: American Institute of Musicology, 1957), pp. 14–5.

APPENDIX

Pieces marked in Caligula A. xiv by the lead point annotator

Folio	Piece	Genre	Literary Form	Dissemination	Liturgical Assigment
7r	Lux vera Christus	introit trope	prose	unicum	St John the Evangelist (26 Dec.)
8r	Dicantur igitur	versus ante officium	prose	unicum	Holy Innocents (28 Dec.)
9v	Deus pater filium	introit trope	prose	pan-Europe	Christmas (25 Dec.)
10r	Adest alma virgo	introit trope	rhythmic verse	pan-Europe	Purification (2 Feb.)
12r	Germinis excelsi	introit trope	hexameters	England	Annunciation (25 Mar.)
15v	Conditor almificus	introit trope	elegiac distichs	England	Feria II in Easter Week
16r	Sanctorum populum	introit trope	hexameters	England and N. France	Feria III in Easter Week
17r	Quos mea perpetuo	introit trope	hexameters	England	Feria IV in Easter Week
23r	Carcere iam liber	introit trope	hexameters	mostly England and N. France	St Peter (29 Jun.)
26v	Splendore sollemni	introit trope	prose	unique version of a S. French trope	Nativity of the Virgin (8 Sep.)
29v	Gemma dei Martinus	introit trope	faulty hexameters	pan-Europe	St Martin (11 Nov.)
33v	Cum venerit verbum	introit trope	hexameters	mostly France	St Thomas of Canterbury (29 Dec.)
34v	Quem caeli cives	introit trope	hexameters	England and N. France	St Oswald of Worcester (28 Feb.)
67r	Exsulta caelum	prose	prose	England, N. France and Sicily	Nativity of St John the Baptist (24 Jun.)

10 The Dates and Origins of Three Twelfth-Century Old English Manuscripts

Elaine M. Treharne

Of the 27 manuscripts listed in N.R. Ker's *Catalogue* which are dated approximately to the twelfth century, many are not dated securely and some have not been assigned a place of origin or provenance.[1] This is no reflection on Ker's magisterial work as it is almost solely to him that we look for information on these manuscripts. In the 40 years since the publication of the *Catalogue*, while many advances have been made in the area of pre-Conquest manuscripts studies, knowledge of the production of vernacular manuscripts in the period *c.* 1100–*c.* 1200 has not been the focus of a great deal of critical debate. No major study of vernacular script or texts in this period has been published beyond the single-manuscript work of Rima Handley, Mary P. Richards, William Schipper, and Susan Irvine.[2] Some scriptoria have been the subject of dissertations and monographs but these focus primarily on Latin manuscript production and do not provide detailed accounts of contemporary Old English copying.[3] Thus it is that scholars can be specific about few vernacular manuscripts of the twelfth century either in terms of their date or place of origin; for example, the large and important Old English codex, London, British Library, Cotton Vespasian D. xiv, is dated variously to the early twelfth century, to the second quarter of that century, and to the middle of the century.[4] This may only be a matter of 40 years in terms of its approximate dating, but to date this manuscript and then use that date as evidence for dating other manuscripts leads to a somewhat circular argument.[5] Vespasian D. xiv is also assigned an origin at either Rochester or Christ Church, Canterbury, these scriptoria often being treated as if they were interchangeable.[6] Such indeterminate localisation creates more difficulties than it solves as it effectively eliminates that manuscript from being used as evidence in assigning a place of origin to other, similar and contemporary Old English codices or fragments; for example, in the case of a manuscript which showed clear palaeographical or textual similarities with Vespasian D. xiv, we would also have to assign it to a non-committal 'either Rochester or Christ Church' designation.[7] That Rochester and Christ Church are not palaeographically identical in this period is outlined by Teresa Webber, for while there seems to have been an identifiable housestyle at Rochester in the first quarter of the twelfth century, the same is not the case at Christ Church.[8] Webber focuses on Latin manuscript production, but it appears that the same principle applies to vernacular manuscripts of the same period: the two scriptoria do not exemplify identical palaeographical or codicological techniques.

The reasons behind the lack of confidence in dealing with twelfth-century material stems in part, perhaps, from the relatively small number of surviving vernacular manuscripts and the lack of definable and developmental features of script which characterise these codices. As a rule, these manuscripts do not form the focus of sustained palaeographical investigation when they are studied. Editors of Old English texts in their indispensable work employ the material copied in Old English in the post-1100 period for collation purposes: to collect variants or to supply texts, or portions of text, missing from pre-1100 manuscripts.[9] The same editors are dealing with a large number of individual manuscripts and cannot usually provide detailed descriptions of the script and place of origin of most of these books for that is not the central purpose of the textual editions. Seldom, then, are the Old English texts from the twelfth century studied in their own right, and within their particular manuscript context, as examples of a continuing tradition of production in the vernacular.[10] Indeed, the limbo in which twelfth-century Old English manuscripts have existed has not made for a lively scholarly debate to date even though there is a great deal to be debated.[11]

In comparison to the numbers of extant Latin manuscripts copied in England in the twelfth century, there is relatively little English material. What does survive, however, constitutes a significant body of vernacular texts which can be analysed comparatively: these codices, charters,[12] fragments, and glosses and corrections to earlier manuscripts provide a sound starting point for a re-evaluation of the importance of the vernacular in the post-Conquest period. There are many developmental aspects of the script that can be traced within these respective extant materials[13] and used to supply a firmer dating and assignation of place of origin when required; and each whole or fragmentary manuscript copied and produced in this period is worthy of sustained and serious scholarly attention in its own right.

Vernacular material in the post-Conquest period can also be compared in relation to dated Latin manuscripts of the twelfth century, the origins of which are identified. This method, however, is insufficient on its own since the datable Latin scripts are often those evident in legal and administrative documents and these are current or semi-current; where Latin bookhands are used for comparison with their Old English counterparts, the Old English scripts frequently demonstrate archaic features attributable either to the careful copying of the exemplar or presumably to the age of the scribe. Because the Old English manuscripts seem archaic in comparison with the Latin, the danger of assigning a date to the former which is too early arises. Such is the case in the arguments of R.S. Cox and Schipper in their analyses of Vespasian D. xiv and Cambridge, University Library, Ii. 1. 33

respectively.[14]

Another difficulty in ascertaining the dates and scriptoria of vernacular manuscripts is that the proliferation of the ascenders and descenders of Insular forms gives to the English text an overall aspect quite unlike that of Latin.[15] Moreover, within one manuscript, there is often no consistency in the copying of letters: for example, Insular *f* and *r* and Caroline *f* and *r* can appear within a single scribe's unilingual stint;[16] *a* might possess a headstroke, or it might appear with a less developed headstroke (akin to a single-compartment *a*) within the same word;[17] and *s* may be high, low, long or uncial. It is also the case that in the copying of Old English, special features current in Latin script at any one time which can be used for dating purposes may not be evident in the copying of English for some years afterwards. Therefore, the dating of a vernacular manuscript on the grounds that it shares specific palaeographical features common to a particular Latin script may lead, once again, to a dating of the Old English that is too early. In Oxford, Bodleian Library, Hatton 115, fols 148–155,[18] for example, a *d+e* ligature is used by the scribe a number of times at the ends of words such as *godcunde* (fol. 148v, line 17) and *lufiende* (fol. 149r, line 2). This ligature, which appears in the form of a round-backed *d* with the bowl and tongue of *e* attached at the top of the ascender, also appears in manuscripts such as London, British Library, Cotton Julius A. ii, fols 136–144,[19] and Cambridge, Corpus Christi College 303, fols 231, 233 and 251–252.[20] This same feature occurs in Latin and French manuscripts discussed in detail by M.B. Parkes.[21] Parkes notes that this ligature is used in a Durham manuscript written in Latin as early as 1096, though it is found more frequently in Latin manuscripts as the twelfth century progresses.[22] The French manuscript on which he focuses, Oxford, Bodleian Library, Digby 23, is dated to the second quarter of the twelfth century and also shows this ligature.[23] The *d+e* ligature may well have been in occasional use in Latin manuscripts as early as the end of the eleventh century, but it does not to my knowledge appear in any English vernacular book before *c.* 1150. It seems that in both French and English vernacular manuscripts the use of this ligature post-dates its appearance in Latin texts, and as such, to use special features of script that occur in Latin manuscripts to help date a vernacular manuscript can be misleading. As all these factors complicate the dating of Old English manuscripts, it is advisable to approach the standard palaeographical descriptions of the period which deal in most part with Latin scripts with caution[24] and to refine the use of features which can help date Latin manuscripts with a close and comparative analysis of the major extant English vernacular materials.[25]

Palaeographical features that are helpful in dating Latin manuscripts in the twelfth century have been subject to some scrutiny and classification.[26] Ker's overview of the elements of Latin script characteristic of the middle of the twelfth century is perhaps the fullest and most useful treatment as it is both retrospective and prospective: he notes that straight lines, angles and shallow curves begin to take the place of full curves in *a*, *b*, *c*, *d*, *e*, *g*, *m*, *n*, *o* and *t*; that instead of forming a triangular projection to the left, the onset of the minim stroke is made like the top of a lozenge; that the abbreviation mark becomes straight instead of being curved or wavy; and that features such as trailing-headed *a* and the horizontal foot of the minim are made more distinctive.[27] These particular elements of Latin script from the middle of the century can be looked for in the English examples as potential guides for dating. To be more precise in dating the script of English texts, however, because of the different linguistic medium, changes in the formation of graphs characteristic of Old English should also be traced to reinforce the general tendencies of the Latin book-hands. This, in itself, is a treacherous business as will be discussed below. It is Ker, once again, who provides the basic information for investigating dating features for Old English hands in the twelfth century: among these is the weakening of the tradition of using the Insular forms of *f*, *g*, *r* and *s* for Old English texts and the Caroline forms for Latin; the increasing use of Caroline *h* in Old English; and the increasingly used distinction between Caroline *g* and Insular *g* for spirants and stops.[28] To these general graphic criteria may be added the developments of ruling in lead, of single columns for Old English manuscripts but double columns for Latin and the use of single vertical bounding lines instead of pairs.[29] Each of these elements is helpful in ascertaining a general date for many manuscripts of the twelfth century, but much more specific descriptions are required for tracing the evolution of the script used for Old English texts. By the middle of the century, for example, when Insular *f* is used, the crossbar often transects the stem; at the same time, the stem of *t* is often seen to push above the crossbar. Other distinctive features which suggest a date around the middle of the twelfth century are the splitting (with a marked serif to the left) or wedging of ascenders; the leftward curve of the descender up to the middle of the century, and then, later, the tapering of the descender to a point; the form of *y* where the tail of the descender flicks to the right; the use of suprascript *s* at the end of words as a space-saver;[30] the occasional 3-shaped form of the *Tironian nota*; the straight suspension mark denoting the omission of a nasal; and the use of transposition marks in the correction of the text.[31] Ligatures also occur more frequently in most hands writing Old English which are approximately datable from the later part of the first half of the century. These include the *ct*, *st* and *or* ligatures.[32] Any of these features, whether they are usually found in Latin or Old English texts or both, when used in isolation within a hand are suggestive of very little, but when all or most of them are found, then a date from about the middle of the century (*c*. 1140–*c*. 1160) is applicable. These criteria would not account for the age of the scribe, however: if he were an old scribe writing in the way in which he was taught, then the actual date of the copying of the manuscript might be somewhat later in the century.[33]

As has been outlined, dating Old English manuscripts in the period *c.* 1100–*c.* 1200 proves problematic for many reasons; exacerbating the situation further is the lack of firm knowledge we possess for scriptoria that produced many of the major books in the twelfth century. Christ Church, Canterbury, Rochester, Worcester and Peterborough have all been identified as definite centres of Old English manuscript copying and writing in the period *c.* 1100–*c.* 1200.[34] These scriptoria were also producing Latin manuscripts, but a number of other centres are also associated with the production of Latin manuscripts such as Bury St Edmunds, Salisbury and Lincoln.[35] The evidence suggests that while many such institutions were engaged in the copying of Latin manuscripts in the period, only a limited number of scriptoria seem to have been copying Old English texts. In addition to those places mentioned above as producing vernacular manuscripts, Ely has been nominated as the possible place of compilation of Cambridge, University Library, Ii. 1. 33;[36] and Southwick is the provenance of the first part of London, British Library, Cotton Vitellius A. xv.[37] The provenance of the extant twelfth-century Old English manuscripts will vary, but the place of origin of them seems to be attributable to one of only a few centres: Christ Church, Canterbury, Rochester and Worcester. Notably, these are all monastic cathedrals,[38] perhaps indicating that vernacular texts were more highly valued or used to a greater extent at these institutions than at secular cathedrals.[39]

Despite the relatively large number of scriptoria and copyists producing Latin manuscripts in the same period, it is notable that some scribes appear to have contributed to the copying of a number of extant Latin books (the output of the *Textus Roffensis* scribe who also writes Old English, for example, or Eadmer, writing at Canterbury[40]); yet, to my knowledge, no one has identified a scribe who is known to write extensively in Latin and/or Old English in different manuscripts. Neither, until now,[41] has the same scribe been identified with certainty in more than one Old English manuscript. As we have so little evidence for the scribes who wrote Old English appearing in other vernacular or Latin manuscripts, potential data for ascertaining the place or origin of a manuscript from comparative sources is almost impossible to find.

Such evidence for tracing the origin of an Old English manuscript is relatively thin on the ground, but there are ways in which this perplexing issue can be addressed. In the following discussion, some examples of Old English script in the twelfth century will be examined initially to give an indication of the complexities involved in analysing specific scribes. From this analysis, some proposals for dating and, particularly, for identifying the place of origin for some previously unlocalised twelfth-century Old English manuscripts will be provided.

To return to a manuscript cited earlier, Cotton Vespasian D. xiv: this is an extensive collection of catechetical, educative and homiletic texts which contains 53 articles in Old English. It has been dated to the first half or middle of the twelfth century and assigned a Rochester or Christ Church, Canterbury, origin;[42] Rima Handley, in a persuasive argument, deduced that it is of Christ Church, Canterbury, origin and maintained the mid-twelfth-century dating; and Mary P. Richards, in her discussion, attributed the manuscript to the second quarter of the twelfth century at Rochester.[43] Richards examines the manuscript in relative isolation, using only the *Textus Roffensis*, Cambridge, Corpus Christi College 303, and one Christ Church manuscript for comparative purposes.[44] She calls upon the presence of some features of eleventh-century Insular script beside the Caroline forms to sustain her assumption that Vespasian D. xiv must have been copied by an English scribe trained in Continental orthographic practices.[45] She believes that Vespasian D. xiv is later than CCCC 303 which she states also originated at Rochester in the first quarter of the twelfth century.[46] One of her main pieces of evidence for this proposal is the 'exclusive' presence of Caroline *g* in the former manuscript together with other, more tenuous features found commonly in Latin and Old English manuscripts throughout the twelfth century.[47] In fact, there are instances of Insular *g* in Vespasian D. xiv at fols 163 and 165, for example.[48] Also, other vernacular manuscripts assigned by Ker to an earlier date than Vespasian D. xiv, such as Oxford, Bodleian Library, Hatton 116 (s. xii^{1})[49] and London, British Library, Cotton Faustina A. ix (s. xii^{1}) use the Caroline form of *g* (as shown, for example, in Plate 16). Later manuscripts, too, such as Bodleian Library, Bodley 343 and Cambridge University Library Ii. 1. 33 (both s. xii^{2}) use the Caroline and Insular forms of *g*.[50] Thus, the scribe's choice of Insular or Caroline letter forms when copying Old English seems to give little firm evidence of date; indeed, in many instances, it appears that the scribe is often following the exemplar's forms thereby complicating the dating process. The main scribe of the *Textus Roffensis*, for example, uses archaic forms of *r* and *y* up to fol. 37. From fol. 38, he uses modernised versions of these letter-forms.[51]

If one is to rely on general palaeographical elements such as the retention or partial retention of Insular characters, there are few manuscripts that will provide consistent datable features. Cotton Faustina A. x, part B, for instance, a manuscript dated to the first half of the twelfth century by Ker,[52] is a copy of the *Rule of St Benedict* which exemplifies the retention of Insular letters and style of script: the letter *e* has a well-developed onset stroke which makes the character a type of archaic horned *e*; *d*, *f*, *g*, *h*, *r* and *s* are Insular as is the *st* ligature with a long *s*. In this careful adherence to these Insular characteristics of script, the scribe could well be emulating his exemplar and can, in this respect, be paralleled with the Christ Church scribes of British Library, Stowe Charter 43 and Campbell Charter xxi. 6, both of which are dated to *c.* 1123.[53] Scribes' attempts at consistency in the twelfth century are often irregular to say the least, and in some instances such inconsistencies do seem to be a result of partial adherence to the exemplar's forms.[54]

The dangers, therefore, of characterising a manuscript on the basis of only a few letter-forms, distinguishing between the Insular and Caroline tendencies of a scribe's hand, or being overly dependent on Latin scripts for comparative purposes, can evidently be misleading, particularly in attempts to date the script. It might thus appear that it is futile to attempt to classify the evolution of script used for copying Old English in the twelfth century, especially considering the substantial amount of variation even within one scribe's stint. The following analysis, however, will address these issues: it will locate and discuss elements of script which might give an indication of place of origin or date of these manuscripts.

The manuscripts on which the remainder of this paper will focus are CCCC 367, fols 1, 2, 7–10 (s. xii^2), and 3–6, 11–29 (s. xii^1); Hatton 115, fols 148–155 (s. xii med.); and CUL Ii. 1. 33 (s. xii^2). Incidental to the discussion are the *Textus Roffensis* (s. xii) and Cotton Faustina A. ix and A. x (both s. xii^1).

Of these manuscripts, a place of origin or provenance has been designated for some: the *Textus Roffensis*, which dates from the first quarter of the twelfth century, with additions from throughout the century, is a Rochester product;[55] Faustina A. x, part A, may be of south-eastern origin as might the first (eleventh-century) portion of Hatton 115, though much of Hatton 115 itself (excluding the folios with which this discussion is concerned) was glossed by the Worcester tremulous scribe;[56] neither of these eleventh-century portions of the manuscripts, however, are localisable with any certainty at present. CCCC 367 is probably of south-eastern origin, though it has a text bound in with it of Worcester origin.[57] Faustina A. ix is of unknown origin;[58] and CUL Ii. 1. 33 has tentative links with Ely.[59]

A cursory glance at this list suggests that Worcester, Rochester and Christ Church are the main contenders for the scriptoria producing or receiving Old English texts well into the twelfth century. In the light of the known continuation of interest in Old English at Worcester,[60] and the evidence recently put forward by Margaret Gibson in *The Eadwine Psalter* for the continued, if subordinate, attention given to the vernacular at Church Church in the middle of the twelfth century,[61] the prominence of these two scriptoria together with Rochester is not surprising. No other scriptoria, bar the possibility of Ely, are among this group of manuscripts' proposed origins or provenances. Still, further precision in assigning these manuscripts (apart from the *Textus Roffensis*) to one or other of these scriptoria is required.

If the manuscripts listed above are examined chronologically, CCCC 367, part II, fols 3–6 and 11–29, and the *Textus Roffensis* appear to be the earliest. This particular portion of CCCC 367, which is now bound together with other vernacular and Latin fragments, is a collection of homilies 'muddled together' as Ker puts it.[62] The composite manuscript — bound from fragments probably for Matthew Parker — contains a booklist of Worcester origin, but the Old English portion of it at fols 3–6 and 11–29 is almost certainly not of Worcester origin. This can be shown by the palaeographical and textual evidence. If these folios of CCCC 367 are compared with Old English text from the part of the *Textus Roffensis* written by the main scribe in the 1120s, the overall aspects of the scripts can be seen to be markedly similar:[63] the same Insular characters, *d, f, g, h, r* and *s*, are retained in both hands, though round *s* is often used in initial position in the *Textus Roffensis*; there are similarities in the slightly backward-looking slant of the scripts, and in their ducts — thick to thin strokes occur in the lower left strokes of the *d, ð, c* and *e* (which are rather angular); the *a* is very similar in both hands with its half-developed headstroke, while the *a* portion of *æ* is formed with barely any headstroke; the *Tironian nota*, the tapering descenders and the split ascenders are similar. Both scribes also use a very low hyphen to bridge a space in the middle of the misdivided word. The *mise-en-page* of both manuscripts is a single-column of writing which often exemplifies an irregular right margin; capitals are offset into the left margin where a new clause corresponds with the line beginning; enlarged initials are in-filled with red; the *punctus* is low; and the abbreviation line for omission of nasals is relatively straight. In contrast, however, a closer analysis of letters-forms signifies most noticeably that the *ð* in this portion of CCCC 367 is quite different from that of the *Textus Roffensis* — its shaft ends in a downward stroke to the left and the character is often drawn as if it were one movement of the pen. The *Textus Roffensis* scribe also employs an *f*, the crossbar of which is above the line and the shaft below, while the CCCC 367 scribe's *f* is typically Insular. Finally, the *e* of the CCCC 367 scribe has an exaggerated tongue which is less evident in the *Textus Roffensis* hand. CCCC 367, fols 3–6 and 11–29, exemplifies — most specifically in the distinctive *d* — correspondences with earlier Old English manuscripts such as Bodleian Library, Laud Misc. 509, dated to the second half of the eleventh century, but also with more contemporary manuscripts such as Cotton Faustina A. x, part B, of the first half of the twelfth century.[64] The weight of palaeographical evidence would suggest that this section of CCCC 367 is of south-eastern origin, and the affinities that it shows with the *Textus Roffensis* might place its origin at Rochester through it is possibly a less practised example of this type of bold, non-compressed script. There are also similarities between this scribe in CCCC 367 and the Latin manuscripts Bodleian Library, Bodley 387, written by a Rochester scribe in the first quarter of the twelfth century, and British Library, Royal 6 A. xii, also written at Rochester in the first quarter of the twelfth century.[65] These similarities would include the general aspects of the scripts, the forked ascenders, the manner of formation of *d*, for example, where the two strokes made by the scribe in the writing of the character are visible in the small overlap, and in the extended tongue of *e*. These are common enough in the twelfth-century scripts of the period, and thus cannot be used as major evidence. A further indication of a south-eastern origin for CCCC 367, fols 3–6 and 11–29, however, is the enlarged and ink-filled decorative initial *M* with its following display script, as seen at fol. 27v, MANEGUM IS CUÐ (Plate 17). This type of initial and the rounded uncial capitals of the display script are akin to those described by Richard Gameson in relation to Christ Church, Canterbury, manuscripts in the post-Conquest period.[66] Similarly formed display script can also be seen in the Rochester manuscript, Bodley 387, fol. 1v.[67]

The textual evidence afforded by CCCC 367, fols 3–6 and 11–29, also points, albeit indirectly, to a south-eastern origin. The texts in this part of the manuscript are bound together in a haphazard fashion and nearly all of them are incomplete. The most comprehensible outline of the contents of these folios is Malcolm Godden's from which the following description is taken.[68] Quire 1 (fols 21, 20, 26) contains homilies for Easter Day (Ixv) and for Easter Monday (Iixvi); Quire 2 (fols 17, 29) contains a homily for Tuesday in Rogationtide; Quire 3 (fols 23, 6, 3–5, 24) includes homilies for the Assumption of the Virgin (Ixxx) and St Bartholomew (Ixxxi); Quire 4 (fols 11–16) is a homily for the Nativity of the Virgin (Assmann x); and Quires 5–6 (fols 28, 19, 27, 18, 22, 25) contain homilies for the Exaltation of the Cross (LS xxvii), St Matthew (II xxxii), St Michael (I xxxiv) and an unspecified occasion (Vercelli iv). Of these texts, the homily for Easter Monday contained in Quire 1 agrees most closely with Godden's manuscript M, CUL Ii. 4. 6, the origin of which is New Minster, Winchester, although its exemplar is south-eastern in origin. Godden proposes a common source for this homily in CCCC 367 and in CUL Ii. 4. 6,[69] which would reinforce evidence for the south-eastern affiliations of CCCC 367. The homily for St Matthew in the final quires agrees most closely with Vespasian D. xiv, Bodley 340 and 342, CCCC 198 and CCCC 162. These are south-eastern manuscripts of the eleventh and twelfth centuries, and the textual evidence here seems, once again, to point to the dominance of south-eastern links in the origin of CCCC 367.[70] Adding to this the palaeographical evidence, it is possible to narrow the 'south-eastern' designation of probable origin to, perhaps, Rochester in the first decades of the twelfth century, before *c.* 1130.

A second manuscript, Hatton 115, fols 148–155, illustrates the same kind of problems as CCCC 367 in ascertaining where it might have been copied. The manuscript is comprised of five booklets which include homilies for unspecified occasions which 'could not have been together until some time after its component parts were copied'.[71] The manuscript as a whole has a Worcester provenance though it is not a product of the Worcester scriptorium.[72] The last two booklets in the manuscript, fols 140–147 and 148–155, were not included in the manuscript's table of contents written in *c.* 1200,[73] which suggests they were not bound in with the first part of the manuscript at this time. It is the date and origin of the final booklet in the manuscript, fols 148–155, upon which I will focus here. This booklet (consisting of two quires of four leaves each) is ruled with pencil and contains 11 prognostications written in a single mid-twelfth-century hand. The last two folios of this booklet are blank; the Tremulous Scribe has written four lines at the top of fol. 154, but has not glossed the text at fols 148–153 (even though the earlier booklets of the manuscript are glossed). This seems to confirm that the booklet was in Worcester by the first part of the thirteenth century when the Tremulous Scribe was working, but that he was not interested in this text *per se*. Additional lines of text concerning the life-span of Adam have been added by a late twelfth-century hand on fol. 155.[74]

Palaeographical and textual evidence afforded by the contents of fols 148–155 suggest that it may be of south-eastern origin. The script is datable to the middle of the twelfth century, or perhaps slightly later (see Plates 18 and 19). For example, the stem of both the Caroline and Insular forms of *f* that are used is pierced by the crossbar; the stem of *t* is beginning to push above the crossbar; the descender of the Insular *g* is often closed by an acute hairline stroke; from fol. 149v, the tail of *y* ends with a distinct flick to the right; the *d+e* ligature occurs; the onset of the minim-stroke is formed with a lozenge shape; and flattish serifs can be seen to the right of the minim-feet. All of these features suggest a date of around the middle of the twelfth century. The scribe's attention to consistency is limited, though, as the variation in the forms of *f*, *g*, *s*, *ð* and *y* attests. This variation (occurring noticeably between fols 148v and 149r) might be attributable to the emulation of the exemplar's forms. While the palaeographical characteristics of the script are helpful in ascertaining date, they are not as helpful for the convincing demonstration of the place of origin of this booklet. Some general links with the script and layout of Cotton Faustina A. ix are illustrated (see Plate 16).[75] The pen-drawn enlarged initials, for example, are very similar, and the overall aspects of the script are similar in that they are very upright, with space between the ruling for relatively long ascenders and descenders; descenders taper to a point sometimes ending with a very slight curve to the left. The abbreviation mark, slightly curved in Hatton 115, is, however, straight in Faustina A. ix, and individual letter-forms are quite different; for instance, Hatton 115 usually uses Insular *g*, Faustina A. ix uses Caroline; Hatton 115 uses Caroline and Insular *f*, Faustina A. ix Insular only. The similarities of script that can be perceived are thus of the most tentative and common kind. As Faustina A. ix is of unknown origin, evidence here becomes cyclical since we are reliant on a comparative analysis with a manuscript that is itself of little help in ascertaining origin. Another manuscript that shares some of the features in evidence in Hatton 115, fols 148–155, is Vespasian D. xiv. The third scribe in Vespasian, who added material at fols 163–166|10 (see Plate 15), shows a rounded form of Insular *g* which is similar to that of the Hatton scribe in that both form their letter in one stroke from the right of the crossbar of the *g*; in both hands, the descender of *p* ends in a horizontal serif to the right; both scribes write a form of *ð* where the top of the crossbar ends in a flick to the left; and the *y* which is formed by beginning the descender from the left limb is also similar in both hands. The Vespasian scribe, though, shows a tendency to form his descenders with a more pronounced curve to the left, and the ascenders have a serif to the left rather than the more common wedge of the Hatton scribe. As Vespasian D. xiv is probably of Christ Church (or Rochester) origin, this might suggest the same place of origin for Hatton 115, fols 148–155, but these general similarities can only provide the most tentative evidence. Other features, then, such as text and dialect might help in clarifying links to determine origin. The 11 prognostications contained in Hatton 115, fols 148–155, are concerned with: the significance of dreams according to the age of the moon; the significance of the moon at childbirth; the significance of the days of the week at childbirth; the harvest according to the days of the week on which Christmas falls; the significance of the wind and sun on the 12 nights following Christmas; the significance of thunder according to the days of the week; the significance of dreams; and the significance of the age of the moon when particular actions are undertaken.[76] Numerous prognostications also appear in Cotton Tiberius A. iii, an eleventh-century manuscript of Christ Church, Canterbury, provenance and possibly origin,[77] and Cotton Vespasian D. xiv. Of these texts, one in Vespasian D. xiv, fol. 75v, which also occurs in Tiberius A. iii in Old English and as an interlinear Latin gloss,[78] is analogous to the fourth item contained in Hatton 115, fols 148–155. In Hatton 115, this is the Harvest prognostic which details the kind of harvest to be expected depending on the day of the week on which Christmas falls. In the Vespasian manuscript, the abbreviated prognostic details the harvest according to the days of the week on which New Year's Day falls[79] but notwithstanding this difference of the day of the year, the general textual similarities between the versions in Hatton 115, fol. 149rv, and Vespasian D. xiv, fol. 75v, are marked. The Hatton text, edited by Cockayne,[80] reads:

> Gif middeswintres messedeg bið on sunnandeg, þonne bið god winter, and lengten windi, and drige sumer, and wingeardas gode, and sceap beoð weaxende, and hunu beoð genihtsum, and eal sib bið

genyhtsummo. Gif he bið on monandeg se middeswintres messedeg, þonne bið gemenged winter, and god lengten, and windig sumer and ystig, and beoð gode wingeardas, and swiþ feorme mannum. Gif he bið on tiwesdeg, þonne bið yfag winter, and windig lengten, and renig sumer, and moni wif sweltað, and scip beoð frecnode, and ciningas forweorðað. Gif seo midwinter bið on wodnesdæg, þonne bið heard winter, and grim, and yfel lengten, and god sumor, and wingeardeas beoð geswencfulle, and hunig byð lesse. Gif heo byoð on þunresdæg, þonne byoð god winter, and windig lengten, and god sumor, and ælc god byð genihtsum in þem selfan geare. Gyf se midwinter byð on frigendæge, þonne byð onwendædlic winter, and byð go[d] leingten and go[d] sumer,[81] and byð genihtsumes micel. Gif se midwinter byð on seternsdeag, þonne byð winter gedrefedlic, and windig lengten, and westmas swincað, and scep cwellað, and ealde men gewitað, and þa clenan beoð leahtrode.

The Vespasian text, edited by Warner,[82] reads:

Đonne forme gearesdæig byð Sunendæig, hit byð god winter, and windig lænctetid, dryge sumer, god hærfest, and scep tyððrigeð, an hit byð grið and wæstme manifeald. Đonne hit byð Monendæig, hit byð scurfah winter, and god læncten, and windig sumer and stormig, and geswyncfull hærfest. Þonne hit byð Tywesdæig, hit byð wæt winter and windig læinten, and wæt sumer, and wifmæn swelteð and scipes forfareð and cynges sweltað. Þonne hit byð Wodnesdæig, hit byð heardwinter and yfel læinten, god sumer and geswyncfull hærfest, and hunig byð gæsne. Đonne hit byð Þuresdæg, hit byð god winter and windig læinten, god sumer and god hærfest. Þonne hit byð Fridæg, hit byð hwerefinde winter, and god lænten and god sumer and god hærfest. Đonne hit byð Sæterdæig, hit byð scurfah winter and windig læinten, and ealle wæstmas yfeles gewænde, scep cwelleð and ealde mænn.

While these texts are clearly not identical, it may be that they share a common ultimate source. That Vespasian D. xiv and Tiberius A. iii contain analogous texts would indicate that the common exemplar for this text was possibly at Christ Church. This would in turn suggest that the Hatton booklet might have been copied there too. The language of the texts might also help in determining the origin of this source. Both texts illustrate a majority of late West Saxon forms:[83] *sceap* in the Hatton text shows diphthongisation of the front vowel after a palatal consonant;[84] in the same text, *drige* and *ciningas* show the late West Saxon feature of *i* instead of earlier *y*;[85] and in the Vespasian version, the late West Saxon compromise spelling of *æ+i* occurs in *dæig* and *læinten*.[86] Late Old English ‹i› and ‹ig› is seen in *moni* and *windi* in the Hatton text.[87] Non-West Saxon dialectal features that can be determined suggest little about the place of composition of either the Hatton 115 text or the Vespasian analogue other than 'southern' perhaps. The *e* for *æ* in *messedeg* in Hatton 115, for example, is a non-West Saxon, possibly Kentish feature;[88] and *byoð* in the same text is also non-West Saxon.[89] The evidence is also complicated by the inconsistency of the Hatton scribe in his spelling. The variety of orthographical forms can be illustrated in the Hatton text by *bið*, *byð* in the singular indicative present form, and *beoð*, *byoð* in the plural; and by names of the days of the week ending variously in *-deg*, *-dæg* and *-deag*.[90] The variant *-dæig* is used on all but two occasions (*dæg*) in the Vespasian version but this indicates little other than that the text is late. As there are notable lexical differences between the two texts, it might be that an analysis of particular lexemes would show affiliation with other manuscripts of a defined area of production. Such lexical items would include the use of *weaxende* in the Hatton text where Vespasian has *tyððrigeð*; *gemenged* in Hatton for Vespasian's *scurfah*; *ystig* in Hatton for *storemig* in Vespasian; and Hatton's *onwendædlic* for Vespasian's *hwerefinde*. Of these, the most interesting are, perhaps, Hatton's use of adjectival *ystig* ('stormy') which occurs otherwise only in the *Paris Psalter* (Paris, Bibliothèque Nationale lat. 8824); the equivalent adjective in Vespasian, *storemig*, appears to be unique in this form and might be a replacement by the scribe of the word found in the exemplar. Hatton's *onwendædlic* 'changeable' also appears to be a unique form, though *onwendednes* occurs in the *Vespasian Psalter* (London, British Library, Cotton Vespasian A. 1).

The language thus points to the typical tendencies of scribes copying Old English in this period to attempt to retain the late West Saxon orthographical forms of their exemplars. This, coupled with the non-West Saxon elements in both texts, points most suggestively to their being southern compositions or copies of such, possibly Kentish. As the Vespasian prognostic is a relatively close, if shortened, parallel to the Hatton version, it may be that Hatton 115, fols 148–155, originated at the same scriptorium. Textual evidence, coupled with the palaeographical links, certainly points to the south-eastern region of England in the mid-twelfth century as the place of origin of this booklet of the Hatton composite manuscript. Sometime after its production, but before the first quarter of the thirteenth century, this booklet was taken to Worcester where the penultimate leaf was used by the Tremulous Scribe, but where the text itself found no favour.

The final manuscripts to be discussed are CCCC 367, fols 1, 2 and 7–10, and CUL Ii. 1. 33. These are both examples of copies of Old English material which can be dated to the second half of the twelfth century though neither has been assigned to a place of origin with certainty.

CUL Ii. 1. 33 is a substantial codex that contains a number of homilies and miscellaneous texts copied, for the most part, by two main scribes. All the codicological evidence points to the manuscript being compiled over a period of time before eventually being bound in its present form. Scribe 1 wrote fols 2–36v and 120v–227v, and Scribe 2 wrote fols 37–120v. Ker notes changes in the appearance of the script which may be attributable to the irregularity of the scribes' hands, or to the changing development of the scribes' scripts as the manuscript copying evolved.[91] Fols 1, 2 and 7–10 of CCCC 367, written by one scribe on vellum upon which he has had to compress his text, are bound in with the manuscript, which has a Worcester provenance. These folios contain parts of Ælfric's rendering of Bede's *De temporibus*.[92] Upon close palaeographical examination, it can be seen that the scribe of this portion of CCCC 367 and the first scribe in CUL Ii. 1. 33 (fols 2–36v and 120v–227v) are the same person (Plate 20 and those reproduced in Schipper's 'A Composite Old English Homiliary').[93] Firstly, the layout of the pages is similar, though in this part of CCCC 367 the scribe is reduced to writing right across the vellum and cramping his lines together as he seems to have had far too little space for his stint. The layout is a single column of text with a relatively ragged right margin; the pen-drawn initials share decorative patternings which are roughly drawn with zig-zag or dot patternings. The general aspect of the script is backward-leaning; ascenders are sometimes wedged; and descenders are tapered or curved slightly to the left. Initials are often offset where the new sentence or phrase corresponds to the beginning of a new line. The most notable features of the script are the well-developed headstroke of Caroline *a*; the relatively straight shaft of round-backed *d*; the protruding tongue of *e*; the Insular *f* with a crossbar that intersects the shaft (though at fols 120 forward in the CUL manuscript, the scribe also employs a Caroline *f* which sits on the line). There are three forms of *g*: Insular *g* which is relatively fluid with a curled bowl which occasionally forms a loop; angular Insular *g* where the descender is made as if it were two distinct movements of the pen; and the rare Caroline *g* with a shallow curved descender. Other notable features are the Caroline *h* which has a right limb curling under the line; the non-symmetrical formation of minim strokes which have small serifs to the right; and the Insular *r* which has a very well-defined, almost 'shepherd's crook', bow and a descender that sometimes curves to the left. Three forms of *s* can be seen: high, round and long, and in CCCC 367 high *s* often has a flattened head. Round *s* has a flattened head with an upward flourish in both manuscripts and can be seen in a similarly shaped fashion in the *Textus Roffensis* addition at fol. 178r[94] and Cleopatra E. i, fols 37v and 38r, a Canterbury manuscript.[95] The left limb of *x* has a very exaggerated descender which curves right under the preceding letter; *y* is dotted (sometimes slightly left of centre) and the descender often ends with a flick to the right; *þ* and *ƿ* (wynn) have pointed bowls and occasionally the descenders curve to the left, though often they merely taper; *æ* sometimes shows the headstroke of *a*, and the *e* portion sits slightly above it with a protruding tongue. *ð* shows variety in its construction: occasionally it is like an upside-down Arabic 4 formed in one movement of the pen; the cross-stroke of *ð* sometimes begins from the right of the shaft ending in a serif downwards; or it pierces slightly through the shaft. The *Tironian nota* has a curved horizontal stroke and the descender is oblique from right to left. Occasionally, it sits on the line. Punctuation is by *punctus* which rests on the line, *punctus elevatus* and *interrogativus*. The abbreviation macron is straight or slightly curved upwards from left to right (sometimes it is joined to the letter on which it sits by a hairline stroke).

Special features include the inconsistent use of the *st* ligature; the *d* and *e* ligature where the bowl of *e* is attached to the top of the shaft of round-backed *d*; suprascript *s* is used to save space; 'primitive Gothic' features of 'biting' such as two *b*'s together are evident;[96] and a very distinctive form of 'capital' *D* which has a narrow top opening into a wide bow, almost like a *B* in shape, is a common feature. High or long *s* where the topmost part is looped is seen occasionally in both these manuscripts: this is rare in English vernacular manuscripts of the post-Conquest period. This particular feature may also be seen in the seventh manumission at fol. 1v of CCCC 140, a Christ Church, Canterbury, manuscript (although it may just be a decorative flourish here as it is on the last line of text).

Assuming for the moment that fols 3–6 and 11–29 of CCCC 367 — the earlier part of the manuscript discussed above in relation to the *Textus Roffensis* scribe — are of possible Rochester origin (which remains tentative until more research provides firmer evidence), a logical step might be to assume that fols 1, 2 and 7–10 of CCCC 367 are also from the same, or a closely linked, scriptorium as they are bound in between one another in the same manuscript.[97] If these latter folios of CCCC 367 are ascribed a Rochester origin, then it seems reasonable perhaps to assume that this particular scribe was doing his copying in the south-eastern region of England in the second half of the twelfth century. It might also follow, therefore, that fols 2–36v and 120v–227v of CUL Ii. 1. 33 are of south-eastern origin also as they are certainly written by this scribe. As there is no certainty about assigning such an origin to either of these portions of CCCC 367 and CUL Ii. 1. 33 by this scribe, corroborating evidence must be sought. The palaeographical evidence for this scribe's work seems invariably to point to similarities with other south-eastern manuscripts as demonstrated above, but what of the textual and linguistic evidence?

Twelfth-century vernacular manuscripts are notorious for the lack of reliable linguistic evidence that they yield as has been shown by the brief analysis of the Harvest prognostic in Hatton 115 and Vespasian D. xiv above: much of the time, scribes are inconsistent in their accidence, orthography and adherence to the exemplar's probable forms. Some scribes are particularly idiosyncratic, which, coupled with the transitional nature of the language in this period, complicates any analysis. Rather than look for particular dialectal features in these manuscripts, then, it is worthwhile to search for notable lexical replacements within the late manuscript texts in comparison to parallel texts in earlier manuscripts.[98]

CUL Ii. 1. 33 sporadically uses *pine* as a lexical replacement for *susle*, as does Bodley 343.[99] Other uses of the word occur in Vespasian D. xiv, CCCC 303, the *Peterborough Chronicle* (Oxford, Bodleian Library, Laud Misc. 636), the Hatton Gospels and the Lambeth Homilies.[100] Other lexical replacements are *þencan* for *smeagan* in CUL Ii. 1. 33 and CCCC 303 and used by the Tremulous Scribe; *synn* for *leahtor* in CUL Ii. 1. 33 and CCCC 303 and in a thirteenth-century gloss in CCCC 303; and *gehatan* or *geclypian* for *geciegan* in CUL Ii. 1. 33 and CCCC 303.[101] These sporadic, but manuscript-wide lexical replacements must suggest that certain elements of vocabulary which were unfamiliar by the middle or later parts of the twelfth century were replaced with synonyms by the scribes in some of the texts they copied. Such lexical replacements occurred perhaps in scriptoria across the country, but can certainly be evidenced in manuscripts copied in the south-east such as CCCC 303.

An unusual calque, *þrimnysse* 'Trinity', which occurs in CUL Ii. 1. 33 a number of times, also occurs in Bodley 343, the *Cambridge Psalter* (Cambridge, University Library, Ff. 1. 23), CCCC 303, Vespasian D. xiv, the mid-twelfth-century Vitellius A. xv, fols 3–94, the *Ormulum* (Oxford, Bodleian Library, Junius 1), and CCCC 162.[102] Of these manuscripts, CCCC 162 and Vespasian D. xiv probably came from Canterbury or Rochester (CCCC 162 may originate in Rochester); CCCC 303 is from Rochester; the *Cambridge Psalter* has been assigned an origin of St Augustine's, Canterbury,[103] and Bodley 343 originated from the region around Worcester but its exemplar may well be south-eastern.[104] Cumulatively, this brief lexical examination and the links it illustrates suggest that the origins of CUL Ii. 1. 33 lie in the south-eastern region of England, particularly at Canterbury or Rochester.

Furthermore, a late thirteenth-century inscription in CUL Ii. 1. 33, *Hoc volumen continet multam copiam sermonum in anglico non appreciatum propter ydioma incognitum*, is written in a hand that resembles the script of a similar inscription in Durham, Cathedral Library, B. III. 32. This eleventh-century manuscript probably originated at Canterbury according to Ker.[105] The inscriber may have been writing in manuscripts possibly at Canterbury as late as the thirteenth century.

Finally, textual links indicate that material incorporated into CUL Ii. 1. 33 has its major base of circulation in the south-east of England. One such example might be the frequent correspondences between CUL Ii. 1. 33 and

Bodley 340 and 342 in its Ælfric material: the former manuscripts originate in either Canterbury or Rochester.[106] Ælfric's translation of Bede's *De temporibus* contained in part in CCCC 367, fols 1, 2 and 7–10, is also contained in manuscripts which originate from Winchester and Christ Church, Canterbury.[107]

In all, the range of accumulated evidence suggests that in CUL Ii. 1. 33, fols. 2–36v and 120v–227v, and CCCC 367, fols 1, 2 and 7–10, we have one competent scribe who copied a range of different material over a period of time. This scribe is a witness to the continuation of interest in the vernacular well into the second half of the twelfth century. The evidence suggests that he was based in the south-east of England, perhaps at Rochester or Christ Church, Canterbury. As such, the suggestion that this scribe might have been responsible for collating CUL Ii. 1. 33 at Ely made by Schipper would seem to require some reappraisal.[108] Indeed, Schipper's interesting argument for CUL Ii. 1. 33's provenance of Ely can be reassessed for a number of reasons. In the first instance, he misreads Ker's dating of the manuscript as second quarter of the twelfth century, when Ker's s. xii^2 clearly indicates the second-*half* of the century.[109] This means that Schipper's corroborative palaeographical evidence is likely to be too early to provide a comparison with the CUL scribes. Secondly, Schipper detects a third hand in the manuscript, Scribe C writing fols 37–52v. This Scribe C may well be the same scribe as Schipper's hand B and Ker's second scribe of the manuscript, but writing at different periods.[110] Schipper analyses the hand of this Scribe C in relation to an Ely *titulus* of 1122 in the *Rouleau Mortulaire* described by Ker.[111] The part of the *Rouleau Mortulaire* that Schipper uses is employed by Ker to illustrate palaeographic features common to the middle of the twelfth century that were already apparent in earlier hands. Furthermore, the round bookhand of the Ely *titulus* in which Schipper detects similarities with the scribe of CUL Ii. 1. 33, fols. 37–52v, can be paralleled with other Latin manuscripts such as Oxford, Bodleian Library, e Mus. 9, fol. 239, of the second half of the twelfth century from Bury St Edmunds,[112] or Manchester, John Rylands, 420, fols 25–26, of the middle of the twelfth century. Evidence for the palaeographical connection of CUL Ii. 1. 33 with this Ely *titulus* is minimal, therefore. Textual evidence linking CUL Ii. 1. 33 to Ely is also rather tenuous. The inclusion of the life of Æthelthryth in the manuscript, and cited as support for an Ely provenance,[113] could have occurred at many other scriptoria as numerous litanies, for example, show a veneration to the saint.[114]

While CUL Ii. 1. 33 might certainly have been taken to Ely after its production in much the same way that CCCC 367 and Hatton 115 discussed above appear to have been taken to Worcester, it was probably not copied there; neither does it seem that the first scribe of CUL Ii. 1. 33 nor the specific scribes of the relevant portions of Hatton 115 or CCCC 367 were themselves working in the scriptoria of Ely or Worcester. The evidence outlined in this discussion points to their working in a south-eastern scriptorium, possibly at Rochester (CCCC 367, fols 3, 6 and 11–29), and Christ Church, Canterbury (Hatton 115, fols 148–155, CCCC 367, fols 1, 2 and 7–10, and C.U.L Ii. 1. 33).

While there are a substantial number of manuscripts from the twelfth century that require firm dating and assignment of place of origin, I have shown that three of these can be more securely assessed by means of comparative palaeographic, linguistic and textual analyses. This essay has also shown that it was quite probably the monastic scriptoria of the south-east that appear to have been chiefly engaged in the production and dissemination of English vernacular texts in the first and second halves of the twelfth century. A major reappraisal and study of all post-Conquest manuscripts containing Old English is required if we are to recognise fully the important continuation of the Anglo-Saxon prose tradition. This continuation of the vernacular heritage was sustained throughout the twelfth century and deserves detailed examination in its own right.

NOTES

1. N.R. Ker, *Catalogue of Manuscripts Containing Anglo-Saxon* (Oxford: Clarendon Press, 1957; repr. with supplement 1990), pp. xviii–xix. I include in this number manuscripts dated s. xi/xii to s. xii/xiii.
2. Rima Handley, 'British Museum MS. Cotton Vespasian D. xiv', *Notes and Queries* 21 (1974), 243–50; Mary P. Richards, 'On the Date and Provenance of MS Cotton Vespasian D. xiv, ff. 4–169', *Manuscripta* 17 (1972), 31–5; William Schipper, 'A Composite Old English Homiliary from Ely: Cambr. Univ. MS Ii.1.33', *Transactions of the Cambridge Bibliographical Society* 8 (1983), 285–98; Susan Irvine, ed., *Old English Homilies from MS Bodley 343*, Early English Text Society, o.s. 302 (London: Oxford University Press, 1993); E.M. Treharne, 'Corpus Christi College, Cambridge, 303 and the Lives of Saints Margaret, Giles and Nicholas', unpub. Ph.D. thesis, University of Manchester, 1992; and Margaret Gibson, T.A. Heslop and Richard W. Pfaff, eds., *The Eadwine Psalter: Text, Image, and Monastic Culture in Twelfth-Century Canterbury*, Publications of the Modern Humanities Research Association, 14 (London and University Park, PA: The Modern Humanities Research Association; The Pennsylvania State University Press, 1992). Recently, R.M. Liuzza, ed., *The Old English Version of the Gospels*, Early English Text Society, o.s. 304 (London: Oxford University Press, 1994), has provided an excellent analysis of the script of the twelfth-century copies of the Gospels.
3. Teresa Webber, *Scribes and Scholars at Salisbury Cathedral c. 1075–c.*

1125 (Oxford: Clarendon Press, 1992); Elizabeth McIntyre, 'Early Twelfth-Century Worcester Cathedral Priory, with Special Reference to the Manuscripts Written There', unpub. D.Phil. thesis, University of Oxford, 1978; K.M. Waller, 'The Library, Scriptorium and Community of Rochester Cathedral Priory c. 1080–1150', unpub. Ph.D. thesis, University of Liverpool, 1980; K.M. Waller, 'Rochester Cathedral Library: an English book collection on Norman models', in *Les Mutations socio-culturelles au tournant des xie-xiie siècles*, Etudies Anselmiennes ive session (Paris: Editions du Centre Nationale de la Recherche Scientifique, 1984), ed. Raymonde Foreville, pp. 237–50; Mary P. Richards, in *Texts and their Traditions in the Medieval Library of Rochester Cathedral Priory*, Transactions of the American Philosophical Association, 78.3 (Philadelphia: American Philosophical Association, 1988), does focus on Old English manuscripts in her monograph but, as shown below, she takes a great deal for granted in her localisation of particular vernacular manuscripts to Rochester Cathedral Priory.

4. By R.S. Cox, 'The Old English Dicts of Cato', *Anglia* 90 (1972), 1–42, at pp. 29–32, Mary P. Richards, 'On the Date and Provenance', p. 31, and Ker, *Catalogue of Manuscripts Containing Old English*, p. 271, respectively. See also Rima Handley, 'British Museum MS. Cotton Vespasian D. xiv', pp. 243–50.
5. As Mary P. Richards, 'On the Date and Provenance', does at pp. 33–4 when dating CCCC 303 in relation to Vespasian D. xiv.
6. By Ker, *Catalogue of Manuscripts Containing Old English*, p. 277, in the first instance.
7. As is the case in Malcolm Godden, ed., *Ælfric's Catholic Homilies: The Second Series: Text*, Early English Text Society, s.s. 5 (London: Oxford University Press, 1979), p. xli: 'The script and language of G [Vespasian D. xiv] ... indicate Rochester or possibly Canterbury as the place of origin.'
8. Teresa Webber, 'Script and Manuscript Production at Christ Church, Canterbury, after the Norman Conquest', in *Canterbury and the Norman Conquest: Churches, Saints and Scholars, 1066–1109*, ed. Richard Eales and Richard Sharpe (London: Hambledon Press, 1995), pp. 144–56.
9. For example, John C. Pope, ed., *The Homilies of Ælfric: A Supplementary Collections*, Early English Text Society, o.s. 259 and 260 (London: Oxford University Press, 1967 and 1968); Godden, ed., *Ælfric's Catholic Homilies*; and D.G. Scragg, ed., *The Vercelli Homilies and Related Texts*, Early English Text Society, o.s. 300 (London: Oxford University Press, 1992).
10. Graham D. Caie, 'Text and Context in Editing Old English: The Case of Poetry in CCCC 201', in *The Editing of Old English: Papers from the 1990 Manchester Conference*, ed. D.G. Scragg and Paul E. Szarmach

(Woodbridge: D.S. Brewer, 1994), pp. 155–62, makes an excellent case for being aware of manuscript context in editing texts. The dangers of editing texts in isolation can be exemplified by the inconsistency of Mary Clayton and Hugh Magennis, eds., *The Old English Lives of St Margaret*, Cambridge Studies in Anglo-Saxon England, 9 (Cambridge: Cambridge University Press, 1994), who state (p. 41) that CCCC 303, one of their main manuscripts, is early twelfth century, and then state (p. 92) that it is dated to the first half of the twelfth century.

11. Currently, scholars such as Mary Swan at the University of Leeds and Susan Irvine at University College, London, are working on various aspects of twelfth-century manuscript production. Indeed, Susan Irvine's *Homilies from MS Bodley 343* has made a considerable contribution to the debate by illustrating the importance of this manuscript and its texts. It is disconcerting that the work of scholars investigating Old English manuscripts in the post-Conquest period is neglected by those scholars who work on Latin manuscripts. See, for example, the summary of scholarship in the earlier part of the period by Richard Gameson, 'Early Anglo-Norman Illuminated Manuscripts *c.* 1066–1125', *Old English Newsletter* 28.3 (Spring, 1995), B-23–29.
12. For legal and administrative documents from 1066–1189, see David A.E. Pelteret, *Catalogue of English Post-Conquest Vernacular Documents* (Woodbridge: Boydell, 1990).
13. Taking into account the different types of script for different purposes: cursive, book-hand, gloss-hand and so forth.
14. Cox, 'The Old English *Dicts of Cato*', pp. 29–32; and Schipper, 'A Composite Old English Homiliary', pp. 285–98.
15. Compare, for example, the work of the *Textus Roffensis* scribe who writes both Latin and Old English text. See Peter Sawyer, *The Textus Roffensis, Rochester Cathedral MS. A.3.5*, Early English Manuscripts in Facsimile 7, 11 (Copenhagen: Rosenkilde and Bagger, 1962).
16. In Oxford, Bodleian Library, Hatton 115, fols 148–155, for example, the scribe suddenly changes from using a Caroline *f*, *r* and *s* to Insular forms between fols 148v and 149r. This booklet is discussed in more detail below. See Plates 18 and 19.
17. For example, Hatton 115, *franlica* (fol. 149r|9) and *wingeardas* (fol. 149r|14). See Plate 19.
18. Dated to s. xii med. in Ker, *Catalogue of Manuscripts Containing Anglo-Saxon*, p. 399, item 332. See Plate 19, line 2, *lufiende*.
19. Dated to s. xii med. in Ker, ibid., p. 202, item 159.
20. This manuscripts is dated to the first half of the twelfth century in Ker, ibid., p. 99, item 57. This date is reappraised to the middle of the twelfth century in Treharne, 'Corpus Christi College, Cambridge, 303', pp. 78–90.

21. M.B. Parkes, 'The Date of the Oxford Manuscript of the *Chanson de Roland*: Bodleian Library MS Digby 23', in his *Scribes, Scripts and Readers: Studies in the Communication, Presentation and Dissemination of Medieval Texts* (London: Hambledon Press, 1991), pp. 71–89. I owe this reference to Dr A.R. Rumble.
22. Ibid., pp. 72–3.
23. Ibid., p. 89.
24. N.R. Ker's *English Manuscripts in the Century after the Conquest*, The Lyell Lectures, 1952–3 (Oxford: Clarendon Press, 1960) is indispensable and is still the best treatment of the codicology and palaeography of the period. Bernhard Bischoff, *Latin Palaeography, Antiquity and the Middle Ages*, trans. Dáibhí Ó Crónín and David Ganz (Cambridge: Cambridge University Press, 1990) is useful. Ker's *Catalogue of Manuscripts Containing Anglo-Saxon*, pp. xxiii–xxxvi, is still the standard palaeographical guide for Old English in the period *c*. 1100 to 1200, though some of his statements require minor revision.
25. This is M.B. Parkes' method in his important essay, 'On the Presumed Date and Possible Origin of the Manuscript of the *Orrmulum*: Oxford, Bodleian Library, MS Junius 1', in his *Scribes, Scripts and Readers*, pp. 187–99.
26. By L.C. Hector, *The Handwriting of English Documents* (Dorking: Kohler and Coombes Press, 1966; 2nd ed. 1980); N. Denholm-Young, *Handwriting in England and Wales* (Cardiff: University of Wales, 1954; 2nd ed. 1964); and B.L. Ullmann, *Ancient Writing and Its Influence*, Medieval Academy Reprints for Teaching, 10 (Toronto: Toronto University Press in association with the Medieval Academy of America, 1980). See also n. 24 above.
27. Ker, *English Manuscripts in the Century after the Conquest*, pp. 34–9.
28. Ker, *Catalogue of Manuscripts Containing Anglo-Saxon*, pp. xxvi–xxxi.
29. Ibid., pp. xxiv–xxv.
30. Although this feature can be seen as early as the beginning of the twelfth century, in CCCC 302 (once), for example, its use becomes more common in the first half of the century.
31. Treharne, 'Corpus Christi College, Cambridge, 303', pp. 82–90.
32. Ker is therefore incorrect when he states in his *Catalogue of Manuscripts Containing Anglo-Saxon*, pp. xxxii–xxxiii, that: 'The ligatures used in Caroline minuscule for *st*, *ct*, *rt*, and *ra* were not adopted for Old English. There are therefore no ligatures in OE writing after about the middle of the eleventh century.' See, for instance, the plate of CCCC 303, in Clayton and Magennis, eds., *The Old English Lives of St Margaret*, p. 100, which shows the frequent use of the *st* ligature in the hand of Scribe B.
33. Parkes' 'On the Presumed Date' illustrates this point.
34. Vespasian D. xiv may originate from Christ Church, Canterbury; the

Eadwine Psalter (Cambridge, Trinity College, R. 17. 1) with its Old English Gloss certainly originated there; from Rochester comes CCCC 303 and the *Textus Roffensis* (Rochester Cathedral MS. A. 3. 5); from Worcester comes Hatton 116; and from Peterborough, Oxford, Bodleian Library, Laud. Misc. 636 (*The Peterborough Chronicle*).

35. See Elizabeth Parker McLachlan, *The Scriptorium of Bury St Edmunds in the Twelfth Century*, Outstanding Theses from the Courtauld Institute of Art (London: Garland Publishing, Inc., 1986); Webber, *Saints and Scholars*, for Salisbury; and Rodney M. Thompson, *Catalogue of the Manuscripts of Lincoln Cathedral Chapter Library* (Woodbridge: D.S. Brewer, 1989), for Lincoln.

36. See Schipper, 'A Composite Old English Homiliary'. Schipper's proposal that CUL Ii. 1. 33 was compiled at Ely is probably incorrect, as I discuss below.

37. Ker, *Catalogue of Manuscripts Containing Anglo-Saxon*, p. xliv. See also Roland Torkar, 'Cotton Vitellius A. xv (pt. 1) and the *Legend of St Thomas*', *English Studies* 4 (1986), 290–303.

38. Peterborough, of course, is the exception here.

39. This is an issue on which I hope to publish soon. My study is an analysis of texts copied into twelfth-century manuscripts which probably originated at these monastic cathedrals and the intended audience of these texts.

40. See Webber, 'Script and Manuscript Production at Christ Church'.

41. See the discussion on CUL Ii. 1. 33 and CCCC 367, fols 1, 2, and 7–10 below.

42. Ker, *Catalogue of Manuscripts Containing Anglo-Saxon*, pp. 271 and 77; see n. 4 above.

43. Handley, 'British Museum MS Cotton Vespasian D. xiv', pp. 243–50; Richards, 'Date and Provenance', p. 31. Richards appears to confuse the term 'provenance' with 'origin' at pp. 31 and 32.

44. This Christ Church manuscript is London, British Library, Royal 1 A. xiv. Offering no evidence, she dates this codex as second quarter of the twelfth century ('Date and Provenance', p. 32), when Ker clearly dates it as second half of the twelfth century (*Catalogue of Manuscripts Containing Anglo-Saxon*, p. 316).

45. Richards, 'Date and Provenance', pp. 33–4.

46. There is little evidence that CCCC 303 belongs to the first quarter of the twelfth century; it is probably closer to the middle of the century. See Treharne, 'Corpus Christi College, Cambridge, 303', pp. 1–90.

47. Richards, 'Date and Provenance', p. 33: 'The twelfth-century closed *g*, a Caroline characteristic, appears exclusively in the MS; there is no trace of insular yogh.'

48. These forms of Insular *g* are, however, in the hand of Scribe C, who added

text to the blank folios. See Plate 15.

49. See Christine Franzen, *The Tremulous Hand of Worcester: A Study of Old English in the Thirteenth Century* (Oxford: Oxford University Press), Plates 4 and 6.
50. See Irvine, ed., *Homilies form MS Bodley 343*, and Schipper, 'A Composite Old English Homiliary', for plates of these manuscripts.
51. Sawyer, *The Textus Roffensis*, vol. 1, pp. 13–14.
52. Ker, *Catalogue of Manuscripts Containing Anglo-Saxon*, p. 194, item 154.
53. Pelteret, *Catalogue of English Post-Conquest Vernacular Documents*, pp. 74–5, item 48. Charles Johnson and Sir Hilary Jenkinson, *English Court Hand, AD 1066 to 1500*, 2 vols (Oxford: Clarendon Press, 1915), reproduce the Campbell Charter as plate Ic.
54. This may even extend to patterns of accenting: in CCCC 303, for instance, accenting is regularly infrequent until pp. 360–2, where a series of double accents on some diphthongs is unique within the overall context of the manuscript; see Treharne, 'Corpus Christi College, Cambridge, 303', pp. 53–4.
55. See Sawyer, *The Textus Roffensis*.
56. Ker, *Catalogue of Manuscripts Containing Anglo-Saxon*, pp. 194–6, item 154, and pp. 399–403, item 332. See Godden, ed., *Ælfric's Catholic Homilies*, p. lxviii, who notes Hatton 115's south-eastern textual connections, and p. lv for Cotton Faustina A. x.
57. Ker, *Catalogue of Manuscripts Containing Anglo-Saxon*, pp. 109–10, items 62 and 63; Godden, ed., *Ælfric's Catholic Homilies*, pp. lvi–lvii.
58. Ker, *Catalogue of Manuscripts Containing Anglo-Saxon*, pp. 190–3, item 153.
59. Ibid., pp. 23–7, item 18; Schipper, 'A Composite Old English Homiliary'.
60. For which the most recent publication is Franzen, *The Tremulous Hand of Worcester*.
61. Margaret Gibson, 'Conclusions: The Eadwine Psalter in Context', in *The Eadwine Psalter*, ed. Gibson et al., pp. 209–13, at p. 213.
62. Ker, *Catalogue of Manuscripts Containing Anglo-Saxon*, pp. 108–9, item 63.
63. Compare Sawyer, *The Textus Roffensis*, vol. 1, fol. 45r, for example, with Plate 17.
64. Ker, *Catalogue of Manuscripts Containing Anglo-Saxon*, pp. 422–4, item 344, and pp. 194–6, item 154B.
65. For Bodley 387, see Ker, *English Manuscripts in the Century after the Conquest*, pl. 12b; for London, British Library, Royal 6 A. xii, see Waller, 'The Library, Scriptorium and Community of Rochester Cathedral Priory', pl. xii.

66. Richard Gameson, 'English Manuscript Art in the Late Eleventh Century: Canterbury and its Context', in *Canterbury and the Norman Conquest*, ed. Eales and Sharpe, pp. 95–144, at pp. 130 and 132. At p. 132, Gameson describes the 'rather mechanical zig-zags, stripes and curves' of the initials in Latin manuscripts; while the initials in this part of CCCC 367 are crude, they do exemplify decoration that can best be called 'zig-zags, stripes and curves'.
67. Andrew G. Watson, *Catalogue of Dated and Datable Manuscripts c. 435–1600 in Oxford Libraries*, 2 vols (Oxford: Clarendon Press, 1984), vol. 2, p. 41.
68. Godden, ed., *Ælfric's Catholic Homilies*, pp. lvi–lvii.
69. Ibid., p. lvii.
70. Ibid., p. lvii. Godden states at p. lvii: 'it is likely that the collection [in CCCC 367] was originally compiled in the South East.'
71. P.R. Robinson, 'Self-Contained Units in Composite Manuscripts of the Anglo-Saxon Period', in *Anglo-Saxon Manuscripts: Basic Readings*, ed. Mary P. Richards, Basic Readings in Anglo-Saxon England, 2 (New York and London: Garland Publishing, Inc., 1994), pp. 25–35, at p. 31.
72. Franzen, *The Tremulous Hand of Worcester*, pp. 38–40.
73. Ibid., p. 39.
74. Ker, *Catalogue of Manuscripts Containing Anglo-Saxon*, p. 402, item 37. The item appears in a similar form in art. 8a, London, British Library, Cotton Tiberius A. iii.
75. Ibid., pp. 190–3, item 153, dated to the first half of the twelfth century and without assignment of place of origin or provenance. See Plate 16.
76. Ker, *Catalogue of Manuscripts Containing Anglo-Saxon*, p. 402, item 332, art. 35a–k. All Old English prognostications are listed and summarily described in Stephanie Hollis and Michael Wright, comps, *Old English Prose of Secular Learning*, Annotated Bibliographies of Old and Middle English Literature, 4 (Woodbridge: D.S. Brewer, 1992), pp. 257–69.
77. Ker, *Catalogue of Manuscripts Containing Anglo-Saxon*, pp. 240–8, item 186.
78. Hollis and Wright, comps, *Old English Prose of Secular Learning*, pp. 257 and 263.
79. R.D.-N. Warner, ed., *Early English Homilies from the Twelfth Century MS. Vespasian D. xiv*, Early English Text Society, o.s. 152 (London: K. Paul, Trench, Trübner and Co., 1917; repr. Millwood: Kraus Reprint, 1975), p. 66.
80. Rev. Thomas Oswald Cockayne, ed. and trans., *Leechdoms, Wortcuning and Starcraft of Early England, Being a Collection of Documents, for the Most Part Never Before Printed, Illustrating the History of Science in this Country Before the Norman Conquest*, 3 vols, Rolls Series, 35 (London:

Her Majesty's Stationery Office, 1864–1866; repr. London: The Holland Press, Ltd, 1961; repr. Wiesbaden: Kraus Reprint, Ltd, 1965), vol. 3, pp. 162–5. I have expanded the abbreviations and supplied modern punctuation.

81. Cockayne, ed. and trans., *Leechdoms, Wortcuning and Starcraft of Early England*, vol. 3, p. 164|8 incorrectly reads: 'onwendædlic winter, and byð god sumer'. In the manuscript *god* is twice written as *goð*.

82. Warner, ed., *Early English Homilies*, p. 66.

83. Though Bruno Assmann, 'Prophezeiung aus dem I. Januar für das Jahr.', *Anglia* 11 (1889), 369, remarks only on the twelfth-century nature of Vespasian D. xiv's language.

84. A. Campbell, *Old English Grammar* (Oxford: Clarendon Press, 1959), p. 69, §185. Late West Saxon smoothing of ‹ea› to ‹e› is evident in the spelling of *scep* seen in both texts (p. 131, §213).

85. Campbell, *Old English Grammar*, p. 132, §316.

86. Campbell, *Old English Grammar*, p. 114, §269.

87. Campbell, *Old English Grammar*, p. 155, §371. Barbara Picard, ed., *Der altenglische Aegidiusleben in MC CCCC 303 (Textedition mit Einleitung und Ammerkungen)*, Hochsammlung Philosophie Literaturwissenschaft, 7 (Freiburg: Hochschulverlag, 1980), p. 022, suggests that this might be a Kentish form.

88. Campbell, *Old English Grammar*, p. 122, §288.

89. Campbell, *Old English Grammar*, pp. 249–50, §768. It may be that this ‹yo› diphthong is the late equivalent of the Kentish ‹io›. For the latter, see ibid., p. 11, §21.

90. D.G. Scragg, *The History of Spelling* (Manchester: Manchester University Press, 1970), p. 17, states that by the twelfth century 'In Latin, ‹æ› and ‹e› had fallen together, while in English ‹æ›, ‹ea›, and ‹a› had done so. The Peterborough [Chronicle] scribes confused all four.' It appears that this is also the case with the Hatton 115 scribe of fols 148–55.

91. Ker, *Catalogue of Manuscripts Containing Anglo-Saxon*, p. 27, item 18.

92. Ibid., p. 108, item 62. See the earlier discussion of CCCC 367.

93. Ker (ibid., p. 27) points out here and at p. 108 that the first scribe of CUL Ii. 1. 33 is 'similar to the hand of no. 62 [CCCC 367, fols 1–2, 7–10]'.

94. Sawyer, *The Textus Roffensis*, vol. 1, p. ii.

95. See also Parkes, 'On the Presumed Date and Origin'. pls. 31a and 31b, for the example of this type of s in a Latin hand of the second half of the century.

96. Bischoff, *Latin Palaeography*, p. 129. Plate 20.

97. This is a yet more tentative suggestion as the manuscript was probably collated in the post-medieval period and has a provenance of Worcester.

98. It should be noted, though, that Ker (*Catalogue of Manuscripts Containing Anglo-Saxon*, p. 27) notes the use of particular non-West Saxon features

in the spelling of the scribe of CUL Ii. 1. 33 with whom this discussion is concerned. Among these features are the use of ‹u› and ‹e› for West Saxon ‹y› and ‹æ›. This same tendency, possibly indicating Kentish dialectal features, can be found in the hand of Scribe C, who copied a small number of pages in CCCC 303, a Rochester manuscript. See Treharne, 'Corpus Christi College, Cambridge, 303', pp. 111–2

99. Pope, ed., *Homilies of Ælfric*, vol. 2, p. xxi, line 201; Walter W. Skeat, ed., *Ælfric's Lives of Saints, Being a Set of Sermons on Saints' Days Formerly Observed by the English Church, Edited from British Museum Cott. MS Julius E. vii with Variants from Other Manuscripts*, Early English Text Society, o.s. 76, 82, 94 and 114 (Oxford: Oxford University Press, 1881–1900; 2 vol. repr. London: Oxford University Press, 1966), vol. 1, no. xix, p. 430, line 238; Irvine, ed., *Homilies from MS Bodley 343*, p. 203, where she states that *pine* might be a Middle English gloss in this manuscript for Old English *wite*.

100. Antonette DiPaolo Healey and Richard L. Venezky, *A Microfiche Concordance to Old English*, Publications of the Dictionary of Old English, 1 (Toronto: Pontifical Institute of Mediaeval Studies, 1980).

101. Treharne, 'Corpus Christi College, Cambridge, 303', p. 122.

102. Roberta Frank, 'Late Old English *þrymnys* 'Trinity': Scribal Nod or Word Waiting to be Born?', in *Old English and New: Studies in Language and Linguistics in Honor of Frederic G. Cassidy*, ed. Joan H. Hall, Nick Doane, and Dick Ringler, Garland Reference Library in the Humanities, 1652 (New York: Garland Publishing, Inc., 1992), pp. 97–107, deals with this word and its occurrences, though she only notes one such occurrence in CUL Ii. 1. 33.

103. Michael Lapidge, 'Abbot Germanus, Winchcombe, Ramsey and the Cambridge Psalter', in *Words, Texts and Manuscripts: Studies in Anglo-Saxon Culture Presented to Helmut Gneuss on the Occasion of his Sixty-Fifth Birthday*, ed. Michael Korhammer (Cambridge: D.S. Brewer, 1992), pp. 99–129.

104. Pope, ed., *Homilies of Ælfric*, vol. 1, p. 18.

105. Ker, *Catalogue of Manuscripts Containing Anglo-Saxon*, p. 147.

106. See, for example, Godden, ed., *Ælfric's Catholic Homilies*, p. xlv.

107. See Ker, *Catalogue of Manuscripts Containing Anglo-Saxon*.

108. Schipper, 'A Composite Old English Homiliary,' pp. 285–98.

109. Ibid., p. 285. See Ker, *Catalogue of Manuscripts Containing Anglo-Saxon*, p. 23.

110. Compare, for example, plates IV ad IIb (Scribe C) with plates III and IIa (Scribe B) in Schipper, 'A Composite Old English Homiliary', pp. 296–8. The forms of *r*, *ð* and the *nota* seem very similar, although the appearance of Insular *g* differs.

111. Ibid., p. 291, and Ker, *English Manuscripts in the Century after the*

Conquest, p. 36.

112. Denholm-Young, *Handwriting in England and Wales*, Plate 10.
113. Schipper, 'A Composite Old English Homiliary', pp. 291–2.
114. Michael Lapidge, ed., *Anglo-Saxon Litanies of the Saints*, Henry Bradshaw Society, 106 (London: Henry Bradshaw Society, 1991).

11 The Ghost of Asser

Andrew Prescott

> The past itself is dead, and the books we write tombs of learning, except insofar as they live in the consciousness of their readers. So conceived, we travel pleasantly, but by the nature of things we never arrive.
>
> V.H. Galbraith, 'Afterthoughts'[1]

THE ALLURE OF LOST MANUSCRIPTS

Manuscripts which have disappeared are often more intriguing than those which survive. There is nothing more tantalising than medieval reports of interesting texts which have now vanished. For the Anglo-Saxon period, one particularly alluring reference is that of William of Malmesbury to an 'obviously ancient book' containing some poetry in praise of King Æthelstan. Malmesbury forbore from including these verses in his chronicle because he found their style too bombastic, preferring instead to transcribe verses by the twelfth-century Peter of Malmesbury. The present whereabouts of this 'ancient book' is now impossible to establish.[2] Equally mysterious is the identity of the 'bella Etheltani Regis' noted in a thirteenth-century catalogue of the library at Glastonbury Abbey, which Michael Lapidge has suggested Malmesbury may also have used.[3] Later centuries also provide similarly beguiling references to lost texts. For the twelfth century, a well-known example is Richard Fitzneal's *Tricolumnis*, a work on Henry II arranged in three columns, one describing the affairs of the English church, another the deeds of Henry and the third other events of interest, particularly court judgments which could be useful as precedents. Richard describes this work in the *Dialogus de Scaccario*, but no manuscript has ever been found.[4]

Presumably these manuscripts vanished at the time of the Reformation, their leaves used to line beer barrels or bind books.[5] Or perhaps they still lie unidentified in an obscure library — it will be impossible ever to be sure. These reports of vanished texts are enticing — indeed, the references to them are so famous that they are perhaps better known than they might have been if they had survived — but the search for them is usually hopeless. More rewarding are those cases where the text survives, but the manuscript does not. Many important medieval texts are known only from a manuscript which survived until comparatively recent times, but was then destroyed. These texts were transcribed or published before the manuscript disappeared, but the loss of the manuscript makes it impossible to establish the accuracy of the transcripts and to answer those questions which modern scholars routinely investigate by reference to the original manuscript, such as the date of the copy, the locality in which the text was produced or the associations of the manuscript. The researcher is left with a ghostly impression of the text, an imprint of the medieval text in various later texts, rather like the impression in the sand of the ship at Sutton Hoo.

A glance at any subject catalogue of medieval manuscripts such as G.R.C. Davis' *Medieval Cartularies*[6] illustrates the dismal hazards of fire, damp and thoughtless destruction to which medieval manuscripts are prey. Some leaves from a fourteenth-century cartulary of Buckfast Abbey were rescued from a wastepaper merchant between 1890 and 1932, who had presumably already disposed of the remainder.[7] Of the surviving cartularies of Coventry Priory, one is now entirely illegible as a result of damp,[8] while another was destroyed in a fire at Birmingham Reference Library in 1879.[9] A cartulary of Loders Priory in Dorset held in the departmental archives at St Lo in Normandy was destroyed when the town was bombed in 1944.[10] The only surviving fragments of a thirteenth-century cartulary of St Mary Overy in Southwark were found being used as drumheads by children in the early nineteenth century.[11] Catastrophes continue to occur. The fine series of pipe rolls, justiciary rolls and other records of the royal government in Ireland dating from the early twelfth century were destroyed in a fire at Dublin Castle in 1922, and are now known only from earlier calendars and transcripts.[12] The Exeter probate records were destroyed when the city was bombed in the Second World War.[13] The beautiful fourteenth-century East Anglian illuminated manuscript, the Douai Psalter, was buried in a canister in the ground to protect it during the First World War. When the canister was dug up again at the end of the war, the psalter had been virtually destroyed by the effects of damp. Although fragments survive, the only way of getting some impression of the original richness and splendour of the manuscript is through black and white photographs taken before the war.[14] Not all manuscripts vanish in such a singular fashion. Simon Keynes was able to trace the descent of the cartulary of Athelney Abbey recorded by William Dugdale as far as a sale of books from Petworth House in 1927, when it simply vanished out of sight.[15] It is not only ancient manuscripts which are at risk; disasters can also happen to more modern records. The service records of soldiers who served in the British Army during the First World War were stored in a building which was bombed during the Blitz in 1940. Over half were destroyed and the remainder were so badly damaged that they cannot be made available to researchers.[16]

Although these manuscripts are now lost, they are of great importance for their respective subjects. Attempting to use the information from a lost manuscript adds an extra dimension to scholarly investigations. If the original manuscript of a chronicle survives, extracts and references to the chronicle in other works are of limited interest. When the manuscript has been destroyed, the original chronicle has to be pieced together from extracts and transcripts in a variety of sources ranging from other medieval chronicles to transcripts by early modern antiquaries, which may differ radically in their treatment of the original source. This process of reintegrating the lost text requires more sophisticated critical tools than are necessary when the manuscripts survive. It can not only lead to the recovery of the lost text but also provide new perspectives on those texts which contain extracts from it. In the case of illuminated manuscripts which have been damaged or destroyed, scholars may become involved in attempting actively to recreate the appearance of the lost manuscript.[17] Scholars working on such badly damaged manuscripts will require often the assistance of technical aids, such as special lighting techniques. Some of the earliest applications of digital technology to manuscript studies have involved the analysis of damaged manuscripts.[18] Moreover, because the original manuscript has disappeared, there is a sense that the study of the text will never be concluded — there is always the possibility that a new transcript or facsimile will turn up and revolutionise knowledge of the manuscript.[19] As a result, the story of the study of texts in lost or damaged manuscripts has a compelling quality, which V.H. Galbraith compared to a good detective story.[20]

For Anglo-Saxonists, the greatest manuscript disaster to date is undoubtedly the fire which broke out at Ashburnham House in Little Dean's Yard, Westminster, on the night of 23 October 1731.[21] Stored in Ashburnham House were two major collections of manuscripts now in the British Library, the Royal Library and the Cotton Library. The Cotton Library is a collection of manuscripts relating principally to medieval and Tudor English history and literature assembled chiefly by Sir Robert Cotton (1571–1631), which contained the largest single accumulation of manuscripts from the Anglo-Saxon period.[22] Keynes has succinctly illustrated the devastating effects of the fire on the Cotton Library by listing some of the manuscripts from the Anglo-Saxon period which were destroyed or reduced to badly charred fragments in just one press, that named after the Roman emperor Otho.[23] These included Otho A. i, an eighth-century collection of texts including a letter from St Boniface to Archbishop Cuthbert, the canons of the council of *Clofesho* and a copy of a charter of King Æthelbald of 749; Otho A. x, which contained the text of Æthelweard's Latin translation of the Anglo-Saxon Chronicle and a copy of a law-code of King Æthelred the Unready; Otho B. ix, a gospel book presented by King Æthelstan to the community of St Cuthbert at Chester-le-Street; Otho B. x, which contained, among a number of interesting items, the unique text of the Anglo-Saxon *Rune Poem*; Otho C. v, part of an early eighth-century Insular gospel book; and Otho B. xi, whose contents included a copy of the Old English translation of Bede's *Historia ecclesiastica*, the 'G' manuscript of the Anglo-Saxon Chronicle, law-codes of Æthelstan and Alfred and an important copy of the Burghal Hidage. The effects in other presses badly affected by the fire, such as the Vitellius press, were equally disastrous.

The way in which the Cotton fire casts a dark shadow over Anglo-Saxon studies is particularly evident in the case of Cotton Otho A. xii.[24] This composite volume contained originally 14 articles, of which the most famous were the first and the third. The first was the only known manuscript of Asser's *Life of King Alfred*, while the third was the unique copy of the Old English poem *The Battle of Maldon*. Transcripts and editions of both these texts had been produced before the fire. The other articles comprised chiefly copies of various Latin saints' lives and related hagiographical material composed in the eleventh and twelfth centuries, including Osbern's Life and Translation of St Ælfheah, Goscelin's Lives of SS Wulfhilda, Æthelburh (Ethelburga) and Hildelitha and Roger of Ford's *Passion of St Ursula and the Eleven Thousand Virgins*. Asser originally comprised fols 1–55, with the second article, two charms, apparently being written on blank leaves at the end of Asser. The manuscript appears to have consisted of six originally separate sections, which were put together into a single volume by Cotton.

Otho A. xii was reported to have been completely destroyed in the fire. During the nineteenth century a number of charred fragments from the manuscript were recovered, but none from the first or third articles. In the case of Asser, the loss of the original manuscript had led to doubts being expressed from time to time as to whether the text is what it purports to be — the earliest biography of an Anglo-Saxon king. These doubts about Asser were most famously articulated by V.H. Galbraith, who pointed to what he felt were anachronisms and inconsistencies in the text, and argued that its true date was not AD 893, but a century or more later. He suggested that the *Life* had been concocted by Leofric, the eleventh-century bishop of Exeter. Despite the comprehensive rebuttals of Galbraith's arguments by such distinguished scholars as Dorothy Whitelock, Michael Lapidge and Simon Keynes, it seems that, without the original manuscript, it is impossible to allay these misgivings about Asser. In a scholarly controversy which achieved newspaper coverage,[25] Alfred Smyth has recently revamped Galbraith's arguments and proposed a new candidate for the title of pseudo-Asser, Byrhtferth of Ramsey.[26]

It would be tiresome to reiterate all the points of this controversy here. Smyth adds very little to Galbraith's arguments, except for the substitution of Byrhtferth for Leofric, some faulty attempts at analysing Asser's Latin and some unnecessarily offensive treatment of other scholars.[27] The case is put much more beguilingly by Galbraith, whose arguments, as Lapidge and Keynes admit, 'make compelling reading'[28] and whose reflections on the text are of interest, even if his arguments against Asser are rejected.

Galbraith was, famously, an historian whose outlook had been shaped by his time as an assistant keeper at the Public Record Office.[29] His historical imagination was fired by the 'almost frightening' quantity in which medieval archives survive and by the way in which their organic unity reflected the history of the state which produced them.[30] The public records seemed to Galbraith to challenge the training he received as an historian. Many of the abstract discussions on which academic historians concentrated seemed far removed from the issues with which those working every day with the records of the medieval period were confronted. Galbraith wrote:

> It is hard, perhaps impossible, for a custodian of the records to preserve the rather abstract cast of thought which is so characteristic of university teaching. Borne down at first by their sheer bulk, the archivist takes refuge in hard facts, in particular lines of cut and dried inquiry, in finding definitive answers to practical questions.[31]

This experience made Galbraith 'doubt the adequacy of the great literary sequence of English history'.[32] He felt the construction of narrative and the identification of historical problems less important than the attempt to engage with and understand the great mass of surviving medieval records and documents. He urged the virtues of what he described as an archivist's history:

> To him the past presents itself as a vast collection of 'original documents'.... To name a century to him is to call up a mental picture of the relevant records, the progress of history appearing to him as a slow pageant of slowly changing records, marked from time to time by the occasional disappearance of one class and the gradual emergence of another.[33]

In Galbraith's writings on history and archives, there perhaps lie the seeds of a new type of history, a textually oriented history, in which the focus would be not on the attempt to discover an objective historical truth, but in a more open-ended exploration of the way in which historical texts are preserved, used and perceived.[34]

Galbraith's historical imagination was fired by manuscripts and the problems posed by them. His most famous discoveries, such as his revolutionary studies of Domesday Book and his work on such chroniclers as Henry Knighton, Thomas Walsingham and Ranulf Higden, reflected this fascination with the way records and texts worked. Galbraith described his study of Asser as 'the most difficult publication of my life', which 'employed my leisure for many years'. This was 'purely and simply owing to the destruction of the original manuscript, Otho A. xii, which was burned in the Cottonian fire of 1731'.[35] Asser thus provided a mirror image of the problems with which Galbraith was most familiar. Instead of attempting to understand how the record or text functioned as an object by establishing how it was put together, the problem confronting Galbraith in the case of Asser was the appraisal of a text without any manuscript evidence.

One way in which this was interesting to Galbraith is that, because of the loss of the manuscript, extracts in other chroniclers are of particular value. Recovering the text of Asser increases awareness of the interaction between medieval texts. This was the theme that Galbraith explored in his first discussion of Asser, in his essay on 'Historical Research in Medieval England',[36] in which he analysed the use made of Asser by 'Florence' of Worcester and Simeon of Durham, and considered the extent to which William of Malmesbury's account of King Alfred was based on Asser. This textual traffic, of course, was not all one way: Asser's work in itself draws on other texts, most notably the Anglo-Saxon Chronicle. Galbraith's concern here was not primarily with the authenticity of Asser. He was more anxious to show how 'the strangest book in our medieval history'[37] illustrates that the use of historical texts during the Middle Ages was more sophisticated than is commonly assumed. However, he did wonder how far the way in which Asser was used suggested that even medieval chroniclers were wary of accepting the whole text.

Galbraith's second essay on Asser, 'Who Wrote Asser's Life of Alfred?', was published at the end of his *Introduction to the Study of History* as an example of 'Historical Research in Action'.[38] This may seem a strange way to have produced what he regarded as the most demanding piece of research he had undertaken, but in so doing Galbraith was intent on making an important point. At the end of a book which emphasised the importance of manuscripts and records at the centre of historical research, he published a study of a problem where the difficulty is precisely that the manuscript has vanished. By this means, he sought to emphasise the uncertainty of historical argument, how 'The longer one studies history, the harder it gets to arrive at results which even the author, let alone the reader, can decently consider to be the truth'.[39] Galbraith saw this example as illustrating 'how shaky are the foundations sustaining the confident narratives we write, and how endless is the work that still remains to be done'.[40] The selection of the essay on Asser to illustrate this point was inspired. Since the manuscript of Asser was not available, Galbraith could focus entirely on how historical reasoning works, taking the evidence that had already been assembled on this question and showing how it could be used to come to other conclusions.

Moreover, by placing at the end of his book discussion of an issue which had arisen because of the loss of a manuscript, Galbraith was also implicitly emphasising the central importance of records and manuscripts in historical study.

Galbraith presented his discussion of Asser as 'an example to be shot down by all who read it',[41] and it was promptly shot down, apparently beyond hope of recovery, by Dorothy Whitelock in her Stenton Lecture, *The Genuine Asser*.[42] In a review of Whitelock's criticisms, Galbraith protested that his most important arguments had not been addressed by her.[43] Galbraith emphasised that he did not consider the ascription to Leofric critical to his position — this had been put forward 'On the principle that "a spoonful of sugar makes the medicine go down"' to 'encourage my young readers to think of Asser as eleventh-century to which it assuredly belongs'. For Galbraith, the central point was the evidence which, to him, pointed to an eleventh-century date for the *Life*, in particular the internal evidence which, he felt, suggested that an earlier draft had spoken of Alfred as dead and had been afterwards imperfectly reworked to portray the king as still living. Galbraith urged those interested in the matter not to rely on Whitelock's portrayal of his argument: 'anyone who wishes to learn what I really said in my book, should first read it for himself or herself, and then read Miss Whitelock.'

Despite Galbraith's rejoinders, Whitelock's position, subsequently further reinforced by Keynes, Lapidge, David Kirby,[44] Janet Nelson[45] and others, has held the field. Galbraith nevertheless continued to brood on Asser, and made an interesting last reference to the controversy in an autobiographical piece called 'Afterthoughts'.[46] In this, he again emphasised how discussion of Asser illustrates general issues in relation to the treatment of historical evidence. Whitelock had referred in passing to the poorly drawn facsimile of the first folio of the burnt manuscript published by Francis Wise in 1722.[47] She suggested that this supported Humfrey Wanley's opinion that the writing of the manuscript resembled that in a charter of 1001. Whitelock also claimed the support of Kenneth Sisam, N.R. Ker, T.A.M. Bishop and Francis Wormald for this comparison, and noted that Wormald also saw a parallel between the layout of the facsimile page and those of two manuscripts of about 1000.[48]

Galbraith seized on this point, denouncing any reference at all to the sketch of the manuscript: 'To anyone whose life has been spent among original documents, this sketch is virtually useless, and to argue from a mere copy is the prostitution of paleography'.[49] This is unfair on Whitelock, since in any case she rested her case more on Wanley's report than on the sketch. Nevertheless, Galbraith, who had spent his life working on the manuscripts and records of the later Middle Ages, which are usually dated and which illustrate at every step the amazing vagaries of scribal behaviour, evidently felt exasperated at the willingness of Anglo-Saxon scholars to hazard dates of astonishing precision for their undated manuscripts: 'No medieval manuscript can be *certainly* dated from its script within much, if any, less than half a century and, even so, it can easily be falsified if reproduced either smaller or larger than the original'.[50]

Galbraith went on again pithily to relate Whitelock's use of the sketch by Wise to broader issues on the role of manuscripts in medieval studies: 'The Asser problem illustrates the inherent weakness of so much English scholarship, which still thinks in terms of the printed word, using evidence of manuscripts only in an emergency to bolster wishful thinking'.[51] For Galbraith, it was better to reconcile oneself to the complete loss of the manuscript and to work with the evidence available rather than to try and call in those high priests of medieval studies, the palaeographers, to pronounce on the matter without sufficient evidence. He saw Whitelock's passing appeal to the Wise sketch as encapsulating the way in which many scholars were inclined to use manuscript evidence as a talisman to validate arguments which were derived primarily from printed texts and secondary literature, rather than as the starting point of research.

Galbraith's work on Asser is thus of interest because of the way it relates to his broader ideas on the relationship of records and history. It is perhaps these aspects of Galbraith's work which will in the end have a greater influence on the study of Asser than his direct attack on its authenticity. In this sense, Smyth's attempts to revive Galbraith's assault on Asser does his work a disservice, since Smyth does not convincingly answer the points made by Whitelock and obscures the subtlety of some aspects of Galbraith's commentary on Asser.

Given that for Galbraith the interest of Asser was in the way it illuminated issues relating to the use of manuscripts by historians, it is surprising that he did not make more play of a strange feature of the manuscript history of Otho A. xii. Galbraith refers to Alistair Campbell's edition of the chronicle of Æthelweard, which points out that at the beginning of the remnants of Otho A. xii in the British Library, at the point where Asser would have been in the volume, are seven badly burnt leaves which are actually from the manuscript of Æthelweard, Otho A. x.[52] One might have expected Galbraith to have pointed out that this curious feature of the present structure of the manuscript is not mentioned anywhere in the enormous literature on Asser. The story of how these leaves came to be at the beginning of Otho A. xii is worth pursuing, both to add something to the tale of the history of Asser, which, in Galbraith's words, 'makes a good detective story',[53] but also because it further illustrates one of the key themes which Galbraith developed in his discussion of Asser, the way in which manuscript evidence is approached by medievalists.

THE RESTORATION OF OTHO A. XII

In all discussion of Asser's *Life of Alfred*, the starting point still remains William Stevenson's critical edition of 1904, and, in particular, the massive introduction in which Stevenson carefully reviewed the evidence bearing on the transmission of the text.[54] Even those scholars who have disagreed with Stevenson's conclusion have nevertheless expressed their admiration at the thoroughness of his analysis. In his attack on Stevenson's conclusions, Galbraith emphasised how his argument nevertheless 'rested upon Stevenson's premises, and has in fact done no more than carry his "unresolved difficulties" to their logical conclusion'.[55] Indeed, Stevenson seems to have been a hero of Galbraith. In his last book, *Domesday Book: Its Place in Administrative History*, Galbraith described Stevenson as 'a scholar of more positive achievement than ... perhaps anyone else — bar Round — of his generation'. Galbraith gave a vivid brief portrait of Stevenson — 'A man of genius, self-taught, and for long obscure, he became an expert philologist as well as a pioneer of English diplomatic' — and recalled how 'When I was young, one read with attention his every article in the *English Historical Review*'.[56] Galbraith's interest in both Domesday Book and Asser's *Life* seems to have been partly due to his fascination with Stevenson's work.[57]

Likewise, another recent Asser sceptic, Alfred Smyth, has observed that Stevenson's 'scholarly commentary has provided the quarry from which all subsequent commentators and translators of the *Life* have drawn liberally and not with due acknowledgement'.[58] Smyth, however, suggests that Stevenson's work encouraged a deluge of annotation and commentary on the *Life* which drew attention away from the text itself. This is difficult to accept, since Stevenson's achievement was precisely the opposite — to clear away the textual detritus which had surrounded Asser and to provide for the first time a reliable text of the *Life*. However, Stevenson's very thoroughness has meant that scholars have tended not to reexamine the detailed evidence presented by him or follow up leads which he provides.

For example, Stevenson refers in passing to a note by John Joscelyn (1529–1603) which states that a copy of Asser was owned by John Stow.[59] Stevenson notes that this was reported in the seventeenth century as being among the manuscripts of Sir Simonds D'Ewes, but does not pursue the matter further. This transcript can be readily identified as British Library, Harley 563, fols 51–119v, which is described by D'Ewes in the list of contents inserted by him at the beginning of the manuscript as 'Asserius Menevensis the Saxon storie of King Alfred in English or his Chronicle never imprinted in that tong'.[60] A note at the beginning of this transcript attempts to demonstrate that 'that whiche in this booke is founde of kynge Alfred is of asserius', and records that it is a translation made for Stow by

Ralph Holinshed in September 1572 of a transcript by Laurence Nowell (d. 1576) of a manuscript in the hands of the executors of the late Nicholas Wotton, Dean of Canterbury.[61] The copy of Holinshed's translation is in the hand of Stow; a colophon reads 'Finis written by John Stow marchaunt taylour of London, and finished the 26 of November Anno dom. 1572 laus deo'.[62] Despite the note at the beginning, this is not a translation of Asser, but of a manuscript containing extracts from the twelfth-century Worcester chronicle formerly attributed to Florence of Worcester, but now generally attributed to John of Worcester. The fact that this is not a copy of Asser is quickly apparent from, among other things, its continuation after Alfred's death, a point which D'Ewes had noted and led him to assume wrongly that the subsequent entries 'seemeth to bee collected & written by John Stow himselfe'.[63]

The confusion between Asser and the Worcester chronicle is easily understandable in view of the numerous extracts from Asser included in the chronicle. Nowell's original notes from the Worcester chronicle are now British Library, Additional 43705. Their source has not identified, but seems to have been related to the recension of the Worcester chronicle which is now London, Lambeth Palace 42.[64] Nowell had originally headed his extracts 'Ex Mariano Scoto notata', and made no suggestion that this was Asser.[65] William Lambarde (1536–1601) added a note to Nowell's heading, recording that the manuscript used was that formerly owned by Wotton and stating that the transcript was made in 1566.[66] Lambarde subsequently struck through this title, and inserted instead a lengthy note in Latin attempting to demonstrate that this was a copy of Asser.[67] It is this note which appears, in translation with an addition recording Holinshed's work as translator and the date it was made, at the beginning of Stow's copy of the text in Harley 563. Nowell made another copy of these extracts, which is now Harley 556. Fols 2v-29v and 64–119 are in Nowell's hand; fols 30–63v are in another unidentified hand which also appears in Harley 357, fols 18–99 and 359, fols 71–103 and 126–216.[68] At the beginning of Harley 556 is a copy by Nowell of Lambarde's note identifying the text as Asser, indicating that he accepted Lambarde's identification.[69] Holinshed, in preparing his translation for Stow, apparently worked from the copy in Harley 556.[70]

Although the Stow reference turns out to be a false lead, Stevenson's annotations contain some other intriguing references which might, at the least, assist in tracing other transcripts of Asser. The list by Joscelyn which mentions the Stow transcript, for example, also refers to other copies of Asser in the possession of Sir George Bowyer and Lady Cheke. It is likely that other transcripts of Asser still survive which are not discussed in detail by Stevenson.

At the heart of the introduction to Stevenson's edition is his description of the history of the lost manuscript. Like Charles Dickens stressing that Jacob

Marley was dead, Stevenson begins by making it clear that no fragments of the copy of Asser in Otho A. xii survived the fire. He notes that some fragments from the manuscript had been rescued and were restored in the nineteenth century, but stresses that 'No portion of Asser has been found amongst them'.[71] He goes on to cite Edward Maunde Thompson, Keeper of Manuscripts at the British Museum from 1878 to 1888 and then Principal Librarian and Director of the Museum until 1909, to the effect that 'no fragments of the Life exist in the Museum, unless in the form of charred and illegible relics of the fire'.

Thus, Stevenson, relying on Thompson, presents a very clear cut picture: 'not a scrap of the MS. has come down to us'.[72] However, such a view is an oversimplification of the history of the manuscript after the fire. It ignores the fact that there were some reports that the manuscript of Asser had survived the fire. It also fails to indicate that at the beginning of the restored Otho A. xii are seven fragments which were identified at some stage as being part of Asser's *Life*, but which are from another manuscript. Indeed, if in 1904 an unwary reader of Stevenson had gone to the British Museum and asked to look at the remains of Otho A. xii, he would have found to his astonishment that there were apparently some fragments of Asser there, with no suggestion that they in fact belonged elsewhere. The reader would probably have been forced to assume, as appears indeed to have been the case, that Stevenson never looked at Otho A. xii, but relied wholly on the testimony of Thompson.

In view of the way in which Stevenson's discussion of the manuscript elides over these important points, it is perhaps worth reviewing again the history of Otho A. xii since the fire of 1731. Otho A. xii has not been totally neglected since the time of Stevenson. Scholars primarily interested in *The Battle of Maldon* have done a great deal of work on attempting to reconstruct the original structure of the manuscript. Of particular note is the account by Helmut Gneuss of the present condition of the manuscript, but again Gneuss does not give much information on how it reached its current state; he assumes that a nameless binder simply pieced together (not very intelligently) the surviving fragments.[73] The process by which the manuscript was rescued and pieced together was in fact more complex.

In the 1732 report of the parliamentary committee appointed to investigate the fire in the Cotton Library, there is a list compiled by David Casley of the manuscripts destroyed or damaged in the fire.[74] Manuscripts which had been 'lost, burnt or intirely spoiled' were marked with an asterisk. Among the volumes so designated is Otho A. xii.[75] Stevenson gives the impression that, because the asterisk was placed at the beginning of the description of the manuscript, the report suggests that just the first article of the manuscript had been lost.[76] In so doing, Stevenson was perhaps trying to reconcile Casley's report that the volume had been destroyed with the fact that some fragments had survived. However, Casley's procedure was clear — that volumes he considered wholly destroyed were marked with an asterisk — and it is evident that, as far as Casley was concerned, the whole of Otho A. xii had gone up in smoke.

It was presumably Casley who was responsible for putting in place of the vanished Otho A. xii a sixteenth-century transcript of Asser, which, Stevenson suggests,[77] was possibly the former Royal 577, probably made for Lord Lumley when the original manuscript was in his library. The identification 'Otho A. xii. 1' in the top left hand corner of the first folio of this transcript is in a hand which closely resembles Casley's.[78] The Cotton manuscripts were kept after the fire in a building constructed as a dormitory for Westminster School, and the surviving manuscripts continued to be shelved there in the emperor pressmark sequence, so this transcript of Asser would simply have stood in place of the original manuscript in the sequence.[79] It was presumably renumbered Otho A. xii* when fragments from the original manuscript were recovered in the nineteenth century.

The attempts made immediately after the fire to preserve and rescue the damaged manuscripts from the Cotton Library are described in the parliamentary report by William Whiston, the clerk in charge of the records kept at the Chapter House in Westminster.[80] Whiston described how the fire had caused animal fat from the vellum manuscripts to melt so that many of the manuscripts were reduced to a congealed fatty mess. These manuscripts were, as far as possible, forced open and dried, sometimes using such expedients as placing leaves on a washing line or opening them in front of a fire. However, despite these efforts, an enormous number of loose fragments remained. Whiston urged that these be 'put either into Covers or Drawers, according to the respective Subjects they treat of, so that the least Fragment may not be lost'.[81] These fragments included the surviving remnants of Otho A. xii, together with many other famous manuscripts which were afterwards to be recovered.

The Cotton manuscripts and fragments languished in the dormitory building at Westminster for 20 years after the fire. Their future safekeeping was only finally assured in 1753 by the establishment of the British Museum as a result of Sir Hans Sloane's bequest. In July 1756, before the Cotton manuscripts were moved to the premises acquired by the Museum's Trustees, Montagu House in Great Russell Street, two detailed reports on their condition were prepared by Matthew Maty, who became the first Keeper of Printed Books at the Museum and was afterwards Principal Librarian from 1772 to 1776, and Henry Rimius. The first of these reports described the main sequence of manuscripts, while the second dealt with the charters, coins and antiquities.[82]

Maty and Rimius made a detailed check of the contents of the shelves at Westminster against Thomas Smith's 1696 catalogue of the collection and

Casley's list of manuscripts damaged in the fire, counting the volumes and comparing the contents of a sample of the manuscripts against the catalogue entries. They found the condition of the presses most badly affected by the fire — Tiberius, Caligula, Galba, Vitellius and Otho — very confused. Some manuscripts which Casley reported as surviving the fire had disappeared, such as Tiberius D. vi, a cartulary of Christchurch Priory in Hampshire, which was said by Casley to have survived the fire largely intact, but could not be found. Maty and Rimius found that the drawers housing the charters also contained masses of 'rubbish of bits of parchment or of paper, scorched by the fire, or consumed by old age'.[83] These were the fragments which Whiston and his colleagues had been unable to place in 1731, which had simply been stuffed away out of sight. They included not only the misplaced material, such as the Christchurch Cartulary, but also fragments of Otho A. xii and other important manuscripts. Richard Widmore, the Keeper of the Library of Westminster Abbey, who had prepared a draft catalogue of the charters, thought that these fragments should be disposed of, but Maty and Rimius wisely urged 'a more particular examination' before any further action, correctly anticipating that 'it is not impossible but some things may still be retrieved'.[84]

Maty and Rimius also managed to locate some manuscripts which Casley thought had been destroyed. For shelf A of the Otho press they reported as follows: 'According to the report consists of 18 numbers all destroyed; yet we discovered the first part of number XII being the Life of Alfred by Asser Menevensis.'[85] It seems unlikely that Maty and Rimius, who were evidently experienced and careful manuscript scholars, could have mistaken the transcript of Otho A. xii for the original manuscript, and if they had been referring to the substitution of the transcript for the original volume, they would have said so. It seems more likely that, in the disorder, they found something which seemed to be possibly the original manuscript of Asser. In 1777, the section of Maty and Rimius' report referring to the supposed rediscovery of Asser was printed in Samuel Hooper's subject catalogue of the Cotton Library,[86] so that this identification of the Asser manuscript has been a matter of public record for over 200 years. However, it has not been mentioned in any of the accounts of the lost manuscript.

This failure to follow up this discovery of Maty and Rimius was perhaps due to the way in which the manuscripts were treated when they got to the British Museum.[87] The bulk of the Cotton manuscripts were arranged on wired presses in emperor shelfmark order. The most badly damaged manuscripts and fragments were, however, put in separate storage, at first in a cupboard in the room where the Harley charters were stored, then afterwards in an upper room away from the public areas known as the charter garret, where they were regarded, as Sir Henry Ellis put it in 1825, as 'perfectly useless to the Museum in every sense of the word'.[88]

Thus, the transcript of Asser was left in the place of Otho A. xii in the main manuscript sequence, while the remnants of the manuscript itself languished in the garret, if not forgotten, at least the object of benign neglect. Any reader who ordered Otho A. xii would have been given the transcript. When Joseph Planta compiled his catalogue of the Cotton manuscripts between 1793 and 1796, he concentrated on the publicly available manuscripts stored in the main emperor sequence, and ignored the fragments stored with the Harley charters. When he came to describe Otho A. xii, he seems to have been almost surprised to find the sixteenth-century transcript in place of the original manuscript, and gives no hint that, 40 years previously, it was reported that Asser had survived and was apparently lurking among the unsorted fragments in a room not far from where he was writing.[89] Nevertheless, Planta confidently stated in the preface to his catalogue that everything worth restoring had been restored. Doubtless, any reader who at this time asked what had become of the leaves from Asser reported by Maty and Rimius was told, as was Sir Frederic Madden when he asked after the Christchurch Cartulary, that nothing from Otho A. xii had survived.[90]

In 1826, however, following discussions with Sir Humphry Davy, a Trustee of the Museum, a method was devised of recovering the burnt fragments by soaking them in a solution and then cutting them open. A major programme for sorting and opening the loose fragments in the upper room was set in hand under the direction of the Keeper of Manuscripts, Sir Henry Ellis, and his assistant, Josiah Forshall, who undertook the bulk of the work. They recovered hundreds of leaves from many important Anglo-Saxon manuscripts, including the unique manuscript of the prosimetrical translation of Boethius (Otho A. vi), the Old English translation of the *Cura pastoralis* (Tiberius B. xi), the Vitellius Psalter (Vitellius E. xviii) and two eleventh-century manuscripts of Ælfric (Vitellius C. v and Vitellius D. xvii).[91] Nothing was recovered from Otho A. xii. The manuscript was named in a list of 'Saxon MSS. wanting' compiled by Forshall.[92] Although a list of the burnt Cotton manuscripts dating from *c.* 1837 states that Otho A. xii was 'preserved',[93] this doubtless refers to the paper transcript of Asser — a detailed list of the burnt Cotton manuscript compiled by Madden in 1841 does not refer to the survival of any fragments but states that 'A paper copy is under this number'.[94] Like Planta, Forshall was convinced that nothing capable of restoration survived among the remaining fragments.

In 1837, Forshall was succeeded as Keeper of Manuscripts by Sir Frederic Madden. On 17 April 1837, shortly before he took over from Forshall, Madden asked him if they could inspect the old charter garret. Madden's diary records what they found:[95]

> Mr Forshall...went, at my request, up with me to the garret called the

> Charter-Room (because the charters were formerly kept here), and where I had always been told there were only a few fragments not worth the bother of dusting or sorting. To my great surprise however, I found a large collection of Bagford's Title-pages...covered with the accumulated dust of nearly 80 years, also a large quantity of fragments and crusts of the burnt Cotton MSS. many of which appeared to me well worth the process of restoration. Mr F. had always assured me he had selected from them every thing worth preserving, but I saw enough before me to doubt the accuracy of his statement, and going on with my searches, I discovered in an old cupboard the identical *Cartulary of Christ Church Twinham* in Hampshire [Tiberius D. vi], which I have so often and so fruitlessly inquired after, and very little the worse for the fire, except being wrinkled up! Is not this very disgraceful of the Keepers of MSS. from the middle of the last century to the present day?... I saw enough to make me resolve in my own mind, to have the entire room cleared out, whenever it should be my lot to be Keeper of the MSS. and I resolved at once to bring down into my own room the two large bundles which formed the Christ Church Cartulary, and a third bundle which apparently contains an English Chronicle. I left up in the garret fragments of crusts of vellum enough to fill several bushel baskets, likewise a box full of receipts of Sir Robert Cotton's and three boxes said to contain the refuse of the Hargrave collection. It is very much to the discredit of Mr F that affairs should have remained thus, and so I believe he felt, when I produced him the long lost Christ Church Cartulary, which he had declared to me over and over again could not by any possibility exist!

Madden afterwards described the fragments as 'sufficient in quantity to load a small cart ... and covered with the dust and dirt of more than a century'.[96] He was determined that his chief aim as Keeper should be the complete restoration of the Cotton library, including the sorting and repair of these fragments.[97] However, the Museum's Trustees did not share Madden's enthusiasm for his discoveries in the garret and were doubtful about the cost of the conservation programme proposed by Madden. Madden had developed a technique for protecting the brittle burnt leaves of manuscripts affected by the heat of fire by inlaying them in heavy paper frames, but felt that the Museum binder, Charles Tuckett, was not equal to this delicate work. Madden was anxious to use a binder who had worked at Oxford, Henry Gough, for this task. It took Madden four years to persuade the Trustees to permit Gough to make trial repairs to some of the burnt vellum manuscripts. Even then, the Trustees were not willing to start work on the fragments from the garret, and it was not until 1845 that Madden finally secured a minute from the Trustees authorising him to 'proceed with the reparation of the burnt vellum MSS. until all which deserve the expenditure are completed'.[98]

At first, Madden was able to identify virtually complete manuscripts on which Gough could work, but as the work proceeded the fragments became more and more intractable and difficult to identify in advance of repair. By 1852, the Trustees were again growing anxious about the length of time the restoration was taking. They asked Madden to indicate 'which of these MSS. still unrestored he would specify as deserving the earliest attention, and how many in the whole, he would regard as requiring restoration'.[99] To demonstrate to the Trustees the difficulty of answering this question, Madden placed before them a selection of burnt lumps and crusts to show them the impossibility of ascertaining their contents 'in their present miserable state of cremation, dirt and neglect'. He also pointed out that 'No portions yet of the very MSS of Æthelweard, Otho A. X, Asser, Otho A. XII, the Peterborough Chronicle, Otho A. XVII, the Winchester Annals, Galba A. XV, the Chronicle of Walter of Coventry and Register of Thorney, Vit. D. V, the Chronicle of Frodoard, Otho B. III and many more have yet to be recovered'. However, he felt 'confident that parts may yet exist among the fragments yet untouched'.[100] Madden was doubtless emboldened in his claim that it was likely some portion of Asser might yet be found by the statement of Maty and Rimius that they had seen the Asser manuscript — in one of his lists of the burnt Cotton manuscripts, Madden had already noted, on the basis of the 1756 report, that 'The first article was discovered'.[101]

As a result of the Trustees' concern about the progress of the restoration, Madden did however propose an important change in procedure.[102] He suggested that Gough should flatten and clean the fragments so as to permit preliminary identification to take place. The fragments could then receive preliminary arrangement and only then be inlaid. Work according to this plan was started in July 1852. Over the next two years, thousands of leaves were flattened, and a large proportion of them identified and inlaid. By 1854, Madden was able to report that 'the entire mass of burnt vellum fragments of the Cottonian Collection ... have now been *flattened* & not a scrap remains *unexamined*'.[103] By the autumn of 1856, the inlaying of the fragments was complete and Gough's 'long and arduous work' was brought to a conclusion.[104]

The task of undertaking the detailed identification and arrangement of these inlaid fragments so that they could be bound up was enormous, and Madden started to involve the junior academic staff of the department in the work.[105] Among these was Edward Maunde Thompson, who had joined the Museum at the age of 21 in 1861, working initially in the office of the Principal Librarian, Antonio Panizzi.[106] Thompson was transferred, at Panizzi's insistence, to the Manuscripts Department, commencing his duties there on 3 March 1862.[107] He began his work in the Department in the time-honoured fashion, by spending his first year describing Additional

Charters.[108] In February 1863, Madden asked him to arrange the inlaid fragments of Vitellius E. viii.[109] The following month he worked on arranging Otho A. x, Vitellius D. xi and Vitellius E viii.[110] During May and June 1863, he worked on a large number of different manuscripts, making some significant discoveries.[111] He found the last 11 leaves of an early manuscript of the chronicle of Roger of Wendover, Otho B. v. 'This is important', Madden declared.[112] On the following day, 'Mr Thompson identified the leaves of the commencement of Tib. A. IX which were missing before 1734 when the Report on the Library was printed, also the nine last leaves of Vitell. A. VIII'. Madden was delighted: 'Mr Thompson is a most useful assistant & his services more valuable than several of the older ones.'[113]

In October 1863, another new assistant had started work in the Department of Manuscripts, Edward John Long Scott. Scott was by training an orientalist, but also very interested in western medieval manuscripts.[114] Like Thompson, he began by preparing catalogue entries for charters.[115] He worked under Thompson's supervision, and his catalogue slips were corrected by Thompson. Madden decided that Thompson and Scott would make an ideal team to complete the work in identifying and arranging the outstanding Cotton fragments. Madden's work diary records that on 10 March 1864 he 'Gave into Mr Thompson's hands the greater part of the remains of the inlaid Cotton MSS. now *identified*, but not *bound*, together with the boxes containing the loose fragments, in order that he and Mr Scott may endeavour to identify or arrange what remains, so as to have the whole put up in cloth boards'.[116] This work was to occupy much of the time of Thompson and Scott until the end of 1864.[117]

The pile of fragments with which Thompson and Scott were confronted came from many different manuscripts, and they only gradually managed to establish which fragments came from which manuscript. The progress of this complex procedure can be traced from the monthly reports submitted to Madden by the two men. In August 1864, Thompson was chiefly engaged in arranging the remnants of Galba A. xvii and rearranging Vitellius A. vii and part of Galba A. xiv. In the course of doing this, he identified individual leaves from Galba A. vi and Vitellius A. vii.[118] At the same time, Scott was arranging fragments from Galba A. i, Otho C. xiv, D. vii and D. ix.[119] It was Scott who, at this time, first seems to have identified fragments from Otho A. xii; he states that his work during this month included 'inserting ff. 3 in and identifying large portions of Otho A. XII and Vit. E. VII (arts. 1, 2, 3)'.[120]

Either Scott seems to have found the fragments of Otho A. xii too complex or felt that they might be of particular interest to Thompson. In any case, in September 1864, Thompson reported that his work for the month had included the arrangement of Otho A. xii 'with additions'.[121] At this point, Thompson and Scott thought they had finally managed to confirm the remarkable discovery made by Maty and Rimius in 1756. In his personal diary for 30 September 1864, Madden states that 'It was reported to me today that a portion of the MS. of Asser's Life of Alfred, in MS. Cott. Otho A. XII (supposed to have been wholly destroyed in the fire of 1731) had been identified among the burnt fragments'.[122] This report was evidently made to Madden by Thompson, since Madden goes on to note that he gave Thompson the remainder of the inlaid paper fragments to sort. Scott, however, claimed the credit for the discovery in his report for October 1864, stating that he had 'identified & arranged Otho A. XII art. 1'.[123]

During 1865, Thompson prepared a list briefly summarising the condition of each of the Cotton manuscripts at the end of the long restoration programme.[124] This list was carefully revised by Madden, and then copied into two interleaved copies of Casley's 1732 list, one of which was placed in the Reading Room.[125] In this list, Thompson (as revised by Madden) stated that Otho A. xii 'now consists of 47 folios, 7 of which belong to article 1, and the rest to Arts. 4, 5, 7, 8, 9, 10, 11, 12 and 13; Articles 2, 3 and 6 are missing'.[126]

As already noted, what Thompson and Scott had found were seven leaves from Æthelweard's Latin version of the Anglo-Saxon Chronicle. They belonged to Otho A. x, another burnt Cotton manuscript from which 11 other very badly burnt fragments had been recovered, and which had been arranged by Thompson in March 1863.[127] These fragments (including those placed at the beginning of Otho A. xii) were first described in detail, and transcribed with the aid of ultra-violet light, by E.E. Barker in 1951, who was finally able to establish the correct order and sequence of the leaves.[128] Barker correctly speculated that the fragments in Otho A. xii had been placed there 'under the erroneous impression that they formed part of Asser's work', but assumed that the mistake was because the leaves had not been properly deciphered.[129] In fact, the annotations afterwards made by Thompson on the paper frame on each leaf indicate that he and Scott had read a surprising amount of the text on the leaves. Whilst it is understandable that the Latin extracts from the chronicle in Asser might be confused with Æthelweard, it must also be wondered how far Scott and Thompson were engaging in wishful thinking: because Maty and Rimius had reported that Asser had survived, they were looking out for fragments from Asser and thought they had found them.

Meanwhile, another misfortune was in store for Otho A. xii. When it was felt that all the surviving fragments had been identified and correctly arranged, the inlaid leaves were sent down to the Museum's binder, Tuckett, to be bound up. In July 1865, the surviving folios of Otho A. xii were among a number of manuscripts (also including Otho A. x) on which Madden, Thompson and Scott had been working which were sent to the

Museum bindery. On the evening of 10 July, a fire broke out which gutted the Museum bindery.[130] A number of repaired Cotton manuscripts were destroyed or damaged. The most notable victim of the fire was Tiberius B. xi, an early manuscript of the Alfredian translation of the *Cura pastoralis*, which was reduced from a 'good thick folio' of 174 folios to eight tiny badly charred fragments. Two volumes of Old English sermons, Galba A. ii and iii, were also completely destroyed, as well as Galba A. i and manuscripts from the Arundel and Additional collections.

Shortly after the fire had been put out, one of Madden's assistants brought over to his residence a 'parcel of vellum manuscripts tied together with tape, which had been found in one corner of the workshop, much burnt on the outside & margins and saturated with water'.[131] These proved on examination to be the remains of several Cotton manuscripts, including Otho A. xii. Madden considered the further damage to this volume, which he still thought contained part of the original Asser, particularly regrettable.[132] The extent of the damage to the volume seems to have been limited to further marginal damage and staining of the leaves. No further folios were destroyed; the folio count remained the same before and after the fire. Madden retired, bitter and disillusioned, the following year. During the second half of 1865, Thompson was engaged in sorting and arranging into boxes the various fragments damaged in the fire at the bindery.[133] In May 1867, the fragments were again flattened, repaired and inlaid in paper frames, this time by Charles Tuckett (the son of the binder about whom Madden had doubts in 1837),[134] and Thompson had once more to set about the laborious task of identifying each fragment and putting it in order.[135] His pencil notes identifying each leaf can still be seen on the paper frames in which the fragments are mounted. Despite being given this second bite at the cherry, Thompson stood by his identification of the seven fragments from Otho A. x as being from Asser. This is even more surprising when it is found that Thompson's pencil annotations on the paper mounts of these fragments explicitly refer to Æthelweard.[136] Thompson completed the final arrangement of the doubly damaged volumes by December 1867, and they were then bound into volumes, thus perpetuating the misidentification of the seven fragments at the beginning of Otho A. xii.[137]

Unlike the other Cotton manuscripts, which had elaborate full-leather bindings, the manuscripts which had been damaged in the bindery fire were bound in more workmanlike half-cloth bindings. The acidic paper used in the paper frames meant that the mounts became very brittle, and some of the misidentified leaves at the beginning of the volume had, by the 1980s, come away from the mount, creating a risk that pieces of the vellum would crumble away. To prevent this, Otho A. xii was disbound in 1987 (the old binding has been preserved separately) and each leaf, still in its nineteenth-century inlay, was placed in an inert plastic sleeve. These sleeves were then placed in a postbinding folder.

ASSER REDIVIVUS

Thompson's belief that Asser had arisen from the flames began to percolate into published literature. In 1876–1877, Henry Howorth published four letters in the *Athanæum* arguing that the text of Asser was spurious.[138] He relied on Thompson in describing the remains of Otho A. xii:

> Mr Thompson, of the MS. Department of the British Museum, than whom it would be impossible to quote a more judicious authority, has obligingly reexamined the fragments of the old MS., which have been rebound, and he authorized me to say that it is written in two distinct hands, one of the eleventh and one of the twelfth century, and that no portion of it is as early as the tenth.[139]

At this stage further confusions pile on top of one another to almost dizzying effect. Thompson at this time still wrongly thought that the first seven leaves of the restored manuscript were fragments of Asser. However, the information he gave to Howorth clearly refers to the whole manuscript. Howorth assumed that Thompson was talking only about Asser (how far he was aware of the existence of the supposed fragments is unclear), and claimed that Asser's text was evidently a composite one, put together at two different periods, and therefore unreliable.

It is surprising that Thompson did not immediately correct this mistake, and it was not until he was pressed on the point by Stevenson, more than 20 years later, that he attempted to clarify the point. By this time, Thompson has realised that the identification of the leaves at the beginning of Otho A. xii was mistaken. In attempting to put the record straight for Stevenson, however, he muddied the waters even further, by stating that 'he was misled into making the statement referred to above through the assumption that the whole of the Cottonian Otho A. xii was in the same handwriting. The fragments upon which this view of the age of the MS. was founded have nothing whatever to do with that of the Life'.[140] Thompson's correction is disingenuous in that he fails to admit that he thought at the time he wrote to Howorth that the fragments did include some from Asser. Moreover, it is difficult to see how an assumption that the whole of the manuscript was in the same handwriting has a bearing on Thompson's earlier comments, since these state that the manuscript is in different hands. Thompson's retraction of 1904 sounds much like the statement of a man who cannot remember why he gave a particular opinion 20 years earlier.

Another scholar led badly astray by the misidentification of these fragments was Henry Bradshaw. In his survey of early Welsh, Breton and

Cornish manuscripts undertaken between 1872 and 1877 and printed in his *Collected Papers*, Bradshaw emphasised the importance of Latin texts of Welsh origin as sources of information on early Celtic philology. He stressed the value of the supposed leaves from Asser as an example of such a text. 'The whole question has to be patiently investigated', he declared,

> and the seven remaining leaves of the burnt Cotton MS. Otho A.XII have to be made to yield up what evidence they are capable of giving. Wherever any vernacular words occur, they are of such unmistakable purity, that it is an absolute impossibility that the work can be a forgery of the XIIth century, as some have wished to make out. The gleanings in the matter of old Welsh words or points of history, are scanty: I have them all copied out and indexed. But they are enough to stir up any one to devote more well-directed efforts towards solving the problem than have yet been made.[141]

This is all very convincing, but, of course, unfortunately refers to the wrong text — to Æthelweard and not Asser.

Stevenson duly chided Bradshaw for suggesting that the manuscript had survived,[142] but does not seem to realise how the mistake occurred. Indeed, Stevenson's discussion of the published literature at this point is thoroughly misleading, since it does not provide the crucial information that, at the time Howorth and Bradshaw were writing, the annotated copy of the parliamentary report in the Museum reading room indicated that part of Asser had survived. It seems likely, in fact, that Stevenson never looked at the reconstituted Otho A. xii, relying instead wholly on information provided by Thompson.[143] Stevenson assumed that Bradshaw had been misled by Howorth, and expresses surprise that 'so careful a scholar' as Bradshaw should have referred to 'the non-existent fragments of the MS. of the Life'. In fact, Bradshaw seems to have been the only one of these scholars to have carefully examined the original manuscript.

The mistaken identification of the seven fragments at the beginning of Otho A. xii was corrected by Sir George Warner in 1878. At the time of Sir Frederic Madden's retirement in 1866, the work on identifying the residue of remaining fragments was still not complete. Under Madden's successor, Edward Augustus Bond, priority was given to the creation of the classed catalogue and the elimination of the arrears of cataloguing which had built up under Madden.[144] Thompson was deeply involved with both these projects and was unable to return to the work on the Cotton fragments. In 1878, Thompson himself became Keeper of Manuscripts. It was decided not to attempt the further integration of the inlaid fragments into the collection, but to bind them up as a series of fragments. The 29 volumes of Cotton fragments were arranged and described by George Warner during 1878.[145] A copy of the handwritten description of this series by Warner is available in the Manuscripts Students' Room at the British Library.[146] It seems to have been Warner who realised the mistake about Asser, presumably in the course of his work on the fragments. The statement that seven leaves from Asser had survived in one of the interleaved copies of the parliamentary report is corrected in Warner's hand.[147] An interleaved copy of Hardy's *Descriptive Catalogue of Materials Relating to the History of Great Britain and Ireland*[148] formerly in the Keeper's Room of the Department of Manuscripts and now in the Students' Room also has an annotation by Warner in vol. 1, page 549, noting that Otho A. xii comprises 47 inlaid leaves, 'but no Asser among them'.

SEARCHING FOR ASSER

The question that inevitably arises from this discussion is: how can we be sure that no fragments from Asser still survive at the British Library? Since 1904, discussion of the manuscript history of the *Life* has rested completely on the statement of Thompson that no fragments of the *Life* are extant in the Library. Given the shaky record of Thompson on this subject, it is worth attempting a more systematic appraisal of the likelihood of some fragments having survived. In discussing this possibility, it is worth trying also to see how far Maty and Rimius' report that they had found the manuscript of Asser in 1756 can be explained.

The first important point is that it is impossible to be absolutely certain that no fragments from any of the burnt Cotton manuscripts survive anywhere. The work of sorting out the burnt fragments and trying to reassemble them into their original manuscripts was extremely arduous, and, not surprisingly, mistakes were often made. For example, N.E.S.A. Hamilton, one of Madden's assistants, worked in 1863 on arranging the fragments of the three Old English manuscripts Otho A. viii, Otho B. x and Otho B. xi. His identifications were not always accurate, and a leaf from Otho A. viii and Otho B. xi can be found in Otho B. x, while Otho B. x also contains leaves originally from Otho B. ii and Otho C. i.[149] Many of the restored volumes have yet to be fully catalogued or edited, and doubtless many more such errors exist. It is quite possible that a fragment from Otho A. xii lurks in another restored Cotton manuscript. Until a detailed catalogue of the entire Cotton collection is available, this possibility cannot be excluded.

Finding such a fragment would be a largely serendipitous process, but the search could be narrowed in some ways. Since any such fragment would come from the material found by Madden in the garret in 1837, it would be more likely to be found in the volumes recorded as missing or destroyed in Planta. Moreover, it is perhaps more likely, though not completely certain, that any fragment would be found in one of the other manuscripts on which Scott and Thompson were working at the time they were arranging Otho A. xii. Possible candidates would include Otho A. viii, Otho A. x, Otho A. xiii, Vitellius A. vi, Vitellius A. vii and Vitellius D. xx. A quick examination of these manuscripts does not indicate that they include any fragments from Otho A. xii, and the one most likely to contain any such fragment, Otho A. x, has, of course, already been fully described and edited. However, until all these manuscripts have been either described in detail or edited, the possibility that a piece of Asser is lurking there cannot be ruled out.

If a fragment of Asser still survives, another possibility is that it is in the residue of material left over after Warner had incorporated the series of Cotton fragments. This comprises three groups of fragments, known respectively as the Case, the Box and the Portfolio, from the form in which they were stored. All this material was described by Eric Millar, Keeper of Manuscripts from 1944 to 1947.[150] It is unclear when these descriptions were prepared by Millar. They were perhaps undertaken as part of the work on a new Cotton catalogue which began after the commemoration of the anniversary of the death of Sir Robert Cotton in 1931. A copy of Millar's handwritten description is available in the Manuscripts Students' Room at the British Library.

The bulk of the loose vellum fragments were kept in the Cotton Case, where they were arranged in four bundles. Previously not available in the Manuscripts Students' Room, these fragments have recently been conserved and placed in protective plastic sheets. They are now numbered Cotton Fragments XXX and can be consulted by readers. These fragments are minutely described by Millar, and it was apparently on the basis of Millar's descriptions that Ker and others were able to include references to these fragments in their descriptions of various Cotton manuscripts. Millar identified in these fragments five further pieces from Otho A. xii, two from the fourth article, Osbern's account of the Translation of St Ælfheah, joining the present fol. 16, and three from the twelfth article, a Life of St Æthelburh, which Millar speculated came from near the present fol. 41.[151]

Millar's work in identifying the tiny fragments in the Cotton Case was remarkable. He was able successfully to identify most of the fragments in Bundle I, but the smaller and more badly burnt fragments in Bundles II–IV caused him more difficulty. In his description, Millar usually indicates the date and subject matter of the fragments, and there is nothing which would appear to be a candidate for a leaf from Asser. Millar also carefully prepared transcriptions, as far as possible, of each fragment, which he placed with the fragment. Again, nothing appears to be part of Asser, but it would be impossible to be absolutely sure that none of these sections of text are from Asser without having access to a searchable text of the *Life*.

The Cotton Portfolio, a now rather battered artist's portfolio of the nineteenth century which has recently been numbered Cotton Fragments XXXI, contains fragments which had been flattened and inlaid by Gough. Unfortunately, the Portfolio cannot be consulted by readers until it has been conserved in a similar fashion to the Case. Almost all the fragments in the Portfolio are paper, with the exception of some fragments from a late medieval cartulary or book of statutes. The Portfolio may perhaps be the remnants of the paper fragments which Madden handed over to Thompson on the day when Thompson told him he had found Asser. The Portfolio also contains some loose leaves from two Birch manuscripts, Additional 4227 and 4337, as well as some pieces of Arundel 152, which was burnt in the 1865 bindery fire.

The Cotton Box, now Cotton Fragments XXXII (also unavailable to readers because it contains some loose fragments which would be easily lost or damaged) comprises again chiefly inlaid paper documents. These are mostly letters and official papers dating from the fourteenth, fifteenth and sixteenth centuries. These include some documents of historical value, such as a letter of 1401 from King Henry IV to the Privy Council, concerning diplomatic negotiations with the Duke of Milan. The material is extensively described by Millar, and again there is nothing which looks as if it might be a fragment from Asser. However, the box also includes seven small medallion boxes containing tiny fragments from Tiberius E. i (approximately eight fragments), Tiberius E. vii (approximately 15 fragments), Otho B. v (one fragment), Otho B. xi (four fragments), Otho D. vii, part 2 (seven fragments), Vitellius E. xiii (more than 20 fragments) and Vitellius E. xv (more than 20 fragments).[152] There are also two boxes containing various unidentified fragments, most of which appear to be from post-Conquest manuscripts, and which are too small or fragile to be easily identified.[153] These are the only surviving completely loose vellum fragments from the Cotton fire. These fragments are generally extremely tiny, and it is impossible to substantiate the identification of them on the boxes. The most interesting of these fragments are perhaps those from Otho B. xi, the celebrated manuscript which contained, among other texts, the 'G' manuscript of the Anglo-Saxon Chronicle. The existence of the larger scrap from Otho B. xi in the Cotton Box was noted by Neil Ker, who reported that it bore the words 'þu eac swilce | am welan ea' in two lines on one side. Ker does not, however, report the two notes on the box containing these fragments, one of which records that another fragment was added to fol. 42 of the manuscript in 1936, while the other emphasises the difficulty of identifying these small scraps: 'The largest fragment, if from the MS. at all, is not from the Anglo-Saxon Chronicle.'

The loose Cotton fragments, then, are so tiny that, if any piece of Asser was among them, it would be virtually impossible to identify it. The other place where one might look for a fragment of Asser is in the series of Cotton fragments arranged by Warner in 1878. Warner's description generally provides an admirably clear account of the contents of this series. The volume which, however, seems to have caused Warner greatest difficulty was the last one, Fragments XXIX, in which he presumably placed all the fragments which were most difficult to identify. When he came to work on this material, Millar went carefully through Warner's descriptions, annotating them and preparing supplementary descriptions of some of the items which Warner had ignored. Fragments XXIX, fols 60 and 61, comprises two leaves which contain, on the verso of fol. 60 and both sides of fol. 61, part of a list of papal bulls compiled in the first half of the fourteenth century. On the recto side of fol. 60, Millar noticed that, inverted, there was a note, apparently in Sir Robert Cotton's hand, reading 'Asserius Menevensis vita [the letters 'As' deleted] Alfredi Regis in Saxon Letters'. Millar convincingly speculated that fols 60 and 61 therefore formed the flyleaves of Otho A. xii.[154]

It seems likely that these flyleaves are the nearest we will ever get to finding fragments of Asser, but, as the preceding analysis has sought to emphasise, we cannot be sure. It seems reasonable to assume that what Maty and Rimius found in 1756 were the two flyleaves of Otho A. xii which are now in Fragments XXIX. Presumably the leaf with the note by Cotton referring to Asser was placed with some other fragments which made them think that the *Life* had survived.

A MORAL?

What is the moral of this story? It does not seem to change our view of the reliability of Asser and does not seem to produce anything which undermines Stevenson's conclusions or suggests that Galbraith's arguments should be revisited. For the most part, it simply adds a further twist to the fascinating tale of Asser, and, as Galbraith emphasised, tales about texts form the best history of all. But this story does also illustrate some points about the way in which manuscripts are used within medieval studies, which Galbraith would doubtless have been anxious to emphasise if he was still alive. First, this story emphasises the potential dangers of relying uncritically on the testimony of experts when dealing with manuscripts. Thompson was, at the least, a compromised witness in the question of the misidentified Asser fragments, rather than the unimpeachable authority everyone assumed him to be. The second moral would be how much work there is still to be done on a topic which, it would seem, had been as comprehensively treated by Stevenson as any topic could be. There is probably still much more information which could be recovered about the history of the manuscript, not to mention the possibility that further transcripts could be traced.

Finally, the story of the modern history of Otho A. xii illustrates an important aspect of the 'archivist's history' propounded by Galbraith. This is that archivists and librarians for various reasons sometimes have to do radical things to manuscripts and that, as a result, the nature of manuscripts continues to change. Many descriptions of Cotton manuscripts give the impression that, once the burnt manuscripts reached the British Museum and were patched up by binders, nothing happened to them. In fact, these repaired volumes represent speculative reconstructions of the original manuscripts, in some cases undertaken over a period of many years. In the case of Otho A. xii, this speculation fell prey to another danger that Galbraith would doubtless have wished to counsel against, that of wishful thinking.

NOTES

A preliminary version of this paper was given at a seminar organised by the Research Group on Medieval Manuscripts in April 1994. I am grateful to Carl T. Berkhout, Michelle Brown and Simon Keynes for commenting on drafts of this paper.

1. In *The Historian's Workshop*, ed. L.P. Curtius (New York: Knopf, 1970), p. 7; repr. in *Kings and Chroniclers: Essays in English Medieval History* (London: Hambledon Press, 1982).
2. Michael Lapidge, 'Some Latin Poems as Evidence for the Reign of Athelstan', *Anglo-Saxon England* 9 (1981), 62–71, who speculates that William's 'obviously ancient book' might be Oxford, Bodleian Library, Rawlinson C. 697, 'but conjectures of this sort cannot be proved'.
3. Ibid., pp. 61–2, n. 6, p. 71, n. 49.
4. Antonia Gransden, *Historical Writing in England, c. 550–c. 1307* (London: Routledge, Kegan and Paul, 1974), pp. 220–1; Charles Johnson, ed., *Dialogus de Scaccario* (London: Nelson's Medieval Classics, 1950), pp. 27–8.
5. Cf. C.E. Wright, 'The Dispersal of the Libraries in the Sixteenth Century', in *The English Library before 1700*, ed. Francis Wormald and C.E. Wright (London: Athlone Press, 1958), pp. 151–6.
6. G.R.C. Davis, *Medieval Cartularies of Great Britain: A Short Catalogue* (London: Longmans, 1959).
7. Ibid., no. 85.
8. Ibid., no. 275.
9. Ibid., no. 277
10. Ibid., no. 595.
11. Ibid., no. 908.
12. Christopher Kitching (for the National Council on Archives), *Archives: The Very Essence of Our Heritage* (Chichester: Phillimore, 1996), p. 25.

13. Ibid., p. 25.

14. John Evans, *English Art 1307–1461* (Oxford: Clarendon Press, 1949), p. 40; Lucy Freeman Sandler, *Gothic Manuscripts 1285–1385* (Oxford: Harvey Miller, 1986), no. 105. Sandler points out that, paradoxically, the destruction of the manuscript can provide a means of finding out more information about the structure of a high grade illuminated manuscript than would otherwise be possible: 'While it is a saddening experience to look at the crumbling fragments of the Psalter, contemporary eyes — and contemporary photographic techniques — can find interesting and unexpected information in the book as it survives. In fact, because of the prevalence of offset images — the painted layer has been peeled away in many cases — the underdrawing is often left visible. The uppermost original layer, which received the final surface details, is also rendered visible by show-through from the offsets. A close study of the technique of the Douai Psalter, made possible by its tragic ruin, would surely prove rewarding'.

15. Simon Keynes, 'George Harbin's Transcript of the Lost Cartulary of Athelney Abbey', *Proceedings of the Somerset Archaeological and Natural History Society* 136 (1992), 149–59.

16. Public Record Office, WO 363. Simon Fowler, William Spencer and Stuart Tamblin, *Army Service Records of the First World War* (London: Public Record Office, 1996). See also the Public Record Office web site at http://www.open.gov.uk/pro/famfacts.htm#ww1.

17. In the case of the burnt Cotton Genesis, British Library, Cotton Otho B. vi, not only have photomontage techniques been used to reconstruct the appearance of the original manuscript, but the inadequacies of photographic reproductions of the fragments mean that scholars have had to resort to drawings of various kinds to provide an adequate record of the surviving fragments. See, e.g., Kurt Weitzmann and Herbert L. Kessler, *The Cotton Genesis, British Library, Codex Cotton Otho B.VI*, Illustrations in the Manuscripts of the Septuagint, 1, Princeton Monographs in Art and Archaeology, 45 (Princeton: Princeton University Press, 1985); M. Wenzel, 'Deciphering the Cotton Genesis Miniatures: Preliminary Observations Concerning the Use of Colour', *British Library Journal* 13 (1987), 79–100; J. Lowden, 'Concerning the Cotton Genesis and Other Illustrated Manuscripts of Genesis', *Gesta* 36 (1992), 40–53.

18. See, for example, A.H. Smith, 'The Photography of Manuscripts', *London Medieval Studies* 1 (1938), 179–207; Kevin S. Kiernan, 'The State of the *Beowulf* Manuscript 1882–1983', *Anglo-Saxon England* 13 (1984), 23–42; Kevin S. Kiernan, 'Digital Image Processing and the *Beowulf* Manuscript', *Literary and Linguistic Computing* 6.1 (1991), 20–7; Kevin S. Kiernan, 'Digital Preservation, Restoration, and the Dissemination of Medieval Manuscripts', in *Scholarly Publishing and the Electronic*

Network: Gateways, Keepers, and Roles in the Information Omniverse, ed. A. Okerson and D. Mogge (Washington, DC: Association of Research Libraries, 1984), pp. 13–43; Andrew Prescott, '*The Electronic Beowulf* and Digital Restoration', *Literary and Linguistic Computing* (forthcoming).

19. As is illustrated by Simon Keynes' recent discovery of Humfrey Wanley's 'Book of Specimens': 'The Reconstruction of a Burnt Cottonian Manuscript: The Case of Cotton MS. Otho A. I', *British Library Journal* 22 (1996), 126–33.

20. 'Afterthoughts', p. 12.

21. Keynes, 'The Reconstruction of a Burnt Cottonian Manuscript: The Case of Cotton MS. Otho A. I', pp. 113–16; Andrew Prescott, '"Their Present Miserable State of Cremation": The Restoration of the Cotton Library', in *Sir Robert Cotton as Collector*, ed. C.J. Wright (London: British Library Publications, 1997), 391–454; Kevin Sharpe, 'Introduction: Rewriting Sir Robert Cotton', in *Sir Robert Cotton as Collector*, p. 5. The report of the parliamentary committee which investigated the fire contains a narrative of the events of that night: *A Report from the Committee Appointed to View the Cottonian Library, and such of the Publick Records of this Kingdom, as they think proper...* (London: Williamson and Bowyer, 1732), hereafter cited as *1732 Report*. This report was reprinted in *Reports from the Committees of the House of Commons...* (London: Hansard, 1803), vol. 1, pp. 443–535. It was reproduced in facsimile from an annotated copy in the reference library of the Department of Manuscripts of the British Library (not Additional 62572 as stated in the introduction) by C.G.C. Tite in his edition of Thomas Smith, *Catalogue of the Manuscripts in the Cottonian Library 1696* (Woodbridge: D.S. Brewer, 1984). Other copies are Additional 24932 and 62572.

22. For an introduction to the Cotton Library, see Colin G.C. Tite, *The Manuscript Library of Sir Robert Cotton*, Panizzi Lectures, 1993 (London: British Library Publications, 1994).

23. Keynes, 'The Reconstruction of a Burnt Cottonian Manuscript: The Case of Cotton MS. Otho A. I', pp. 115–16, which gives further bibliography for each of the manuscripts mentioned.

24. Helmut Gneuss, 'Die Handschrift Cotton Otho A.xii', *Anglia* 94 (1976), 289–318; D.G. Scragg, ed., *The Battle of Maldon* (Manchester: Manchester University Press, 1981), pp. 1–4; H.L. Rogers, '*The Battle of Maldon*: David Casley's Transcript', *Notes and Queries*, n.s., 32 (1985), 147–55; Donald Scragg, ed., *The Battle of Maldon AD 991* (Oxford: Basil Blackwell; The Manchester Centre for Anglo-Saxon Studies, 1991), pp. 15–16; Leslie Webster and Janet Backhouse, eds., *The Making of England: Anglo-Saxon Art and Culture AD 600–900* (London: British Museum Press, 1991), no. 234; N.R. Ker, *Catalogue of Manuscripts*

Containing Anglo-Saxon (Oxford: Clarendon Press, 1957; reissued with supplement 1990), nos 171–2.

25. *Times Higher Educational Supplement*, 8 December 1995: 'Alfred Smyth ... has just written one of the most controversial Anglo-Saxon history books ever, rampaging through the hill fort of orthodoxy and leaving behind the rubble of bitter rivalry and broken friendships.' I am grateful to Simon Keynes for providing a copy of this article.
26. *King Alfred the Great* (Oxford: Oxford University Press, 1995), 149–70.
27. Just as Whitelock vanquished Galbraith's attack on Asser, so Smyth's arguments have, it seems to me, been comprehensively demolished by Simon Keynes, 'On the Authenticity of Asser's *Life of King Alfred*', *Journal of Ecclesiastical History* 47 (1996), 529–51.
28. Simon Keynes and Michael Lapidge, trans., *Alfred the Great: Asser's Life of King Alfred and Other Contemporary Sources*, The Penguin Classics (Harmondsworth: Penguin Books, Ltd, 1983, repr. 1984), p. 50.
29. R.W. Southern, 'Vivian Hunter Galbraith 1889–1976', *Proceedings of the British Academy* 64 (1978), 406–8: 'he brought to the PRO a more vivid sense of history than any of the officials whom he found there, and it was in the stacks that he discovered his personality as a historian.'
30. *Studies in the Public Records* (London: Thomas Nelson, 1948), pp. 1–19. In Public Record Office mythology, however, Galbraith was remembered as having seen his Assistant Keepership as a 'stick in the mud' job, although he doubted whether he could find any nicer mud to stick in (J.D. Cantwell, *The Public Record Office 1838–1958* [London: Her Majesty's Stationery Office, 1991], p. 406).
31. Ibid., pp. 5–6.
32. Ibid., p. 6.
33. Ibid., p. 7.
34. A reading of the preface to *The Study of Public Records*, pp. v–vii, and *An Introduction to the Study of History* (London: C.A. Watts, 1964), esp. pp. 1–21, is instructive in this respect. They almost seem to look forward to a kind of wholly relativistic, textual history which Roland Barthes and Michel Foucault might have found sympathetic. Galbraith cites (*Study of Public Records*, p. vi) the remark of Sir Ernest Barker: 'There is no end of the things that were, and there is no end of the stories which might be told about them. But are such stories history?'. Galbraith answers this with a resounding 'Yes'. Where Galbraith would doubtless have differed with Foucault is that Galbraith would have stressed the objectivity of the record and the spuriousness of Foucault's archaeology of the intellect. But, on the other hand, Foucault's fascination with archives and archival documents suggests that there might be more in common between them than might at first be imagined.
35. 'Afterthoughts', p. 12.

36. *Historical Research in Medieval England*, The Creighton Lecture, 1949 (London: Athlone Press, 1951); repr. in *Kings and Chroniclers: Essays in English Medieval History* (London: Hambledon Press, 1982).
37. Ibid., p. 24.
38. *An Introduction to the Study of History*, pp. 88–128.
39. Ibid., p. vi.
40. Ibid., p. vi.
41. Ibid., p. vi.
42. *The Genuine Asser*, The Stenton Lecture (Reading: University of Reading, 1967).
43. *Medium Ævum* 38 (1969), 178–81.
44. D.P. Kirby, 'Asser and His Life of King Alfred', *Studia Celtica* 6 (1971), 12–35.
45. E.g., Janet L. Nelson, 'The Problem of King Alfred's Royal Anointing', *Journal of Ecclesiastical History* 18 (1967), 145–63; '"A King Across the Sea": Alfred in Continental Perspective', *Transactions of the Royal Historical Society*, 5th ser., 36 (1986), 52–3; 'Reconstructing a Royal Family: Reflections on Alfred from Asser, Chapter 2', in *People and Places in Northern Europe 500–1600: Essays in Honour of Peter Hayes Sawyer* (Woodbridge: The Boydell Press, 1991), pp. 47–66.
46. 'Afterthoughts', p. 12. Galbraith reiterated many of his ideas on Asser in a very lively fashion in a series of charming letters to Tomás Kalmar, now a Professor at California State University, Monterey Bay, who had met Galbraith while he was at Berkeley. I am grateful to Professor Kalmar for letting me see these delightful letters, and hope that he will publish them. In a letter of 28 December 1966, Galbraith notes that 'No one, repeat N. One has either (sic.) accepted my paper on the subject — I refer of course to reviewers: but equally no one (reviewers) has attempted to meet its arguments.' However, he had 'continued to brood on Asser, without in any essential way doubting the truth of my conclusion, viz. that it was written in the 11th century'.
47. The sketch is reproduced in William Henry Stevenson, *Asser's Life of King Alfred* (Oxford: Oxford University Press, 1904; repr. with new introduction by Dorothy Whitelock, 1959), pl. facing p. xxxii.
48. *The Genuine Asser*, p. 17.
49. 'Afterthoughts', p. 12.
50. Ibid., p. 12.
51. Ibid., p. 12.
52. A. Campbell, ed., *The Chronicle of Æthelweard*, Nelson's Medieval Texts (London: Thomas Nelson and Sons, Ltd, 1962), p. xi. Galbraith refers to Campbell's apparent reservations about Asser in *An Introduction to the Study of History*, p. 89. The implication here appears to be that Campbell was one of those scholars who had decided against editing Asser for

Nelson's Medieval Texts. This is supported by a letter of Galbraith to Tomás Kalmar, dated 28 December 1996. Galbraith summarises Campbell's position as follows: '"It may be 9th and may be 11th — no matter what it is very *unreliable*." But Alistair is 60 years of age, and I have here in a drawer 24 pages of foolscap typed 20 years ago — in which he shows that there is no *philological* proof of the early date — and he is our best living philologist.'

53. 'Afterthoughts', p. 12.
54. *Asser's Life of King Alfred*; see n. 46 above.
55. *An Introduction to the Study of History*, p. 122. In a letter of 9 May 1964 to Tomás Kalmar, Galbraith emphasised his view that Stevenson knew privately that Asser was dubious, but was unwilling to admit that a text on which he had lavished so much learning was false. Galbraith emphasised that 'No one has ever known as much about the Life as W.H.S.'
56. *Domesday Book: Its Place in Administrative History* (Oxford: Oxford University Press, 1974), p. 11. Indeed, if anyone could be regarded as an archetypal 'outsider' in English academic circles, it would be Stevenson. The *Dictionary of National Biography* article on him by A.L. Poole states that he was the son of a Hull timber merchant who, after leaving school, worked in his father's office on Queen's Dock, and became interested in Scandinavian languages because of his father's business connections. He learnt Norwegian from a Norwegian sailor. He cut his scholarly teeth on preparing calendars for a variety of bodies ranging from Nottingham Town Council to the Public Record Office. He never took a university examination, receiving an Oxford M.A. degree by decree of convocation after his election to a fellowship at Exeter College.
57. Like Galbraith, Stevenson also had close connections with the Public Record Office. He produced the *Calendar of Close Rolls* for the reigns of Edward I and Edward II and the first six years of Edward III (*Dictionary of National Biography*, s.n.).
58. *King Alfred the Great*, p. 151.
59. *Asser's Life of King Alfred*, p. xxxiii, n. 3.
60. Harley 563, fol. 1*v.
61. This note reads as follows: 'Loke John Bale in the lyfe of asserius menevensis folio 151 [*recte* 125; see Additional 43705, fol. 2v] and you will graunt that, that whiche in this boke is founde of kynge Alfred is of asserius. He shall also informe you yf I be not deceyved, who added the residew, but yf that may not suffice you loke what John Leland hathe in his comentaris of the swans songe the 90 leafe and thos thyngs whiche he citethe forthe of asserius ye shall fynde the same in this booke in manar worde for word. Adde that where he speakethe of wise men given to hym and called forthe by alfred, he speakethe withe bashfulness of hymselfe Asserius in the xiii leafe. As to that that pertaynethe to the rest, ye may

see that whiche are had in the lefe 54. The originall copie is in the hands of doctor wottons admynystrators, which was sence copied by Laurence Nowell, and now englyshed by Raffaell Holenshed for John Stowe. Anno doi 1752 in the monithe of September.'

62. Harley 563, fol. 119v.

63. Harley 563, fol. 66; cf. also fol. 51. D'Ewes had evidently compared the text in Harley 563 with a printed edition of Asser. In the list of contents for this manuscript, he describes the continuation after the death of Alfred as follows: 'A continuation alsoe of his storie ab a^{o} 900 ad annum 1101 a quodam Anonymo; and of this there is noe continuance at all in the imprinted latine copie.'

64. R.R. Darlington and P. McGurk, eds., *The Chronicle of John of Worcester* (Oxford: Clarendon Press, 1995), vol. 2, p. xlv, n. 16.

65. Additional 43705, fol. 3.

66. Additional 43705, fol. 3.

67. Additional 43705, fol. 2v.

68. Andrew G. Watson, *The Library of Sir Simonds D'Ewes* (London: British Museum, 1966), p. 311. There are also slips inserted at various points in Harley 556, which are in another hand and contain additional extracts from the Worcester chronicle which are not in Additional 43705. These were apparently inserted under the direction of Nowell, who has annotated a number of them, e.g., fols 5, 41, 78v, 88, 113, 120–122. I am grateful to Carl T. Berkhout for identifying the hand of Nowell in Harley 556 for me.

69. Harley 556, fol. 2v. Presumably the fact that Harley 556 does not contain Nowell's original title, 'Ex Mariano Scoto', or Lambarde's cancelled addition to it indicates that Harley 556 was made from Additional 43705 after Lambarde had added the note about Asser, but the possibility of a more complex relationship cannot be excluded.

70. Darlington and McGurk, eds., *The Chronicle of John of Worcester*, vol. 2, p. xlv, n. 16.

71. *Asser's Life of King Alfred*, p. xxxii.

72. Ibid., p. cxiii.

73. 'Die Handschrift Cotton Otho A.xii', pp. 317–18.

74. *1732 Report*, pp. 15–139.

75. Ibid., pp. 50–1.

76. *Asser's Life of King Alfred*, p. xxxii.

77. Ibid., p. liii.

78. Examples of Casley's hand are British Library, Additional 44919, fol. 102, an autograph proposal for publication of his catalogue of the Royal Manuscripts, and Harley 7632, the autograph manuscript of his catalogue of the Royal Manuscripts. Casley's transcript of *The Battle of Maldon*, Oxford, Bodleian Library, Rawlinson B. 203, is also reproduced in

Scragg, ed., *The Battle of Maldon AD 991*, pp. 2–14.

79. For this and all further details of the post-fire history of the Cotton manuscripts, see Prescott, '"Their Present Miserable State of Cremation": The Restoration of the Cotton Library', where full references are given.
80. *1732 Report*, pp. 11–15.
81. Ibid., p. 15.
82. These reports are briefly noted in Edward Miller, *That Noble Cabinet; A History of the British Museum* (London: Andre Deutsch, 1973), pp. 60–1. They are in the British Museum Archives, CE 3/1, 102–106 (23 July 1756) and 110–114 (30 July 1756). They are printed in full in Prescott, '"Their Present Miserable State of Cremation": The Restoration of the Cotton Library', pp. 435–9.
83. Prescott, '"Their Present Miserable State of Cremation": The Restoration of the Cotton Library', p. 438.
84. Ibid., pp. 398, 438.
85. Ibid., p. 437.
86. S. Hooper, *A Catalogue of the Manuscripts in the Cottonian Library* (London, 1777), pp. xii–xiv.
87. Prescott, '"Their Present Miserable State of Cremation": The Restoration of the Cotton Library', pp. 398–9.
88. Ibid., p. 404.
89. *A Catalogue of the Manuscripts in the Cottonian Library Deposited in the British Museum* (London: Hansard, 1802), p. 365: 'This cannot be the MS. that was originally in the Cottonian Library under the above reference, and which is said to have been used by Archbishop Parker: Since that appears to have been of an ancient date, in Saxon letters and on vellum, whereas this is of a modern hand, and on paper.'
90. Cf. Prescott, '"Their Present Miserable State of Cremation": The Restoration of the Cotton Library', pp. 400–2, 408–9.
91. Ibid., pp. 404–6.
92. Additional 62576, fol. 52rv.
93. Additional 62576, fol. 4. This list may be dated from an 1837 watermark. In '"Their Present Miserable State of Cremation": The Restoration of the Cotton Library', p. 439, I give too early a date for this list (*c*. 1830).
94. Additional 62576, fol. 29v.
95. Diary of Sir Frederic Madden, 17 April 1837, cited in Prescott, '"Their Present Miserable State of Cremation": The Restoration of the Cotton Library', p. 408. Madden's personal diary is Oxford, Bodleian Library, Eng. hist. c. 140-182. Extracts are printed by kind permission of the Bodleian Library. A copy is in the British Library: MS. Facs. *1012. It is hereafter cited as MJ.
96. In his resignation memorial of 12 July 1866, a copy of which is Additional 62041, fols 88v–89.

97. For the following, see Prescott, '"Their Present Miserable State of Cremation": The Restoration of the Cotton Library', pp. 409–19.
98. Additional 62007, fol. 62.
99. Additional 62033, fol. 56v.
100. Additional 62033, fols 56v–61v
101. Additional 62576, fol. 29v.
102. Prescott, '"Their Present Miserable State of Cremation": The Restoration of the Cotton Library', pp. 417–18.
103. Ibid., p. 418.
104. Ibid., p. 418.
105. Ibid., pp. 428–30.
106. *Dictionary of National Biography*; Miller, *That Noble Cabinet*, p. 258.
107. Additional 62021, fol. 41v.
108. Additional 62021, fols 42–48, which gives details of the hundreds of charters calendared by Thompson during his first months on the Department of Manuscripts. When I began work in the Department of Manuscripts in 1979, my first task was also the description of Additional Charters, as indeed was the case with my colleagues Michelle P. Brown and Scott McKendrick when they joined the Department seven years later. In 1864, when Frederick Gemmer complained virulently in a pamphlet about the inadequate training he had received when he joined the Department of Manuscripts, he reserved particular scorn for the practice of using the description of charters as a training exercise; see his *Memorial Addressed to the Trustees of the British Museum* (London: J.R. Lynn, 1864), a copy of which is British Library, Printed Books, pressmark 011903.bb.23(2). Madden considered Gemmer's charter descriptions to be 'Filled with gross blunders and worthless': Additional 62021, fols 54–55. The Museum response to Gemmer's pamphlet is to be found at British Library, Printed Books, pressmarks 011902.bb.23(1) and 11900.n.54.
109. Additional 62021, fol. 47.
110. Additional 62021, fol. 47v
111. Additional 62021, fols 48v–49.
112. Prescott, '"Their Present Miserable State of Cremation": The Restoration of the Cotton Library', p. 430.
113. Ibid., p. 430.
114. Additional 62021, fol. 51v; *Dictionary of National Biography*; Miller, *That Noble Cabinet*, p. 291.
115. Additional 62021, fols 51v–54.
116. Additional 62016, fol. 2v; cf. MJ, 10 March 1864.
117. Additional 62021, fols 54–57v.
118. Additional 62021, fol. 56.
119. Additional 62021, fol. 56.
120. Additional 62021, fol. 56.

121. Additional 62021, fol. 56v.
122. MJ, 30 September 1864.
123. Additional 62021, fol. 57.
124. Thompson's draft description is Additional 62578. Thompson's authorship of this brief catalogue is confirmed by his monthly reports for February–June 1865: Additional 62021, fols 59–61.
125. Now Additional 62573 and Department of Manuscripts Reference Library; see further Prescott, '"Their Present Miserable State of Cremation": The Restoration of the Cotton Library', p. 433.
126. Additional 62572, fol. 45.
127. Additional 62021, fol. 47v.
128. 'The Cottonian Fragments of Æthelweard's Chronicle', *Bulletin of the Institute of Historical Research* 24 (1951), 46–62.
129. Ibid., p. 50.
130. Prescott, '"Their Present Miserable State of Cremation": The Restoration of the Cotton Library', pp. 419–21.
131. MJ, 10 July 1865; Prescott, '"Their Present Miserable State of Cremation": The Restoration of the Cotton Library', p. 419.
132. Ibid., p. 421.
133. Department of Manuscripts Archives, Returns of Service 1865–1878, fol. 152.
134. Tuckett's bill for inlaying Galba A. xix, Otho A. i, Otho A. x, Otho A. xi and Otho A. xii is in a volume of memoranda relating to the Keepership of Edward Augustus Bond in the Department of Manuscripts archives. It is dated 21 May 1867. The 80 fragments from these volumes took 70 hours to flatten, mend and inlay, at a cost of nine pence per hour.
135. Department of Manuscripts Archives, Returns of Service 1856–1878, fol. 159v.
136. E.g., on the frame of Otho A. xii, fol. 2v, Thompson has written 'Ethelwerd. Lib IV. cap. 3 (death of Guðrun) [Mon. p. 517 c]' and on fol. 3 'Ethelwerd, iv. 3 (891) [Mon. p. 517 D–E]'.
137. Tuckett's bill for binding up the inlaid leaves is also preserved in Bond's memoranda in the Department of Manuscripts archives. It is dated 7 December 1867. It is for six volumes in half cloth lettered in three parts. The cost of each volume was four shillings and sixpence.
138. H.H. Howorth, 'Asser's Life of Alfred', *The Athanæum* 2526 (25 March 1876), 425–6; 2535 (27 May 1876), 727–9; 2549 (2 September 1876), 307–9; and 'Ethelweard and Asser', *The Athanæum* 2597 (4 August 1877), 145–6.
139. *The Athenæum* 2526 (25 March 1876), p. 426.
140. *Asser's Life of King Alfred*, p. cxiii.
141. *Collected Papers of Henry Bradshaw, Late University Librarian ... Edited for the Syndics of the University Press* (Cambridge: Cambridge University

Press, 1889), pp. 467, 485.

142. *Asser's Life of King Alfred*, p. cxii, n. 3. Stevenson also notes that Bradshaw 'asserted that the Cottonian MS. came from St Augustine's abbey, Canterbury, but he adduced no authority for this statement and we have been unable to find any proof for it', *ibid*., p. xxxv. Bradshaw's authority for this statement was an examination of the manuscript purporting to be Asser at the British Museum, a manuscript which Stevenson never saw. Bradshaw's only fault was the understandable one of not realising that Thompson and Scott had caused him to be presented with the wrong manuscript.

143. Stevenson's papers are preserved in the archives of St John's College, Oxford. They are uncatalogued and difficult to access, so it has not been possible for me to examine them. The College Archivist advises me that they contain no material relating to Stevenson's edition and no correspondence with Thompson, but nevertheless I feel they would repay investigation.

144. Miller, *That Noble Cabinet*, p. 288.

145. Department of Manuscripts Archives, Returns of Service 1865–1878, fol. 404; Department of Manuscripts Archives, etc. of the British Museum, 1879, p. 11.

146. Colin G.C. Tite, 'The Cotton Appendix and the Fragments', *The Library*, 6th ser., 15 (1993), 52–55, at p. 52.

147. This is the copy in the Department of Manuscripts Reference Library which was reproduced by Colin G.C. Tite in his 1984 edition of Thomas Smith's catalogue; see further Prescott, '"Their Present Miserable State of Cremation": The Restoration of the Cotton Library', p. 450, n. 254.

148. London: Longman, 1862. The copy annotated by Warner is currently at pressmark 20a in the Manuscripts Students' Room.

149. Prescott, '"Their Present Miserable State of Cremation": The Restoration of the Cotton Library', p. 429.

150. Tite, 'The Cotton Appendix and the Fragments'. On Millar, see further *The Eric George Millar Bequest*, special number of *British Museum Quarterly* 33 (1968–1969), 1–89.

151. Cotton Fragments XXX, Bundle I (4). The existence of these fragments is noted in Ker, *Catalogue of Manuscripts Containing Anglo-Saxon*, p. 221, n. 1, and Gneuss, 'Die Handschrift Cotton Otho A. xii', p. 293.

152. Millar states that there were also fragments in the Box from Tiberius A. x, Otho B. iii and Royal 9 C. xi, apparently stored in four envelopes, but these could not be found when the contents of the Box were checked in June 1997. Presumably the fragments from these manuscripts are those which were found loose in the Box in 1957 and put in a new container.

153. Millar only refers to one box of unidentified fragments. This is presumably the box with the pencil note 'Cotton. Various Small

fragments', which contains just one fragment from a late medieval manuscript. The second box of unidentified fragments contains fragments found loose in the Box in 1957, which probably comprise fragments of Tiberius A. x, Otho B. iii and Royal 9 C. xi.

154. These flyleaves are not recorded by either Ker or Gneuss. Cotton's description of the manuscript as being 'in Saxon letters' presumably influenced James Ussher, who in 1639 described the manuscript as being 'characteribus Saxonicis' (Stevenson, *Asser's Life of King Alfred*, p. xli). Spelman also apparently followed Cotton in referring to 'Saxon letters' (*ibic.*, p. xliii). Wise's sketch of 1722 was made in order to demonstrate that the manuscript was not written 'characteribus Saxonicis' (*ibid.*, p. xliii). These references to the manuscript being in 'Saxon letters' provide a further illustration of the influence of Cotton's own descriptions of his manuscript; cf. Tite, *The Manuscript Library of Sir Robert Cotton*, pp. 41–77.

Index